What is Britain's future in Europe? This book [illegible] t for dramatically new times. The old arg[illegible] detachedness' from Europe and wheth[illegible]. The new times are the crisis in th[illegible] the European Union's future. While [illegible]tion, the politics associated with the EU's [illegible]nificant and possibly insurmountable challenge. [illegible]n stand? What future should Britain want for the EU? [illegible]portant is continued membership of the EU for Britain's future? [illegible]ok offers new answers to these questions from the perspective of an author who has combined experience at the heart of the British government – as Tony Blair's European adviser – with understanding of Europe from the inside – working at a senior level in the European Commission. This book will be essential reading for anyone interested in the future of British and European politics.

In the series:

After the Third Way: The Future of Social Democracy in Europe
Edited by Olaf Cramme and Patrick Diamond
ISBN: 978 1 84885 992 0 (HB); 978 1 84885 993 7 (PB)

Europe's Immigration Challenge: Reconciling Work, Welfare and Mobility
Edited by Elena Jurado and Grete Brochmann
ISBN: 978 1 78076 225 8 (HB); 978 1 78076 226 5 (PB)

Left Without a Future? Social Justice in Anxious Times
Anthony Painter
ISBN: 978 1 78076 660 7 (HB); 978 1 78076 661 4 (PB)

Progressive Politics after the Crash: Governing from the Left
Edited by Olaf Cramme, Patrick Diamond and Michael McTernan
ISBN: 978 1 78076 763 5 (HB); 978 1 78076 764 2 (PB)

Governing Britain: Power, Politics and the Prime Minister
Patrick Diamond
ISBN: 978 1 78076 581 5 (HB); 978 1 78076 582 2 (PB)

The Europe Dilemma: Britain and the Drama of EU Integration
Roger Liddle
ISBN: 978 1 78076 222 7 (HB); 978 1 78076 223 4 (PB)

Roger Liddle

the europe dilemma

Britain and the Drama of EU Integration

Published in 2014 by I.B.Tauris & Co. Ltd
6 Salem Road, London W2 4BU
175 Fifth Avenue, New York NY 10010
www.ibtauris.com

Distributed in the United States and Canada Exclusively by
Palgrave Macmillan
175 Fifth Avenue, New York NY 10010

ISBN: 978 1 78076 222 7 (HB)
ISBN: 978 1 78076 223 4 (PB)

A full CIP record for this book is available from the British Library
A full CIP record is available from the Library of Congress

Library of Congress Catalog Card Number: available

Typeset in Great Britain by Data Standards Ltd, Frome, Somerset
Printed and bound in Great Britain by T.J. International, Padstow, Cornwall

'Roger Liddle's analysis of "how we got here" is interesting and as expected well informed, but it's his reflections on the approach pro-Europeans should take that could add a new dimension to the debate. Pro-Europeans have sometimes seemed to be in a competitive bidding process with Eurosceptics as to what powers we can repatriate, and how far we can chip away at the role of the EU. This is dead-end reasoning. Liddle makes a compelling case for an alternative and bolder British EU agenda.'
Julian Priestley, secretary general of the European Parliament 1997–2007

'Roger Liddle offers a fresh and shrewd account of the many missed opportunities in Britain's relations with the EU – including a frank assessment of the disappointments of Tony Blair, whom he served as an adviser in Downing Street. He concludes with an alternative view of how the UK could still play a positive and constructive role in Europe.'
Peter Riddell, director of the Institute for Government

'Riveting and realistic, this book offers by far the best-informed analysis I have read of the European dilemmas facing modern British governments, as well as the most cogent argument for European solutions to our national challenges.'
Stephen Wall, formerly Britain's permanent representative to the European Union

'This is a hard-hitting account of the frustrating politics of British European policy across the decades from an insider who persists in holding to a positive case for full-hearted British engagement in Europe. Roger Liddle provides a fine-grained analysis of the squandered opportunities as well as the achievements of New Labour's period in office and offers salutary comments on the dilemmas facing the Conservative Party and future governments. He is surely right in arguing that for the British to be at ease with Europe requires conviction in their souls and not only appeals to their pocket books.'
Helen Wallace, emeritus professor in the European Institute, LSE

About Policy Network

Policy Network is a leading thinktank and international political network based in London. It promotes strategic thinking on progressive solutions to the challenges of the twenty-first century and the future of social democracy, impacting upon policy debates in the UK, the rest of Europe and the wider world.

Through a distinctly collaborative and cross-national approach to research, events and publications, the thinktank has acquired a reputation as a highly valued platform for perceptive and challenging political analysis, debate and exchange. Building from our origins in the late 1990s, the network has become an unrivalled international point-of-contact between political thinkers and opinion formers, serving as a bridge between the worlds of politics, academia, public policy-making, business, civil society and the media.

www.policy-network.net

Contents

Glossary of Abbreviations

AECR	Alliance of European Conservatives and Reformists
AES	Alternative Economic Strategy
AfPak *or* Af-Pak	Afghanistan and Pakistan
ANZAC	Australian and New Zealand Army Corps
ASTMS	Association of Scientific, Technical and Managerial Staffs
AUEW	Amalgamated Union of Engineering Workers
BoE	Bank of England
BRIC	Brazil, Russia, India and China
BSE	Bovine Spongiform Encephalopathy *or* 'mad cow disease'
CAP	Common Agricultural Policy
CDU	Christian Democratic Union of Germany
CFSP	Common Foreign and Security Policy
CND	Campaign for Nuclear Disarmament
COREPER	Committee of Permanent Representatives
COSAC	Conference of Community and European Affairs Committees of Parliaments of the European Union
EAEC	European Atomic Energy Community *or* Euratom
EBA	European Banking Authority
EC	European Commission
ECB	European Central Bank
ECHR	European Convention on Human Rights
ECJ	European Court of Justice
ECR	European Conservatives and Reformists
ECSC	European Coal and Steel Community
Ecu	European Currency Unit
EEC	European Economic Community
EFSF	European Financial Stability Facility
EFSM	European Financial Stabilisation Mechanism
EFTA	European Free Trade Association
EMS	European Monetary System
EMU	Economic and Monetary Union
EPP	European People's Party
ERDF	European Regional Development Fund
ERM	European Exchange Rate Mechanism
ESDP	European Security and Defence Policy
ESDU	European Security and Defence Union
ESM	European Stability Mechanism
ETA	Basque Homeland and Freedom
EU	European Union

FCO	Foreign and Commonwealth Office
FDR	Franklin Delano Roosevelt
GDP	Gross Domestic Product
GSM	Global System for Mobile Communications *originally* Group Spécial Mobile
IMF	International Monetary Fund
IRA	Irish Republican Army
JHA	Justice and Home Affairs
LPC	Labour Party Conference
MEP	Member of the European Parliament
MP	Member of Parliament (UK)
NATO	North Atlantic Treaty Organization
NEC	National Executive Committee (Labour Party)
NHS	National Health Service
NIC	United States National Intelligence Council
ODS	Civic Democratic Party of the Czech Republic
OECD	Organisation for Economic Co-operation and Development
OEEC	Organisation for European Economic Co-operation
OSCE	Organisation for Security and Co-operation in Europe
PES	Party of European Socialists
PiS	Law and Justice Party of Poland
PISA	Programme for International Student Assessment
PJN	Poland Comes First Party *or* Poland is the Most Important
PLP	Parliamentary Labour Party
PS	Socialist Party of France
PSOE	Spanish Socialist Workers' Party
PVDA	Labour Party of the Netherlands
QMV	Qualified Majority Voting
REACH	Registration, Evaluation, Authorisation and Restriction of Chemicals
SEA	Single European Act
SFIO	French Section of the Workers' International
SPD	Social Democratic Party of Germany
TCE	Treaty establishing a Constitution for Europe
TGWU	Transport and General Workers' Union
TUC	Trades Union Congress
UEN	Union for a Europe of Nations
UK	United Kingdom
Ukip	United Kingdom Independence Party
UN	United Nations
US *or* USA	United States of America
USSR	Union of Soviet Socialist Republics *or* Soviet Union
VVD	People's Party for Freedom and Democracy of the Netherlands
WTO	World Trade Organization

Preface

This is a book of reflection based on personal experience, which I hope may help Britain resolve its European dilemma. It was my privilege – and it was a great one – to be entrusted with working for ten years from 1997 as political adviser on Europe, first in Downing Street to Tony Blair and then from 2004 in Brussels to Peter Mandelson, trade commissioner, and José Manuel Barroso, Commission president.

In 2010 when I started work on this book, 'Europe' seemed a 'dead' issue in British politics, so comprehensively had the British political class apparently taken to heart David Cameron's infamous piece of advice to Conservative MPs and activists to 'stop banging on' about it.[1] I am grateful to my publisher for thinking that the venture might be remotely worthwhile. By the time I finished, much behind schedule, but in some ways fortuitously, Cameron's January 2013 promise of 'renegotiation and referendum' had made the European question once again immediate and central.

I owe it to the reader to be upfront about where I am coming from. I am a social democratic pro-European, but by no stretch of the imagination a classic 'Europeanist'. Before I started my job with Blair, I had no experience of the European institutions, diplomacy or working abroad. The only foreign language I can read is French and, to my shame, I can barely converse in it. The reason I define myself as a 'European' is a deep commitment to a brand of modernising social democratic politics which has pro-Europeanism at its core. That explains why in the 1990s I became a passionate Blairite. The central part of the book is an account of that Prime Minister's unfulfilled European hopes, based on my own experiences at the heart of European policy-making. But this is not a 'kiss and tell' memoir. It attempts to be an honest, intellectual analysis of Blair's failure on Europe in the context of the troubled history of Britain's post-war relationship with our Continental neighbours and to reflect on its lessons for Britain's present European predicament.

My pro-Europeanism was shaped through my political formation. I was brought up a strong chapel socialist in a family that was Labour to the core. My father was a Carlisle railway clerk; my mother's father had been a

Labour pioneer in the Cumbrian coalfield. As a 17-year-old in 1964, I experienced two life-changing events. First, I won a scholarship from Carlisle Grammar School to The Queen's College, Oxford, where my tutors, the late R. A. C. ('Alistair') Parker and Kenneth Morgan (now Lord Morgan), greatly deepened my understanding of history and politics. Second, having imagined 'heaven on earth' had arrived with the election of the Wilson government, cold reality gradually set in. Many of that 1960s generation swung to the left in disillusionment with Harold Wilson (a disillusionment which I now think exaggerated and unfair): I swung to Europe. Nation state social democracy seemed incapable of either securing fairness and prosperity in Britain or exercising moral leadership in the world. Northern nonconformity's idealistic internationalism was noble in inspiration, but a Britain of diminished economic strength and political clout was an increasingly enfeebled vehicle for delivering its hopes. Moreover, in the moves across the Channel towards a united Europe, started by the Common Market Six (which I had initially followed my adolescent political hero, Hugh Gaitskell, in rejecting), I began to see something unique and remarkable. Its rejection of nationalism chimed with my gut instinct that modern Britain had to ditch its imperial illusions. Its commitment to the 'European social model', the 'social market', social partnership and social cohesion steered a progressive 'third way' that long eluded Britain between heavy-handed state interventionism and the unfettered free market. And I felt close to the core values of European social democracy as a project of emancipation – to enable all citizens, whatever their class or background, to lead a full and fulfilling life. I have stuck to these views ever since, without of course forgetting that, in human affairs, all our idols have feet of clay!

My positive view of Europe was much reinforced by the Labour politicians whom I came to admire. From the distance of student politics, Tony Crosland and Roy Jenkins offered the most coherent liberal, egalitarian and social democratic way forward: both were then committed pro-Europeans. At a more personal level I owe a particular debt to the late Frank Pickstock, who in the 1930s and 1940s had made the remarkable transition, with the help of the Workers' Educational Association, from a railway office in Stoke to the Extra Mural Delegacy in Oxford. In 1960 he had been a founder of the 'Gaitskellite' Campaign for Democratic Socialism and in 1971 helped me become a Labour councillor in Oxford at the tender age of 23. The late Philip Williams of Nuffield College, Gaitskell's official biographer, gave me a life-long detailed fascination with the 'twists and turns' of post-war Labour politics. Bill Rodgers (now Lord Rodgers of Quarrybank), who had organised the 69 Labour MPs who voted against the party's three-line whip to secure British entry to the European Community in October 1971, gave me my break onto the national political scene when he appointed me his Special Adviser in 1976. As a judge of politics and an example of courage, he has few equals.

In the 1981 Labour split, the most devastatingly traumatic and upsetting moment in my life, I ended up in the Social Democratic Party (SDP). I got to know Roy Jenkins well: he is for me the most remarkable figure I have ever come across in politics. I also married into Europe: I met my future wife Caroline, the daughter of the late George Thomson (Lord Thomson of Monifieth), Labour's first European commissioner; she has gallantly put up with my political obsessions for the past 30 years, which I hope has not got too much in the way of her own success. My ambition has always been to play a part in building a modern social democratic party of the moderate left that would move beyond the narrow confines of 'class' and 'interest' and be an electable alternative to the Conservatives. For me, it was a *sine qua non* that such a party would be pro-Europe.

When the SDP failed in 1988, I became a firm and consistent advocate of Lib–Lab cooperation. Labour's firm embrace of Europe, under Neil Kinnock's brave leadership, made this yearning for a broad-based 'progressive alliance' both realistic and appealing: my view remains that this is where the best future for British politics lies. I began to work closely with Peter Mandelson (Lord Mandelson of Hartlepool and Foy), whose commitment to Europe has never been in doubt and whom I had got to know well in the struggles against 'Red' Ted Knight's rule in the London Borough of Lambeth in the late 1970s. Peter introduced me to both Tony Blair and Gordon Brown: I discovered they both shared my strong pro-European commitment. With Tony Blair's election as Labour leader in 1994, I decided to rejoin Labour, though it may surprise some to learn that Blair himself for a while tried to dissuade me on the grounds that he wanted people inside the Liberal Democrats keen to argue for Lib–Lab cooperation! For 40 years my politics have therefore been of a distinctive pedigree in which Europe has played a major genetic part. I have been strongly but not uncritically pro-European, but Europe was always about domestic politics too: what kind of broad-based alternative to the Conservatives the left is trying to build; what kind of open and internationalist Britain we were trying to shape.

The reader is entitled to ask what sort of pro-European I am. While I do feel a strong sense of cultural identity as a European, my aim is not to establish a new country called the United States of Europe. All of us have multiple political identities, of which for me the most important remains my northern roots in Cumbria and the Union – the United Kingdom that is. Yet I regard the doctrine of the indivisibility of Westminster sovereignty as hopelessly outmoded. There is a need for multiple tiers of governance both below and beyond the classical nation state, each with its own independence of action and democratic legitimacy. For all that, I still see myself as a British patriot who believes that my country's 'greatness' can in modern times only be realised through our full and committed membership of the European Union (EU).

For me, the 'pooling of sovereignty' is not some great issue of principle. The increasing realities of global interdependence place sharp limits on national sovereignty. National sovereignty is of little use where political action can only be effective if taken as part of a wider collectivity than the nation state.

I rather agree with Harold Wilson's quip when asked in a 1967 television interview about the dangers of a loss of sovereignty involved in the Labour government's decision to make a second application for European Community membership. Wilson replied that he regarded the pooling of sovereignty as 'a mark of an advancing civilisation'.[2] If that was true in 1967, it is far truer today that nation states have to accept significant limits on their absolute sovereignty in order to act together effectively if politics is to be able to shape our people's destinies, and not be powerless in the face of anonymous global forces. Globalisation is a man-made phenomenon and the great democracies should work together to shape it better in the public interest. Europe of course is not the only level of governance that is needed beyond the nation state: the United Nations, the North Alantic Treaty Organization (NATO), World Trade Organization (WTO) and many others all play an essential role. However, there is no better example than the EU of proud 'nation state' democracies sharing a commitment to work together and reach agreement around a common table of constant negotiation and compromise: this is not a denial of their nationhood, but the only means of fulfilling it in modern times. In an interdependent world our EU membership is crucial: a logic which for Britain grows more compelling, not less as many Eurosceptics believe, with the dramatic shift in the global balance of power to the East. As Tony Giddens puts it, the EU offers us 'sovereignty plus'.[3]

The EU is different from other international organisations in the nature of the commitment it requires of its members. The EU has achieved so much precisely because it has been much more than an association of sovereign nation states cooperating in peace and harmony. The essential insight of the EU's founding fathers was that peace, democracy and European unity could not be built simply on airy statements of goodwill, but rather on a series of practical steps to pool sovereignty. As the Schuman Declaration in May 1950 put it:

> Europe will not be made all at once or according to a single plan. It will be built through concrete achievements which first create a de facto solidarity [...] The solidarity [...] thus established will make it plain that any war between France and Germany becomes not merely unthinkable, but materially impossible.

The concept of sovereignty pooling succeeded brilliantly in bringing about reconciliation and an end to war on the European continent. It has institutionalised a shared commitment to reach agreements for the common good. With that historic achievement now secure, the case for further European integration today should hopefully be judged pragmatically, but with the disintegration of the EU that the disorderly break-up of the eurozone could trigger, all bets for the future would be off.

There is absolutely nothing of merit in transferring powers to Brussels for its own sake. There is a lot wrong with the way the EU works which needs radical reform. Deciding important issues of public policy at European level does raise significant questions of democratic legitimacy, although the EU's critics often forget that Westminster, our national political parties and the Brussels institutions are all held in equally low regard. There is an undesirable irreversibility about transfers of powers to Brussels which become part of a difficult-to-change 'acquis'. The European system at present provides nothing comparable to a general election in which the voters can 'throw the rascals out' or even the intense pressure under which Parliament and the media can put British ministers. These issues all have to be addressed if pro-Europeans are to make a renewed case for sovereignty pooling. In the meantime there is a simple test to which supranational sovereignty pooling should be subject. Can a case convincingly be made that the nation states of the EU will achieve significantly more through any new measure of sovereignty pooling than they could achieve on their own – in other words by the test of whether it delivers results?

Among British pro-Europeans there are wide and legitimate differences of view about what membership of the EU implies. The issue of Britain's position in the EU as a euro-out is part of a much wider debate about the necessity for 'variable geometry' in an enlarged EU in order to accommodate diversity of circumstance, different stages of economic development and varying national preferences, about which for at least two decades there has been much theorising. Personally I am not against 'variable geometry', but I am instinctively opposed to Britain opting for second-class status in the club. A flexible 'pick and choose' Europe offers a convenient device for squaring awkward circles, but, in my opinion, for Britain to adopt it as a positive goal of policy implies that our EU membership will never be a genuine community of equals with France, Germany and other 'core' member states. The question is whether, with Britain outside the euro for the foreseeable future, we must now face up to permanent exclusion from an integrated inner core. This book argues that for a euro-out, there is a credible alternative, at least for the decade or so ahead.

So this is a transparently pro-European book. This is not to concede that its arguments lack reason or objectivity. Rather the book's target reader is the genuine sceptic, in the true meaning of the *Oxford Dictionary of English* – 'a person inclined to question or doubt accepted opinions'. Such a person, by definition, remains open to rational persuasion. This remains where, on the European question, the majority of the British public still stands, although for a sizeable minority Europe has become the worrying embodiment of an alien 'otherness' against which people define themselves, somewhat akin to anti-Catholic feeling in eighteenth-century England.[3] The EU has become the whipping boy for society's wider ills, with EU withdrawal presented as a simplistic solution to complex issues that are rooted in the social tensions caused by the realities of globalisation such as migration, the declining economic fortunes of the low skilled, and the decline of a traditional sense of community. Pro-Europeans have yet to find emotional arguments to counter this prevalent hostility to Europe, which is constantly ventilated through a hostile press. It involves a wholesale rethinking of the traditional British pro-European case.

The informed vantage point for this book's reflections was the author's position of special adviser in the No. 10 Policy Unit, to which I was appointed in 1997. Special advisers have been more or less an accepted feature of British government since the 1970s. But I was the first ever political appointee to be given a European brief in No. 10. I decided early on that my job was not to join the fierce competition to hang on to the Prime Minister's coat-tails so that I could be the successful courtier whispering in the great leader's ear! Rather I saw my job (and Blair approved of this) as to get 'out and about', touching base with opinion-formers at home, networking extensively across the Continent, particularly with the political class to whom most diplomats cannot easily relate, but whom British politicians too casually ignore, so that I could offer the Prime Minister an independent view.

For over seven years I worked alongside the British officials responsible for European policy. Although Tony Blair was at times frustrated by the quality of civil service advice, I rarely heard him complain about the professionalism of the 'Rolls Royce machine' that runs Whitehall's European policy. I share that respect. Once aboard this European 'Rolls Royce', I interpreted my job as to offer backseat advice on the pace and direction of travel, not to try to seize control of the steering wheel. There are too many officials to name them all, but I would like to put on record my thanks for much tolerance, generous hospitality (when abroad on numerous trips) and balanced wisdom in particular to Sir Brian Bender, Sir Colin Budd, Robert Cooper, Martin Donnelly, Sir John Grant, Sir John Holmes, Michael Jay (now Lord Jay of Ewelme), John Kerr (now Lord Kerr of Kinlochard), Matthew Kirk, Anne Lambert, Sir Paul Lever, David Madden, Sir David Manning, Sir Michael Pakenham and Sir Nigel Sheinwald. Most of all I owe a great debt to Sir Stephen Wall, for four years my colleague in No. 10, and the giant among the Europeanists of his generation. Many of the insights that inform this book are his.

There is no point in writing a book of this kind unless one is prepared to be rigorously self-critical, often of positions and attitudes I struck myself. In writing as I have, I speak for no one but myself. If I offend, that is not my purpose and no criticism is intended to be personal. I have the highest regard for Tony Blair, Gordon Brown and Peter Mandelson – all three – who framed New Labour's case for Europe. My first encounter with Gordon Brown was well before John Smith's death. We talked for nearly two hours. It was the most intensive grilling I had ever experienced on policy and politics in decades of political activism, displaying a depth of intellect and understanding that deserved to put him among Labour's 'all-time greats'. Tony Blair has an instinctive political feel combined with communication talents that are so rare I doubt there will ever be the like again in my lifetime. As for Peter Mandelson, he has shown toughness in adversity, transforming himself from spin-doctor through 'disgraced' minister to wise statesman, even a national treasure in some quarters. And he has been a very loyal friend. The mood now is very critical of New Labour, in my view unfairly, but far, far more could have been achieved.

There was a period in the first years of Blair's leadership of a 'once in a generation' sense of movement in the frozen landscapes of party politics. One is left with a painful sense of missed opportunity, nowhere more so than on Europe, particularly as there is now a significant question mark hanging over future British membership.

Many people have helped me with this book. I am grateful for the support I have received from my publishers, especially Joanna Godfrey. In particular I would like to thank Lord (Giles) Radice, my predecessor as chair of the thinktank Policy Network, a prolific author in his own right and a font of wisdom; Olaf Cramme, the director of Policy Network, Michael McTernan, his deputy, and Emma Kinloch, Simon Latham and Séamus Nevin who have helped me a great deal. My long-time friends Rt Hon. Peter Riddell and Tony Halmos who read the book in draft; and Gregg McClymont MP corrected me on points of Labour history. Most of all I would like to thank Patrick Diamond, who has been a constant source of advice and encouragement, and Caroline, my wife, who helped me edit the whole thing. Andrew, my son, has been his usual jolly and supportive self. The book is dedicated to my late parents, Jack and Betty Liddle, without whose inspiration and determination I would never have got anywhere.

Roger Liddle
November 2013

A Drama in Three Acts

> This is the story of fifty years in which Britain struggled to reconcile the past she could not forget with the future she could not avoid.
>
> The opening sentence of Hugo Young's *This Blessed Plot*[1] chronicling the history of Britain and Europe from Churchill to Blair

> The drift to isolation must stop and be replaced by a policy of constructive engagement.
>
> Tony Blair's speech at Chatham House, 1995[2]

> When the referendum comes, let me say now that if we can negotiate such an arrangement I will campaign for it with all my heart and soul.
>
> David Cameron's speech at Bloomberg, 2013[3]

This book is a drama in three acts with no clear ending yet in sight. The drama is the troubled story of Britain's relations with the EU. Running through the three acts of the drama is a set of key questions, once we set the daily froth of politics aside:

- What are the fundamental causes of the continuing 'British problem' with Europe? And is there any solution?
- Tony Blair made putting Britain's EU relations on a more positive basis a key objective of his premiership, but he failed. Why, and what lessons of long-term significance can be drawn?
- David Cameron announced in January 2013 a new policy of 'renegotiation' of our terms of membership and an in/out referendum on the outcome. Do his tactics stand a better chance of successfully bringing about a sustainable British–EU relationship for the longer term?
- The eurozone crisis that started in 2008 is said to be leading to a fundamental reshaping of the EU, with the creation of a more politically integrated 'hard core'; yet the emergence of a 'hard core' has been forecast for more than two decades, but has not so far arrived. Is it now unavoidable that a two- or three-tier Europe will develop, with Britain in the outer tier or, as some might put it more emotively, in the 'second or third division'?

- Is there a more positive social democratic British vision for Europe, what might it entail and how could a political case for it be won? Or is there no feasible alternative other than (for pro-Europeans) a resigned acceptance either of Britain's EU withdrawal or a more semi-detached relationship?

Act One: Missed Opportunity

Act One puts the European question in its historical context. The half-century from Britain's rejection of the Schuman Declaration in 1950 to the European travails of the Major government saw many 'missed opportunities' in Britain's relationship with the EU. In the immediate post-war period, when Britain's reputation was at its highest, Britain could have 'led in Europe', but we flunked it. Trapped by our history and imperial past, Britain repeatedly underestimated the dynamic of European integration on the Continent. Bevin rejected the Schuman Declaration in 1950; Eden failed to join the Messina talks in 1955, closing the door on Britain becoming a founder signatory of the Treaty of Rome; there was no national consensus around EEC membership under Wilson and Heath, even when it became possible after de Gaulle's departure in 1969; Britain hesitated over joining the EMS in the closing stages of the Callaghan government, leading subsequently to long and bitter arguments about our membership under Thatcher; she then railed against the single currency but could not halt the project's momentum; Major, by contrast, suffered the illusion that he had side-stepped the problem by negotiating the Maastricht Treaty opt-outs. In Blair's own words, 'the history of our engagement with Europe is one of opportunities missed',[4] but then of course he went on to fail in his attempt to lead Britain into the euro.

Roy Jenkins first characterised the UK relationship as 'semi-detached' in 1983 on the tenth anniversary of our European accession.[5] Why has this image so accurately cast a three-decade-long shadow? What has made Britain come across as 'the awkward partner'?[6] Jean Monnet characterised Britain's troubled post-war attitude towards European integration with brilliance and acidity as 'the price of victory'.[7] Yet there was then a legitimate question over Britain's 'European vocation', as General de Gaulle put it. When Britain first applied to join the Common Market in 1961, the 'Six' represented a mere fifth of our trade and Britain's self-image was still that of a great imperial power with global reach, the third member, with the USA and the Soviet Union, of the wartime Grand Alliance that had defeated Nazism. Arguably the structural obstacles to positive engagement should have become less powerful over time with the end of Empire and the permanent shift in trade patterns away from the old 'sterling area' towards Europe. The EU single market today represents half our trade. In the 1980s, Britain's long post-war period of relative decline against France and Germany came to an end. Logic might suggest that Britain could then have dealt with its partners in more self-confident terms, making our engagement easier. The eurocrisis has understandably led to increased negativity towards the EU, but it has equally underlined our close economic interdependence with the Continent, to an extent that was simply not the case half a century ago. In the 2010 Parliament, that interdependence was the Chancellor of the Exchequer's constantly repeated excuse for the delay in meeting his economic targets. In the short term it is good politics to heap the blame on Europe, but in the longer term should not the admission of European interdependence make the case for European engagement stronger?

In the last decade and a half, the rapid shift in the global balance of economic power makes the 'decline of the West' a reality, a new world in which a Britain outside the EU surely runs the risk of marginalisation. The USA looks more to the Pacific. Defence is undergoing major retrenchment after a decade in which the British Army has been forced to withdraw in Iraq and Afghanistan, with its military objectives at best half-secured, and at great cost in blood and treasure. Britain's position in the world is now far more defined by our place in Europe.

To an extent, reality has won through, though it is barely acknowledged. Our security relationship with France has never been closer since Suez. While not all EU members share the Franco-British sense of global responsibility (with some adopting the mindset of a 'greater Switzerland'), on questions of 'soft power' such as trade, climate change, international development or human rights, Britain shares with its partners the same broad objectives, and the benefits of collective EU action ought to command a wider consensus.

Geopolitically, Britain's weight in the world is declining fast due to the phenomenal rise of Asia; this has happened simultaneously with an unprecedented decline in the living standards of the average British family. The brute facts of our shrinking clout might superficially be thought to reinforce the case for deeper cooperation with our nearest European neighbours whose vision for society and the globe compares most closely with our own.

Yet Britain's attitude towards the EU remains deeply ambivalent. Has our national capacity for objectivity about our position in the world, and the global transformations underway, deserted us? Yet the path of historical determinism is not and never has been easy. Myths and politics get in the way of logic and leave a permanent mark on political perceptions and discourse.

The falsehood is often repeated that, when we signed up to join the European Community in the 1970s, we only joined a free-trade area, not a project for a 'federal superstate'. Our partners find this line of argument incomprehensible. For them, Europe has always been much more than a free-trade area, but much less than a federal superstate. Their motive for economic cooperation has always been at root political: to end the possibility of war on our continent (in which the EU has been a brilliant success) and, step by step, build a unity between our nation states that would make Europe count for more in the world. These political arguments for British membership were fully accepted, and publicly argued for, by Britain's political leaders in the 1960s and 1970s. But it is a delusion that Europe's political leaders today have as their aim the construction of a 'federal super state' or a 'United States of Europe'. The whole lesson of the eurocrisis is that the EU will, in Mario Draghi's famous words, 'do whatever it takes' to preserve the achievements of European integration; but throughout the crisis, EU leaders' reluctance to surrender national sovereignty is palpable, unless they really have to. Britain appears unable to face up to the reality of the 'EU of member states' as it is and prefers to fight a federalist bogey of its own fevered imagination. What are the roots of the psychological and political obstacles to a pragmatic recognition of our national interests? How does one explain the myths and identity crises that mean we cannot confidently deal with the reality of the EU?

Act Two: Blair's Failure

Act Two analyses the failure of the 1997–2010 Labour governments to end our 'semi-detached' relationship. For a committed New Labourist, failure is a blunt and absolute word. The apologist can plead in mitigation many important successes in Britain's European policy in this period: for most of it, British influence in Brussels was probably never higher. But domestically, in terms of how Britain judges its relationship with the EU, the end result was abject failure.[8] The forces of pro-Europeanism had by 2010 been scattered to the winds. Whilst the cancer of Euroscepticism then seemed dormant, little had been done to excise it from the body politic and it remained a critical threat to Britain's place in Europe. In terms of the national psychology, as measured both in opinion polls and the attitudes of the political, government and media elite, Britain and Europe ended up as far apart as ever. Yet to transform how the British feel in their guts about Europe was New Labour's ambition, and we failed.

New Labour's pro-Europeanism was deep and genuine, but its motivations lay in domestic politics, not in a clear vision for Britain's future in the EU. For New Labour, to be pro-Europe was to stand for a brand of modernising social democratic politics, as Tony Blair and Gordon Brown did. To be pro-European in Labour terms was to believe in the market economy, recognise the need for fiscal and economic discipline, and desire an end to the destructive politics of class division and industrial conflict. It was to oppose the traditional left's isolationism and unilateralism and view Britain as committed to the idea of 'the West'. Pro-Europeanism was a crucial part of Labour's modernisation and slow return to electability after the party's near-death experience in the early 1980s: it was essentially a project for British social democracy, not a project for the future of the EU.

New Labour did in time frame a European strategy. Many of its key planks – for example, for a more open and economically liberal Europe, for a deeper single market, for EU budget and wider economic reforms, for an EU led by its member states through the European Council, not dragooned by the European Commission, for more subsidiarity and a stronger role for national parliaments in EU decision-making – bear strong similarities to the reform agenda that David Cameron appears to advocate. Yet, although Blair achieved some notable successes (for example, the commitment in principle to the wide-ranging Lisbon agenda of economic reform, the Lisbon Treaty's formalisation of the role of the European Council), there were flaws and contradictions in Blair's objectives and they achieved mixed results. What are the lessons here for David Cameron's ambition to negotiate a 'new relationship' with the EU?

Analysis of the failings of the New Labour governments has been dominated by the Blair–Brown 'soap opera'. Labour's record of achievement would undoubtedly have been more substantial if the party's two leading figures had worked together more effectively. Yet whereas Blairites heap blame on Brown for most of the government's failings, the contemporary consensus is that, on the battle to take Britain into the euro, Blair was wrong and Brown right. Had Blair got his way on the euro, many argue that

Britain's economic problems since 2008 would have been more serious, because the pre-crisis boom would have been the greater on the back of lower ECB interest rates; in the consequently deeper bust, the sense of national resentment against the Brussels 'diktats' to which our economic policy would have been more subject, without the flexibility to depreciate sterling, would have stirred an even fiercer anti-Europeanism that might even have triggered the break-up of the single currency and possibly the whole EU in its wake. Yet there is an alternative view. By not joining the euro, the Treasury and the Bank of England kept their freedom of action, but their record of continued misjudgement has been breathtaking, with the result that Britain's economic performance has been more lamentable than much of the eurozone.[9] Had Britain become a member of the euro in the early 2000s, it could only have been on the basis of a less overvalued exchange rate. Britain would have had to pursue more prudent fiscal and regulatory policies. As a result, prior to 2008 the economy would have become less unbalanced. In the crisis, Britain would have had more say in shaping Europe's response. George Osborne, as chancellor of the Exchequer, would have shared Angela Merkel's misguided dogmatism on austerity, but he might have tipped the balance in favour of faster and more resolute collective action to tackle fundamental problems in the European banking system, which could have facilitated a faster UK recovery. To many in Britain, the whole euro venture now seems extraordinarily misguided, and the debate about British membership no longer relevant. Will this prove another historic 'missed opportunity' in the longer run?

Apart from staying out of the euro, did the Blair and Brown governments leave much of a European legacy? The St Malo Declaration[10] in 1999 paved the way for European defence and much closer cooperation on security issues between Britain and France, despite the public drama of the Blair–Chirac rift over the Iraq War. The British, and Tony Blair personally, left a major imprint on the four intergovernmental treaties that were signed in the New Labour period, but, in arguing for them, the government as a whole took the low road of appeasing Euroscepticism, rather than the high road of confronting it head on. As for perhaps Blair's biggest contribution to the course of European history – his passionate support for the most rapid possible enlargement of the Union to embrace the new democracies of central and eastern Europe – this commitment led him to wave aside any question of the imposition of transitional controls on the free movement of labour in 2004, with major consequences for domestic politics. The salience of immigration as an issue in our politics soared as a result and gave the opportunity for UKIP to link immigration to our EU membership.

None of these achievements ended British 'semi-detachedness'; indeed the unanticipated influx of east Europeans to Britain after 2004 may well have accentuated it. What does this failure tell us about the underlying structural obstacles to a bolder and more explicit Europeanism and how they might be overcome?

Act Three: Cameron's Gamble

The centrepiece of Act Three is the speech David Cameron felt compelled to deliver in January 2013 announcing a new European policy of 'renegotiation and referendum'.[11] He pledged that, should the Conservatives win the 2015 general election, an in/out referendum on Britain's EU membership would be held by 2017. At the time of writing, this Act is therefore by definition unfinished. The post-2015 prospects for the future of Britain's EU relationship are at best uncertain: the risks of 'accidental exit' can no longer be dismissed.

Not many people expected this turn of events. In the 2010 general election, the European question lay dormant. David Cameron's clear wish was for the European question to be downgraded and sidelined. His inner circle were said to believe that Europe had become a 'dead issue'. Cameron may well have welcomed the creation of the Conservative–Liberal Democrat Coalition as a means of moving the Conservative Party onto the centre ground and 'detoxifying the Tory brand'. On Europe it seemed a new consensus had now been reached: a cautious, conditional and heavily pragmatic Euro-realism. Some hailed this as the true lasting legacy of the Blair–Brown commitment to end Britain's semi-detachment. But this complacency proved misplaced.

The eurocrisis changed the political weather. It led to a serious loss of confidence in the EU and its institutions across the whole of Europe. But for British Eurosceptics, it presents a heaven-sent chance to loosen, even sever, Britain's European ties. In their hearts the most committed Eurosceptics want to believe that the euro is a doomed project, the eventual break-up of which will prove a decisive point in reversing post-war European integration, while liberating Britain from its shackles. Yet in their heads rational Eurosceptics recognise the strength of our partners' political commitment to sustain the euro. Their way of reconciling this tension is by arguing that the euro project can only survive by some giant leap towards fiscal, economic and ultimately political union of which they take for granted Britain could never be part. It is this 'remorseless logic'[12] that presents them with the opportunity they have long awaited for Britain to achieve a fundamental loosening of its relationship with the EU. They rarely ask themselves how far our eurozone partners share the logic of this giant federal leap: the true picture appears to be an acceptance of the need for more integration, but on a pragmatic 'step-by-step' basis, which may or may not offer an opportunity for major treaty change or suit a British timetable of 'renegotiation'.

The Cameron speech was a remarkable turn in British European policy. For the first time since the 1970s, a British prime minister declared that the present basis on which Britain is a member of the EU was no longer acceptable. This is quite different from the type of argument Blair made for 'reform', or Thatcher advanced in her 1988 Bruges speech for a nation state Europe. Cameron has endorsed the proposition that the present 'terms of our membership' are no longer acceptable to the Conservative Party. He has reopened the 'terms of entry' argument that Harold Wilson imagined he had closed with the 1975 referendum. Furthermore, he is the first British prime minister in the post-war era to volunteer Britain's consignment to the outer ring of a two- or three-speed Europe. An essential continuity in British foreign policy since the 1960s has been the conviction that if Britain wants to maintain its global position and punch above its weight in the world, it not only has to be a member of the EU, but it has somehow to maintain a position of leadership parity with France and Germany within it. Cameron argues that a looser relationship, effectively in Europe's outer tier, is an inevitable consequence of Britain's decision not to join the euro, but few people pose the question the other way round: can a proud nation like Britain define for itself a sustainable future within the EU if it voluntarily opts for outer tier status?

Cameron's speech was a testament to how much the case for Europe in Britain has weakened and the power of Eurosceptic thinking grown. Until Cameron made his speech, the pro-Europeans had largely vacated the battlefield. The timidity and weakness of the 'pros' is not matched by an equivalent circumspection on the part of the 'antis'. Among Conservatives, anti-Europeanism remains virulent among the influential 'party in the media' – the columnists of *The Times*, *Telegraph*, *Daily Mail* and *Spectator* – as the political scientist Tim Bale described them[13] in his thoughtful analysis of the Tory Party's long period in opposition and subsequent recovery. Among the ranks of Conservative MPs, there are significant numbers for whom unthinking Euroscepticism was a condition of success in their parliamentary selection. Some may be looking for an excuse, which Cameron's renegotiation may provide, to retreat from what they know to be an unrealistic policy of withdrawal. Others, however, would like either to get out of the EU altogether or drastically to limit the EU's powers. UKIP's success in the 2013 local elections, presaging a major opportunity for them in the European Parliament elections of 2014, has edged a collective Tory Party neurosis about Europe nearer to a complete psychological breakdown. Many Conservative MPs believe that the way to handle the UKIP threat is to appease it. But the absolutism of UKIP's core position on EU withdrawal makes appeasement problematic. Also, the core of UKIP's electoral appeal is not so much about Europe but a deeper emotional rejection of establishment politics and protest against immigration and modernity.

The Adullamite cave of Conservative Euroscepticism is internally divided. For a minority, a 'failed' renegotiation is a necessary prelude to a referendum in which Britain votes to pull out, which, in their quixotic view, would hand a British government a strong hand to negotiate a free-trade agreement with our EU partners. Yet, there are few historical precedents for a nation like Britain negotiating favourable economic terms with a trade bloc that accounts for nearly half our trade but only 8 per cent of the rest of the EU's. Others are more genuine that a new relationship within the EU can be renegotiated. Their goal is an association of sovereign nation states committed to the single market, but without an excessive burden of regulation, with the federalist trappings of the European institutions cut down to size, and the EU's role in our national life confined as far as possible to 'trade and political cooperation'. Yet there are big doubts whether a 'looser Union' of this kind is either credible in its own terms or remotely negotiable.

How would the implied weakening of the supranational institutions, especially the Commission and the Court of Justice as upholders of member-state obligations under the treaties, be consistent with the British Conservatives' professed aim of strengthening the single market? Who intervenes to prevent member-state business interests seeking national shelter from the cold winds of free competition? How does one prevent 'loosening' turning into a messy disintegration if the mentality becomes 'If they can do just as they want, why can't we?' As for negotiability, who amongst our EU partners shares this vision of an EU that is little more than a free-trade area and a framework for intergovernmental political cooperation? On the Continent, the growing forces of Euroscepticism on both right and left are not the Conservatives' natural allies: they are anti-Europe because in part they oppose the deepening of the single market and economic liberalisation that the Conservatives want to see. On the single market the Conservatives do have allies in the 'northern liberal' camp, but this group tends to be comfortable with a degree of supranationalism and political integration with which British Conservatives find it hard to live.

Cameron's 2013 speech on Europe glossed over these difficult questions. He successfully dampened the risk of a public backlash from business by expressing his personal commitment to Britain's continued membership and couching his plan for renegotiation in terms of a very general set of reforms that appeared reasonable and balanced and Tony Blair could have endorsed. Yet his acquiescence in an in/out referendum on the basis that our existing terms of membership of the European club are unsatisfactory is an extraordinary policy turnaround: for all their previous promises of referendums on new EU treaties, Conservative leaders have never before committed to a referendum on the fundamental issue of Britain's actual EU membership.

On the European question, Cameron's modernisation project now faces its supreme test. It is difficult to believe that someone of Cameron's background and political disposition would regard it as practical Tory statecraft for Britain to come out of the EU, even if he possesses little emotional commitment to the idea of Europe. Every Conservative prime minister since Harold Macmillan has judged membership to be in our national interests, including Margaret Thatcher for all the time she held office. Yet the negotiating ground on which the national interest and internal party preferences can be reconciled looks extremely narrow, if indeed they can be reconciled at all. In terms of party management, Europe remains a far more problematic issue than any other. The Conservative tradition of statecraft has almost always emphasised the pragmatic importance of gaining and holding power rather than inflexible adherence to any particular policy or ideological viewpoint: when it has not, as on the repeal of the Corn Laws in the 1840s or the question of tariff reform in the 1900s, the party has divided with fatal consequences for its electability. Can Cameron, and any Conservative successor, persuade the party not to repeat this historic mistake? And if it can't be done, where will a politician with Cameron's instinct for power come down?

Either way, the old argument about Britain's semi-detachedness has been completely reframed. Whereas in 1997 the European question was defined in terms of whether Blair could achieve his ambition to end British semi-detachedness, by 2013 the question had become whether Prime Minister Cameron could somehow dress up some ill-specified codification of greater semi-detachedness as a 'new relationship with the EU' that the British people would be prepared to endorse in a referendum. Tony Blair was determined to bring to an end the state of ambivalence in Britain's EU relationship; now ambivalence seems the best that a British pro-European can hope for. What accounts for this depressing slide from Blair's vaunting ambition to Cameron's defensive promise of a renegotiated relationship? What will it ultimately mean for the future of the EU and Britain's place within it? Or is the more realistic question what will be Britain's place outside, or in some form half-outside?

The Plan of the Book

Act One, 'Missed Opportunity', explores in more detail the constraints and myths that historically had made Britain the 'awkward partner'. Chapter 1, 'The Conservative Legacy', describes how and why the Conservatives made themselves the party of Europe and then proceeded to throw that precious achievement away. Chapter 2, 'Europe and the Failure of Labour Revisionism', considers why it took Labour four decades to come to terms with our EU membership. Chapter 3, 'Labour's Turn to Europe', analyses the formation of New Labour's pro-Europeanism as a story of principled commitments and tactical retreats.

Act Two, 'Blair's Failure', comprises the central section of the book and analyses the lessons of the New Labour record. Chapter 4, 'In Power without a Policy', recalls Labour's first days in office up to October 1997 and how then it saw its European ambitions. Chapter 5, 'Policy-Making at the Red Lion', describes how and why a euro referendum in Labour's first term was effectively ruled out and how then Blair tried to rethink his European policy after this setback. Chapter 6, '(Half) Making the Case', discusses how Blair chose to make the case for Europe. Chapter 7, 'Reforming the Club Rules', turns to the unavoidable necessity of institutional reform. Chapter 8, 'Reforming Member State Economies', describes why and how making the case for economic reform was seen as essential to making the case for Europe. Chapter 9, 'Drafting, Ditching and (90 per cent) Reviving Europe's Constitution', draws lessons from the story of the attempt to draft a European constitution. Chapter 10, 'Blocked on the Euro', discusses why Blair lost his battle to join the euro. Chapter 11, 'A Glass Half Empty', offers an overall assessment of the New Labour record.

Act Three, 'Cameron's Gamble', examines prospects for the future; why and how we have reached a point where our position as a euro-out may lead to unintentional exit as a Europe-out; and what alternative, if any, the left can offer. Chapter 12, 'The Unexpected Return of Europe to British Politics', considers why Europe came back as a huge issue during the Cameron Coalition. Chapter 13, 'Renegotiation and Referendum', analyses the viability of David Cameron's strategic response to Eurosceptic pressures. Chapter 14, 'A Progressive Alternative', argues that there is a credible and more positive alternative to the present choice being offered to the British people between permanent semi-detachedness and withdrawal. A brief Conclusion, 'Britain's Unresolved Choice', summarises the argument for resolving Britain's dilemma by staying in.

The Prelude

> What is at stake in the European controversy in British politics is a major choice about Britain's role in the global political economy which involves questions of interest, ideology and identity. Such choices occur rather rarely but when they do they often trigger political realignments which can constitute major turning points in the life of parties and governments [. . .] (The European issue) fuses together issues of sovereignty and identity with political economy in a novel and powerful way. Andrew Gamble. The European issue in British Politics.[1]

Most accounts of Britain's troubled EU relationship depend on the 'pro' or 'anti' prejudices of the writer. For 'pros', their favourite explanation is the feebleness of Britain's political leaders in displaying a lack of leadership in the face of the obstacles posed by a fiercely hostile press, much of it foreign-owned. The 'antis', however, tend to see the issue in terms of outraged public opinion, tricked into voting for membership in 1975 on the basis that Britain was joining a free-trade area not a political union, and angered by successive surrenders of sovereignty to Brussels by an out-of-touch political elite. The 'antis' are right that most of the governing elite in politics and business accept the reality of our EU membership as being in our national interest, but in a grudging way that deliberately forswears enthusiasm and obscures political responsibility. Their largely technocratic approach drains our EU membership of any idealism and at the same time reinforces the myth of domination by a Brussels bureaucracy. The conduct of Britain's EU policy is constrained by deeply embedded interpretations of UK national interests based on ideas and 'myths' that transcend individual politicians, parties and governments.

Most politicians, perhaps unsurprisingly, like to think of history as a story of 'great men'. However, our political leaders are not free agents making free choices about the policies they choose to pursue: they are constrained by the ideas, interests and institutions that have for decades shaped the policy options that are seen as realistic. That pattern of path dependency has been evident in Britain's relations with Europe. The prevailing consensus can be challenged by a leader willing to risk 'making the weather': but 'making the weather' requires a boldness in challenging assumptions and 'myths', which, particularly on Europe, few politicians have the confidence and power to do. This theme runs through every Act of our European drama.

The Fundamental Problem is not British Public Opinion

The degree of public hostility to our EU membership has fluctuated over 40 years rather than grown. Six months before the 1975 referendum, the polls suggested that a large majority would vote to exit; the referendum result was two to one in favour of staying in. Since then, public attitudes to our membership tend to track perceptions of Europe's success or otherwise, what academics call its 'output legitimacy'. In the recession of the early 1980s, a clear majority backed UK withdrawal as the extravagant promises of our membership were unfulfilled. The Continent appeared in the grip of what *The Economist* called 'eurosclerosis'. At the same time, Margaret Thatcher was 'hand-bagging' our partners to secure a British budget rebate. Opinion became more favourable towards the end of the 1980s when business enthused about the potential of the single market and Jacques Delors' '1992 programme'. Support waned after the debacle of John Major's withdrawal from the ERM in 1992 and during the 'beef wars', but grew again in the early years of Blair's premiership. Although the polls always showed a majority against joining the single currency, in the early 2000s, a clear majority of the public expected Britain to join the euro eventually. Given the travails of the euro since 2010, it is hardly surprising that support for the EU, and even more for the euro, has plummeted: this is not just a British phenomenon, but applies across most of the EU. Yet polling also suggests that the public are open to increased European cooperation to tackle unemployment, improve the environment, fight crime and promote our security.[2] True, they have little confidence or trust in EU institutions, but this is no special triumph for Euroscepticism: levels of trust in the EU institutions are around the same depressing lows as for national government, Parliament and the UK political parties.

For all the public's mistrust, Europe is not generally in the public's top ten concerns. In pollsters' language, its salience is low. There is a significant section of the electorate who are irreconcilably opposed to our EU membership, perhaps more than a third, while positive support is registered by less than a sixth of voters. The remainder fall into the category of people who claim to know little about the EU, and do not much like what they know, but are open to persuasion that membership nevertheless remains in our national interest. In the pollster Peter Kellner's judgement, if David Cameron recommends 'revised terms' for our membership in a referendum, he has a good chance of winning, with a result not dissimilar to 1975. The surprise is that this remains the position, despite the constant bias of the popular press against the EU and the consistent feebleness with which the pro-European case has been argued.

The Problematic View of Europe among Britain's Political Class

The root of the British problem with Europe lies not so much with public opinion, but with the failure of our political class to make the case for our membership. The reason is in part fear of media attack: the anti-European press have a track record of treating pro-Europeans ruthlessly. More important, though, is that in both of our main political parties there is a lack of emotional commitment to Europe. At the Conservative Party base, among the diminished ranks of elderly constituency activists, dogmatic opposition flourishes. In Labour's case, our EU membership is something the party in principle favours, but is best not talked about. Labour has fought every European Parliament election on national issues and never made the case for why strong Labour representation in the European Parliament would make a difference. Since UKIP became a force on the national scene, and up until the time of writing, Labour has preferred to ignore its presence rather than attempt to demolish its arguments, largely because Labour believes that UKIP will do more damage to the Conservatives than to them. Party advantage trumps the national interest.

In the Conservative Party, the pro-European position is much weaker. Since 1990 the dominant voices have been hostile. The bitter parliamentary battles over the Maastricht Treaty's ratification were followed by front-bench Conservative opposition to every new European treaty that Blair signed, coupled with the demand for a referendum on every single one. Who now remembers what of significance the Treaty of Amsterdam or the Treaty of Nice contained – or even when they happened? As for the more high-profile Lisbon Treaty, it would be interesting to discover how many Conservative MPs can remember three significant changes that were made as a result of it. It was about Europe: therefore they opposed it and, in doing so, they could bask in the approval of their tiny band of constituency activists and become heroes of the columnists of the right-wing press.

As a result of the weakness of the British political class in allowing anti-Europeanism to fester, a huge gap has opened up between internal party politics and the realities of modern statecraft. In modern Britain, senior ministers spend a significant part of their time handling European issues. They may not particularly enjoy aspects of this process, especially lots of tiresome late-night negotiations in Brussels, but its importance rarely escapes them. Few emerge from the experience with the conviction that Britain should sever its EU ties. Nigel Lawson, 25 years after he ceased to be chancellor of the Exchequer, has expressed this view, but he is perhaps the eccentric, if distinguished, exception. Yet few have been prepared to invest their political capital in explaining to the public why Europe matters. There is a deep emotional reserve. Why? The big themes running throughout our three-act drama are: the constancy of Britain's global, not continental, outlook; the role of myth in the political and public imagination; the hold of the 'Westminster model'; and the significance of the European question in intra-party faction fights and personal struggles for power.

The Constancy of Britain's 'Global Outlook'

Throughout this drama, one constant – shared by our main political parties – has been the assumption that Britain's interests and outlook are global and not just European, and that in this we are very different from our Continental partners. Britain's self-image remains that of a global power with global reach. The most famous exposition of this self-image was Churchill's description of Britain at the centre of 'three circles' of influence:[3] the Empire and Commonwealth, the transatlantic 'special relationship' and Europe. This imagery has exerted extraordinary power through the decades. For Harold Wilson, Britain's frontier lay on the Himalayas. For Blair, Britain was a global 'pivot';[4] for Cameron we are a 'network' power.[5] This self-regarding imagery subconsciously, of course, puts Britain at the centre of the world and reinforces the view that Britain should not commit itself to Europe at the expense of its global role.

To be fair to Churchill's greatness, he was the least of successive sinners in this respect. With wonderful magnanimity and foresight, he led the post-war call for Europe to unite, but he was ambiguous about Britain's role. He supported 'unity', but did he want Britain to be part of a 'union'? Churchill was vague. As prime minister after 1951 he accepted (perhaps reluctantly in the face of pressure from Anthony Eden) that we are 'with them, not of them' as he once famously minuted.[6] One still hears this argument today: the eurozone should integrate more, but that is for them, not for us. Britain's boundless horizons are set by the global transformations that are opening up new opportunities in Asia and other parts of the world.

Strategically this global commitment has found expression in the overriding priority Britain has given to NATO and the US security relationship, while reserving sentiment and tradition for the Commonwealth with the British monarch as its head. In 1945 Britain saw itself, perhaps then legitimately, as a victor in war, in an altogether different and bigger league than the devastated nations of Continental Europe. Britain endeavoured to hang on to its 'great power status' as one of the wartime 'big three'. Yet it quickly became apparent that an economically enfeebled Britain lacked the resources to sustain an independent global role. As Peter Clarke's *The Last Thousand Days of the British Empire* brilliantly describes,[7] by 1947 the Attlee government had granted independence to India, withdrawn British forces from Palestine and Greece, and exhausted the US loan that Keynes, in his final noble act of service to the British state, had negotiated to support Britain's balance of payments after the abrupt American cancellation of lend-lease at the end of the war. Yet the political class found it difficult to recognise the implications. In one sense, one can but admire the sense of global responsibility that post-war Britain accepted. Despite the evident 'writing on the wall' for Britain's great power pretensions, the Attlee government sustained a huge defence budget, complete with its costly military research and development and industrial complex. The huge defence build-up at the time of the Korean War in 1950 demonstrated Britain's commitment to the West. Hugh Gaitskell, as Labour's chancellor, backed rearmament all the way, despite the National Health Service (NHS) economies that it necessitated, and the fateful consequences for Labour unity as a result of the Bevanite resignations that the Labour cabinet's decision triggered. At almost the same time, Britain refused to take part in the first moves to a united Europe; acceptance of the Schuman Declaration in 1950 would, in the view of the policy-making elite of the time, have wrongly prioritised Europe over all else.

The decisive jolt to Britain's great power illusions came at Suez when it became clear that President Eisenhower was prepared to pull the plug on American support for sterling unless the Anglo-French intervention was called off. These fateful events all occurred around the same time as the Messina talks that led to the founding of the European Community in the

Treaty of Rome, famously dismissed by the Conservative 'second-in-command', 'Rab' Butler, as 'some archaeological excavations at an old Sicilian town',[8] of no conceivable relevance to the UK. The Suez disaster forced Eden's successors to become more open to Europe, but in considerable part as a way of rebuilding London's broken relationship with Washington, given the priority that Presidents Truman, Eisenhower and Kennedy all gave to closer European integration in which they wanted Britain to play a key role. The 1960s and 1970s were decades when Britain accepted the realities of its reduced international position. But Margaret Thatcher's Falklands victory in 1982 restored a national sense that Britain's place in the world was somehow special. For all his pro-Europeanism, Blair followed her in perpetuating that global self-image through his advocacy of 'humanitarian interventionism' and his elevation of the 'special relationship' to new heights post 9/11.

But this global view has been integral to the UK's economic outlook as well. This global perspective has often been ascribed to the role and influence of the City of London. Yet in the early post-war years the City had sunk into relative decline and only revived as a global financial centre against New York in the late 1960s, boosted successively by the end of exchange controls in 1979, the 'big bang' in 1986 and the emergence of integrated global trading banks in the 1990s. However, a major success for the City has been its emergence as the financial centre of the EU single market and euro-denominated trading, following the liberalisation of the EU's wholesale financial markets and the creation of the single currency in the 2000s. For all the aftershocks of the 2007–8 banking crisis, and a legitimate debate about the potential risks of hosting one of the world's greatest financial centres with assets and liabilities in many multiples of UK GDP, the City's global fortunes are intrinsically bound up with our EU membership.

Britain harbours an image of itself as a global trading nation. Yet the pattern of our trade has changed dramatically. The Lancashire cotton industry is no more, but in the late 1940s it was still exporting around a third of its output to India, and Britain was also then still the world's largest shipbuilder. In manufacturing, Britain is now a far larger exporter to the rest of Europe than it was in the early post-war decades and has been much less successful in penetrating emerging markets overseas than the French and Germans, despite our supposed 'global reach'. We often presume that Britain, with its distinctive 'global outlook', together with the advantages of speaking English, the quality of our professions and our historic reputation for political stability and the rule of law, is well placed to foster a new generation of 'merchant adventurers' seeking their fortune across the world's high seas. One would like to think so, but whether these merchant adventurers can gain access to new markets without the negotiating weight and influence of the EU trade bloc behind them remains an open issue.

The Power of Historic Myth

This view of the uniqueness of Britain's global role has been reinforced by the power of historic myths that have held the public and political imagination in their grip. Britain is rightly proud of the stability of its institutions in contrast to the revolutionary upheavals and foreign invasions that most countries on the Continent have had to endure in the past and previous centuries. Whether this sense of uniqueness has been due as much to the luck of being an island, as to the adaptability of our pre-democratic parliamentary institutions, this has reinforced a view of Britain's specialness, if not uniqueness, in contrast to our Continental neighbours. And many politicians on both the right and left of the spectrum attribute what they see as special about Britain to the indivisible sovereignty of the House of Commons. This was what enabled Britain to 'stand alone' against Hitler. That same indivisible sovereignty was what in the immediate post-war era enabled the Attlee government, with its large majority in the Commons, to build the welfare state, create the NHS and take the first giant strides towards a British socialist commonwealth. This perceived strength of the Westminster model has reinforced myths on both right and left that have over the decades inhibited Britain's full engagement in the EU.

The 'Dunkirk myth' of how Britain 'standing alone' faced up to Hitler's might, reinforced the ahistorical view, ignoring the experience of previous centuries, that Britain could survive and prosper by keeping clear of Continental engagement. In the immediate post-war era, it was the lingering ties to Empire reinforced by the Dunkirk myth that explained much of the emotional blockage on the right about Europe: Conservative views only began to change after the debacle of Suez. On the left, the idea of Empire never had universal appeal, with independence for India celebrated as one of the Attlee government's outstanding achievements, but in its place was substituted a new myth about 'Britain's unique potential for moral leadership in the world' as head of the Commonwealth and a leading backer of the United Nations (UN). The conceit of the Campaign for Nuclear Disarmament (CND) was that a unilateral gesture by Britain could rid the world of nuclear weapons. This conceit was of course rejected by the Labour right. But Hugh Gaitskell came out against the Common Market in 1962 because he worried it meant the 'end of the Commonwealth'[9] – though within a decade, with Britain remaining outside the Common Market, the influence and role of the Commonwealth had considerably waned. Privately it was the alliance for freedom (as he saw it) with the USA to which he attached top priority, despite the insistent urgings of the Kennedy administration that Britain should engage in moves towards a united Europe.

But it is in terms of domestic political economy that the myths of indivisible Westminster sovereignty have proved most stubborn. On the left, the Attlee government's achievements were seen as a triumph of nation state social democracy: the 'spirit of '45' has left a lasting imprint on Labour thinking. Despite British economic weakness and our extreme dependence on securing US loans and restoring Britain's overseas trade, the Attlee government was able to build the post-war welfare state. It did this behind a protective wall of import controls, domestic rationing and the suppression of personal consumption, particularly by an increasingly aggrieved middle class. The collective spirit of wartime lasted long enough for Labour to achieve this. But the nation state model of central planning and economic controls captivated Labour activists for more than a generation. When the Wilson government model of planning in a mixed economy failed to deliver the growth it promised, the left reverted to the Bennite 'alternative economic strategy' (AES), which rejected Europe for the very good reason that its 'dirigiste' model of state planning and direction of industry was inconsistent with the Treaty of Rome: from his perspective on this issue, Benn was correct. After 'nation state' Bennery had contributed to Labour's 1983 electoral disaster, the Kinnock reconstruction of the party showed a new openness to European integration. Blair and Brown were enthusiasts for this, but in time they also constructed a new model of nation state social democracy in which national economic autonomy was secured by central bank independence and fiscal rules, the market was left free to deliver growth, and the role of New Labour governance was to redistribute the proceeds of that growth to improve public services and tackle poverty. In their New Labour model of nation state social democracy, Europe became a desirable option, not a fundamental essential.

On the right, Thatcherism initially embraced Europe as the driver of the 1992 programme of liberalisation to bring about the single market. However, the 'spill-over' consequences, which extended the reach of Europe into (for Thatcherites) unwelcome action in social and environmental fields, and revived the project for monetary union, turned Thatcherites against European integration. They developed an alternative political economy based on the idea of an 'offshore Britain'. In this model, a myth was created of Brussels as a regulatory monster which, in terms of intrusiveness and its attendant economic costs, not to mention the grave economic consequences of a misguided single currency, held back the UK's economic potential. For 'offshore Britain', the opportunity lay in a flexible and deregulated Britain taking advantage of the quickening pace of global transformation.

The Hold of the 'Westminster Model'

Our adversarial style of politics and the consensus style of European decision-making are a poor match. British politicians tend to believe in what they call 'strong government'. General elections hand parties a 'mandate', legitimised by winning a Commons majority, based on the manifesto on which their party fought the election. The mandate gives ministers their mission to deliver: to enable them to do this, they should be all-powerful masters of their department (with the role of an independent civil service as 'guardians of the state' increasingly under challenge), accountable only to the Commons for their actions. This constitutional theory, if it deserves the accolade of 'theory', is riddled with obvious problems. Few voters are aware of what is in most party manifestos. In Britain's 'first-past-the-post' electoral system, a majority in the Commons can now be secured on the back of the support of little more than a third of those who voted in the election and a far smaller proportion of the electorate as a whole. When the general election of 2010 did not deliver a majority to any party, the Conservative–Lib Dem Coalition agreement substituted for the manifesto mandate and the style of British government carried on largely as before. In the Westminster model, ministers take firm decisions and pull off undisputed triumphs, which their own side can cheer and the opposition duly denounce.

The European way of doing business is very different. The essence of the EU is not a 'federal' commitment to build a United States of Europe. At its core is the principle that its member states will work together around a shared table to find common solutions to the problems they face together. This principle is formally constitutionalised through complex treaties and reinforced informally through the sheer daily habit of working through common problems. Compromise is not just the inevitable outcome: it is a way of life. For British politicians schooled in the 'Westminster model', the idea of compromise is deeply alien – and even worse when it is with foreigners. The consequence is that ministers try to mask the significance for our national life of the EU policies, to which, as members of the Council of Ministers, they have assented, except on the relatively rare occasions when they feel they can ride into some high-profile political battle with our EU partners 'standing up for Britain'. Who can imagine a ministerial statement to the House of Commons in the following style?

> In Europe we face a genuine common problem of A, but our sovereign member states have somewhat different approaches as to how it should be tackled. The French advocated B; the Germans C; and several other member states D ... I am, however, able to report to the House that I was able to persuade our partners of X and Y, which I feel meets 80% of UK objectives. However, in order to reach this agreement I have agreed that the United Kingdom will in addition support Z. Left to ourselves we would not have gone as far as Z, but on balance the overall agreement is strongly in our national interest. Of course, as the House will be aware, the compromise we have reached in the Council of Ministers will not necessarily be the final outcome. The European Parliament has to agree to the package and may propose amendments of its own. But I am confident, on the basis of the European Parliament's past record, that the detailed scrutiny they will give our proposals [*unlike most domestic legislation which is forced unamended through the Commons by the Whips – probably best left unsaid!*] will result in important details being improved. And it is on this basis that I commend this European compromise to the House.

This of course is an exaggeration to make a point, but in the British political mindset, such a statement is countercultural. Hence in our politics the role of Europe is kept opaque and as far as possible unmentionable, except when political capital can be won by attacking it.

The Role of the European Question in Intra-Party Politics and Manoeuvres

These assumptions and myths have all played a crucial part – not so much in the electoral competition between the parties, as in the internal struggles for power within them. In modern politics, the most destructive effects have been seen in the Conservative Party. The idea of 'offshore Britain' became central to the Thatcher myth: that she had been right about Europe all along, whereas it was a pro-European conspiracy by Michael Heseltine, Geoffrey Howe and others that had brought her down. Within the Conservative Party, the power of this myth became greatly strengthened by the ERM debacle in the early 1990s, membership of which Thatcher had opposed and only embraced reluctantly under extreme pressure from the pro-European forces who were later held responsible for her downfall. This led to the internal divisions that destroyed the Major government, as vividly described by Norman Fowler. The Conservative Party is still living through the consequences. Anti-Europeanism led to the successive leadership defeats of Kenneth Clarke by William Hague and Iain Duncan Smith. It also led to the ambiguities of David Cameron's 'modernisation' project, which tried to deal with the European question by avoiding it – successful in opposition but deeply damaging in government.[10]

However, Labour too has seen its fair share of the European question playing its destructive part in internal party manoeuvres. Harold Wilson's about-turn on Europe in 1971, when he switched from support of membership to opposing it 'on the Tory terms', had devastating consequences for Labour unity and destroyed the real chance of a national consensus behind our EU membership, but arose from his (quite reasonable) fear that James Callaghan might successfully challenge him for the party leadership on a populist anti-European platform of nation state social democracy. Similarly Gordon Brown used the European question as a means of undermining Tony Blair's leadership by currying favour with the anti-European press (though to be fair to Brown, Blair himself was not entirely innocent of similar tactical ploys), although as prime minister, the reality of Brown's pragmatic pro-European stance was to disappoint the Eurosceptic admirers he had so assiduously cultivated.

Europe has always mattered far more in the internal politics of our parties than the febrile influences of public opinion. This more than any other factor explains the problematic nature of the European question in British politics. The rest of this book develops these themes.

Act One: Missed Opportunity

> If the British Empire and Commonwealth should last for a thousand years, men will still say this was their finest hour.
>
> Winston Churchill, 1940

> Churchill's words still resonate. Of course the British Empire lasted barely another two decades. The British people had to reconcile the pride in their wartime achievement with the relative poverty in which it left us and the twilight of our role as a world power.
>
> Stephen Wall, 2008[1]

CHAPTER 1

The Conservative Legacy

The European legacy that Blair inherited in 1997 was essentially a Conservative story in two distinct halves, with Labour's Harold Wilson occupying the stage at times decisively, at other moments mercurially. The first half of the Conservative story is the one-time party of Empire somehow by the 1960s turning itself into the party of Europe. Then, this remarkable achievement is gradually cast aside and the story becomes one of steady drift towards Euroscepticism with consequences that are apparent to this day.

The Conservative Turn to Europe

Harold Macmillan deserves the accolade of a prime minister who 'made the weather'. To put membership of the European Community on the agenda of British politics was a major change of direction and part of a wider reassessment of Britain's role in the world following the 1956 Suez debacle. Amazingly for a protégé of Churchill, he accepted the imperative of rapid withdrawal from Empire.[1] He ended conscription and gave impetus to a process of bringing Britain's defence commitments in line with constrained resources. He was the first prime minister to recognise and grapple with Britain's decline. The motivations for his turn to Europe were a mixture of high strategy and low politics, with both economic and foreign policy justifications playing a part.

At the level of electoral politics, Macmillan sensed an opportunity to enhance the credentials of the Conservatives as a party of the future: the party best equipped to modernise Britain and meet the growing aspirations of a newly enfranchised consumer society, as opposed to a Labour party stuck in its old world of class politics, trade union power and the culture of the 'cloth cap'. Macmillan famously boasted that Britons had 'never had it so good'. Privately, however, he came to recognise a less optimistic truth. The West German 'economic miracle' was by then well underway. The economic balance of power in Europe was shifting rapidly, rather as the rise of China has altered the global balance of economic power in the last 15 years. Britain was rapidly being overtaken by Germany – not only in terms of growth and relative gross domestic product (GDP), but in terms of competitiveness and quality. Britain was rapidly losing ground in world export markets. As Geoffrey Owen has argued, the protectionism of imperial preference facilitated a strong export revival after 1945, but damaged Britain in the longer term by focusing our exports on slowly growing markets.[2] In the 1930s, public policy had actively encouraged cartels and monopolies, in part to protect key sections of Conservative core support in the depression, who might have been attracted by fascism: for example, retail price maintenance protected small shopkeepers (like Margaret Thatcher's father in Grantham). But these lingering monopolies and restrictive practices needed to be exposed to tougher competition if British productivity was to rise. The best route was thought to be through participation in the Common Market's rapid growth and the 'cold shower' of competition it would bring.

Failing to Secure Free Trade

Politics, however, made it difficult for the government to acknowledge publicly the realities of Britain's reduced economic position. Macmillan's first preference was to find a technical solution to Britain's trade problem that would not open up a seismic political debate. Hence Britain's 1957 proposal for a European free-trade area aimed at securing unimpeded access for our exports to the Common Market, while avoiding the imposition of the Six's common external tariff on Britain's Commonwealth imports. At the same time, a free-trade area would weaken the importance of the integrated political structures that the Six had agreed in the Treaty of Rome.[3] This position had some potential for support in Germany. Chancellor Adenauer's heir apparent, Ludwig Erhard, the author of the West German *Wirtschaftwunder*, feared that too close an embrace of the French might result in protectionist policies threatening his ordo-liberal economic achievement.[4] Yet Britain's diplomatic potential to build a credible free-trade alliance had been greatly weakened by its stand-offish attitude to the Messina talks. For Adenauer, the Treaty of Rome was the top political priority, believing as he did that European integration was the only way that Germany could regain international legitimacy and its own sense of nationhood after World War II. He was in no mood to abandon it.

The failure of Macmillan's 'free-trade area' initiative is now largely forgotten. Yet there is also a crucial lasting lesson that Macmillan was forced to learn, but today's Eurosceptics forget. When Eurosceptics argue that when Britain joined the Common Market we 'simply joined a free-trade area', they do not know their history. A European free-trade area 'without Brussels strings' proved impossible to negotiate when European integration was in its infancy. For the UK, creating the European Free Trade Association (EFTA) Seven to rival the Common Market Six proved a poor and inadequate substitute, both in terms of its market size and political clout. The episode has contemporary echoes. Macmillan was trying to get most of the economic benefits of being an 'in' and avoid the political risks of the 'ins' caucusing in ways damaging to UK interests, while preserving British sovereignty as an 'out': a classic example of Britain wanting to participate in the benefits of European integration, but in a highly conditional way that our prospective partners found unacceptable. When the proposal for a wider European free-trade area foundered, the big political choice on Community membership could not be circumvented. But the realities of brute power were hard for 'Great Britain' to acknowledge and therefore the public arguments were fudged.

The Strategic Case for Europe

Macmillan also recognised the strategic significance of the Schuman Declaration and the Treaty of Rome. In part there was idealism in his support for a united Europe that would end the risk of mass slaughter in which so many of his compatriots and friends had died. It was tinged, however, with steely cynicism and 'realpolitik'. He feared the emergence of a united Europe across the Channel from which Britain would find itself excluded. A united Europe without Britain would, he reckoned, eventually be dominated by Germany. As he once minuted the Treasury's permanent secretary, 'it is really giving them on a plate what we fought in two world wars to prevent'.[5] Also, a united Europe without Britain would diminish the UK in the eyes of Washington. Here crude politics mixed with Macmillan's traditionalist view of Britain's global role. Conservative electoral strategy required Britain visibly to maintain its 'seat at the top table' in world affairs. Just as Churchill in the first half of the 1950s had sustained the image that he could deal with Eisenhower and Stalin in a British-led initiative to end the Cold War, so Macmillan relished international summitry with Khrushchev and Eisenhower, and as the statesman father figure to the young Jack Kennedy. The claim that under Macmillan the Conservatives could be trusted with foreign policy[6] and Britain would maintain its seat at the top table featured strongly in their 1959 election victory.[7] The flaunting of the closeness of Britain's relationship with the USA was Macmillan's means of assuaging a national pride wounded by the decline of Empire: on it rested his famous boast that Britain could be the 'Athens' to the new 'Rome'.[8] Macmillan also depended on the Americans to supply the Polaris nuclear missiles to deliver Britain's independent nuclear deterrent and sustain this continued badge of great power status. The turn to Europe enabled Macmillan to rebuild the strained 'special relationship' with America and at the same time hand him some electoral trump cards. His policy was a curious mixture of idealism, statesmanship and genuine belief in a European vocation for Britain, on the one hand, laced with crude cynicism, loathing of the Germans, great power illusion and electoral showmanship, on the other.

Overcoming the 'Dunkirk Myth'

To achieve his goals, Macmillan and the succeeding generation had to overcome, or rather circumvent, the 'Dunkirk myth'. The most enduring hold of this myth was of British exceptionalism – how 'standing alone' became Britain's 'finest hour', bolstering a legacy of pride in Britain's independent role in the world which outlived reality and fed a deep suspicion of Europe and its entire works.[9] Ironically, pre-war this same basic mindset had led to appeasement and the shameful resonance of Chamberlain's words at the time of Munich about an abandoned Czechoslovakia as a 'far away country of which we know little'. Post-war, of course, no one seriously argued that Europe could be ignored. The Soviet tanks were too close and threatening. Nevertheless, the Continent remained largely a world of alien 'otherness' with lingering hatred of the Germans and deep suspicion of the French. For these reasons, the domestic politics of European Union (EU) membership had the potential to be extremely destabilising within the Conservative party. Here was the traditional party of Empire proposing to join an entity that would impose tariffs on the vital exports of white Commonwealth countries on the other side of the world, whose soldiers had fought to defend the home country on battlefields as far flung as Gallipoli, Burma, North Africa and the Western Front. Here was a European Community committed to a common agricultural policy (CAP) that at this time alarmed British farmers so much that 'Rab' Butler warned Macmillan it was 'dynamite *for* and to the County constituencies'.[10] Here was a system of agricultural protection that could deny working-class families access to cheap New Zealand lamb and butter that had become staples of the household diet.

Macmillan's inner resolve was firm and clear: he wanted to join the Common Market and sidelined the sceptics in his cabinet, cleverly ensuring that all the key players in the ministerial negotiations were firm supporters of British entry. Yet he publicly positioned his historic change of policy as a tentative application – 'talks about talks' – an exploration of whether joining the Community could be in the UK's interests. By positioning Britain's application as *conditional*, he ran the risk that the more the government stressed the importance of the 'terms of entry', the greater the possibility that others would suggest that the price might be too high, or that they could in future negotiate a better deal:[11] the Labour opposition was duly to oblige. A more successful negotiating strategy might have been to accept as the starting point the Treaty of Rome in full, but argue that various derogations and transitional arrangements were necessary to meet the essential interests of the UK and Commonwealth. De Gaulle's veto of the British application in January 1963 would then have been more difficult. Also, the priority Macmillan gave to the USA backfired in Europe, or at least with the only person who really mattered: the Nassau agreement to supply Britain with US Polaris missiles may have pushed de Gaulle over the brink to exercise his veto on the grounds that the British could never be trusted to be genuine Europeans.

The obvious contrast is with the post-war international settlement of the 1940s. The Labour government did not announce that it was only prepared to sign up for the International Monetary Fund (IMF) or North Atlantic Treaty Organization (NATO) as long 'as the terms were right'– despite the fact that both international engagements were major limitations on British sovereignty by comparison with the pre-1939 world. Rather, the government was unequivocal that these were the right choices for Britain and that the obligations that went with them had to be accepted without qualification. Opposition in Parliament was simply faced down. If, in the European case, the issue had been presented as a clear, straight choice, the immediate politics might have been more difficult, but a definitive resolution obtained a lot earlier.

Macmillan's tactics set five major parameters that were to weaken Britain's 'national strategy' for Europe over the next half-century. First, the commitment to Europe has always been pitched as a conditional one. In 1961, the Conservatives set three conditions for entry; Labour expanded the list to five. Harold Wilson rejected the terms Edward Heath had negotiated in 1971, but then 'renegotiated' them in 1975. This same tentative approach was applied to virtually every further move in European integration: the 'Madrid conditions' for joining the exchange rate mechanism (ERM); Labour's 'five tests' for membership of the single currency. If the government itself was not 100 per cent convinced, why should the British public ever be?

Second, the focus on the 'terms' turned the question of membership into a largely economic calculus. This was convenient for governments in diverting attention away from awkward debates about the political nature of the Community and its implications for national sovereignty. But it also accentuated a divergence of views with our partners about the main purpose of the Community. In the 1980s, for example, most of our partners believed the single market was about the 'construction of Europe', not just a conscious policy of liberalisation. Similarly, the single currency was mainly seen on the continent as a political, not primarily an economic, project. Our partners regard the British habit of looking at Europe mainly on the basis of an economic calculus as very strange.

Third, the US relationship was publicly given pride of place. Macmillan's emphasis on the transatlantic 'bridge' – joining Europe as a means to remain relevant to the Americans – was broadly adhered to by successive governments.[12] This priority for Britain's global role made our partners feel that Britain was by definition semi-detached. Britain's commitment was always *conditional* on whether it was seen to help achieve, and not contradict, our wider global interests. This was a quite different attitude of mind to our partners.

The project of European integration succeeded, not primarily because of an ideological or idealistic commitment to a federalist vision of a United States of Europe: in some senses, quite the opposite was true. The original Common Market Six judged that moves toward European unity were *the only means* by which their sense of sovereignty and nationhood[13] could be restored after World War II. The carefully limited, but nonetheless hugely significant, supranationalism of the original Monnet/Schuman Declaration for the Coal and Steel Community was accepted as being essential to the national interests of the six signatories. Restoration of industrial growth on the Continent required that the post-war suppression of German industrial power should be relaxed. Sovereignty pooling constituted a guarantee that never again would the coal and steel industries become destructive engines of war production. It was the *sine qua non* of European economic recovery. Post-war British governments never thought in this way about Europe.

Fourth, Britain has had to pay a continuing price for its late arrival. De Gaulle's veto kept Britain out of the European Economic Community (EEC) effectively for its first crucial decade and a half. As a result we had no say in shaping the CAP, resulting in negative associations with higher food prices that persist to this day, especially among working-class women. It also led to the original unfairness in the British contribution to the EU budget, not out of Continental conspiracy, but simply as a consequence of the fact that our agricultural sector was then a lot smaller than that of all our partners, yet agriculture spending consumed the bulk of the original EU budget. That in turn provided the political backcloth for the virulent 'I want my money back' wars fought by Margaret Thatcher in the early 1980s.

Fifth, the long delay in Britain joining led to a decade and a half of adversarial domestic debate that has never really gone away. It was in the nature of our 'winner takes all' politics that the issue became highly contested. The 1975 referendum 'yes' was historic in guaranteeing Britain's place in Europe (for 40 years at any rate), but it was a grudging place and it did not end the argument. The British European debate never broke out of the argument 'for' or 'against' membership. In that sense the referendum did not settle the European question. The 'antis' felt they had been cheated: as time went on, they convinced themselves that if only the British people had been told the 'truth', the result would have been different. This has hampered intelligent debate about what kind of Europe Britain wants and diverted attention from the real choices facing the country.

Edward Heath ultimately succeeded in achieving Macmillan's historic goal of EU membership, but the legacy of that struggle in its qualified and conditional commitment to European integration, and its reluctance to embrace its real political significance, has left a mark that has cramped Britain's European policy ever since.[14]

Thatcher and the Creation of a New European Myth

The past three decades have seen a gradual fracturing of the Conservative internal coalition between consensus-driven moderates; free-market and 'big business' liberals; and British nationalists. Committed Conservative pro-Europeanism has been destroyed in the process. A Thatcherite myth gained an ideological hegemony over the party: the myth of 'offshore Britain'. This involved rejection of Continental social market capitalism in the frame of European economic integration in favour of a neo-liberal competition state, secured through the indivisible sovereignty of the

Westminster model.[15] Believers in the 'offshore myth' hold that Britain outside the EU can be an exemplar of success in the world of globalisation: economically free to compete on the basis of a Thatcherite model of a 'small state', competitive taxes and light regulation without being shackled by a sclerotic, bureaucratic, corporatist, centralising EU with its rigid single currency that denies its members the flexibility to adjust; politically outward-looking in a world where the European continent counts for less and less, and Britain is released to engage in a plural range of bilateral contacts and networks to advance our interests and values.

Initially the significance of the Thatcher revolution for Britain and Europe was little noticed. When Peter Riddell first published his well-regarded account of *The Thatcher Government* in 1983, he chronicled with great objectivity the profound impact Thatcherism was making on British economy and society, but the question of Europe and its place in the Thatcherite legacy scarcely featured.[16] Yet Margaret Thatcher was ejected from office in significant part as a result of her mishandling of European policy. John Major's European policy differed little from what Margaret Thatcher's had been for her first decade in office, but she now allowed an ideological anti-Europeanism to become the defining feature of her legacy, which for her ardent followers took on the nature of quasi-religious belief.

Where did Thatcher's Euroscepticism come from? If it was a deep personal conviction that she had held throughout her political career, then in her 20 years as an MP before becoming prime minister she had kept it under wraps. She was never a Euro-enthusiast in the manner of Edward Heath and Willie Whitelaw, or Kenneth Clarke, Michael Heseltine and Douglas Hurd in a younger generation, but she had kept her distance from the Powellite 'antis' too. Once in office, her way of dealing with Europe was to stand up unapologetically for national interests as she saw them. For her, our membership of the EU was a zero-sum game in which those who were toughest delivered the best results: what mattered was what played well back home. Her toughness over the EU budget provided her supporters in the tabloid media with welcome copy to distract their readers from the Conservative government's domestic difficulties. The political consequence was a souring of the public mood towards Brussels.

Distinguished British diplomats have argued that there was no alternative to her 'hand bagging' our partners to correct an obvious injustice in terms of Britain's budgetary contributions.[17] Yet a pro-European government could have pushed for EU programmes of genuine cross-border value from which Britain could draw more benefit, which would have given Britain the moral authority to argue for fundamental CAP reform. The reality of Thatcher's victory on the rebate was that, as a result, Britain never gave top priority to CAP reform. In all this, Thatcher showed little real interest. Once she had publicly 'won' her budget battle, she then quietly accepted Delors' proposals for a doubling of the EU budget. What mattered to her was her public relations success, not the substantive outcome. Her successors have mainly followed down this Thatcherite road: fighting a glorious battle in the Eurosceptic press rather than achieving the substance of real reform.

The middle phase of Thatcher's European policy was the big push for the single market. By the mid-1980s the Thatcher government had put in place a more or less coherent neo-liberal national strategy for Britain: prioritising inflation over unemployment, privatising nationalised monopolies, breaking trade union power, abandoning industrial 'lame ducks', opening up Britain's doors to foreign ownership and overseas investment from any part of the world. From that perspective, it must have seemed exceptionally heart-warming when in 1985 a reinvigorated EC under Jacques Delors followed UK promptings and embraced market liberalisation to tackle 'eurosclerosis'. For British officials dealing with European business, the single market was a 'once in a career lifetime' breakthrough that enabled Britain to get on the front foot in the EU. The key to progress was the treaty change embodied in the 1985 Single European Act. Thatcher hesitated: initially she wanted to block a new treaty, arguing that it was unnecessary to achieve the single-market objective, but found herself outvoted at the European Council on the decision to launch an intergovernmental conference. However, unlike David Cameron in December 2011, she was shrewd enough not to claim a 'veto' of a treaty that did not as yet exist. Instead Britain negotiated actively on the text. Thatcher was eventually persuaded by officials to sign up, notably by David Williamson (now Lord Williamson of Horton who went on to be secretary general of the Commission). Only later did she claim to have regretted it.

What Thatcher and her British advisers failed to anticipate was the dynamic the single market would give to wider European integration.[18] The single market had seemingly handed British pro-Europeans the trump card in favour of membership for which they had long been searching. Business rallied strongly behind the EU. With growth and jobs in prospect, public support for Europe strengthened significantly: few foresaw the force of the coming Eurosceptic backlash. The gap between the Thatcher and Delors visions of the single market widened as the reach of European integration quickly extended to 'flanking legislation' in the consumer, environmental, health and safety, and social domains. For Thatcher the single market was all about deregulation and breaking down barriers to business. For Delors it was about re-regulating a 'social market' at European level. He unwisely and incorrectly boasted that soon 90 per cent of all legislation would originate from Europe, and he pushed the argument that the inexorable logic of a single market was a single currency.

Thatcher, seemingly secure in her Downing Street bunker after her third successive general election victory in June 1987, began to see Europe as a 'big problem'. In part this was personal. Thatcher found she could not dominate the European Council as she dominated her cabinet: despite her powerful personality, she found herself periodically thwarted, out-manoeuvred and (doubtless she imagined) double-crossed.[19] The style of doing European business effectively was not hers: she wanted her way and in Europe she could not get it.[20] But there is also a deeper ideological explanation. The impact of her famous speech in Bruges in September 1988 was heightened by its proximity to Jacques Delors' pro-European rallying cry to the Trade Union Congress (TUC) the previous month. Delors' speech made the case for European economic integration with a deepened single market at its heart, but with social action an essential accompanying part: its success recruited British trade unionists as friends and allies. But he lost Thatcher.[21] The ideological edge of Bruges was its clear rejection of the social-market model of European political economy that Jacques Delors was advocating. It was a carefully argued case for a different kind of Europe, not an argument that the Conservative Party should become anti-European: in many respects a familiar restatement of the case for a Europe of nations where sacrifice of sovereignty was the carefully agreed exception and did not become the norm over ever-widening domains of domestic policy. Nonetheless, Bruges' tonal shift marked the beginning of a new era in UK–EU relations. Two competing visions of Europe were now publicly on offer.

Thatcher deserves credit for gradually recognising that there was a huge gulf between the kind of Britain *she* wanted to create and the kind of Europe the majority of the European Council were set on trying to build. One may not agree with her, but there was an intellectual honesty about her position that the nuances of Foreign Office negotiation and compromise could not successfully paper over. Yet her increasingly strident tone jarred with the generally pro-European spirit of the times. The internal cabinet rows over the ERM and single currency were regarded by the public more as a sign of an increasingly divided government than anything else.[22] During the 1989

European Parliament election campaign, Conservative Central Office raised the bogey of Brussels as an over-regulating 'bureaucratic conglomerate', in Margaret Thatcher's own words, with posters featuring unwanted 'Brussels sprouts'. This attracted widespread derision.[23]

Europe was the trigger for, but not the fundamental explanation of, Thatcher's deposition. There was massive disaffection among Conservative MPs because of the 'poll tax' and the huge damage they felt this would cause to their prospects of holding their seats. Concerns about Thatcher's handling of European questions reflected more her style than substance and her seeming inability to work amicably with colleagues who had served with distinction in the engine room of the Thatcherite revolution. However, the trigger was Thatcher's ostensibly total rejection of British membership of a single currency at the Rome European Council. The resignation speech by her deputy prime minister, the pro-European Geoffrey Howe, sparked the fatal challenge. The pro-European Michael Heseltine led the charge. The pro-European Kenneth Clarke told Thatcher bluntly after the first ballot that her career as prime minister was over. Maybe the Conservative Party should have felt gratitude to this band of pro-European regicides when John Major won their fourth general election victory in April 1992, but any such feelings were short-lived in the debacle of Britain's forced withdrawal from the ERM that September.

The purpose of the ERM was to re-establish the exchange rate stability of Bretton Woods in Europe through a system of fixed, but ultimately adjustable, parities. Thatcherites like Nigel Lawson were attracted to it because it provided a monetary anchor for macroeconomic policy given the failure of their experiment with monetary targets. Against this view were monetarist economists who supported 'free-floating', as well as unreformed Keynesians who thought it essential to retain the 'freedom to devalue'. It was not clear how far Thatcher engaged in these intellectual arguments. The loss of sovereignty she cared about was her political control over interest rates, which she judged crucial to her political base among homeowners. Having ruled against the majority of her cabinet in 1985, ERM membership came up again in 1989 when the Prime Minister was effectively cornered by her Chancellor and Foreign Secretary. She gave ground, dropping her opposition in principle and agreeing to the so-called 'Madrid conditions' for membership. She agreed to join when her chancellor, John Major, forced the issue in 1990: having lost Nigel Lawson the year before, she could not afford politically to lose a second chancellor.

It was not a happy decision. Britain joined at the wrong time, at the wrong rate and for the wrong reasons. It was the wrong time because the UK was locking into an exchange rate system when domestic interest rates were at a cyclical high. It was at the wrong rate because high interest rates were sustaining an artificially high parity between sterling and the Deutschmark. And it was for a wrong reason, because the main motive was political – to ease criticism of the government by doing something that a majority of the commentariat had wanted. The government showed its short-termist mindset by using the market credibility gained by joining to reduce mortgage rates in time for the Conservative annual conference. The early 1990s recession was not caused by the ERM; responsibility there lay with the laxity of Lawson's fiscal and monetary stance post-1987 and the 'hubris' that the Thatcher 'miracle' had transformed Britain's growth and productivity performance, when it clearly had not. (There are some parallels with Gordon Brown two decades later.) However, John Major's decision to join the ERM in 1990 meant that, in order to sustain the exchange rate parity, interest rates had to be kept high for longer than they would have been, as the recession deepened. The situation was made worse when the Bundesbank raised German interest rates to deal with the inflationary consequences of unification. When Britain was forced out of the ERM in September 1992, interest rates fell quickly as the pound was in effect devalued by 25 per cent against the mark. The pain, however, continued. Fiscal policy had to be tightened severely to correct the public sector deficit. Tax increases ('twenty-two tax rises', as Labour skilfully labelled them) and harsh spending cuts were introduced in seeming defiance of Conservative pledges at the 1992 election.

The consequence of this policy disaster, following hard on the heels of the deposition of Thatcher, was a shift to Euroscepticism in the British polity, which was seismic at the Conservative base. The recession was particularly brutal in the Tory heartlands of the South and Midlands, unlike the Thatcher recession of the early 1980s which hit the old industrial areas hardest. Many small- and medium-sized enterprises went bust, or had to downsize radically, as a result of sustained high interest rates. Particularly hard hit by this were successful small-business people who played a key role in local Conservative associations: 'our people' as Margaret Thatcher would have described them, or the new generation of 'garagistes' as Conservative traditionalists derided them. The Conservative base was perhaps never as Euro-enthusiast as its leadership cadre from Macmillan on. Its 'officer class', with close links to the armed forces, the Church of England and the land, was first and foremost traditionalist and patriotic. However, among the generation who had experienced the horrors of war, some were instinctively sympathetic to the European cause. Also this 'officer class' had traditionally shown fierce loyalty to its leaders. Since Anthony Eden's departure in 1957, the key figures in the party leadership – Macmillan and Douglas Home, and then Heath and Whitelaw – had been strongly committed to Europe. Heath in particular inspired a generational shift towards pro-Europeanism, winning over converts like Peter Walker and inspiring a whole group of prominent Conservative MPs who first became active in politics in the late 1950s and 1960s, such as Geoffrey Howe, Michael Heseltine, Douglas Hurd, Leon Brittan, Kenneth Clarke and John Selwyn Gummer.

The Conservative shift to Euroscepticism was first in public view at their party conference in October 1992, an occasion convulsed by anger, a toxic mix of lingering bitterness about Thatcher's demise and resentment against Britain's European entanglement in the ERM, against which Thatcher's warnings now appeared prophetic. On Europe, Margaret Thatcher, it seemed, had been proved right all along. This anti-European shift had a huge impact. In the short term, it stiffened opposition to the Maastricht Treaty within Conservative parliamentary ranks: it was impossible for the whips to threaten rebels with de-selection given the state of opinion at the grass roots. The internal ideological struggles of Conservatism spilled over into the media, where battle was joined on a daily basis. The *Mail*, *Sun*, *Telegraph* and *Times* became filled with columns obsessing about the European issue. More seriously, it emboldened those eyeing the Conservative leadership, like Michael Portillo and John Redwood, to behave, as John Major was heard to observe, like 'bastards', making the conduct of European policy fraught and difficult.[24] More seriously still for pro-Europeanism within the Conservative party, it became virtually impossible for committed pro-Europeans to be selected as parliamentary candidates. The party fell into the hands of Thatcher's Eurosceptic children.

Another Missed Opportunity

In the mid-1980s, Delors' single-market programme had opened up real possibilities for British leadership in Europe. Nothing in the EU's history, except for enlargement, owed more to British inspiration and encouragement. It brought significant benefits to Britain in terms of trade and inward investment – and the boost to jobs and growth that came with it. But it could have been much greater in its impact – in services, for example (which in the last three decades have grown dramatically in economic significance) – if successive British governments had portrayed themselves as 'good Europeans' in a more single-minded pursuit of the single market's implementation. Ideologically the single market 'meshed very strongly with British values and interests' – it 'seemed Thatcherite in its essentials', but also chimed with Labour's greater acceptance of market mechanisms from the late 1980s on.[25] Such coalescence of interests even led contemporaries such as Charles Powell to sense that Europe was 'moving our way'.[26] However, Thatcher's increasing obsession with its sovereignty implications, her ideological opposition to what she saw as interventionist social and economic policies of the Delors Commission, her long-standing resistance to British membership of the ERM and her refusal to engage in the growing single currency debate turned the chance of being seen as good Europeans irredeemably into the perception of the British as the 'awkward partner'.[27]

Had Britain more pragmatically accepted the argument that a single currency was in principle a logical and desirable extension of a single market, this need not have been the case. Britain was too slow in putting forward gradualist approaches to the achievement of a single currency, such as the hard Ecu or some form of parallel currency. These ideas might have won more political traction if advanced at an earlier stage by a government that sounded sympathetic to the single currency as a long-term aim. Arguably, gradualism would have been more sensible in economic policy terms, enabling the single currency to expand as member states converged and satisfied the conditions for the creation of an optimal currency area. After Thatcher had departed, the Major government, by giving priority in the Maastricht negotiations to securing its single currency 'opt-out', surrendered the potential for policy leadership on the design and timetable of the single currency project. Politically, the single currency project saw a reassertion of Franco-German leadership in Europe. By 1997 the choice for the Blair government on the euro had become whether Britain wished to be a 'taker' of what had already been agreed and many recognised as flawed; the opportunity to be a 'shaper' had been missed.

The 1997 European Legacy

By the time Labour came to power in 1997, a national consensus of sorts in favour of EU membership had at long last been established across the leadership of the major political parties. However, the national strategy underlying it remained equivocal. The commitment remained heavily conditional. It prioritised America over Europe. It took it for granted that Europe needed unspecified but radical 'reform'. It was largely seen through the liberalising prism of the single market. As a result of successive failures of vision, interspersed with episodes of political feebleness, 'Europe' was never viewed at home as a British project in British interests, but came more to be seen as a Franco-German conspiracy against the British people. Britain's prolonged enforced absence from the EEC's conception and early development created the sense that the European project represented some Continental 'other', and this was exacerbated by the fact that Britain continued to approach European integration from a fundamentally different philosophical and practical perspective that was fixated with its own national decline.[28]

The legacy of the Thatcher period has been profound. On the one hand, the commitment to the single market reinforced a new 'neo-liberal' consensus over economic thinking, which, until the 2007–8 financial crisis, was accepted virtually without challenge. Its hold over both politicians and the ranks of the civil service has had a profound impact on the framing of Britain's Europe policy. Europe has been seen as a Continental extension of a domestic agenda of liberalisation and open markets. The single market became the almost exclusive prism through which a positive case for Europe could be made. On the other hand, for Eurosceptics, the single market backfired as a project as it became a source of unwanted and intrusive rules and regulations 'holding Britain back'. The EU became increasingly portrayed as a monster of bureaucratic and over-costly regulation; Europe's social and employment rights, with its 'health and safety culture' – not to mention the European Convention on Human Rights (ECHR) – have been portrayed as the enemy of freedom and flexibility. Thus, the past both institutionalised a neo-liberal approach to our membership of the EU and laid the basis for a new neo-liberal myth opposed to it. This myth has grown in strength as globalisation gathers pace and Europe's economic dominance in the world weakens. In the Eurosceptic world view, the EU ties Britain down with its shackles. Whereas post 1945 the power of the ahistorical 'Dunkirk myth' made it difficult for Britain to come to terms with Europe for three crucial decades, a new global myth of 'offshore Britain' may cause the UK profound damage in adjusting to the realities of our position in the twenty-first century.

CHAPTER 2

Europe and the Failure of Labour Revisionism

Prior to 1997, Britain's 'national strategy' towards Europe was mainly a Conservative story. Nevertheless, the Labour government of Attlee and Bevin had dismissed the Schuman Declaration. Gaitskell is most remembered for his claim that joining the Common Market would mean 'the end of a thousand years of history'.[1] Wilson was perceived as constantly on European manoeuvres. Labour's 1983 election manifesto actually proposed withdrawal – it was the only major British political party ever to have done so, at least as yet.[2]

How was it that a party so proudly internationalist in its traditions rejected European integration for so long? As The Prelude to this book indicates, the roots of Labour Euroscepticism owe much to two myths: beliefs in both a commitment to a nation state social democracy[3] and Britain's 'unique capacity for moral leadership in the world'.[4] The Labour leadership's unwillingness or inability to break the hold of these myths made Labour's path to Europe exceptionally tortuous. Europe was both symbolic of, and fundamental to, Labour's wider revisionist failure.

The Inadequacy of Nation State Social Democracy

The 'spirit of '45' has left a lasting legacy: a Labourite commitment to the 'Westminster model' that rationalises the party's raison d'être as winning democratic control of the central levers of the British state on the basis of a transformatory manifesto that a Commons majority would then force through. Labour's leaders have never sought to challenge this model; rather their revisionist efforts have reinterpreted and 'modernised' the transformatory goals to be achieved. Against this overriding domestic goal, European integration has always been at best second order, possibly a distraction, and at worst might get in the way. The belief that British Labour could autonomously build its own socialist commonwealth was key to the rejection of the Schuman Declaration. It was literally true, as Herbert Morrison notoriously remarked: 'it's no good, we can't do it, the Durham miners won't wear it' on the evening of 2 June 1950 when the Acting Prime Minister (on one of Attlee's many absences due to illness) interrupted his dinner at The Ivy to sign the letter declining to participate.[5] The newly nationalised coal and steel industries were the crowning achievement of post-war democratic socialism. To have put their ultimate control under a supranational authority, as Jean Monnet had proposed, was unthinkable without the assent of the National Union of Mineworkers in which the 'leadership-loyal' Durham Federation held decisive sway.

Labour's foreign secretary, Ernest Bevin, had spotted the grand, long-term ambitions of the Schuman Declaration for what they were, and they remain glaringly obvious to any reader today. This was not just a plan for coal and steel. 'Europe will not be built in a day' but through a succession of steps. The innovative institutional machinery Schuman proposed was clearly intended to establish a broad direction for European integration. Bevin objected vehemently to France's insistence, at Monnet's instigation, that, before entering discussions, Britain should accept in advance the principle of a supranational authority; this contradicted his previous insistence that the Organisation for European Economic Co-operation (OEEC), set up to administer the Marshall Plan, should operate intergovernmentally.[6] Bevin did not object *because of* the USA, but rather in contradiction to clear US preferences: the Truman administration enthusiastically approved of Schuman's text, on which Monnet had consulted them in advance. Bevin was not anti-Europe. In order to strengthen Europe against communism, Bevin desperately wanted European unity. The paradox was that, on defence, Bevin accepted that an attack on an ally would automatically be treated as an attack on the UK, a fundamental limitation of British sovereignty on questions of peace and war, much resisted in the pre-1939 world. Bevin had made this sacrifice of sovereignty first with the French and then Benelux, all before NATO was formed with the US security guarantee. But for British Labour reasons, pooling sovereignty on economic questions was, in Bevin's view, simply not on.[7]

These hostile sentiments were set out with vigour and clarity in a Labour pamphlet *European Unity*, published around the time of the Schuman launch.[8] Drafted by a young Denis Healey, the party's then international secretary, the text was the property of the Labour National Executive (NEC) International Committee, chaired by Hugh Dalton. Ben Pimlott's classic biography of Dalton is essential reading for anyone who wants to understand this brilliant and complex figure who was Labour's dominant politician-intellectual from the 1920s to the end of the 1950s, and an inspiration to generations of social democrats. A high-minded internationalist, his bitter experiences of World War I had also made him an ardent Germanophobe. On the Schuman Declaration, Dalton's bottom line was clear. 'This country could not lose control over its own budgetary and financial policy, or over controls necessary for our planned economy.'[9] This theme was given pride of place in the document signed off by the full NEC, at which Attlee as leader was present. Attlee later complained to Dalton about the pamphlet's excessively tendentious tone. Dalton pointedly reminded the Prime Minister that he had been present at the meeting at which it was approved: Attlee's sole contribution had been to demand insertion of a sentence requiring protection for the horticultural industry! He hadn't thought the subject of European unity important enough to justify him reading the document thoroughly.

By the end of the 1950s, however, the 'planned economy' argument against Europe had weakened in political force. The Labour leadership, after three successive election defeats where the Conservatives successfully identified themselves with the rise of the consumer society, sensed that the electorate had little appetite left for ration books and direct controls. On Common Market membership, Gaitskell sought advice from James Meade and Sir Donald McDougall, two of his economic advisers as chancellor. Both concluded that the economic costs and benefits of joining more or less cancelled each other out: the judgement should be made on political grounds. Labour set 'five conditions' for membership. Three were the same as Macmillan's: the safeguarding of British agriculture, the Commonwealth and our EFTA partners. Labour added two more. Britain must remain free to:

- 'conduct our own foreign policy';
- 'introduce whatever measures of socialist economic planning we consider necessary for the welfare of Britain'.

The ironic parallel with the 'five tests' for British entry to the euro cannot have been lost on Gordon Brown. The 'five tests' served the same purpose as the 1962 'five conditions': they covered up indecision on a central issue. As George Brown, the Labour deputy leader, quipped, so many people were trying to sit on the fence that it would sooner or later collapse. Four months before the 1962 Labour Conference, Gaitskell's leading trade union allies privately sought guidance on how to steer their conference delegations. Gaitskell's reply was equivocal: 'The Labour Party is not committed to going in, nor is it committed to staying out,' but it was 'gravely misleading to suggest that we shall not be able to conduct our own economic policies'. He warned that 'if we stay out, we run the risk of becoming nothing more than a little island off Europe'.[10]

His tone had changed, however, by the time of his October 1962 Conference speech. The memorable phrase that entered the public consciousness was Gaitskell's claim that membership would be 'the end of a thousand years of history'. This came at the end of a tightly argued paragraph that still resonates. With typical intellectual honesty, Gaitskell addressed head-on the 'idea and ideal of a Federal Europe'. He did not criticise the ambition of Europe's founding fathers: 'We would be foolish to deny, not to recognise and indeed sympathise with the desire of those who created the European Community for political federation. That is what they mean, that is what they are after.' He then set out starkly the implications for Britain:

> It means that if we go into this, we are no more than a state in the United States of Europe, such as Texas and California [...] That is what it means [...] it does mean the end of Britain as an independent nation state [...] it means the end of a thousand years of history. You may say 'let it end', but my goodness, it is a decision that needs a little care and thought. And it does mean the end of the Commonwealth.[11]

After Gaitskell's untimely death in January 1963, Wilson's approach to Europe was totally different. He avoided Gaitskell's language of fundamental choices. He brushed aside questions of sovereignty, seeing shared sovereignty as an inevitable fact of modernity and human progress. He refused to engage in debate about what might be Europe's *finalité:* he chose to deal with the reality of the European Community as it was, and dismissed talk of closer political integration as irrelevant speculation of no consequence, at least in his lifetime.

Labour won the 1964 election on the by then well-established thesis of national economic decline. The 1964 election slogan 'Let's go with Labour' conjured up images of a National Plan, forged in the white-hot heat of a technological revolution that would transform growth prospects, finance expansion of public services and modernise the face of Britain. However, Labour's ambitions ran up against balance of payments constraints. The July 1966 sterling crisis marked the National Plan's effective abandonment. The Plan's driving force, George Brown, moved to the Foreign Office. A strong pro-European, Brown's move pitched Europe up the government's agenda, but with little obvious reluctance from Wilson. Wilson had already quietly ensured that Labour's 1966 manifesto opened the door. 'Britain, in consultation with her EFTA partners, should be ready to enter the European Economic Community, provided essential British and Commonwealth interests are safeguarded.' This now seemed logical for a British growth strategy that had been, in Wilson's words, 'blown off course'. Wilson's efforts to build a consensus behind Europe were meticulous, skilfully manoeuvring through no fewer than seven full cabinet meetings. He successfully whittled down opposition to the point where even Barbara Castle, Wilson's old ally on the Bevanite left and a fierce anti-European, softened, at least in the privacy of her diary; she mused: 'we are going into Europe because we haven't applied economic policies which are a real alternative. In such a situation entry might be politically more tolerable than just drifting on our deflationary path rather than devaluation.'[12] Castle was half right: with the National Plan's demise, the government was thrashing around for a new modernisation strategy for Britain. But even if General de Gaulle had this time said yes, it was not enough – nor realistically, could it ever have been – to avoid the devaluation that Wilson had fought so hard against and the tough economic choices made in its wake.

The 1968 devaluation was the root cause of Labour's 1970 general election defeat. In the election run-up, the polls flattered to deceive. Wilson fully expected victory but Labour activists detected large-scale working-class abstention, in all likelihood in reaction to squeezed take-home pay. Incomes policies had narrowed skilled workers' differentials. Higher taxes had been necessary to pay for an expanded welfare state. In the aftermath of defeat, the trade unions and the Labour left called for a more interventionist socialist economic policy. This was seen as antithetical to all that the Common Market was seen to represent, as well as the politics of the 'mixed economy' that Labour's pro-Europeans stood for. There was a tragic irony here. Labour had renewed the EEC membership application after de Gaulle's abrupt resignation in 1969. If Labour had won re-election, it would have accepted the terms that Heath obtained in 1971. A national consensus would have been established across the leaderships of our political parties that EEC membership was in the national interest. But it was not to be. A leftist vision of nation state social democracy was to dominate the party's outlook for the next 15 years.

Britain's Unique Capacity for Moral Leadership in the World

Labour's fierce debates on foreign policy took place within a common frame – Labour's duty to offer 'moral leadership' to the world. This was the left's inheritance from Britain's imperial legacy. Labour saw itself as the party of colonial freedom. Independence for India became a powerful element in the Attlee myth. Commitment to the United Nations Association was *de rigueur* for all shades of Labour opinion. Tackling global poverty united all sections of the party. Labour was after all more the party of Methodism than it was of Marx. Against these high-minded ambitions, some thought a commitment to Europe diminished Britain's global responsibilities. This view bridged what became the party's key foreign-policy divide between the Labour right's anti-communist Atlanticism and the left's opposition to nuclear weapons and Britain's unconditional commitment to 'the West'.

The first generation of Labour leaders were ethical socialists for whom an idealistic internationalism was a critical part of their political make-up. For Keir Hardie, a self-taught Lanarkshire miner who became Labour's first leader, socialism was about the brotherhood of man (and sisterhood too, as he was an early supporter of women's emancipation).[13] He travelled tirelessly throughout Europe and the world, speaking out against racialism in South Africa, colonialism in India, and the rise of nationalism in Europe, bringing to his politics an eclectic mix of Gladstonian morality, New Testament teaching and Marxist analysis.[14] A stalwart of the Second International, the inability of his German Social Democratic Party (SPD) friends to stop the outbreak of an 'imperialist' war in 1914 broke his heart.[15] Ramsay Macdonald, also a Scot and an illegitimate child who became Labour's first prime minister, concluded the 1906 pact with the Liberals that first gave Labour a secure Westminster foothold. He, more than any single individual, was instrumental in dislodging the Liberals in the 1920s as the second party of the state and turning Labour into a national party with a broad-based, non-class appeal. Internationalism was central to this. His lonely and courageous opposition to World War I appealed in the 1920s to many former Liberals, strait-laced nonconformists as well as Bloomsbury aesthetes. Macdonald dedicated his foreign policy to disarmament and righting the wrongs of Versailles.

Yet idealistic internationalism was always contested within Labour. There was a strong tradition of working-class, patriotic populism, particularly among trade unionists, except among nonconformist temperance reformers in the Gladstonian tradition. The Parliamentary Labour Party (PLP) backed World War I and were happy to see the party's general secretary, Arthur Henderson, join Lloyd George's coalition government in 1916. But the patriotic tendency lost out, as Britain reacted against the war's huge loss of life and apparent pointlessness. Yet, idealistic internationalism was to provide no answers to the rise of the fascist dictators. Labour's approach to foreign policy went through a tormented but radical change. The leadership eventually abandoned the pervasive early socialist idea that war was an inevitable product of capitalism and imperialism, and that only the prior transformation to socialism could prevent it. A new approach to collective security was gradually forged based on support for rearmament, but the process was bitterly fought between foreign policy 'realists', on the one hand, and an eclectic alliance of socialist idealists, Christian pacifists and communist fellow travellers, on the other. The most symbolic moment came in the middle of the 1935 Abyssinian crisis when Labour accepted the principle of sanctions against Mussolini, but George Lansbury, Labour's leader from 1931 to 1935, insisted on making clear his own personal commitment to pacifism; this occasioned Bevin's notorious public assault that Lansbury was hawking his 'conscience around from body to body', finishing off Lansbury's leadership.[16]

The inter-war years were formational for those who sought to build a new international order after 1945. Bevin had been one of Britain's earliest opponents of Nazism, partly because he knew personally of the terrible fate that had befallen fellow German trade unionists. At the outbreak of the 1939 war, Attlee as leader since 1935 (who had hovered indecisively during many of the fierce pre-war arguments) went so far as to declare 'Europe must federate or perish'.[17] But after 1945, federalism in Britain was tainted by its link to 'third force' ideas: the notion of building a bloc independent of both the USA and USSR, consisting of Europe and the Commonwealth (led of course by Britain) which the backbench 'Keep Left' group flirted with. To Labour's leaders, these ideas smacked of anti-Americanism, neutralism and weakness in face of the Soviet Communist threat. As was often quipped, Bevin treated the Soviet Union with the same venom and contempt as if it was an unofficial breakaway from his beloved Transport and General Workers Union. His anti-communism was unbending and decisive. The differences between the realist and idealist camps continued in one form or another to divide Labour until the end of the Cold War, stretching from the fierce debates over German rearmament in the early 1950s, through the Campaign for Nuclear Disarmament (CND) storms that almost toppled Gaitskell's leadership, to the conclusive triumph of unilateralism at the 1980 party conference. For the Labour left, 'Europe' was as much a part of their critique of 'the West' as was Britain's commitment to NATO and nuclear weapons. In these debates there were many shades of grey.

Opposition to the Common Market appealed as much to those who wanted Britain to offer independent moral leadership in the world as part of some putative 'third force', as it did to fellow travellers who saw European unity as aimed at weakening Moscow. These battles played a crucial role in determining whether people thought of themselves as being on the right or left of the party.

Yet Gaitskell's 1962 conference speech on Europe temporarily appealed across the party's traditional left–right foreign-policy divide. The decisive argument was that European engagement would represent a grievous loss of Britain's capacity for moral leadership in the Commonwealth and wider world. His 1962 speech struck a powerful chord, when he said:

> I sometimes wonder whether the great problems of the world today are to be found in the unity or disunity of Western Europe. I would have said there are two problems outstanding above all others: the problem of peace and the problem of poverty. The problem of East West relations that plagues us and the problem of the division of the world into the 'haves' and 'have-nots'.[18]

The relationship that Gaitskell most cared about, though, was the alliance with the USA. Just before his fatal illness took hold, conscious that he might be prime minister within two years, Gaitskell sent a revealing personal memorandum to President Kennedy.[19] Worried that Kennedy might misunderstand his opposition to Common Market membership, he emphasised his total commitment to Atlanticism as the anchor of his post-war politics. 'As I think you know, Mr President, no one has fought harder than I against neutralism and anti-Americanism. More than once I have staked my whole career on this.' The Americans were mistaken in seeing a united Europe as an unmitigated blessing: 'I believe a new powerful European state may well seek to become that third force after which, as I think mistakenly, some Europeans have long hankered.' Gaitskell's commitment to the USA was at the core of his political being in the post-war world: he was determined Britain would be a reliable partner in what he saw as a global struggle against the evils of totalitarianism. There is a strong parallel between Gaitskell and Blair. Had Gaitskell become prime minister, he might well have sent British troops to Vietnam. It would have been totally consistent with the stance he took in the Korean War that nothing, simply nothing, should stand in the way of rearmament and the deployment of British troops. As chancellor, he was prepared to put the British economy and the unity of the Labour cabinet under tremendous strain to meet that overriding obligation.

Wilson was very different. In 1951 he resigned from the cabinet with Aneurin Bevan on an apparently trivial difference over National Health Service (NHS) charges for teeth and spectacles, arguing that the Korean rearmament programme was putting too great a strain on the economy. As prime minister he offered President Lyndon Johnson moral support on Vietnam, but refused steadfastly (despite what we now know to have been extreme pressure) to send British troops. For Gaitskell the relationship with America was the *sine qua non* of Britain's role in the world, whereas the question of Europe was a sideshow. Gaitskell's instincts are an object lesson in how, in politics, the most admirable of qualities can also be the most dangerous. His commitment to the idea of Britain's global moral leadership, standing together with America in the fight for freedom, still casts a long spell – across the deserts of Iraq and the mountain ranges of Afghanistan.

Europe and the Failure of Labour Revisionism

Labour's reluctance on Europe in the early post-war decades is perhaps understandable. Against the beckoning prospect of a British 'new Jerusalem', European integration appeared an unattractive flight of fancy. Also from a British Labour perspective there was little to look for in mainland Europe for inspiration. Communism threatened democratic socialism in France and Italy: its revival was feared in Germany. There was little sympathy for the Catholic corporatism of the Continental centre-right. To the extent a model was thought worthy of emulation, it was neutral Sweden's 'people's home'. Mostly, on the rare occasions when the social democratic left looked overseas, it was to FDR's New Deal, or Labour experience in Australia and New Zealand.

Yet Labour's attachment to nation state social democracy was not an exclusively British phenomenon rooted in British exceptionalism. As Donald Sassoon points out,[20] most social democratic parties initially adopted a sceptical, even hostile stance towards European integration. Only the Benelux socialists were committed federalists. In France, the Section Française de l'Internationale Ouvrière (SFIO), under Guy Mollet's leadership, did back the Schuman Declaration strongly and later, as prime minister, he pushed the Treaty of Rome through the National Assembly; this was no mean feat given the previous failure of the European Defence Community in face of both Communist and Gaullist opposition, but Mollet's motivation was the French national interest, not a distinctive left argument.[21] The social democratic parties in Austria, Denmark, Finland, Norway and Sweden reacted negatively, as surprisingly did the Germans and Italians. Kurt Schumacher, the SPD's first post-war leader, notoriously denounced the Schuman Declaration as 'a Europe of the four Ks: konservativ, klerical, kapitalistich, and kartellistisch.'[22] In choosing the nation state road, Labour was little different to most social democrats in the immediate post-war years; the interesting question is why others changed, but Labour took so long.

The key shift was that of the German SPD. First, the SPD abandoned neutralism as a possible basis for Soviet assent to reunification and accepted Adenauer's strategy of embedding the Federal Republic in the structures of the West: this took them further away from the Labour left. Second, the 1960 revision of the party's fundamental programme at Bad Godesburg was highly significant ideologically and for Europe. The SPD's new principle – 'the market wherever possible, planning wherever necessary' – was a world away from Labour's bitter and unresolved debates about nationalisation and public ownership. In the task of revisionism, the SPD succeeded where Gaitskell failed. As a result the SPD bought into a model of market-based European integration, governed by social rules, that Labour was simply not ready for.[23]

In the early 1960s the public debate on Britain's relative economic decline opened up. Michael Shanks published his influential *The Stagnant Society* in 1961.[24] A vocal section of informed opinion, particularly in the political and economic planning thinktank and *The Economist* magazine, argued forcefully for Common Market membership as a modernisation strategy for British industry. This angle of the 'decline' debate left Labour largely untouched. The European question hardly featured in Labour's revisionist ferment. Europe is scarcely referred to in Crosland's 1956 *Future of Socialism*[25] and there is no reference in the index of the 1964 revised edition, despite Crosland's strong pro-Europeanism at the time.[26] For most shades of Labour opinion, revisionists included, the answer to Britain's growth problem was better domestic economic management, not Europe. The internal party debate obsessed about the role of public ownership. Even among revisionists, who accepted the market, the solutions to slow growth were framed in terms of more sophisticated state interventions to improve economic performance and Labour's claim to deploy the presumed all-powerful tools of Keynesian demand management more skilfully than the Conservatives. The dynamic benefits of being part of a growing Common Market were given little weight.

One interpretation of Gaitskell's 1962 Europe speech is that he deliberately chose to appeal to the left wing and unite Labour after its fierce divisions over Clause Four and unilateralism. He was closing a chapter on the efforts of Labour's revisionists, at least until after an expected election victory. It deeply upset some of Gaitskell's most ardent allies in the party's inner struggles. Gaitskell's wife, Dora, famously remarked from the platform, 'all the wrong people are cheering'.[27] Bill Rodgers, the newly elected MP for Stockton on Tees and secretary of the Campaign for Democratic Socialism that had organised for Gaitskell, sat with his arms firmly folded throughout the standing ovation. On Europe there was to be no reconciliation of view between Gaitskell and his closest political friends before his tragic death in January 1963. In the same month de Gaulle's veto avoided Labour having to make a difficult choice on acceptance or rejection of the Tory terms.

The 1964–70 Wilson government was not a bad government from a social democratic perspective. Wilson recognised that to overcome relative decline, Britain had to make major structural reforms. The list was extensive: bad industrial relations; inattention to science, engineering and skills; too elitist an education system; an overbloated military presence overseas; the 'cult of the amateur' in the civil service and the senior ranks of British society; neglect of the regions and essential infrastructure; inefficiency and overcapacity in the nationalised industries; pervasive poor management and over-cosseted inefficient firms in the private sector; and of course inadequate presence in the EEC markets with then the greatest growth potential. The Wilson governments attempted to tackle all these structural issues, including EEC membership. Wilson may fairly be criticised for sometimes a lack of boldness or consistency of purpose, but the criticism comes ill from those who believed that better macroeconomic policies could have provided some alternative magic fix. It was the strength of the belief in the miraculous potential of nation state Keynesianism that led to difficult political issues being ducked. At the time it was fashionable to argue in social democratic circles that Wilson's opposition to devaluation was totally wrong-headed and typical of the short-termism and opportunism that was said to characterise his approach to politics. Yet Wilson's uncertainties about devaluation appear more understandable today. Whilst the 1967 devaluation did lead to an extraordinary turnaround in the balance of payments in the second half of 1969, the favourable impact did not last and by 1971 Britain was back in a crisis of stagflation. The key failure was to reform industrial relations, but here the obstacle was not just opposition from the trade unions and the traditional left (indeed, Barbara Castle, the Tribunite heroine, was leading the charge). The home secretary and former chancellor, James Callaghan, publicly opposed the government's *In Place of Strife* policy at the party's NEC. With an eye to his future leadership prospects, he rallied the PLP's trade union right to oppose reform.

The virulence of the post-1970 party split on Europe was in retrospect only in part Wilson's fault. Acceptance of the pro-European consensus that Wilson had laboriously constructed proved skin deep after the party's unexpected 1970 defeat. The reason that the European question split Labour from top to bottom was a toxic mix of high politics, tribal loyalties and an ideological swing to the left. There was the 'high politics' of conflicts of ambition and manoeuvrings for leadership among the elite of the party – not only between Wilson, Callaghan and Jenkins at the very top, but with Crosland and Healey positioning themselves for the future as not too factionally 'right wing'. There was the reassertion of 'tribal loyalties' against what was then seen (remarkably in retrospect) as Heath's extreme right-wing Tory government. Finally there was the 'ideological shift to the left' in the trade unions, PLP and constituency parties, in reaction to the Wilson government's perceived betrayals. Europe and British Labourism came to be seen, by supporters and opponents alike, as paths leading in totally opposite directions.

Wilson faced a terrible dilemma of leadership: whether to fight his party or manage it. Maybe a less tactical politician would have behaved differently, but in retrospect, through all his twists and turns, Wilson stuck consistently to his pro-European goal. Wilson's position was weak. His personal morale had been hit hard by his 1970 defeat. The foundations of his leadership were increasingly insecure. First, his standing with the public had fallen from its previous stellar heights: in the words of a controversial BBC documentary of the time, he was one of *Yesterday's Men*.[28] Second, his relationship with the trade unions had been badly soured by the *In Place of Strife* white paper, with the two largest affiliates, the Transport and General (TGWU) and the Amalgamated Union of Engineering Workers (AUEW), swinging sharply to the left under Jack Jones and Hugh Scanlon,[29] casting their 'block votes' in favour of left policies and for left candidates for Labour's governing NEC. Third, his PLP support was fragile. The air had been thick with PLP plots against his leadership, particularly in 1968. After six stormy years as prime minister, Wilson's relations with his one-time allies on the left had badly weakened, yet little of the venom felt towards him due to his opportunistic opposition to Gaitskell had diminished on the party right.[30]

Wilson's feelings of anger and insecurity must have intensified when in May 1971 Callaghan made a calculated bid for the leadership by attacking Europe in highly emotive terms. Picking up on an understandable remark President Pompidou had made that, despite his acceptance of British membership, French would remain the official language of the European Community, Callaghan launched into a populistic defence of 'the language of Chaucer and Shakespeare'. If sacrificing our identity was what Common Market membership meant, 'the President can have his answer – in French – non merci beaucoup'.[31] Significantly Callaghan, who was to advocate a 'yes' vote in the 1975 referendum, somehow failed to recall this episode as worthy of inclusion in his own memoirs. But Wilson knew he faced a potential leadership challenge. Jenkins, the then deputy leader, pledged his full support for Wilson if he stood behind a pro-European line. Together they probably would have been able to hold a PLP majority, but Wilson would still have faced a conference vote against Common Market membership and found himself in a more isolated position than Gaitskell on unilateral disarmament in 1960, without any obvious means of reversing the conference decision.

Wilson decided that the only viable course was to argue against membership 'on the Tory terms'. As Jenkins remarked, his speech at a special Labour Conference in July 1971 was like watching from the shore as a slave ship containing an old friend, who had been captured and was being sold into servitude, gradually slipped over the horizon. For Labour pro-Europeans this was a great betrayal of principle: it confirmed all their worst feelings about Wilson as a tactical, opportunist and unprincipled politician.[32] Sixty-nine Labour MPs, including the future leader, John Smith, courageously voted in favour of British membership in October 1971 in defiance of a three-line whip, the largest post-war rebellion inside the PLP until the March 2003 Iraq vote. The rebellion was badly received at Labour's grass roots. The left argued tendentiously that the pro-Europeans had kept the Tories in power: with the support of Conservative anti-Europeans, a united Labour vote could have forced Heath into a general election. Tony Benn, originally a pro-European Labour moderate, on a long journey from Anthony Wedgwood Benn to Tony Benn, began pressing the case for a referendum on Europe. His critique of the 1964 government drew on the 'events of 1968'. Labour had been too technocratic and top-down: he identified a yearning for a new politics of participation that embraced movements from below. This led him to reject hierarchy and the old elitist model of Labour decision-making. But the purpose of 'participation' and a reinvigorated internal party democracy was to strengthen Labour's commitment to seize the central levers of nation state power in order to implement a new 'alternative economic strategy', a comprehensive plan for a more dirigiste nation state social democracy.

Wilson retreated to the bunker. To the astonishment of colleagues, he accepted the principle of a referendum on the Europe question in the belief that it would enable him to hold the party to a position of opposition to membership 'on the Tory terms'. Jenkins promptly resigned as Labour deputy leader, alongside three other members of the shadow cabinet, arguing that a referendum was wrong in principle and, given likely public opinion, in practice a commitment against membership. In retrospect the pro-Europeans made a huge mistake. Instead of accepting political realities, once they had staked out their own European commitment, they should have sought to re-establish relationships with Wilson in order to secure a successful renegotiation and a positive referendum outcome. Their resignations only confirmed their isolation. Jenkins threw away his position as leadership 'heir apparent'. The general mood was to blame the pro-European 'right wing' for the perceived betrayals of the Wilson years. Jenkins and his supporters became objects of vilification and abuse: demands for parliamentary re-selection first began to be heard. The pro-Europeans felt this isolation themselves: for the first time some began to think that Labour, if not yet a 'lost cause', was on its way to becoming a party in which they were no longer welcome as members. Yet the irony was that the European cause was far from lost.

Wilson persuaded a narrow Conference majority to oppose a policy of outright EEC withdrawal, but only by threatening union leaders in person that he would resign as Labour leader if defeated. He won support for a policy of 'renegotiation' should Labour return to power. To pacify the anti-Europeans he made the renegotiation hurdle sound rhetorically very challenging, but without burdening himself with over-specific commitments. Once safely back in government he accepted 'terms' that involved no renegotiation of the UK Treaty of Accession, which he knew was impossible to achieve with our partners. 'Renegotiation' was largely a cosmetic exercise, in essence a collection of policy changes and paper assurances. But Wilson understood his Labour electorate. One of his great renegotiation 'triumphs' was to secure higher quotas for cheap New Zealand lamb and butter, popular with working-class housewives and at the same time a gesture of emotional resonance with the Australian and New Zealand Army Corps (ANZAC) who had sacrificed so much for the 'old country' in World War II. The other 'coup' was Wilson's invitation to the German chancellor, the SPD's Helmut Schmidt (a one-time Panzer tank commander), to speak in brilliant English at a special Labour Conference and argue the case for Britain to share a common European future with Germany. The Labour Conference still voted two to one against the renegotiated terms, but the ground had shifted. Wilson's inglorious tactics ultimately resulted in a two-to-one 'yes' vote in the 1975 referendum. Wilson had manoeuvred, but in the end he had won. His tactical retreats and verbal convolutions eventually produced the outcome he had almost certainly wanted all along.

Winning on Europe, but Losing the Party

Yet the price of winning on Europe was to set back the cause of Labour revisionism for a generation. The internal stability of the party suffered a devastating blow from which it took more than two decades to recover. There was bitterness at the top between the towering figures that dominated the Labour governments of the 1960s and 1970s. This was not just true of Wilson, Callaghan and Jenkins: Healey's indecisiveness (in the autumn of 1971 he changed his position three times in a matter of weeks) was widely ridiculed. The close personal friendship between Jenkins and Crosland since their Oxford student days broke apart as Crosland, with half an eye on a future bid for the Labour leadership, ignominiously abstained rather than vote with the 69 pro-European rebels and claimed, unconvincingly (to those that knew him of old), that Europe did not rank in the issues he really cared about.[33] The party's traditional governing coalition splintered. The left attacked on all fronts, from demands for nationalising the top 25 companies to support for Clay Cross councillors who had defied the law on raising council house rents. Their demands coalesced around 'the alternative economic strategy'. The manifesto on which Labour was unexpectedly elected in February 1974 was allowed to contain many proposals which the leadership had little intention of implementing: their attitude simply fed alienation and anti-leadership feeling at the grass roots. The Attlee generation of Labour activists was literally dying out. Many local parties had become ossified and the Old Labour right appeared bankrupt. A new generation of 1960s graduates came into the party, radicalised by 1968 and opposition to the Vietnam

War. This new generation had new concerns: women's rights, gay rights, racial equality and the 'limits to growth'. Many convinced themselves that they had no 'enemies to the left'. They misread the early 1970s wave of shop-floor militancy as a desire for a wider transformation of society against which the old structures of the party and its parliamentary representatives were an obstacle. Europe was *not* the cause of this 'cultural revolution', but it was the major reason why the party establishment was paralysed in its response.

There proved to be still some life in Old Labour yet. After Wilson's retirement in March 1976, Callaghan remade himself as a highly successful prime minister, popular in the country and effective in reuniting a divided party. Yet his misjudgement in not going to the country in September 1978 was on the same scale as Gordon Brown's mistake in not calling an election in the autumn of 2007, prior to the financial crisis. In the 1978–79 'Winter of Discontent', Labour's claim to governing credibility fell apart. The party's governing model for the 1960s and 1970s lay in ruins. It could no longer claim that because of its close relationships with the trade unions, it could make the post-1945 welfare settlement work better than the Conservatives. It laid the basis for Margaret Thatcher's insistence that there was no alternative to her policies.

After Labour's 1979 defeat, the central issue for the party was whether, and then how quickly, the trade unions would come to terms with reality and enable the leadership to reassert control and re-establish the party's governing credibility. Tragically it did not happen in time to avert the SDP breakaway. Europe played a significant part, perhaps more than the defectors consciously realised. First it persuaded senior social democrats to put aside their personal rivalries and act together. In May 1980, John Silkin (a long-standing anti-Common Marketeer, who had been secretary of state for agriculture in the Callaghan cabinet) launched a campaign for Labour to recommit itself to EEC withdrawal. He thereby triggered the first public démarche by David Owen, Bill Rodgers and Shirley Williams, the newly dubbed 'Gang of Three', declaring that they would not go along with EEC withdrawal. Shirley Williams later went on to announce that she would not re-stand as a Labour candidate on a manifesto that contained such a pledge. Yet Labour's autumn 1980 conference, by a majority of five to one, carried a motion supporting unconditional withdrawal on a card vote, after a mere half an hour's debate at the end of a long afternoon, despite the referendum vote only five years before. In the left's mindset, the sovereignty of the party conference mattered far more than the sovereignty of the British people.

This anti-Europe vote did not itself lead to the SDP break. Pro-Europeanism would have been a poor issue on which to rally public support for a new party. Also, for the Gang of Three, there were far deeper issues facing the party. The SDP judgement was that the post-1979 move to the left was so fundamental that it would prevent Labour ever again offering a credible alternative to the Conservatives. With hindsight this judgement proved faulty, but not by that wide a margin. In the early 1980s Labour still enjoyed powerful structural bases of support within British society. Over 6 million people still worked in manufacturing; there were over 10 million trade union members; and over 50 per cent of the population still described themselves as working class. Nonetheless, Labour only survived the SDP breakaway by the skin of its teeth. Had the tiny margin of Denis Healey's victory over Tony Benn for the party's deputy leadership in September 1981 been reversed, and had the Falklands War not rescued Margaret Thatcher from deep unpopularity, history might well have turned out differently.

The 'elite' rebellion of Labour's pro-Europeans did therefore lead to Labour's greatest ever crisis. It demonstrated how control of the party was slipping out of the hands of the leadership structures that had sustained Labour as a party of government in the post-war era. It fatally divided and weakened the old right. An extra parliamentary tide, including many shades of ultra-leftism, such as the entryist Militant Tendency, was allowed by the party authorities to overrun dozens of constituency parties. The 'legitimate left' of the parliamentary party initially allowed themselves to be swept along. For them it was payback time. After decades of being worsted by the Labour right in factional disputes, they expected the one-time Gaitskellites and Jenkinsites (who had relied on trade union block votes and the support of the 'old right') to live with the party's 'democratic decisions'. Those who left for the SDP were not playing the game, as they saw it. The split proved a catalyst for the wave of Bennite self-destruction that led directly to Labour's catastrophic defeat under Michael Foot in 1983. The credibility of Labour as a party of government suffered a devastating blow from which it took a decade and a half to recover.

Europe was a big ideological undercurrent. It was a proxy for a wider unresolved struggle for Labour's soul. Full-hearted acceptance of the 1975 referendum result was another 'Bad Godesburg' opportunity that Labour once again passed by, as it had when it spurned Hugh Gaitskell's efforts to reform Clause Four in 1959 and when Harold Wilson chose to oppose EEC membership 'on Tory terms' in 1971. Commitment to the EEC could have been the opportunity to cast aside the myths that prevented Labour emerging as a modern social democratic party. Those who left for the SDP wanted Britain to adjust to a realistic appreciation of her place in the world, whereas the left's response was to renew the call for Britain to take a moral lead on nuclear weapons. The heart of the left was still beating with the illusions of Britain's unique capacity for moral leadership in the world. Also SDP-ers drew lessons from the economic disappointments of the 1960s and 1970s that were the exact opposite of the left's. They yearned for a party that recognised the limitations of nation state social democracy and had come to terms instead with the task of turning Britain into a modern social market economy. Against these views the Bennite 'alternative economic strategy' (AES), based on import controls and state-planning of industry, aimed to give nation state social democracy a second chance. Only as 'Bennery' imploded in the late 1980s, and Labour's commitment to AES-type policies was gradually ditched, did this lead to a new Labour interest in the Continental social market and a more European model of welfare-state capitalism.

CHAPTER 3

Labour's Turn to Europe

This chapter examines the part Europe played in Labour's long path to recovery as a potential party of government. What led to this post-1983 pro-European shift and was it as profound as on the surface it seemed? Within a month of becoming leader, Neil Kinnock abandoned the 1983 manifesto commitment to unconditional EEC withdrawal – a first indication of his courageous determination to remake Labour as a credible force. In the way of politics, Kinnock justified a major shift on tactical grounds. In a visit to Labour MEPs in Strasbourg, he argued that EEC withdrawal should only be a last resort if Labour's efforts to build a more socialist Europe failed.[1] For the left of the party, the currents of the time seemed favourable: popular protest against the deployment of US cruise missiles on European soil, the case for a 'Euro-Keynesian' coordinated stimulus and 'Euro-communist' ideas for industrial policy intervention. Nonetheless, Labour still remained outside the pro-European mainstream, opposing the Single European Act. It was not until Labour's 1988 Policy Review that the option of EEC withdrawal was finally abandoned.

Labour's Conversion Experience

For Kinnock personally, his initiative on Europe was part of a gradual rethinking of traditional 'left' positions. As shadow education secretary after 1979, he had rejected the knee-jerk leftism of 'reversing Tory cuts'. Along with a sizeable group of Tribunite MPs, he abstained in the final round of the 1981 deputy leadership contest, in effect handing victory to Healey over Benn. His pro-European shift was not driven by opinion polls (they continued to show strong public hostility to UK membership), but by a strategic judgement on where a modern party of the left needed to be.

Pro-Europeans remained prominent in Labour's senior ranks, despite the SDP defections. In addition to Roy Hattersley as Kinnock's deputy, figures such as Jack Cunningham, Giles Radice and George Roberston were strong pro-Europeans. Most prominent of all was John Smith, trade and industry spokesman after 1983, shadow chancellor after 1987 and leader from 1992 until his death in May 1994. Although criticised for being a tactical trimmer in the 1980–81 party crisis, and later for his 'one more heave' strategy as leader, on Europe Smith's commitment was consistent and clear. As one of the 69 Labour rebels in 1971, he told the Commons:

> I am willing to give up some national sovereignty to gain a sovereignty which will be able to do something [...] the fundamental of democratic socialism is that economic forces must somehow be brought under popular control and be fashioned towards social and political ends that the people determine.[2]

Smith had an edgy relationship with Kinnock, but their meeting of minds on Europe allowed a new pro-European consensus to emerge. This was greatly helped by developments in France. The credibility of the 'alternative economic strategy' suffered a major blow from the failure of the Mitterrand 'experiment' in 1981–83. As market pressures on the French franc strengthened, Jacques Delors, as French finance minister, persuaded Mitterrand to ditch nationalisation and the 'dash for growth' that had been the basis of his victorious electoral pact with the Communists – and work within the ERM framework of macroeconomic discipline. In a move of wide political significance, once Mitterrand accepted this abandonment of nation state social democracy, he became a strong advocate of European integration. With Delors soon installed as Commission president, and in a 'grand bargain' with Thatcher, France gave its backing to the single-market project in the belief that structural reforms would increase Europe's growth potential, at the same time as new rafts of 'flanking' policies – increased structural funds to assist weaker regions, stronger consumer and environmental protections, and extended workers' rights – would ensure more equitable market outcomes. As the breadth of these ambitions became apparent, Labour began to look at Europe differently.

The turning point was Delors' appearance at the TUC in September 1988. Much of his speech was a dry, intellectual lecture on the progressive case for market liberalisation. But his call for increased structural funds appealed to regions ravaged by Thatcherite deindustrialisation. His advocacy of a 'Social Charter' enthused trade unions demoralised by industrial and political defeat. His support for 'every worker's right to be covered by a collective agreement' so excited Ron Todd, the then TGWU general secretary, that in a dramatic response to Delors he threw over three decades of hostility to Europe:

> in the short term we have not a cat in hell's chance in Westminster. The only card game in town at the moment is in a town called Brussels.[3]

Three weeks later at the Labour conference, Clive Jenkins, the general secretary of the Association of Scientific Technical and Managerial Staffs (ASTMS), who had long been a scourge of Labour pro-Europeans, recanted on his past errors, which he self-critically described in his memoirs as 'learning from life itself'. These conversion experiences on the left were reinforced by Margaret Thatcher's apostasy on the right. Turning her back on her 'grand bargain' with Mitterrand, her Bruges lecture, delivered the same month, reignited Euroscepticism with its affirmation that 'we have not defeated socialism at home only to have Europe reimpose it through the back door'.[4] For a Labour movement that felt unloved and excluded, with the front door slammed in its face, progress through the European back door seemed highly alluring.

Europe and Labour's Return to the Social Democratic Mainstream

At the end of the 1980s, Labour's conversion to Europe was a crucial part of the biggest ideological shift in the party's history: from belief in the centrality of state-planning to embrace of the market; from crude Keynesianism to support for anti-inflationary discipline; and from 'free collective bargaining' to a framework of workplace law, underwriting a Social Charter of individual employee rights. With Smith and the rising star Gordon Brown in the lead, the ERM became the cornerstone of Labour macroeconomics. Tony Blair, as shadow employment secretary, trumpeted individual workplace rights under Delors' Social Charter, in the process largely accepting the Thatcherite industrial relations reforms on collective rights. In the run up to the 1992 election, Labour's leaders energetically worked the 'prawn cocktail' circuit, emphasising to business Labour's strong European commitment as a badge of economic competence and trust.

Pro-Europeanism became part of a larger progressive tide. The collapse of the Lawson boom raised doubts as to whether Thatcherism really had transformed British economic performance. There was renewed interest in the contrasting successes of the 'Rhineland model'. Michael Heseltine made the virtues of social market capitalism his central critique of Thatcherism. Giles Radice wrote an influential book on *The New Germans*. The economic commentator, Will Hutton, developed the ideas that would lead to his sensationally successful *The State We're In*. Academics launched a genre of studies in 'varieties of capitalism'. For a time the 'European social model' became a British intellectual fashion.[5]

Constitutional reformers also looked to Europe. The longer the Conservatives stayed in power with only a minority of the popular vote, the more progressives questioned the Westminster model of 'winner takes all'. The debate on electoral reform, as a means of promoting consensus against the extremes, resurfaced. Europe was seen as entrenching social rights against the tyranny of an unrepresentative parliamentary majority. European Court of Justice (ECJ) judgements were seen as broadly progressive. Support grew for a Bill of Rights, incorporating the Strasbourg Convention fully into British law. Devolutionists looked to regional decentralisation in Italy, France and the new democratic Spain.

The Baleful Consequences of the ERM

Within Labour, however, the commitment to the ERM remained controversial. Its attraction to Smith and Brown was as a guarantee of economic discipline to fend off Conservative attacks on Labour profligacy. Because the Thatcher government was deeply and publicly split on whether Britain should join, it offered a perfect combination, both enhancing Labour's economic credibility and highlighting Conservative division. But for some elements within Labour, the ERM prioritised fighting inflation over tackling unemployment: it therefore fell into the same category of deflationary unacceptability as the Thatcherite monetarist experiment. Bryan Gould, Labour's shadow trade and industry secretary, after 1987 remained deeply opposed. A former Oxford law don with a formidable intellect and excellent presentational skills, he had been a consistent advocate since the 1970s of export-led growth based on a competitive exchange rate and increased public investment, if necessary, buttressed by import and exchange controls. Gould knew perfectly well that this alternative was inconsistent with EEC rules but, as a native New Zealander with Eurosceptic instincts, he didn't care. Gould eventually lost the argument and his economic portfolio. In a significant drama of high politics, Kinnock moved him in autumn 1989 to lead Labour's campaign against the poll tax, with Brown taking his place. Labour's official policy moved quickly from an ill-specified Euro-Keynesianism to a clear commitment to a European currency peg.

For Brown, the September 1992 ERM crisis was as big a crisis as it was for the Major government. Had Labour won in the April 1992 election, a Labour government would of course have faced the same crisis. But Labour might have been able to negotiate a multilateral exchange rate realignment keeping Britain within the ERM; after all, it was not Labour that had decided to join the ERM in November 1990 at an unsustainably high rate. Labour's economic diplomacy would also have been more subtle. John Smith would not have got himself into Norman Lamont's position at the Bath meeting of European finance ministers in September 1992, which ended in a shouting match between the Chancellor and the Bundesbank president, Hans Tietmeyer, over the Germans' refusal to lower interest rates. Anyone with the slightest sensitivity to the way the Bundesbank had built its reputation over the previous four decades would have known that such a semi-public démarche was a total non-starter.

Unfortunately though, from the impotence of opposition, Labour was totally powerless to manage events. For Brown, now shadow chancellor, this proved a searing experience. Not only was Labour's economic credibility on the line, as Labour had hitched its wagon to a failing policy, Brown's personal credibility was on the line too. This huge blow fell as Brown was also struggling to change public perceptions of Labour as a 'tax and spend' party. He fought bruising battles with shadow cabinet colleagues whose every instinct was still to attack 'Tory cuts' and make spending promises of their own. A section of the PLP was out for Brown's blood: those who originally agreed with Bryan Gould's opposition to the ERM, and the 60-odd Eurosceptic Labour MPs who had defied a three-line whip to vote against the Maastricht Treaty on its second reading. Worryingly these included younger, recently elected 'soft left' MPs like Roger Berry and Peter Hain, who opposed what they saw as deflationary policies being forced on Europe as a result of the Maastricht criteria. Inside the PLP, Brown became less popular and MPs began to look more favourably on the more emollient Tony Blair, who performed brilliantly as shadow home secretary. The new mood created the conditions whereby, when John Smith suffered his sudden fatal heart attack in May 1994, Brown's bid for the leadership was swept aside by an avalanche of shadow cabinet and PLP support for Blair. Brown could never reconcile himself to this: in his eyes Blair had, ruthlessly and without sentiment for his close friend, who for nine years had been the accepted senior figure in their relationship, seized the claim to leadership that he thought was rightfully his.

Blair and Brown United by Fate on Europe

In analysing how politicians behave, the formational influences of early political experiences are typically underplayed. Of course individual views change over time, as in any rational person they should. Yet often early events shape a politician's 'world view' and retain a lasting hold as they rise through the party system. In the same way that interpretations of the fall of Thatcher have cast a long shadow among Conservatives, so in Labour politics have perceptions of the 1980s.

Europe was a crucial formational influence on Blair and Brown. They reacted against the visceral anti-Europeanism of large sections of the Labour Party they joined, seeing it as part of a destructive left politics that had led Labour to the brink of extinction. Blair was a highly atypical outsider in the Labour tribe, discovering politics late by the standards of the conventionally ambitious. However, one of his first acts as a politically inactive Oxford student was to vote 'yes' in the 1975 referendum.[6] At his selection conference in the Durham constituency of Sedgefield in March 1983, he was asked about his view of Europe: he did not deny his pro-European views, but promised to stick loyally to Labour policy.[7] Before he was elected to Parliament he had a settled view on a key issue that differed from the conventional 'soft' left wisdom in the London Labour world in which he and his wife, Cherie, moved.

Brown by contrast had been a political obsessive since he arrived at the University of Edinburgh aged 17. Yet he was an unconventional socialist in terms of the entrenched left and right positions that divided the Scottish Labour Party establishment. What first brought him to notice was his support for Scottish devolution on left-wing grounds, a position he argued in the 1975 *Red Paper on Scotland*. Even if the pull of tribal loyalties would have drawn Brown towards the 'anti' camp in the referendum, intellectually he would have been influenced by Tom Nairn, the Scottish Marxist and equally passionate left devolutionist, who in his earlier 1973 book *The Left against Europe* stood out of the crowd by arguing that the left's opposition to Europe was fundamentally misguided.[8] Brown was a politician with a capacity to think things through unconventionally and for himself.

What made Blair and Brown stand out as newly elected MPs in the PLP in 1983 was their desperation for Labour to recover its position as a party of government. Anti-Europeanism had been a source of disabling internal party conflict and division. The SDP breakaway had deprived Labour of a whole generation of political and policy-making talent. Despite the prevalent anti-Europeanism of Labour's traditional working-class support, the pledge of EEC withdrawal had not prevented their desertion en masse in 1983: anti-Europeanism simply strengthened adverse public perceptions of Labour's 'fitness to govern'. Europe thus became a totem of both Brown and Blair's modernising politics.

Europe's Place in the New Labour Project

Pro-Europeanism was vital to where Blair, now ensconced as leader, aimed to take the Labour Party and Britain. He wanted to create a broad-based governing Labour majority. He wanted to change British political history, reversing the dominance of the Conservatives. He sought a long-term transformation in Britain, brought about by a durable period of 'progressive' government, implementing gradual social improvement, and sustained by a 'big tent' progressive majority. Europe was an essential prop of that big tent. First, it was a common platform on which a progressive alliance with the Liberal Democrats could be built that might pull them gradually inside. Second, Europe was crucial to opening the big tent's doors to a business community, increasingly disillusioned with Conservative Euroscepticism. Third, it offered the tempting prospect of weakening and possibly splitting the Conservatives, just as had happened over repeal of the Corn Laws in the 1840s and tariff reform in the early 1900s. Blair's pro-Europeanism was not in its prime motivation a British project for Europe. Rather, it was a very clear pro-European project for Britain.

How far did Brown buy into Blair's vision? The post-'94 Brown was in a difficult position: determined still to become leader when Blair departed, he had to retain the position of 'heir apparent', at the same time as being part of a governing 'duo' with Blair. Brown also liked to hide his views behind a veil of tactical caution: the more one committed oneself publicly in politics, in his view, the greater the risk one ran and the more likely that one's words would be seized on by opponents to undermine and attack. But there were also innate differences of emphasis with Blair. Whereas Blair thought superficially in terms of a 'big tent', Brown thought more deeply about constitutional reform. Intellectual logic leaned towards a federal Britain, with a written constitution, a reformed electoral system and multi-party politics, but there was always a tension between the intellectual ideal and the politics of becoming leader of a party with a deep-seated commitment to the traditional Westminster model. Despite occasional public hints of an instinctive radicalism, Brown largely kept his thoughts to himself for tactical party reasons and because he was never totally confident of what final conclusion to draw.

The same Brown caution applied to Blair's embrace of the Liberal Democrats. Most Labour MPs disliked the idea of an ideological affinity with Liberal Democrats, whom they thought of as a bunch of unprincipled opportunists, changing their message from street to street in order to garner votes. They did not understand that the 'first-past-the-post' system left the Liberal Democrats with little alternative if they were to win seats without a committed class base. Brown himself was more positive: he was keen to explore common ideological ground with the Liberal Democrats, admired their leading intellectuals, particularly Ralf Dahrendorf and David Marquand, and was fascinated by the innovative policy positions the SDP had struck in the 1980s. Both Blair and Brown wanted Labour to be a broad-based 'big tent' party on the model of the US Democrats, not a party of the 'labour interest', still less an ideologically driven left that had to work in a permanent multi-party coalition as in many Continental countries. They both recognised that Labour might need the Liberal Democrats to govern, and a strong pro-Europeanism was part of the common ground this putative 'progressive alliance' shared.

Brown was publicly more supportive of Blair's overtures towards big business. Odd as this may seem, this was safer ground in the party than closeness to the Liberal Democrats: after long years in the wilderness, the party was flattered by the attention of business, and few expressed concerns about the subtle long-term influences on policy that pro-business overtures inevitably entailed.

Prior to 1997, Blair and Brown were largely at one on the European question. In private, Brown was deeply troubled by the difficulties an incoming Labour chancellor would face. The spectres of the 1960s and 1970s loomed large in his mind. His nightmare was that party and union pressures would lead to an unsustainable surge in public spending that would overstrain the economy, worsen the balance of payments and put pressure on sterling. Brown's worst dread was that he would become another in the line of Labour chancellors forced to devalue the pound or, worse still, to seek emergency help from the IMF. These political nightmares were combined with a rock-solid conviction that currency depreciation was a temporary fix that solved none of the long-term problems facing the British economy. No one in the inner circle was unaware of this. This view he held with the Presbyterian rigour of his mentor, John Smith: in the September 1992 ERM crisis Brown had memorably taken to the airwaves to declare that 'devaluation was not our policy at the last election, is not our policy now and will not be our policy at the next election'.[9] The 'Iron Chancellor' was the soubriquet he positively cultivated.

This bundle of nightmares and convictions made Brown instinctively sympathetic to the concept of a single currency: membership would at a stroke abolish the sterling problem that had been the bane of post-war chancellors. He recognised there were great difficulties in going for British membership, both political and economic, but the perception that he was from the start hostile to the whole idea is quite wrong. Prior to 1997, Brown had not ruled out a bold move to euro membership once in office, in the same way as he was to move decisively to make the Bank of England independent: he remained open to what would be an economic game-changer.

Blair's gut instincts were also profoundly pro-European, but different in nature. He always argued that, for him, and for young people of his generation (and, it might be added, educational background and class), pro-Europeanism 'seemed the natural thing'.[10] Blair did not have Brown's deep historic sense of how the question of sterling had derailed previous Labour governments – and, unlike Brown, he had lived through the ERM episode at one remove. For Blair, what other future might there be for Britain than as a leading player in the EU? Blair simply could not relate to the fevered passions of the British anti-Europeans. The emotional attachment to an indivisible Westminster sovereignty that marked out a Michael Foot or Enoch Powell just left him cold.

Blair and Brown were both instinctive Atlanticists as well. Some argue that their admiration for the USA ran much deeper than their commitment to Europe and that explains why Britain went to war in Iraq and never joined the single currency. Frankly this is trite. What marked out Brown and Blair as rising Labour politicians in the 1980s and 1990s was not whether they were more pro-Europe than pro-America, or vice versa, but that they were passionately pro-both. They had no time for the traditional Labour left's rejection of the 'idea of the West' and its long history of simultaneous suspicion of, if not antagonism towards, both America and Europe. Brown was an avaricious follower of the currents of American intellectual and political debate and loved holidaying on Cape Cod with one of his brothers, doubtless devouring the latest tomes of political and economic wisdom that he had picked up in the Harvard bookshops on his way. Blair preferred France or Italy for summer holidays with Cherie and their children. But these holiday preferences were without wider significance. Brown and Blair were treading a path familiar to previous

Labour generations before the party adopted the isolationist positions of the early 1980s. They both identified with the US Democrats, sharing the post-war tradition of the moderate left in Europe that thought of the USA as a beacon of liberal and social democracy, a progressive 'city on a hill'. But also, for both Brown and Blair, Europe mattered to their modernising politics: they saw 'Europe' as something significantly more than an exercise in pragmatic statecraft.

Tactical Constraints and the 1997 General Election

In the run up to 1997, Blair and Brown's overriding concern was to ensure victory after four successive defeats. Extreme (and objectively irrational) nervousness about Labour's prospects trumped all other considerations. The 1992 defeat had been cathartic, with Labour's campaign damaged beyond repair by the Conservative assault on 'Labour's tax bombshell'. Blair and Brown feared that, even if they rebuilt public trust on 'tax and spend', the Conservatives would next turn to Europe as the vehicle for mobilising an anti-Labour media campaign. Constantly in fear of being outmanoeuvred, in their own minds they exaggerated the risk that the Conservatives could successfully make Europe into a 'dividing line'. Deep government divisions, and Kenneth Clarke's unwillingness to play politics on the issue, in truth made this difficult if not impossible. As long as Clarke remained chancellor, he was determined that no pre-emptive step would be taken to prevent an incoming Labour government taking Britain into the single currency.[11] Clarke steadfastly resisted pressure to rule out membership in the next Parliament, a striking instance of a politician prepared to put his view of the country's interests before his party's, even when he wanted so much to become its leader. In the bovine spongiform encephalopathy (BSE) crisis, John Major temporarily tried to raise the stakes by launching the so-called 'beef wars', announcing that Britain would veto every measure that came up in the Council of Ministers until a European ban on British beef exports was lifted. Major was forced into a humiliating climb-down, as he had been warned by his senior officials, but, in a telling example of Labour's fears, Blair went along somewhat lamely with the government's ludicrous posture. Labour's tactical judgement was that on Europe they should minimise policy differences with the Major government to ward off any possibility of their pro-Europeanism being used as a weapon of attack. This had the added bonus of enabling Labour to keep the focus on the Conservatives' own divisions, with the destructive behaviour of the Eurosceptics readily offering their own helping hand.

These tactics represented a political judgement that Labour had to work within the constraints of a more Eurosceptic mood. The parliamentary ratification of the Maastricht Treaty had run into deep trouble. The initial Danish 'no' vote in June 1992 followed by Britain's ERM debacle in September had emboldened Conservative rebels. The treaty debate fired up the single currency issue, rather than dodge it as John Major with his 'opt-out' had hoped.[12] On the Continent, a fierce debate raged in Germany about the risks of giving up the Deutschmark. In the mid-1990s, there was no clarity about whether the single currency would go ahead as planned, or at all, or with how many members. This Continental clamour fed the complacent British attitude that 'it will never happen', or, as John Major notoriously put it, the single currency had 'all the quaintness of a rain dance and about the same potency'.[13] Within the UK, single currency sceptics spread far beyond the ranks of traditional anti-Europeans. Former Conservative chancellors Lawson and Lamont argued that the single currency was a flawed idea and would never work. The former Conservative European commissioner, Christopher Tugendhat, expressed strong reservations. The former SDP leader, David Owen, opposed it. The ranks of UK economists were divided and the press was sceptical. If a Labour government genuinely wanted to pursue a pro-European, pro-single currency policy, it would somehow have to change the political weather. This task could not be undertaken in opposition: Blair and Brown were clear that they first had an election to win.

The Decision to Offer a Referendum on the Euro

The crucial pre-election retreat was Blair's decision to offer a referendum on the single currency. Brown, to his great credit, fiercely resisted making this commitment. As Labour's future chancellor, he wanted to retain maximum freedom of manoeuvre. Blair's rationale was to neutralise Europe as a general election issue by promising a separate vote on the single currency. The referendum pledge made it more likely that the Murdoch press would endorse New Labour, while retaining their hostile stance on Europe. These were tactical gains. Against them, the referendum pledge was a major victory for Euroscepticism. Labour's decision to accept a 'referendum lock' on euro entry hugely raised the stakes. There could never be a certainty, however favourable the circumstances, that such a referendum would be won. Defeat, on the other hand, could easily prove a turning point in the electorate's love affair with New Labour and foreshorten the party's grip on power.

In a strange paradox, Blair's anxieties over the referendum were assuaged by Roy Jenkins, who by this stage had become a Blair intimate. Wilson's offer of a referendum had triggered Jenkins' resignation as Labour deputy leader in 1972. But in his view 1975 had shown how a Europe referendum could be won and, on an issue as significant and controversial as the euro, where there was no national consensus, in principle it was wise to seek the people's full-hearted consent. Jenkins may have been right, but he failed to spot the big difference compared with 1975. For Wilson the referendum was a political imperative and an unavoidable risk. Without it, he could not have kept Labour even tenuously united or hung on as leader. Furthermore, without a referendum in 1975 Labour would never have gathered up sufficient unity and strength to address the formidable economic problems facing the country. On the euro there was no political compulsion on the Labour leadership to take what was always going to be a risky gamble.

The Appeasement of Murdoch

After Labour's 1992 defeat, the myth that 'it was the *Sun* that won it'[14] gained almost mystical power. Despite that, John Smith made no special effort to soften up Murdoch: in his view, hostility from that quarter came with the job of Labour leader. The 'modernisers' were determined to change that, in part to demonstrate how genuinely 'new' New Labour was. Murdoch had been the bogeyman of the left since the 'Winter of Discontent'. His struggle to break the print unions had been ferocious and symbolic of Thatcherism's ideological victory, with Labour, under union pressure, imposing a formal boycott on News International contacts. Rebuilding relationships with Murdoch was a signal that Labour was burying its past. Few around the leadership cavilled at Blair's audacity, or questioned what of value, along with the past, might be buried.

Alastair Campbell, Blair's newly appointed press secretary, was cheerleader in chief, but Blair himself was willing to go to enormous lengths, flying halfway across the world to address News Corporation's management conference and treating his relationships with the Murdoch family as one would treat long-standing family friends. The most egregious example of Blair's appeasement of Murdoch was his 'Why I love the pound'[15] article shortly after the *Sun* came out for Labour in the 1997 campaign.[16] For pro-Europeans this provided compelling evidence of a New Labour pact with the devil. When I saw a draft of the article, I protested vigorously to Peter Mandelson in Labour's Milbank headquarters. Peter's response was to read out the *Sun* piece line by line, pausing to ask after every sentence whether anything was being said which would actually constrain a Labour government's actions. I was forced to admit that the piece conveyed the desired impression that Blair would be no 'pushover' without making a single binding commitment. It was a classic example of the best and worst of New Labour 'spin'.

But was it necessary to go to the lengths Blair did, given Labour's overwhelming lead in the polls? It was, according to Blair. Four days before polling day Blair still displayed a striking lack of confidence: at his home in Islington, he insisted that Labour would have a majority of no more than 40. New Labour had lived through 18 long years of unelectability and the grievous disappointment of 1992: nothing was to be allowed to stand in their way this time, but that striking lack of confidence was to have a major influence over future European decisions.

Murdoch, Europe, Hyper-Globalism and New Labour

What sway over government policy did Blair's attitude hand to the Murdochs? Blair insists none, and on specific policies I agree with him. Yet there were more subtle and deeply significant influences. One, as we shall see later in the book, was on the internal struggle for power between Blair and Brown, which gave the Murdoch press huge leverage to exert pressure. Another can only be described as ideological. In Blair's eyes, Murdoch was not a traditional anti-European. He was neither of the 'British establishment' nor a Westminster sovereigntist. According to Blair, Murdoch's view of Europe was framed by a deep objection to Continental 'corporatism' that simply did not 'get' globalisation and the economic revolution it entailed. Blair and Brown attentively listened to Murdoch's espousal of his hyper-globalist world view. Of course he was by no means alone in expressing this view, but the perceived electoral power of his newspapers obtained for them a ready attention.

How far did New Labour buy into this hyper-globalist viewpoint and to what extent did it lead down a dangerous blind alley? Arguably it subtly moved New Labour from being a project of social democratic modernisation that had at long last come to terms with the centrality of a competitive market economy, to one that made an overenthusiastic accommodation with the excesses of financial capitalism. This is highly relevant to the academic debate about whether New Labour represented a further legitimate phase of social democratic revisionism, or whether it represented an accommodation to neo-liberalism outside that tradition. This is also relevant to the separate but related question of whether New Labour represented a leadership coup by a small elite 'against the rest of the party', or whether a genuine transformation of attitudes towards a New Labour 'world view' had taken place across the wider Labour movement, giving substance to Blair's claim that Labour was a 'new party'.

New Labour devoted considerable intellectual energy to thinking about its project for the country and developing a coherent strategy for power. It entered office with what it imagined was a clear set of governing principles that had been internally debated and thought through. On Europe, the pro-European shift was a genuine movement of opinion in the wider party, not the result of manipulation by a leadership elite. It was in advance of public opinion, which remained highly problematic. Rather, the pro-European shift represented a clear change of view among activists within the trade unions, in Labour local government and in the PLP towards a more positive recognition of the EU's achievements and potential. It reflected a hesitant but nonetheless real acceptance of the limitations of nation state social democracy in the face of the seeming dominance of Thatcherism. Ideologically, it represented a more realistic appreciation of the difference a Labour government at Westminster might be able to make in a modern market economy and a dawning of the realities of economic interdependence in a world of increasing economic integration. The essence of the New Labour domestic pitch was that the market reforms implemented by the Thatcher/Major governments, especially privatisation and trade union reform, had been necessary and would not in essence be reversed; rather, Labour's mission would be to address the negative consequences that Thatcherism had inflicted on British society: the scars of long-term unemployment and poverty; the neglect of public services and public investment; and the rejection of the idea of 'society'. This New Labour mission amounted in simple terms to making Britain more like a modern European country – a social market economy with more equality of opportunity, less poverty and a higher-quality public realm. This amounted to a significant reappraisal of the possibilities of British social democracy.

Yet New Labour's governing principles were always capable of being bent or overridden by Blair and Brown's profound nervousness about

Labour's electoral prospects. New Labour was first and foremost a project to win elections. That required radical change in public perceptions of the Labour Party. Of course this meant an element of accommodation to the electorate's perceived wishes, as reflected in focus groups and opinion polls. In the process, New Labour clearly became something different to the precepts of north European social democracy. The simple idea that New Labour wanted Britain as a society to become more like Europe and less like America became impossible for New Labour to articulate. Not only did it conflict with the anti-European thrust of the British press that closer association with Europe would 'hold Britain back', it was also deeply offensive to the world view of the 'hyper-globalisers', including the Murdochs, who swarmed around Blair and Brown once it was clear Labour was on the threshold of power. America to them was the beacon to the world of free enterprise, innovation and dynamic growth. Europe was the home of a sclerotic, failing social model. As a result, Blair and Brown both shifted to a more positive view of globalisation than many on the European left would find palatable. 'Hyper-globalism' made a convincing turn to Europe ideologically much more difficult.

One telling episode was the Blair–Brown sidelining of Will Hutton's concept of the 'stake-holder society'. Peter Mandelson and I were finalising *The Blair Revolution* at the time.[17] Peter was anxious to find out from Blair what he thought about stakeholderism. The answer we got back was 'put plenty of it in'. By the time the book was published, the position had changed. The 'stakeholding' idea had been seized on with enthusiasm by the trade unions with the risk that it might be attacked as implying a return to 1970s corporatism with unions seeking seats in company boardrooms. The truth is that this was a complete distortion of what Hutton was proposing. Also, if New Labour had taken stakeholding as seriously as it should, it would have had to argue for policies that would address corporate short-termism: 'hyper-globalisers' would have found that deeply uncomfortable.

Of course the 'hyper-globalisers' made some points that at the time appeared valid. The US record in new business growth and innovation appeared much more impressive than Europe's. In terms of productivity growth, the USA in the late 1990s looked to be accelerating away from Europe. Also, Europe's social models did need major reforms, particularly if they were to withstand the strains of coexistence within a single currency. Yet Europe's 'hyper-globalising' critics tended to ignore reforms in some European countries, particularly the Nordics and the Netherlands, that had already demonstrated their ability to carry through major change without destroying the essence of their social models. The hyper-globalisers wilfully ignored the growing lack of distributive legitimacy in the US model. A huge share of US productivity gains was being siphoned off to the top 1 per cent of the population. While this rampant growth in corporate greed and inequality was not so apparent in New Labour's early days, 'trickle down' was clearly failing. Of course it is simplistic to think in terms of a binary choice between American and European models, but the 'hyper-globalising' world view distorted the essential core of the New Labour narrative and led both to caution on Europe and to a failure to espouse the European social model of social market capitalism.

A European Message with a Harder Edge

This all contributed to Labour's message on Europe becoming harder-edged than had been its tone in the early 1990s. A simple way of showing this is to look at the references to Europe in Blair's conference speeches. In his first speech in 1994, Blair attacked the Conservatives for 'playing politics' with Europe, to which he responded: 'I will never allow this country to be isolated, cut off or left behind.'[18] The statement received massive applause and had only one implication: if the single currency went ahead, Britain should be part of it.

In 1995, Blair was equally forthright: 'we cannot be half in or half out forever.' But the language was more qualified: 'Of course Europe needs reform […] if there are further steps to integration, then we are the first to say the people should give their consent at a general election or in a referendum.'[19]

By 1996, Blair had toughened up even more. In bulldog tones, he declared: 'I will not scrap Britain's veto in Europe.' On the single currency, the language that we could not be half in and half out forever had changed to a much more conditional statement: 'Our options on the single currency should remain open, to be determined according to our national interest. Any change will only come with the full consent of the people.' So not only would there have to be a referendum, Labour was keeping its options open with the possibility that it might not be in Britain's national interest to join. There was also a more instrumental approach to Britain's EU membership. Blair spoke about how 'with a good relationship with Europe, we can get more out of it'. Of his ten vows to the country, Blair promised on Europe an unspecific 'new and more constructive relationship'.[20] For the moment at least the passion and commitment of earlier speeches had been put firmly back in a box marked 'Britain's national interest'.

Blair and Brown's mission was to devise an election-winning and governing project for Labour, of which they judged a commitment to Europe to be a necessary part. To be sure of winning the 1997 election, however, this shared strong commitment to Europe became overlaid by tactics and caution, characteristic of predecessors such as Harold Wilson and Jim Callaghan in contrast to whom they had been so determined they would be different. On Europe, Blair was willing to make whatever tactical concessions he judged necessary. He insisted these had not deflected from his pro-European purpose. Yet his decision to pledge a referendum on Britain's membership of the single currency, his appeasement of the Eurosceptic media, and his acceptance of a particular account of globalisation that would in time shape his own world view were to raise big hurdles to the achievement of his ambitions. Once firmly esconced in office, Blair and Brown were to expend much energy in a restless and unresolved attempt to reconcile a European commitment that they both felt to be important, with the constraints of 'preference accommodation' to public and media opinion and a set of assumptions about the 'national interest' that they uncritically inherited and imbibed.

Act Two: Blair's Failure

CHAPTER 4

In Power without a Policy

I started my job as special adviser in the No. 10 Policy Unit a couple of weeks after Blair's momentous 1997 landslide, taking on the Europe brief in the belief that this represented one of the central challenges facing New Labour. Yet I experienced a cold shower of disillusion early on. At the first full meeting of the Policy Unit, chaired by its then acting head, an exuberantly youthful David Miliband, we went round the room discussing priorities for the new government's first term. The Policy Unit was made up, with one exception, of politically appointed special advisers, most of whom had worked full time for Blair in opposition. I knew my new colleagues quite well, having worked closely with them in a voluntary capacity before the election. Yet if I was part of their circle, it was on its outer edge. As a newcomer to the team, I started off my contribution a little hesitantly, not quite knowing what to expect. Europe, I began, was central to the strategic objectives of New Labour: at this there was a lot of smirking and some titters round the table. I then argued that the politics of the first term would need to be dominated by building support for British entry to the single currency. At this point the room broke into 'you must be joking' laughter. I was taken aback. Clearly the people who had worked with Blair most closely on a day-to-day basis were at best cynical about New Labour's European commitment. The 'operation', as it liked to describe itself, was clearly not fully bought-in to what I had imagined was a central Blair priority. And it meant something, because the office was an 'echo chamber' of Blair's off-the-cuff remarks and instinctive reactions: they saw him in a much more tactical and opportunist light than at that time I did.

Their reactions conflicted with everything I had heard or been told. Because of our friendship, Peter Mandelson had told me about a lot of the discussions that he, Blair and Brown had had. That 'Trio', as well described in Giles Radice's book of that title, had worked together closely for a long time: until John Smith's death, it had been a remarkable three-way relationship of high intensity, mutual empathy and deep commitment. Yet all my past discussions with Peter had taken for granted that the 'Trio' saw Europe and the single currency as one of New Labour's greatest challenges and ambitions. This had been reinforced by my own 'one-to-one' contacts with Blair and Brown before 1997. For the first time, the thought crossed my mind whether Peter's commitment to Europe, which had been genuine and consistent throughout his political life, was of an order of strength much greater than that of the others. Was he (and by extension, me) being played along as an 'outrider' to persuade a pro-European constituency that there was a stronger commitment to Europe than in fact there was? Certainly Labour came into government with a strong pro-European instinct and a predisposition in favour of the single currency, although in public the leadership had been careful to be non-committal, or more accurately ambiguous. But there was no worked-out European strategy or single currency timeline. At first the government improvised. Then 'events' led to the 'half in, half out' October 1997 single currency statement, which Blair immediately recognised to be glaringly inconsistent with his rhetoric of 'leading in Europe' on anything but a holding basis. It took the following 18 months for Blair's strategy for Europe to crystallise.

But Europe was no exception. Labour had arrived to power without a set of well-worked-out policies, still less a governing mindset. The prime motivation in devising the New Labour electoral programme had been defensive: to remove the negatives that the public still felt about Labour from its past, and to convince sceptical voters that Labour could be trusted with power. It took time for New Labour in office, at first cautiously and then more confidently, to pursue the classic priorities of a centre-left social democratic government – better public services, action to tackle joblessness and poverty, a more active role for the state in creating new opportunities and addressing underperformance – in a manner commendably shorn of ideology and political correctness, and taken forward in a framework of economic prudence and fiscal responsibility, at least for the first six or seven years of government. Yet Blair's rhetoric and conversation conveyed a sense of wanting to achieve far more: a new politics, a new party, a progressive alliance to put the Conservatives out of power for a generation, and an end to Britain's semi-detachedness in Europe. To a wide circle of contacts in the press, politics and business, Blair had not conveyed the impression that for him Europe was a dispensable add-on: rather, it was presented as central to his political being.

New Labour's Initial Weaknesses in Government

As an area of policy, there was nothing atypical about Europe in its level of vagueness prior to 1997. New Labour was brilliant at politics and opposition, but its leadership had little practical experience of government. In Blair's first cabinet, only Margaret Beckett, Jack Cunningham and Ivor Richard had previously held office – and then in junior capacities prior to 1979. Of the senior ministers, only the home secretary, Jack Straw, had government experience as a special adviser in the health and environment departments in the 1970s under Barbara Castle and Peter Shore. The Attlee and Wilson governments all came into office with vastly more Whitehall knowledge. In political 'green-ness', the only historic parallel was the first Ramsay McDonald government of 1923. The contrast between Tony Blair and David Cameron is also instructive. Cameron had been a special adviser in the Treasury and Home Office after the 1992 elections. Blair had no experience inside government whatsoever, or for that matter of working inside any large organisation.

Inexperience explains a major part of the lack of New Labour policy innovation in Blair's first term. The first term did fulfil some major manifesto commitments, crucially on constitutional reform and the national minimum wage, but these were hangovers from the Smith leadership. At the Treasury, Brown made important policy innovations – Bank of England independence, a new regime of financial supervision, 'welfare to work' and tax credits, on which he and Ed Balls had organised serious preparatory work before the election. Elsewhere (with education an exception) the government adopted a 'tick box' approach to its manifesto commitments. Blair himself initially saw government, as he had seen the task of opposition, as a permanent campaign to respond to public opinion as largely defined by the press and media. In the first term, some members of Blair's policy unit still saw policy-making as working out how to respond to stories in the *Daily Mail*. Blair gradually became conscious of these weaknesses, but it took him two or three years to develop a clear sense of direction.

Blair's was the first government of the '24-hour news cycle'. Of course politicians have always been obsessed with the media, as any reader of the diary accounts of the Wilson governments can only be aware. But the 24-hour news cycle has changed the nature of politics, as the fast-moving news cycle gives politicians less time to react. It gives the media an incentive to keep a story moving, inflating every twist and turn of events, exposing an organisation as complex and diffuse as 'the government', headed by ministers with conflicting egos and ambitions, to the hazards of (often unintentional) contradiction and confusion. Critical to the public's sense of the competence of a modern political party and government is whether it can manage this media roller-coaster successfully. Central to the rise of Blair and Brown had been the fact that, with Mandelson's and then Campbell's help, they had grasped this insight. However, they were not naive about the dangers of being dragged down by the hand-to-hand warfare of the daily media grind. They constantly obsessed about 'strategy', but it was not strategy as most ordinary mortals in the world of business would define it. Once, early on, an irritated Peter quipped that 'what Tony means by strategy is what's in the weekend papers'. This remark was exaggerated and unfair, but it contained a grain of truth.

Blair's hallmark as a leader and prime minister – and how he wanted the rest of the world to see him – was summed up in the phrase 'leadership not drift'. To lead successfully, leaders had to know where they wanted to go, or at least convey some sense of it. This may sound a statement of the blindingly obvious, but it is less so when one reflects on the political style of the prime ministers who both preceded and succeeded him, including David Cameron. Every Sunday that Blair spent at Chequers, he would sit down, almost without fail, and write a long note to the office with his thoughts on the strategic direction of his government and the principles that should determine its policies. These strategy notes could sometimes be repetitious and superficial. For historians they will provide a unique account of Blair's personal development as prime minister. For Blair himself, his strategy notes – and the very process of writing them – were an invaluable lifeline in giving him a sense of direction down a clear path. They prevented him from being drowned in the domestic storms and the media turbulence that constantly threaten to engulf any government in the modern age. Yet initially Blair conceived of strategy as essentially about communications. The central question in his mind was 'has the government got a credible message about what it is trying to achieve?' His thinking about policy was insufficiently rooted in hard analysis of the real challenges and constraints that the government faced. What he at first called strategy was in reality 'position': defining broad goals and political messages, rather than identifying what needed to be done and what were the key levers for change.

In the first term, the culture of Downing Street reinforced Blair's tendency to think in this way. The dominant figure until 2003 was of course Alastair Campbell as head of communications. He was on his own admission 'not a policy man', although this was no reflection on his quick intelligence. Campbell cast a magnetic spell over most people he encountered, including the senior civil service. He was at once brilliant and courageous at his job, brutal and highly entertaining, loyal, honest and straightforward in his dealings with others and committed to Blair because he was wholly committed to Labour. But like all of us he could get things wrong – and when he did, he had the personality to do it in a spectacular way. There was also in Alastair a strong desire to be counted as a 'big player' in New Labour, which he was: in his mind, a true equal of the original 'Trio' of Blair, Brown and Mandelson. This led at times to counterproductive rivalry with Peter, which was to have particularly unfortunate consequences in the manner of Mandelson's second forced resignation from the cabinet in January 2001. But it also initially had negative consequences for the government's European policy. Alastair had been the architect-in-chief of New Labour's rapprochement with the Murdoch press and the European question had a habit of getting in the way. As a result, from a pro-European perspective, Campbell's domination of No. 10 was a mixed blessing, in part because there was no one of his political weight and stature employed within the Blair operation with a more governmental outlook. The October 1997 'Red Lion' fiasco on the single currency was a direct consequence of treating the single currency as a media handling issue rather than a crucial policy decision.

Most of No. 10 was in awe of Campbell. David Miliband, as head of policy, was at that stage no match. He was the young man everyone liked, highly valued for his compendious knowledge of detailed policy and his ability to provide intellectually interesting justifications for the positions Blair had decided to take, but he was still in the process of putting down his own political roots. On Europe, he was instinctively a strong 'pro', but uncertain at that stage about expressing his views because he was not clear where others in No. 10 were coming from and was reluctant to be seen as too close to Mandelson.

Sally Morgan, the political secretary, saw herself essentially as the voice of the 'soft left' inside the PLP, particularly among the new generation of 'Blair's babes' elected in 1997. Their support was rightly seen as crucial to the stability of the Blair leadership inside the party; her role at this stage was to warn and steer, not to push policy in dangerous radical directions, though she much later became a committed public service reformer. On Europe, she was sound but cautious, and she had a difficult relationship with Mandelson who had not wanted her in that role. Anji Hunter had been with Blair since he became an MP and was a friend before then. She had a good sense of politics, and moved in circles most Labour people didn't; she was a channel for outsiders to get to Blair and offered him a different non-tribal perspective, which he found invaluable. She got on well with Peter, but had tricky relationships with Sally Morgan as well as Blair's wife, Cherie, and Alastair's partner, Fiona Miller, adding a further dimension of complexities in the Blair court.

With Jonathan Powell, the chief of staff, matters were much more straightforward. He played an absolutely pivotal role for Blair throughout his premiership, acting as troubleshooter, diplomat and his loyal protector. He was at all times strongly pro-Europe and pro-British membership of the single currency, arguing the case in his distinctively eclectic way. Even though his title gave him seniority, in the early years of government, he seemed unduly conscious that he was operating in a court of competing influences, not a well-organised office of which he was in full charge as chief executive. The office was by definition incoherent, but that, I concluded early on, was how Blair wanted it to be. As a consequence, the task of converting aspiration and position into policy and implementation was not given the attention that it deserved – and there were counterproductive tensions in the Blair inner court.

This all deeply affected the handling of the European question. It was always mixed up in everyone's minds with the relationship with the Murdochs, the growing tensions with Brown and the position of Mandelson in No. 10. It became symbolic of who was in charge in the government – Chancellor or Prime Minister – and who was the dominant influence on Blair – Mandelson or Campbell.

The 'Real' Tony Blair

There are many faces to the 'real' Tony Blair. Indeed, answering the question of 'who is the real Tony Blair?' is almost impossible. This is not to suggest that as prime minister Blair was a deceitful opportunist. He was not. He had clear core convictions that he constantly came back to as an anchor, as regular attenders at his office meetings will testify, always tempered by an acute sense of, as he would put it, 'where people are on all of this'. The extraordinarily energetic and empathetic Philip Gould reported to him weekly on shifts of opinion in his 'focus groups'. This combination of real convictions, tempered by sensitivity to focus groups, gave Blair his political compass. His was not an intellectual approach based on a well-worked-out, coherent framework of political economy. He depended on his office to provide the intellectual rationale for what he had decided to do, particularly David Miliband, Peter Hyman and Andrew Adonis, and later Matthew Taylor and Patrick Diamond.

Blair always liked to feel he had a strategy. He was at his most brilliant at top-level strategy – positioning New Labour in the right place to hold together his electoral coalition and win elections. He could also be very good at articulating the governing principles that should shape policy in particular domains, though inevitably he had a better feel for some areas than others. At the task of transforming those governing principles into implementable policies, he was less good, because he had an uneven grip on detail and a low boredom threshold where he thought the detail didn't matter. In meetings he would start tapping his hands on his chair in frustration if some hapless official or adviser began explaining a problem to a level of detail he felt he did not need to know. His natural intellectual curiosity was limited. On the other hand, when he had no alternative but to get to grips with an issue, he reverted to being the young barrister who mastered the brief overnight, before the court appearance. Every speech that bore his personal stamp – and on Europe they all did – became an Oxford essay crisis, often with the final version dashed off in his own hand with extraordinary fluency and speed (just in time for the tutorial, as it were) in the early morning of the event.

Blair was not superhuman and did not try to be. Unlike Margaret Thatcher, whose strategic sense he admired, he did not regularly spend the hours past midnight absorbing official papers over a glass or two of whisky. He was therefore more reliant on good advisers if this part of the strategic process was to work well. Better though to have a leader with some measure of clarity on the 'big picture' than one who is so enmeshed in the detail that they cannot develop an overall sense of direction. Even worse is a leader who cannot make up their mind, because they are clever enough and so obsessively and intellectually absorbed in the detail as to see the flaws on all sides of any issue. This was a problem Gordon Brown shared with Tony Crosland in a previous Labour generation. As a senior civil servant once put it, 'we can cope with ministers who are either a control freak, or an indecisive ditherer, but not someone who is both at the same time'. Happily Blair was in most cases neither and he learnt fast on the job.

Blair liked performance and knew he was good at it. It was almost as though when he walked through a door to a meeting, he asked himself 'what role am I playing now?' And his skill as a 'big tent' politician was in being empathetic to, and seductively charming with, virtually everyone he met. People almost always left the room thinking he was on their side. Blair is helped in this by a remarkable facility for words. This was something first pointed out to me by Derry Irvine, one of the few great reforming Lord Chancellors of history and Blair's one-time pupil-master. Derry and I had been given the task together in the 1997 general election of preparing Blair for his big television interviews. 'Listen to him carefully,' Derry warned me in admiration, 'I have never come across anyone with a greater verbal skill in avoiding being pinned down.' That struck me as quite a claim from one of the bar's leading and most fearsome cross-examiners! The basis of Blair's power was his enormous public appeal based on his remarkable communication skills. This ability and appeal enabled him to step over the heads of his ministers, the PLP and established party structures. As long as he maintained his reputation as a winner he felt he would remain all-powerful. That made him dependent on a very close court of advisers who could anticipate up-and-coming problems and react to events. Particularly in his first term, Blair spent huge energy and time shoring up his political capital, rather than working out strategically how to use it. The Roy Jenkins metaphor of the man 'carrying a vase of priceless Chinese porcelain over a slippery floor' summed up the pre-Iraq Blair brilliantly.

Blair initially operated to a large extent in isolation from his ministerial colleagues. Famously, in the early days, cabinets turned into a 45-minute political chat. Cabinet ministers felt isolated from the central direction of the government. The idea in that first six months of government that the handling of Europe and the central issue of the single currency might be a suitable subject for collective discussion by cabinet colleagues would have been greeted with derision in No. 10. Blair preferred to exercise control over his ministers informally, through his network of No. 10 advisers who were specifically trusted to keep ahead of emerging issues and, as far as possible, enforce No. 10's will. When necessary, Blair would hold bilateral meetings with cabinet colleagues. This was the basis of 'sofa' government for which he was later to be much criticised by the civil service establishment. One reason why Blair so disliked cabinet and committees was he thought they would always leak: he had no wish to see a repeat of the dramas lovingly retold in the pages of the Benn, Castle and Crossman diaries under the Wilson governments. He was also reluctant to put himself in a position where he might find himself in an awkward minority. With his first cabinet, he was suspicious that many did not share his basic New Labour instincts. It was almost as though he thought of his leadership as a 'coup' against the Labour Party. He minimised collective discussion because he wanted to retain his freedom of manoeuvre.

The one figure that Blair always turned to at times of trouble was Mandelson. Throughout all the ups and downs of his leadership of the party and Peter's own career, Blair was desperate to keep Mandelson as a close intimate. On questions of political judgement, in terms of coolness under pressure and clarity of thinking, Peter has no equal. Some would say Peter was never able to apply the same qualities to himself, yet, in the case of Mandelson's second resignation from the cabinet, it was Blair's judgement and character that was shown to be more at fault. But Blair was equally desperate to prevent the rest of the world, particularly the rest of the Labour Party, from realising the extent of his dependence on Peter. Blair's decision to stand for the leadership in 1994 forced him to build a wider base of political support within the cabinet and party. Here he had to bring on board many people who liked and supported him, but had over the years formed a deep mistrust of the tightness and perceived machinations of the Blair, Brown and Mandelson 'Trio'. This led to behaviour which was frankly weird on Blair's part and 'up with which' Peter should never have put. In the 1994 leadership election, Mo Mowlam and Jack Straw were officially designated as heading the Blair campaign, even though Mandelson in effect directed it. This pattern of secrecy and attempted deception continued throughout the Blair leadership and premiership. Peter was around but unacknowledged. It was rather like a husband who has a long affair in a marriage, which the wife and children all know about but never dare mention. This immensely complicated the Blair and Brown relationship at the centre of the government and New Labour's handling of Europe.

The Blair–Mandelson relationship was fundamentally one-sided. Peter was a safety valve for Blair – someone to whom he could pour out his deep frustrations, especially with Brown, without having to live with the consequences of having to act in the way he felt. Yet, because of Mandelson's own personal commitment on Europe, the Mandelson–Blair relationship was of key importance. While Blair often followed Peter's advice, at key points in the Europe story he failed to do so. In the single currency fiasco of October 1997, Peter had not been brought into the communications loop: if he had, it would have been handled differently. In 1999, Blair significantly retreated on the decision he and Peter had taken to start campaigning for the euro. In 2002–3, Blair paid scant attention to what Iraq would mean for his European strategy and his leadership of the party, despite Peter's warnings. In 2004, Blair gave way to Jack Straw on the issue of a referendum on the Constitutional Treaty without consulting Peter. Peter was powerful, but not all-powerful.

Blair and Mandelson's Starting Point: 'Bring Back Bruges'

Blair was always acutely conscious that either the government would be successful in setting its own agenda for Europe, or it would find it being set for it by others. At home this would mean the government's agenda being driven by the obsessions of the Eurosceptics in the Conservative Party and media. In the EU itself, it would mean sitting back and waiting for the next Franco-German initiative to set the parameters of the debate. Occasionally Blair allowed his eye to slip off the ball, but for the most part he was absolutely determined to avoid either of these eventualities.

But the government had first to have a European strategy to promote. This took many months to put in place and was never achieved satisfactorily. Where essentially was Blair coming from? What did his gut Europeanism mean for the future of the EU? This question had not been thought about very much by anyone close to Blair or Brown. The civil service was strikingly absent from the field. To my knowledge there was no civil service paper, either from the Foreign Office or the European secretariat in the Cabinet Office, handed to ministers outlining a potential European strategy for the incoming government. Of course, many detailed and thorough papers were prepared setting out the agenda of forthcoming EU business and recommending how the UK might handle the key dossiers. In the summer of 1997 the focus of senior officials was very much on the final stages of negotiations over what became the Amsterdam Treaty. Labour ministers bought largely into the official brief; they had no real time to get abreast of the issues themselves. The civil service were of course much relieved: they knew they would have encountered far more troublesome 'noises off' had the Conservatives been re-elected.

Labour's published statements in advance of the 1997 election had given little indication of how in practice Labour's European policy would seek to be different from that of the Major government. As Stephen Wall has noted, the striking thing was 'the similarity, rather than the differences between the manifestos in 1997'. He points out that in the campaign, Blair had made a virtue of this: 'the real issue [between the parties] is one of leadership and clarity'.[1] The tone might be more positive, and the issue less divisive in the cabinet and party, but where was the substance?

In a well-ordered, rational government, one might have expected that an early act of the prime minister would be to request that the foreign secretary provide him with a European strategy paper. Yet, from a No. 10 perspective, it was striking how initially absent the Foreign and Commonwealth Office (FCO) was from the scene. In part this was because of the rocky start Robin Cook had as foreign secretary. He enjoyed the confidence of neither Brown nor Blair. There was no natural intimacy or trust between him and the two of them. His relationship with his new department also got off to a bad start, made worse by the FCO's decision to block the appointment of Gaynor Regan as his diary secretary. Gaynor was later to become Robin's wife, after the newspaper exposure of their affair led to his highly public divorce from Margaret Cook that summer. Furthermore, the FCO suspected Cook of harbouring deep prejudices against the diplomatic service, as a result of the 'arms for Iraq' inquiry during the Major government. Extraordinary as it seemed to me, Stephen Wall, then serving as UK permanent representative in Brussels, was one of those that Cook apparently had in his sights, but any risk that he might be removed was firmly scotched by Blair and Jonathan Powell.

The one European policy area where the FCO showed some signs of life was planning the six-monthly British presidency of the EU in the first half of 1998. In theory, the presidency presented a rare opportunity for Britain to set Europe's direction. The rotating presidency, before it was radically reformed by the Lisbon Treaty in 2009, was an enormous undertaking for the member state privileged (or burdened) to hold it. For six months, the presidency not only hosted and chaired a vast number of ministerial (and official working-group) meetings of the Council of Ministers. It was also responsible for setting agendas and steering deliberations towards a consensus conclusion, handing the member state holding the presidency a brief but sometimes decisive hold on power.

The presidency was also regarded as a public relations opportunity to showcase the country to the rest of Europe and build support for Europe at home – or so it was blithely assumed. Some political leaders found to their discomfort that their electorates resented the time spent on European business, involving an apparent succession of well-publicised 'jollies' at the national taxpayers' expense. However, for officials working on European business, making a success of the presidency was often seen as the high point of their careers. It was the diplomatic equivalent of the Olympics, something where the Brits could still prove we were a class act by comparison with the Luxembourgers or the Finns, even the French and the Germans, whereas the poor Greeks were dismissed as the nadir of incompetence.

Each presidency tended to choose a theme. This was often related to their geographical position or historic ties. So it was no surprise when the Finns chose the 'northern dimension', the Portuguese 'Africa' and the Spaniards 'Latin America'. As a result of the presidency, this theme was dutifully given pride of place for six months before slipping back to normal in the routine order of business. Officials had great difficulty in coming up with a powerful theme for the UK presidency that carried any conviction or resonance. In retrospect this was a telling illustration of Britain's inability to conceptualise a confident message about its place in Europe. As a nation that still thought of itself as having a global role, Britain could hardly choose as its theme 'the world', yet to be more specific would be insulting to its own pretensions. The FCO eventually came up with the bland idea of a 'people's Europe'. This was intended to convey the idea that, under British leadership, the EU would concentrate on practical reforms that reconnected Europe with 'the people' and stop navel-gazing over grand institutional designs. The problem was that the list of measures proposed had little coherence or public impact. As Churchill might have said when presented with the UK's agenda of forthcoming EU business, 'this pudding lacks a theme'. The presidency remained something of a blank page waiting for Blair to decide what his European strategy really was.

With the FCO, temporarily at least, 'hors de combat', Blair turned to Mandelson, then serving as minister without portfolio in the Cabinet Office. He sought advice on the background to UK policy from Colin Budd, an FCO official then serving in the Cabinet Office, as chair of the Joint Intelligence Committee. One of the first things Blair and Mandelson took upon themselves to do was to re-read Thatcher's Bruges speech. This was also a result of the unconscious prompting of Mandelson's (and Blair's) friendship with Carla and Charles Powell, Jonathan Powell's elder brother and former foreign policy adviser to Thatcher.

Blair and Mandelson both reflected on how much of Bruges they agreed with. The answer was a surprising amount. First, they were more inclined to a Europe of freely cooperating sovereign nation states, not a 'federal' Europe, although the large grey area between these extremes was at this stage very fuzzy. Second, they wanted an economically liberal Europe, committed to the single market and free trade, which they saw as axiomatically in the interests of growth and jobs in Britain. On the other hand, in their view Thatcher had been mistaken in allowing the pragmatic view of sovereignty pooling she had taken in 1985 in signing up for the Single European Act to be overtaken by far too dogmatic resistance to any further surrender of sovereignty in the single currency debate in 1990. They also thought that the Bruges speech had been misguided in painting the EU as a threat to the pro-market principles for which Thatcher stood. For a start, this all depended on the policies the EU chose to adopt, over which an actively engaged UK should be able to exert a decisive influence. The prevailing mentality that every EU move should be seen as a plot against Britain was mistaken: rather, the reverse was often true. A successful single currency was in principle a major step towards a more economically liberal Europe because greater price transparency would increase competition. Barriers to free exchange would come down. Finance would flow without currency risk to where it would earn the greatest returns.

Social Europe Shunted into a Siding

British officials had mistakenly imagined that Blair would want to promote an expansive legislative agenda for a more 'social Europe'. This was an over-literal reading of Labour's pledge that it would sign up for the Social Chapter. This gesture was executed with much fanfare in the first week of the new government by Douglas Henderson, the first of the FCO's many (far too many) Europe ministers in the Labour years. The Social Chapter opt-out had of course been central both to John Major's claim of 'game, set and match' at Maastricht and to the long parliamentary battles over the ratification of the treaty. Yet because of the manner in which the Conservatives had chosen to make the Social Chapter a symbol of both British exceptionalism and unwanted Brussels interference, it was not a policy domain where New Labour wanted to signal a substantive further shift. 'Signing up', however, made a real difference to employee rights in the UK. It meant that directives setting minimum standards on maternity leave and protecting part-time workers' rights would now apply within the UK. It also resolved the dispute the previous government had had with Brussels about the applicability to the UK of the Working Time Directive as a 'health-and-safety' measure to which the Social Chapter opt-out did not apply. The practical significance of this was important for working people: for the first time every worker in Britain won a statutory right to four weeks' paid holiday, a major social reform which Blair initially made little of. It was several years before Labour figures were prepared to argue strongly for the significant role Europe was playing in strengthening the minimum floor of individual rights to which British workers were now entitled.

Early in Labour's first term, the flags of celebration for the Social Chapter were quick stored away. Mandelson, as minister without portfolio, acted quickly to dampen any impression that the Prime Minister supported an expansive social agenda. Brian Bender, the admirably efficient and wise head of the Cabinet Office's European secretariat, was requested to produce a list of EU social legislation potentially in the pipeline and, by reply, handed a much shorter list of measures that might be acceptable to the UK. Why did Blair take this position? To have done otherwise would have been anathema to British business, whose support, or at least sympathy, was seen as crucial both to New Labour's electoral 'big tent' as well as to its European strategy. Soon after the 1997 election, the Confederation of British Industry (CBI) declared its firm support for British membership of the single currency and urged the government to get on with setting a timetable for when Britain would join. The CBI's support was seen as critical by Blair to any future chance of success in a euro referendum but, when it came to questions of social partnership and labour market regulation, even under the enlightened leadership of Adair Turner, there was not much progressive spirit in the CBI Council: the industrial relations scars of the 1970s and 1980s still greatly troubled British business. Turner did persuade the CBI reluctantly to accept a national minimum wage, and limited statutory rights to union recognition, but this was the most they would happily stomach. Antagonism was especially strong among their smaller- and medium-sized company membership: the big multinationals tended to be more relaxed. The last thing the CBI majority wanted was for New Labour to open up some new route for trade union advance through a social Europe.

Even under the moderate leadership of the TUC's John Monks, the path to Continental-style social partnership remained blocked. To please the CBI, and to the understandable outrage of Monks, in 1998 Blair persuaded the Germans to block a draft Commission proposal to give employees in small- and medium-sized firms, with between 50 and 2000 employees, statutory rights to information and consultation. In retrospect, this was a significant missed opportunity. This could have been the basis for a new consensus behind social partnership in the UK. It potentially provided a route to greater employee engagement at workplace level on something like the German Works Council model. But Blair was unwilling to force British employers down this road against their wishes. When a watered-down version of the directive obtained the necessary qualified majority after the 2001 general election, the opportunity to use it as the platform for a new advance in social partnership had been squandered.

Strategic First Steps

The Policy Unit held an initial discussion of European strategy at Chequers in July 1997, with Blair and Mandelson present. Blair focused on three questions. First, was there any prospect that the rest of Europe might share Britain's vision of European cooperation as opposed to the traditional view of integration? Blair's way of posing this question revealed what would prove an abiding tension throughout his premiership. He was strongly pro-Europe in the sense that he took the view that the scope of EU policy-making would and should deepen and widen over time. But his clear preference was for the decision-making *method* to be intergovernmental rather than 'federal'. He wanted to strengthen the European Council and shift the balance away from the classic community method where the right of policy-making initiative rested with the Commission, and decisions were taken by majority vote in the Council of Ministers and European Parliament. His reasoning was simple: if Europe was to be seen as legitimate by its citizens, the member states had to be seen to be in charge. In this, his thinking was classically French and a bit Gaullist: pro-Europe, but pro a Europe of sovereign states. In reality a 'Federation of Nation States' summed up his view of Europe perfectly, but it was regarded as impossible for a British politician to use the misused and misunderstood 'f' word in polite company.

Blair's second question was whether Britain could achieve a thorough shake up in Europe's institutions with which the Prime Minister felt there was a fundamental problem. Blair was in part reflecting his negative reactions to his first experiences of EU business. In part he was also making a judgement about 'where the public are on Europe', which British public opinion polling has consistently shown. There is public support for more European cooperation, but huge negativity about Brussels. Europe's institutions are seen as remote, unaccountable, costly, wasteful and bureaucratic, always instinctively promoting an agenda to expand the reach of Brussels. This gives continuing life to the Eurosceptic charge that the British people are trapped on an upward-moving escalator to something called a United States of Europe.

Blair's instinctive disregard for the institutions did not go without wider notice. The practice within the EU has been for most incoming prime ministers to make a trip to Brussels in the first months of taking office to pay their official respects to the president of the Commission and the European Parliament. Blair, however, did not pay an official visit to

Brussels until the second half of 1999 (leaving aside the April 1998 European Council, which he had to attend). Blair did later qualify this casual approach to the Brussels institutions with recognition that the EU was inevitably a 'hybrid' entity of the intergovernmental and the supranational: as time passed, he understood better the essential role of the supranational element. He came to recognise that the Commission as an institution – and not just the British commissioners who served in it – was usually a reliable ally of Britain on single-market and competition issues. He even softened his initial disdain for the European Parliament, eventually turning himself into one of its star performers in the British presidency of 2005. That said, Blair's goal was a better functioning 'hybrid' with the nation states firmly in the driving seat: hybridity was not for him a staging post en route to a United States of Europe. This was what he meant when he drew a distinction between *cooperation* and the *traditional view of integration* (my emphases). Early on he sensed that his opinion was widely shared among Europe's leaders; getting other leaders to acknowledge that publicly would be difficult, but nonetheless worth a try.

Blair was greatly exercised by the 'problem of the institutions', as he put it. He had no clear way forward. Blair did not suggest at that stage that Britain should open up a whole new round of European constitution-making. He was looking for an agenda of hard-headed practical proposals for reform, at the same time as itching for the opportunity to launch a great debate about the 'new Europe' New Labour wanted to emerge. This exposed a large eternal contradiction. Most British pro-Europeans complain endlessly about what they see as the EU's tendency to indulge in institutional navel-gazing. At times Blair joined in this chorus, calling in his Malmö speech in June 1997 for the EU to stop talking about European theology and start doing things from which real people can see real benefit. But the truth of his position was much more complicated: he always hankered after a radical institutional shake-up. This explains why in 2001 he eventually went against official advice and agreed to the establishment of the Constitutional Convention, which led to the ill-fated Constitutional Treaty.

Blair also sensed the strategic significance of enlargement, alongside the single currency as the two transformative projects on which the EU was embarking. He was an unqualified enthusiast for enlargement but recognised that it would also bring in its train equally profound change. The Conservatives consistently refused to accept that enlargement automatically entailed a radical institutional rethink. The institutions designed for a Common Market of the Six were not likely to be fit for purpose for a Europe of 27 and more. The 1998 Treaty of Amsterdam was supposed to deal with these questions, but had failed. To the inexpert eye, the so-called 'left-overs' represented a lot of boring, technical details about the size and organisation of the Commission, how it was chosen and to whom it was accountable, the functioning of the Council of Ministers, the scope of majority voting and what constituted a 'qualified majority', the role of the European Council, and the future of the Council presidency. Yet these questions are central to the efficiency as well as legitimacy of the EU, the 'federal versus intergovernmental' debate, as well as the distribution of power between member states. They were to take the EU a further decade to resolve in the Treaty of Lisbon – and then not satisfactorily.

Blair instinctively grasped what few British politicians are prepared to recognise: that the EU is fundamentally a political project. It is not some glorified free-trade area. Nor is it an international organisation, of which, like a whole array of others, the UK happens to be a member. It is about building a polity called the European Union, through which member states pool sovereignty in order to achieve specific purposes that they cannot achieve on their own or even as sovereign nation states cooperating together. The rules for governing how sovereignty is pooled are therefore not a distraction; they are of existential importance. They determine whether the Union can act effectively and whether its actions are perceived as legitimate and democratically accountable. For all the acute difficulty in talking about these questions in Britain, where most politicians behave as if talking about their sex lives in front of a maiden aunt, Blair had no hang-ups. He knew what the debate was all about: the question was how to sell the institutional changes the EU needed to make to the British Parliament, media and people.

The third big question at that Chequers away-day was: how can Britain lead in Europe when the dominant issue for our partners is how to make a success of the single currency? It was here that the gap between tactical considerations and Blair's strategic vision was to prove most glaring, to which we turn in the next chapter.

CHAPTER 5

Policy-Making at the Red Lion

From the outset of his premiership in 1997, Blair recognised that the EU itself was on the threshold of an epoch-making decision: whether to go ahead in 1999 with the single currency on the Maastricht timetable. Blair saw the creation of the single currency as a bold historic step in the process of European integration, as significant as the Schuman Declaration in 1950 or the Treaty of Rome in 1957, possibly more so. He instinctively felt that the single currency was a huge, incalculable risk. He recognised that it would inevitably entail further steps towards European integration of an unknown, and in detail unknowable, dimension. The whole venture, he accepted, was a giant act of faith, but in the secrecy of the confessional box my firm view was that he would have counted himself among its true believers. The reason was simple and political: he wanted Europe to unite and he believed Britain must be part of it.

Blair was also acutely conscious, however, that this belief set him apart from the main body of political opinion in Britain. In his own cabinet and party, there were many whose instincts were pro-Europe, but on the euro they were more questioning, genuinely sceptical and pragmatic. Whereas Chancellor Kohl of Germany managed somehow to treat the economic questions as 'second order', despite the intense controversy in Germany about the end of the Deutschmark and its economic consequences, the British debate allowed our politicians no such leeway. The British discourse obsessed (and who can say it was wrong) about whether genuine economic convergence would be achieved and the risks entailed in the irrevocable locking of exchange rates, perhaps because sterling crises had played such a dramatic part in Britain's story of post-war decline. So there was no alternative but to treat the question of British membership as one, at least in part, of pragmatic calculation. On the other hand, Blair was more acutely aware than many of the British political class that the coming of the euro raised the hugely difficult question that if Britain were to decide *not* to join, how could it remain a key player in the EU in the long term in the light of that fact? Blair was far-sighted enough to recognise the strategic importance of this question, even when the *immediate* consequences of not joining did not seem that serious as against the political and economic risks of attempting to join. Indeed, for most of the ensuing decade the problems of being an 'out' were to prove less damaging than initially feared. The result was a decade of double illusion: the illusion of complacency among the eurozone members about the long-term consequences of being 'in' and the degree of further integration required to make the single currency work; and the illusion of inconsequence in Britain about the long-term impact on Britain's position in Europe of being 'out'.

Blair's acute understanding of the 'big picture', however, did not prevent the handling of one of the central questions facing his premiership from descending into farce. Within days of Blair's victory, business began to call on the government to set a date for Britain's euro membership: as always, business wanted the certainty that politics can hardly ever provide. As the deadline loomed for Britain's formal decision on whether to join the single currency in the first wave, the markets began to show signs of impatience with a government that appeared to offer no clear direction. The Prime Minister's seeming irresolution proved too much for his Chancellor, who felt the need to buy the government more time for the decision, by giving the markets more certainty. The result was a bungled press briefing that in effect ruled out a euro referendum in Labour's first Parliament. In practice this scuppered the best chance Blair had of fulfilling his ambition for Britain to 'lead in Europe' and it was mainly his own fault. It seems improbable that this was the definitive outcome that either Blair or Brown had actually wanted at that time – but the retrospective judgement has to be that it was on such a confused basis that Britain's future in Europe was determined.

Ambiguity and Dither

Labour had come into office with what it trumpeted as a clear policy on the euro – but it was a position for opposition, not a policy for government. The 1997 manifesto had said:

> Any decision about joining the single currency must be determined by a hard-headed assessment of Britain's economic interests. Only Labour can be trusted to do this: the Tories are riven by faction. But there are formidable obstacles in the way of Britain being in the first wave of membership, if EMU takes place on 1 January 1999. What is essential for the success of EMU is genuine convergence among the economies that take part, without any fudging of the rules. However to exclude British membership of EMU forever would be to destroy any influence we will have over a process which will affect us whether we are in or out. We must therefore play a full part in the debate to influence it in Britain's

> interests. In any event there are three pre-conditions which would have to be satisfied before Britain could join during the next Parliament: that the Cabinet would have to agree; then Parliament; and finally the people would have to say 'yes' in a referendum.

I was very familiar with this piece of text, having laboured hard over it. It was a piece of studied ambiguity to see Labour through an election. It did of course set out a series of dilemmas that remain relevant to this day. First, 'in or out' of the euro, Britain is affected by it: outside, we lose leverage over a hugely important piece of economic policy affecting growth and jobs in Britain. Second, genuine and sustainable convergence is necessary for a single currency to work smoothly. The manifesto stressed that on the question of membership Britain's economic interests should be decisive – not issues of sovereignty. On the timing of the decision it balanced the 'formidable obstacles' to being in the first wave, with the possibility that Britain 'could join in the next Parliament'. The manifesto contained no commitment to the 'five tests' or a Treasury-led economic assessment that were only to become 'holy writ' in the October 1997 statement.

Although the obstacles to membership were real, the manifesto did not close the door: in truth it was rather obvious that it was deliberately being left open. That was why, from the moment of the decisive election result, business clamoured hard for a date so that they could begin to plan for the changeover. One might have imagined that a strong government with a huge majority would, in these circumstances, have immediately ordered officials to begin a thorough analysis of the modalities of taking a decision to join, including how long a currency changeover would take to put into effect based on the model of decimalisation in the early 1970s. One might also have imagined that No. 10 would have asked the Cabinet Secretary for advice on how Britain's national economic interests might best be assessed. This would not have been a final commitment to membership, but it would have been a commitment to an orderly process for taking a decision. There was, however, no such immediate move: Brown waited on Blair and Blair dithered.

As often on matters European, the economics and politics of the decision moved out of alignment. At the point Labour was elected in 1997, there was uncertainty as to whether the single currency would go ahead on the January 1999 deadline provided for in the Maastricht Treaty for the start of Stage 3. There was still debate about which member states would be deemed to fulfil the criteria for membership. The election of the French

Socialists in June 1997 temporarily added another element of uncertainty, as they were committed to full employment policies that, superficially at least, seemed incompatible with the anti-inflation mandate of the European Central Bank. The British public discourse predictably played up those doubts and uncertainties. The belief that 'it will never happen' is always strongest among those who don't want something to happen. Against this background Labour was understandably reluctant to come out publicly and back membership of something that was still not a 'racing certainty'. Domestic politics favoured a policy of 'wait and see'.

On the other hand, the economics of early membership were becoming trickier. Brown made a bold and right decision, at the same time as he announced Bank of England independence on first becoming chancellor, to raise UK interest rates by 2 per cent to curb the risks of an incipient upturn in UK inflation. This increased the interest rate differential between sterling and the Deutschmark and put upward pressure on the pound. In the short term at least the British and German economic cycles were moving out of sync. Business opinion, while overwhelmingly committed to British membership, feared the sterling–mark parity might rise too high for entry. There would clearly have to be some interval in which British inflation would be squeezed down, UK interest rates would eventually converge more to German levels and sterling would stabilise at a more competitive rate. But there was no reason to presuppose that this process would pre-empt a decision in the first Parliament. A British announcement of a referendum and a timetable would in itself impact on sterling.

Policy-Making from the Red Lion

Amidst dithering and indecision, it was unclear what the real intentions of Blair and Brown were, if indeed they knew themselves. The weaknesses of Blair's governance model were fully evident. The first discussion of European strategy was purely political during a Policy Unit away-day at Chequers. The civil service would not have seen my presentation on Europe had I not copied it to them, and I had to tell John Holmes, then the foreign affairs private secretary in No. 10, what had been the outcome. Blair's whole tone at that discussion was that Britain would be wise to steer clear of the 1999 start date. He assumed the French and Germans would find a way of pressing ahead despite what he described as 'the present terrible mess'. Blair dismissed the current talk about the postponement of the start date, hyped of course to a near certainty by much of the British commentariat. Postponement would only occur if the newly elected Socialist government in France refused to comply with the fiscal disciplines of the Maastricht criteria. While this was widely rumoured after Jospin's victory, he ended up doing nothing of the sort, as Blair expected. Had postponement occurred, Blair claimed to be attracted to reviving the hard ECU/common currency plan for a gradual transition to a single currency. In the same breath, however, he added that he wanted to avoid what might appear as a 'wrecking manoeuvre: therefore best to wait and see'.

The first big meeting to discuss European strategy at which officials were present involved the Prime Minister, Chancellor and Minister without Portfolio (Blair, Brown and Mandelson). When the No. 10 diary secretary put round a note calling the meeting, I received an urgent phone call to go over to the Cabinet Office to meet the head of the European secretariat, Brian Bender. 'We just wanted to ask you, Roger, a small point about this meeting. It's very unusual in our experience for the prime minister to have a meeting to discuss Europe without the foreign secretary being present. Can you tell us why this might be so?' I paused. The internal machinations of the New Labour tribe were still then pretty much under public wraps, but I decided that, for the sake of my future relationship with officials, I should be open. 'They will want to discuss the handling of the euro. Tony will want to have worked out a common line with Gordon and Peter before he discusses it more widely in the government. He doesn't trust Robin on this.' At that point there was another awkward pause until Brian said, 'Ah yes, I understand,' when clearly he thought this a recipe for totally dysfunctional decision-making, as indeed it was to prove.

At this July meeting, in addition to his economic adviser Ed Balls, Brown brought along Sir Nigel Wicks, his top official with immense experience and authority stretching back to the 1960s on international monetary matters. So respected was Wicks by his European peers that they had elected him chair of the monetary committee of senior officials that did all the preparatory work on the euro for meetings of European finance ministers. No single individual in Britain knew more about the single currency. The two-hour-long meeting mainly took the form of a fascinating tutorial with Wicks answering the Prime Minister's questions with an objectivity and balance which was truly enviable. The general thrust was that the euro was certain to happen, most likely with a wide membership, but that it represented a 'leap in the dark' with many uncertainties for the future. Wicks forecast with great prescience that major problems would arise if the member states with a historic tendency to inflation could not live within a framework of monetary policy that would effectively be the same as the Bundesbank's. The big uncertainty was whether domestic reforms would be made by those weaker countries, particularly in terms of making their labour markets more flexible, to prevent the weaker economies becoming uncompetitive. Italy featured high in his concerns. The question was whether the creation of the single currency would prove a 'positive shock' forcing reforms, or whether countries would continue as before with the problems of lack of competitiveness gradually building up.

As far as the UK was concerned Wicks did not see insuperable obstacles to British participation, given the domestic reforms that had taken place under the Thatcher and Major governments to make the economy more flexible. However, there were important questions of timing that would determine the smoothness of UK entry, of which Wicks put emphasis on the dollar–euro exchange rate and its impact on sterling. The tutorial went on for some considerable time.

The meeting then switched to a more political discussion. The Chancellor pressed the Prime Minister on the possibility of postponing the euro start date, with the clear implication that if it could be put back for two years then Britain might be in a position to join at the start. Blair, however, said he thought there was no prospect that Kohl would agree to postpone the start date and was reluctant to raise the possibility with him on the grounds that this would immediately paint the Brits into the corner of the 'awkward partner'. He also thought it would be easier to persuade people at home of the case for membership if the single currency was already 'up and running' successfully. His political instinct was that it did not make sense for Britain to join in the first wave. In an inconclusive discussion, Brown at that stage came across as the more committed to early entry, but it was unclear whether the markets would wait for Blair to make up his mind.

Nothing happened until September. Robert Peston, then the economics editor of the *Financial Times*; wrote a seemingly well-sourced story, splashed on the front page, that the government was about to take its historic decision to join. It was widely rumoured in No. 10 that the source of the story was the economic secretary, Geoffrey Robinson, a rich and generous Brown ally with a colourful business past, who had been a consistent supporter of export-led growth driven by a 'competitive' exchange rate. The Treasury wanted to correct the market expectations that the Peston story had generated. The means chosen to do this was to arrange for a few well-chosen words from the Chancellor – in fact, a few paragraphs of answers to questions – to be faxed over to Philip Webster, the political correspondent of *The Times*, which the newspaper was to present as a 'Brown interview'. Although the words faxed to *The Times* did not precisely say that membership of the single currency had been ruled out in the present Parliament, in the process of briefing them this interpretation was confirmed. The intended correction became an over-correction: the government ended up effectively ruling out a decision on entry for Labour's first Parliament. This was confirmed in a statement Brown made to the Commons the following week.

In the now voluminous accounts of Blair–Brown rivalries, there are many descriptions of the so-called 'Red Lion affair', the Whitehall pub where on the evening of Friday 17 October, Charlie Whelan, the Chancellor of the Exchequer's spokesman, was heard bawling down his mobile to journalists that British membership of the single currency had been ruled out for the current Parliament. At the time, much No. 10 anger and outrage was vented at Whelan, which was ultimately to force his resignation, alongside that of Mandelson, in the 'Geoffrey Robinson home loan' affair just over a year later in December 1998. Although Whelan's briefing methods were, to say the least, ill-advised, he became the fall-guy for an extraordinary failure in policy-making, as much the responsibility of Tony Blair as Gordon Brown, which given the importance of the issues at stake for the country's future is hard to credit.

The Red Lion affair had profound consequences for the framing of the single currency debate within the government. First, an inevitable consequence of the furore was that a policy had to be developed at short notice for the Chancellor to announce in Parliament. Drafts of a statement flew to and fro between the Brown and Blair private offices, with Mandelson playing an important role, at the same time as Blair was chairing the Commonwealth prime ministers' conference. Senior officials were largely excluded from this process: as Brian Bender, head of the European secretariat, put it at a meeting of senior officials in the Cabinet Office, the content of the draft statement was 'above my pay grade'. The essence of the statement was to resuscitate the five tests for entry which Ed Balls and Gordon Brown had allegedly invented in the back of a taxi in Washington in 1996. Frankly, these tests were intended to convey a spurious objectivity to what were essentially questions of judgement. However, the language of the statement was positive: firm that the government favoured membership in principle; clear that sovereignty was not a decisive objection; and left open the possibility that, should circumstances change, the government might return to the issue later in the Parliament. The tone was assertively upbeat: this government would 'prepare and decide', in contrast to Major's 'wait and see'. It contained some hostage to fortune that the outcome of the assessment of the tests should be 'clear and unambiguous', but at the time this was seen to be no more than a typical New Labour rhetorical flourish, not a statement that the Treasury later would come to regard as of immense significance. At the time no one in No. 10 took the tests that seriously.

The Red Lion Aftermath

It is now commonplace to argue that Blair's ambition to join the euro was done for when he conceded that the decision would be taken out of his hands by the Treasury and become conditional on the favourable outcome of an assessment that they would conduct. This presupposes, however, that in October 1997 Brown had already made up his mind that Britain should not join the single currency. The truth in my opinion is more nuanced. Blair's indecisiveness on the issue since the May election, and the market turbulence that had been experienced on the basis of rumour and counter-rumour in the autumn, convinced the Chancellor that, for reasons of sound economic management, the political decision on membership had to be firmly within his own personal control. Hence Brown's insistence that the primacy of the Treasury judgement be clearly stated as government policy. This also fitted in with Brown's interpretation of the infamous 'deal' between him and Blair when he accepted that he would not run for the Labour leadership after John Smith's death in 1994. As is now known, this had been codified in an exchange of faxes in which Blair ceded that Brown would have control over a wide swathe of economic policy. The events of the first months in government convinced Brown that if Britain were to join the single currency, it should in the first instance be his call.

Although Blair baulked at any public acknowledgement that he was in some way in hock to his Chancellor – he was after all the 'First Lord of the Treasury' – he also saw some advantages in the perception. It would help convince sceptics that the economics of the decision were being given full and proper consideration. It would reassure that a recommendation for entry was not being made for a mix of ideological or political reasons. However, Blair remained convinced that in the end Brown could be persuaded, or lent upon, to come out with a 'yes' to membership – a view he continued to hold, in my opinion, until the late summer of 2003 – even after the announcement of the first negative assessment of the five tests. It was not to be Gordon Brown – but the political aftermath of Iraq – that ultimately blocked him.

The political consequences of the Red Lion affair were, however, more destructive. Blair was furious that his government had made an appalling communications mess of such a crucial issue, but showed little sign of remorse about the decision that had actually been taken, almost by default. Yet Blair could have decided on an alternative course of action. Blair was being urged by Roy Jenkins to announce a commitment in principle to join the single currency, with a referendum to take place relatively soon, probably in 1998. Jenkins' proposal was to separate the political from the economic decision to join. Assuming a 'yes' vote in a referendum on the principle, the actual timing of entry would then be left for the Chancellor to decide, enabling Britain to join when the economic circumstances were most appropriate. Jenkins' political argument was that the government would have enough political capital to win a referendum early in its term, as the government had done successfully on devolution for Scotland and Wales. In addition, the Conservatives were weak and divided and would not be able to mount a credible 'no' campaign. Blair was not convinced. He argued forcefully for caution. Labour had to prove its capability as an effective party of government before it could recommend such a momentous decision to the British people. However, by opting for an 'in principle' referendum, Blair would have been able to respect his Chancellor's perfectly reasonable wish to have full control over the timing of entry that would best suit the circumstances of the British economy. Blair worried such a ploy could backfire. The 'antis' would argue that the electorate were being invited to buy 'a pig in a poke'. Yet the 'in principle' referendum might have been the best means of keeping Brown on board. He would have lost his veto. But then it was not at all clear that in 1997 he wanted a veto. What he wanted was to be a successful chancellor by demonstrating his ability to manage the economy.

The truth was that Blair and Brown had run away from a decision laden with risk: the inevitable political risk that a referendum might not be won (however small at that point) and the risks inherent in the single currency project itself, which were unknowable and might have threatened Blair's ability to win a second term for New Labour. There was a possibility that a positive referendum result, even by a sizeable winning margin, might not have settled matters for the future. Any adverse change in economic circumstances might have been seized upon by the Conservative opposition to reopen the euro argument in a general election, with the likelihood of the Murdoch press in full cry against Labour's re-election. On the other hand, a successful referendum would have destroyed the internal unity of the Conservative Party and greatly weakened the pretensions of the Eurosceptic press.

The Red Lion episode had a serious impact on the internal functioning of the government. It was the first serious blow-up between Brown and Blair over a central question of policy. The dispute was not so much about the content of the policy as about who had been responsible for the catastrophic manner of its presentation. Blair was furious that Charlie Whelan had made the government look so casual and inept. But the fault lay in his own approach at that stage to government decision-making. Brown had not acted on his own in briefing *The Times*. Alastair Campbell was fully in the picture and had spoken to Blair on the phone about it, allegedly in the middle of an awkward conversation Blair was having with the mercurial Clare Short about an unfortunate incident between her and a police constable at the Labour Party Conference.

There had been a complete failure to establish proper processes for fully involving the expertise of the official machine when considering key policy options. British membership of the euro raised policy issues that affected the responsibilities of a number of key Whitehall departments. For example, prospects for overseas inward investment were the proper responsibility of Trade and Industry, not the Treasury. And the Treasury had a long record of Euroscepticism: if the decision had been left simply to them, Britain would probably never have joined the Common Market in the first place.

From Blair's perspective, however, the issue probably at the top of his mind was how to make a success of running his government, given the unique and special position he had conceded to Brown. Conscious of his own dependence on Brown's intellect and strategic sense, his ideal was a government where Blair and Brown and their respective courts worked together cohesively. Yet 'court' politics are full of inherent tensions, as any historian who had studied power would have told him. History is full of tense and dysfunctional relationships between kings, their queens and their crown princes. Democratic election does not make that much difference. Court politics was institutionalised by the fact that when New Labour won office, Blair and Brown brought into government their own courts of advisers and assistants. Court politics develop an internal dynamic of their own. The Red Lion episode strengthened the already ingrained introspective defensiveness of the Brown court. In their eyes, the Blairites were gunning for Charlie. Brown became convinced that Blair was all presentation and no substance. His people behaved as though if only Mandelson could be got out of the way, the Blair regime would collapse from within.

Brown also knew that his only chance of succeeding to the premiership was if he could maintain his standing as the 'crown prince' against any emerging rival. There was a fundamental insecurity about Brown's position. If he became weak or unpopular, Blair might move against him. This made a distancing from Blair inevitable. Brown was forced into a position where he had to be seen not only as the leading force in the government, but also as the leading force inside the party opposing the government at the same time. When in the second term Blair decided to go out on a limb on public service reform, to the annoyance of established interests in the party and trade unions, this gave Brown the opportunity to present himself as the voice of 'real Labour'. Equally, Europe was the issue where, because of the press's overwhelming opposition to the single currency, he could strengthen his media defences against Blair. The merits of the issues counted for little in what became a raw struggle for power. More and more this became a major factor in the chequered history of the development of the government's European policy.

Strategy after the Red Lion

The Red Lion fiasco temporarily blew Blair's position in Europe out of the water. Britain's apparent decision not to join the single currency was received with great disappointment by many of our European partners. Relations with Britain had become so difficult in the latter days of Major that many on the Continent had convinced themselves that Blair would execute a dramatic pro-European change of course. Britain, in the eyes of many, had a golden opportunity to seize the leadership in Europe, and with Blair's popularity and the Conservatives' disarray a referendum victory would largely be a formality. This acute sense of disappointment was shared by pro-Europeans at home, who felt that another historic opportunity had been missed that no one could be certain would become available again. By the end of October 1997, therefore, the Labour government was in a worse position on Europe than it had been on winning power that May. Where stood its historic mission on Europe without a clear strategy for the future? Over the next year and a half Blair was to succeed, at least in part, in rebuilding that sense of his European mission. But it took him time.

The most important developments did not occur until towards the end of the British presidency in the first half of 1998. The special European Council held in Brussels in April 1998 administered a real electric shock to Blair's system. The meeting's purpose was to settle the outstanding questions on the launch of the single currency, including who would be the first president of the European Central Bank (ECB). Germany had indicated its support for the Dutch nominee, Wim Duisenberg. The ECB president could not conceivably be a German because of the earlier decision to base the institution in Frankfurt: it was unprecedented for any member state, however powerful, to claim both a new institution's seat and its presidency. Moreover, Duisenberg was as near in outlook to the Bundesbank ideal as any German could wish for. At the last minute, however, France put forward its own nominee, Jean-Claude Trichet. No one disputed Trichet's credentials for the job, or suggested he would be the stooge of the French government. Before the council met, Kohl had assured Blair that a satisfactory compromise could be found whereby Duisenberg served four years and then Trichet would take over. The difficulty was that it seemed no one had properly taken responsibility for telling Duisenberg this. As the meeting opened, Duisenberg, having discovered what others had apparently decided about his future, stood on his dignity: for the European Council to instruct him to stand down, a mere four years into the eight-year term provided for in the Maastricht Treaty, would be contrary to the ECB's independence from political interference. The blazing row in Brussels went on all night. Spats between the French and Dutch have a history of always being very difficult. Blair's job as chair was to broker a typical EU compromise, whereby Duisenberg promised to consider resignation of his own volition after the desired period.

The messy episode conveyed two lessons to Blair. One was the EU's (and soon to be eurozone's) totally inadequate governance procedures for the scale of the common tasks it had decided upon: it was handling the challenges of twenty-first-century interdependence with the toolkit of nineteenth-century nation state diplomacy. The glaring weaknesses of managing a single currency with the diplomatic techniques of the Congress of Vienna were only to become apparent after the eurocrisis broke in 2010. The second, and more important to Blair personally, was that Blair found the experience of Britain being a euro-out acutely uncomfortable: a chairman without real authority, a foretaste of the marginalisation he feared to come. He came back from Brussels determined that Britain had to find a way of setting the European agenda, but on what and how?

Trying to be Positive about the Euro

Realising the potential problem, Blair became keen in the autumn of 1998 to find some way of demonstrating his personal commitment to the euro without changing the essence of the October 1997 policy. A paper was commissioned from the Treasury on what was meant by 'convergence'. This was duly prepared. The fact that a paper had come back to No. 10 from the Treasury at all was some demonstration that relationships were still in reasonable order between the Prime Minister and his Chancellor. The Treasury paper occasioned considerable debate among Blair's advisers about whether there was any significant economic advantage in delaying the euro decision.

For the late Derek Scott, the Policy Unit's economic adviser and an old SDP comrade-in-arms, there would never be a right moment to join the euro. In his view, exchange rates should be free to respond to changes in a country's competitive position. If the nominal exchange rate was fixed, then real exchange rates would need to adjust through internal changes in the price level, a difficult and painful process that could cause sustained losses of output. Even if there was apparent convergence, the British economy might be subject to future shocks which were different from the rest of the euro area – so better not to abolish the exchange rate's essential adjustment function. Yet Derek's arguments presupposed a rationality about the way foreign-exchange markets function that historical experience defied. The massive structural imbalances that persisted between different parts of the world, and proved a significant factor in the 2007–8 banking crisis, suggested that floating exchange rates were some way from adjusting perfectly. Foreign-exchange markets were subject to bubbles. Exchange rates could be out of line with 'fundamental equilibrium' for long periods, with hugely damaging economic effects. The virtues of free-floating were a textbook myth. In my view, a willingness to tolerate a prolonged period of sterling misalignment was the major economic error of the New Labour years, with a heavy cost in lost jobs and a structural weakening of our balance of payments. Hence the sharp decline in UK manufacturing which occurred under Blair and Brown without the government or the Treasury spotting (or visibly caring about) what was going on.

The person who had most influence over Blair's economic judgement was his then Treasury private secretary, Jeremy Heywood. Probably the most brilliant civil servant of his generation, Jeremy has an extraordinary capacity for clear thinking and succinct explanation that absurdly long hours of work never seemed to dull. Heywood's advice to Blair on the euro was that whenever a decision was made to join, there was bound to be some unavoidable period of uncomfortable adjustment as the economy shifted from being governed by one macroeconomic policy regime to another. It was therefore right to time membership when the degree of disturbance was likely to be the least damaging. However, some upheaval and awkwardness could not be avoided. This made a lot of sense to me.

Blair indicated to the Treasury that he wanted to make the statement to the Commons on the 'national changeover plan', which was due for publication early in the New Year of 1999. This gesture was clearly intended to signify a great deal, as the plan itself was in effect a relatively uncontroversial implementation of the 'prepare and decide' policy that the Chancellor had announced to the Commons in October 1997. Blair's pro-European advisers in No. 10 urged him to use this statement to make clear the government's firm intention to join the single currency *when* the five tests were assessed as positive. The Chancellor presented the purpose of the five tests as to decide *whether* the economics were right for Britain to join. The change of tone No. 10 wanted was to affirm that all questions of principle, economic as well as political, had been resolved.

Three main arguments were made for making this move. First, business needed more certainty to be able to plan ahead. The commitment to a currency changeover was, for many of them, costly in the short term. If preparations seriously got underway, there would be an element of irreversibility and inevitability about the decision. Second, Blair had to convince our partners on the Continent that he was serious about the euro: a more positive commitment to join would greatly strengthen Britain's bargaining position in the EU in the years ahead. Third, a firm statement of clear intent was needed to persuade the Liberal Democrats and most of all the pro-European Conservatives, such as Ken Clarke and Michael Heseltine, to join publicly a cross-party alliance to campaign for Europe and the euro.

Blair toyed with this idea for some weeks. Brown was not at all keen. The Campbell diaries tell us that on the Sunday evening before the week in which the changeover statement was due to be made, a worried Brown tried to persuade Blair to drop the whole idea of making a parliamentary statement. This Blair declined to do as he knew such a course would have been judged very negatively by the people the statement was designed to reassure. However, Blair did agree, as a concession to his Chancellor, that the statement would represent a 'change of gear', not a change of policy. On the morning of the statement's delivery, Blair still had not finally decided what he was going to say. Mandelson – at that time in exile from the cabinet following his resignation as a result of the Geoffrey Robinson home loan affair – was on the phone several times to Blair carefully going through the draft wording of the statement in an attempt to make it as positive as possible. I pitied the No. 10 private secretary that was duty-bound to show these revisions to the Treasury!

The eventual statement[1] was not as forward as the pro-Europeans had been pressing for: 'Our intention is clear: Britain should join a successful single currency, provided the economic conditions are met. Our membership is conditional: it is not inevitable. Both the intention and the conditions are genuine.' Blair attempted to reassure the Treasury by the sharp distinction he drew between the politics and economics of the issue.

> We have as a government resolved the political issues in favour of the principle of joining, should the economic tests be met. But they must be met. The manner in which we joined the exchange rate mechanism is a standing monument to the danger of joining a monetary arrangement on purely political grounds.

Of course, few pro-euro supporters would have disagreed at the time with Blair. The comparison with the 'manner' of joining the ERM put the emphasis on the question of timing, not more fundamental questions on the merits of permanently locking in exchange rates that more sceptical economists such as Derek Scott had raised. The mainstream critique of the ERM saga had essentially been about one of entering too late in the UK economic cycle and at too high an exchange rate. On a similar logic, in the case of the euro, the key factors that appeared relevant were the size of the interest rate differential between the UK and the euro area (soon expected to decline), and whether the exchange rate at which sterling would enter the euro was at a level that could be sustainable. This is what was meant by making the argument about 'when' not 'if'. The 'changeover' statement sought to establish a more rational approach to the euro decision. The *Sun* responded by describing Blair as 'the most dangerous man in Britain'.

CHAPTER 6

(Half) Making the Case

In all frankness, my feelings as a Blair adviser swung erratically back and forth between rose-tinted admiration for his ambitions and (perhaps over-emotional) disappointment at what might have been. On this roller-coaster of emotions, the high points were really good. One of the most moving was when Blair received the Charlemagne Prize and declared his 'bold aim [. . .] that over the next few years Britain resolves once and for all its ambivalence towards Europe'. He went on: 'I want to end the uncertainty, the lack of confidence, the Europhobia.' That morning in Aachen was rich in symbolism – not that this was how it had felt the night before. The Prime Minister's entourage had flown in the previous evening to a somewhat inauspicious modern hotel on the outskirts of the city, where at a meeting in a hotel bedroom an exhausted and rather tetchy Blair asked the team 'what's this speech trying to say?' The draft that the Downing Street collective had provided was the normal curate's egg of good arguments ending with evasive conclusions. In the discussion, Alastair and Jonathan placed themselves at the bold end of the spectrum. Then the Prime Minister came in: 'Look everybody, I think it's rather simple. As a country we've messed around on Europe far too long. It's time we make up our minds.' A tired Blair burnt the midnight oil, adding his own personal stamp onto the new paragraphs that his team were providing, as he was to do with all his major European speeches. As we were getting into the cars the following morning, Blair came over with that typical look of stage fright on his face: 'Do you think it's alright, Roger?' This was a big speech that he intended would resonate throughout Europe, as well as embolden pro-Europeans at home.

The symbolism began with High Mass in the magnificence of Aachen Cathedral. The then Anglican Blair took communion without hesitation: in a more mundane act, but of equal symbolism, my role was to supply him with a 'soon to disappear' Deutschmark note for the collection. At the end of the service, the Archbishop led him by the hand to pray at Charlemagne's tomb. Few of us had realised, but it was Ascension Day: how appropriate a choice of date to commemorate a Europe united peacefully as never before in the first capital of the Holy Roman Empire, and how, under the EU's benevolent umbrella, Germany had risen from the ashes of World War II. The Blair party then processed to the Town Hall through the old medieval streets, lovingly reconstructed as best they could by the good burghers of the city after 1945, all bearing witness to the mix of Catholic tradition, civic virtue and Rhineland enterprise that had created the democratic miracle of the post-war Federal Republic. Britain had played a crucial role in the creation of modern Germany: Churchill – bravely defiant after Dunkirk in the struggle against Nazism, but wonderfully magnanimous in calling for a united Europe after 1945; Bevin – instrumental in committing the USA to the Marshall Plan that saved Europe and the German people from starvation and communism. Yet somehow, from the 1950s onwards, Britain had thrown its influence away. From those days to this, we had never been capable of committing ourselves without inhibition to the success of the democratic Europe our people's bravery and sacrifice had helped bring into being. By this measure, wasn't the scale and audacity of Blair's ambition that day in Aachen simply breathtaking?

Blair's Political Arguments for Europe

The main themes of Blair's Charlemagne speech recurred constantly in his argument for Europe. First, pro-Europeanism is 'modern patriotism'.

> To be pro-British you do not have to be anti-European. We treasure our national identity as you [Germans] do. But in creating the European Union we have the chance not to suppress our national interest, but to advance it in a new way for a New World by working together.

Domestically he was later to turn this theme into an attack on Conservative anti-Europeans. Nothing riles Conservatives more than to have the patriotism card played against them.

Second, the case for Europe had changed since the days of the founding fathers, but that European unity remained as relevant now as it had been then. This was Blair's riposte to the argument that the EU had been a brilliantly successful 'peace project' from the 1950s to the 1980s but, with its founding rationale achieved, was no longer needed: 'Our first phase was peace within the EU; our second phase is meeting the new global challenge. The next era must be about how we build Europe's strength, power and responsibility vis-à-vis the outside world.' Blair listed various areas for more effective EU action in the economy, defence, enlargement and to tackle crime, drugs and the environment under the familiar Blairite mantra of 'reform'. In his Warsaw speech two years later, he more pithily summarised the modern EU's purpose: 'prosperity, security and strength'.

Third, he explicitly rejected the common British tendency to argue 'thus far and no further'. He accepted that for the future the EU would be a dynamic, not a static entity. Rather, the guiding principle for its future development should be to 'integrate where necessary, decentralise where possible'.

Fourth, the EU was a political project with a unique identity:

> I do not believe that Europe is likely to grow into a replica of the United States of America. But no more do I think Europe will simply be a mere free-trade area. It will be a new and different sort of entity. In reforming our European structures we should not imitate the constitutional theory of a sovereign state, but rather build the structures we need to achieve our objectives, recognising the unique nature of the Union.

He was later to develop this thought into a clearer plan for reform of the European institutions, but at Aachen he explicitly recognised for the first time the need for a 'strong Commission', with a European Parliament that 'holds the Commission to account', marking a crucial declaration of support for the role played by the supranational institutions. The distinctively Blairite touch was the call for 'a new partnership' between Commission and Council, where the European Council 'should set the strategy'.

In Warsaw two years later Blair described his view of Europe's institutional development as a 'third way'. He contrasted 'two opposite models': one Europe as a free-trade area 'beloved of British Conservatives. The difficulty is that nowhere near answers what our citizens expect from Europe.' However, the contrasting view of Europe as a 'superstate, subsuming nations into a politics dominated by supranational institutions' is that it too 'fails the test of the people'. Blair's vision was 'a Europe of free independent sovereign states who choose to pool that sovereignty in pursuit of their own interests and the common good, achieving more together than we can achieve ... this unique combination of the intergovernmental and the supranational [can] in its economic and political strength be a superpower, not a superstate'. In 2001, in talking of a 'superpower', Blair was not looking backward to the Cold War, but thinking ahead to the extraordinary shifts in the global balance of power underway in Asia and Latin America and the need for Europe to unite if it was to shape globalisation.

The final leg of Blair's argument addressed the attitude of the UK. 'Maybe history would have been different if we had been there at the very beginning, if we had felt we were creating it, rather than joining it. However, my generation has a new opportunity.' The 'missed opportunity' theme came up again and again in his speeches. 'We did not shape the institutions that make up euro. We were not part of the historic Franco-German compromise that had made another war unthinkable. We thought we didn't need to: we had won the war after all.'[1]

In autumn 2001 at Birmingham, he argued:

> Britain's future is inextricably linked with Europe [. . .] the tragedy for British politics – and for Britain – has been that politicians of both parties have consistently failed, not just in the 1950s but on up to the present day, to appreciate the emerging reality of European integration. And in doing so they have failed British interests.

Blair spoke of 'opportunities missed in the name of illusions'. In a direct dig at Gaitskell, 'we had to recognise even in the 1960s that a "thousand years of history" were not enough. Because yesterday's heritage did not guarantee today's influence or tomorrow's prosperity.' Britain had to 'adjust to the facts. Britain's future is in Europe.'

Could Blair Have Made a More Persuasive Case?

Blair was keen to argue for Europe from a position of confidence about Britain's economic standing and its continuing role in the world. He had little time for the 'declinism' that had characterised the pro-European case in previous decades. A classic of this genre is Christopher Soames' well-publicised (and at the time effective) quip in the 1975 referendum campaign: 'at this moment in our nation's history, you'd think twice about withdrawing from a Christmas Club, never mind the Common Market! We need all the friends we can get.' Soames was speaking as the UK inflation rate approached the levels of the apocryphal Latin American banana republic. The general undercurrent of the pro-European case of the time was that, with loss of Empire, Britain was left with no alternative but to look to the Continent. Of Churchill's three circles, by the 1970s the Empire was gone (and the Commonwealth survived on ties of sentiment, not real community of interest), while our 'special' relationship with the USA depended on our being fully committed partners in Europe. Equally, the hard facts of trade, jobs and growth in Britain depended on Europe. Blair in the 1990s did not believe that declinist pessimism was either any longer accurate or a proper representation of the national mood. Rather, pro-Europeans needed to recognise and not disguise the essentially political nature of the European project. With the notable exception of Edward Heath, this dimension of Europe had been publicly downplayed by most British statesmen. Blair believed it had to be addressed head on if British feelings of ambivalence were to be overcome.

Oliver Daddow, in his interesting study of New Labour's discourse on Europe,[2] argues that Blair set himself an impossible task in trying to rewrite the history of Britain and Europe as the British typically perceive it. Blair argued that for centuries Britain had been a 'European power'. But this flew in the face of popular historical understanding of Britain as separate from Europe. Closeness of geography never overcame deep emotional and psychological barriers to thinking of Britain as part of Europe. Daddow points out how this attitude betrays itself in common remarks such as 'the biggest mistake Britain ever made was going into Europe'. Large sections of the public fear Europe as some Continental 'other'. Popular understanding of Britain's history of engagement with the Continent is generally seen as one of war, grief and sorting out other people's problems. Daddow concludes that, in challenging the 'Dunkirk myth' that Britain was at its finest when it stood alone, Blair was attempting the impossible.

Daddow may be right about the British public's predominant psyche. His insight may explain the puzzling paradox of modern Britain that, while millions of us lead lives intertwined in so many different respects with the Continent, these social trends have apparently done little to lessen suspicions of European integration and the feeling that Britain should remain separate. Perhaps Blair could have pitched his pro-European argument less on history and more to erode the factual basis of the idea of British 'separateness'. Blair might have done more to stress the interlinkages between British life and the rest of Europe in terms of where people go on holiday, live, work, retire, study, play and watch football. Europeans are people with whom British citizens and their children and grandchildren partner and marry, and with whom they conduct all forms of human intercourse. The EU provides so many vital underpinnings for these human and commercial ties through its core policies of free movement and the single market, touching the lives of millions.

Blair might also have made more use of historic symbolism to counter the false consciousness of UK separateness. There was nothing natural or automatic about the Franco-German rapprochement in the decades after 1945: it had been rich in high emotion and symbolism. Both sides worked hard at it in every generation, from Adenauer attending mass with de Gaulle in Rheims cathedral, to Kohl holding hands with Mitterrand in front of the war memorials at Verdun. Blair tried some of this: he started his Warsaw speech with a tribute, well received in Poland, to the Polish airmen who had played an absolutely critical role in giving Britain its narrow edge over Germany in the Battle of Britain. (The 60th anniversary had been celebrated a few weeks before his speech.) Yet far more could have been made of gestures of this kind. For example, the church bell that tops the reconstruction of the *Marienkirche* in Dresden was made in Coventry: the ceremony should have been attended by either the Prime Minister or the Queen. However, in Britain there remains a high level of touchiness about attempts to reinterpret 'our finest hour'. In Blair's in-tray there were still pleadings for recognition from groups who felt that their sacrifice in World War II had somehow been marginalised: women who had worked in the munitions factories, Japanese prisoners of war, Bomber Command. Symbolic gestures towards our former enemies carried unpredictable media and political risks.

Gordon Brown saw Britain's problem with Europe as essentially about how the British see their identity. He became convinced that success in defining a modern and confident sense of British identity was central to winning some of the most crucial political arguments: not just for strong British engagement in Europe, but to defeat Scottish nationalism and to make a success of multicultural Britain. He was deeply troubled by the growth of 'Englishness', which in his eyes was an affront to multicultural Britain, fostered the break-up of the UK and encouraged the political forces that wanted to 'pull up the drawbridge' with the rest of Europe. Brown, encouraged by Michael Wills, the deepest thinker in the Brownite 'court', made several major speeches about Britishness. However, he was never satisfactorily able to translate what he identified as distinctive British values into a set of concrete guiding principles about Britain's role in the world, particularly after he became more reluctant, for tactical political reasons of his own, to show his cards on Europe. He worried away at these issues to the end of his own premiership, by which time he had become convinced that one had a better chance of renewing a real sense of British identity on the back of a general commitment to internationalism than pro-

Europeanism. For all the difficulties Brown was to cause Blair on Europe, the paradox was that at heart he remained the internationalist idealist that his Church of Scotland upbringing had made him. His belief in 'Britain's unique capacity for moral leadership in the world' burned ever brighter. Hugh Gaitskell would have been proud of him.

The question of how to define and promote a modern sense of British identity became for a time the subject of intense discussions in the Blair–Brown circle. Blair, however, never really bought into Brown's obsession with identity, or at least only at a superficial level. He probably thought it all too difficult and too abstract. And he may have suspected that Brown had started looking for reasons as to why the European argument was too difficult to win.

A more telling criticism of Blair's efforts to make the European case is that they were occasional and inconsistent. One early jibe was that Blair was only willing to make the case for Europe abroad: yet that flaw was corrected, and in terms of the coverage and impact of his big speeches it mattered little where they were made. A more telling point was that when he did make a big speech there was little follow-up. This was largely the result of the government's policy on the euro, into which Blair had, by accident or design, locked himself. A strong pro-European intervention by the Prime Minister inevitably triggered speculation that a positive move to euro membership was about to be made. The problem was that the October 1997 parliamentary statement had effectively put British policy on the euro into commission until the assessment of the five tests had taken place 'early in the next Parliament'. So Blair was forced to kill the speculation that he was about to change his own policy. This meant in practice that No. 10 attempted to shut down as quickly as possible the media interest that the initial speech had generated. The government spin doctors thereby ended up killing their master's efforts at persuasion.

The Failed 1999 Push on Europe

Blair wanted 1999 to be the year that he made a significant push on Europe. As we saw in the previous chapter, that was the reason he decided himself to make the euro-changeover statement to the House of Commons in February; it had no political purpose other than reasserting his and the government's commitment to joining the euro. But he also intended the statement to herald the launch of a cross-party campaign, at the same time as there was a 'step change' in the government's efforts to lead in

Europe. But by the end of the year there had been no decisive breakthrough across the Eurosceptic lines; rather, the government was stuck in the trenches, with signs that, behind the scenes, a war between its generals had broken out.

Within the House of Commons the euro-changeover statement was well received by those it was most intended to influence. Michael Heseltine described it as a 'marked step forward in the intention of the government' and called on the Prime Minister to put himself at the head of an all-party campaign. Kenneth Clarke agreed it was 'a marked change of tone'. All seemed set fair for the launch of the cross-party Britain in Europe campaign. The statement was, however, in February; the campaign launch was delayed until mid-October, largely as a result of the difficulties that Blair had in persuading Brown to participate on terms acceptable to Clarke and Heseltine.

Blair was badly rocked by the ferocity of the reaction, to his parliamentary statement both from the *Sun* and his own Chancellor. The *Sun*'s description of Blair as 'the most dangerous man in Britain' raised the question of whether the implicit pact between Blair and Murdoch had been irretrievably breached. How could the 'most dangerous man' conceivably be judged worthy of re-election as prime minister in two years' time? Only around this time did Blair fully grasp the depth of Murdoch's objections to the euro. Initially he had imagined that Murdoch might be persuaded to accept the euro if Blair could demonstrate that Europe was set on fundamental economic reform. Murdoch did not share Blair's gut feeling that, for Britain, commitment to Europe was an expression of modern patriotism. He saw no problem with Britain as a larger Switzerland, as long as Britain remained a firm and strong ally of the USA. It was around this time that Blair realised, in my view, that he could only pull off the central mission of his government by confronting Murdoch. Yet his overriding priority in 1999 was to become the first ever Labour prime minister to win a second full term. So he compromised with himself by deciding to keep Europe and the euro on the boil, but not allow the brew to boil over. Significantly, Alastair Campbell, who never instinctively empathised with Blair's passionate pro-Europeanism, became much keener on the prospect of a euro referendum as the opportunity for a decisive confrontation with the media. Blair's attitude was more like St Augustine's: 'Lord, make me pure, but not just yet'.

Relations with Brown also became more difficult following the euro-changeover statement, which the Chancellor regarded as an attempt to 'bounce' him. Its only purpose had been to devalue the significance of, and undermine the objectivity he attached to, his euro assessment, which he was determined would remain under his control. The launch of the Britain in Europe campaign was not therefore an easy one. Superficially it was impressively staged at the newly opened IMAX cinema near London's Waterloo. On the platform were five of the most popular politicians in Britain – Tony Blair, Gordon Brown, Kenneth Clarke, Michael Heseltine and Charles Kennedy (who had just succeeded Paddy Ashdown as leader of the Liberal Democrats). The campaign had prominent business backing, with Colin Marshall of British Airways as its chair. Simon Buckby, its director, had put together a talented campaign team, including the young Liberal Democrat Danny Alexander as press secretary (he was to become chief secretary to the Treasury in the post-2010 Coalition). But the process of getting all the ducks in a row had been fraught.

Blair hesitated about 'going up again' against the Eurosceptic press. Brown then suggested that *he* launch the campaign without Blair, making clear that the campaign would be wholly consistent with government policy: a campaign for Europe and for British membership of the euro, but only if the economic tests for membership had been met. Blair was firmly advised (which he knew anyway) that Clarke and Heseltine would not participate without his personal commitment and attendance. Eventually Brown accepted that Blair should lead the launch, but he won the point about the campaign's heavily conditional commitment on the euro. This proved to be a major barrier to the campaign's effectiveness. The campaign made the judgement that, as Brown's support for euro membership was crucial, little would be done without the approval of the Brown office. This was a mistake. The pro-euro campaign needed outriders, not pro-government loyalists.

Standing Up (or Not) for British Interests

1999 proved a troublesome year in handling EU business. On 15 March, the European Commission was forced to resign. The French commissioner, former Socialist Prime Minister Édith Cresson, had employed her dentist (to whom she was close) as an adviser to her cabinet on a consultancy contract, for which the services rendered were unclear. Although an independent report exposed serious irregularities, Cresson, with the backing of the French government, refused to resign. Jacques Santer, the Commission president, had no power to sack her and was put in the unenviable position of possibly losing a vote of confidence in the European Parliament. To avert this, the whole Commission resigned 'en bloc'. The episode appeared to confirm that European institutions were tainted by bad management, sleaze and corruption.

The first half of 1999 also saw a number of high-profile clashes between Britain and our EU partners. The final stages of negotiation on the EU's seven-year budget were made even more fraught than usual by the need to deal with the costs of enlargement. These discussions raised entirely predictable alarums and diversions in the British media about 'threats' to the British rebate, before being settled at the European Council in Berlin at which Blair secured a highly advantageous settlement for the UK. Then the UK's success in lifting the EU ban on British beef following the BSE scandal was marred by the French government's refusal to comply immediately with the Commission's ruling, even after the ECJ had ruled against France's position. Finally, a serious row about EU tax policy burst onto the scene. This had been ignited in the British media by early statements from the incoming Red Green government in Germany in favour of tax harmonisation. Elements in the City of London chose to treat the proposed EU Savings Directive as an existential threat to London's Eurobond market.

All of these issues were toxic in the British media. They required a government response that calmly but firmly dealt with the issues raised on their merits, but rebutted scaremongering. For example in the Prodi Commission that succeeded Santer, Neil Kinnock was to drive forward a radical process of administrative reform. On enlargement and the EU budget, it was not other member states 'ganging up' against Britain, but everyone accepting that enlargement, of which Britain was the strongest advocate, had a cost and necessitated EU policy reforms. On the beef ban, French obstructionism was frustrating, but France did eventually comply with the ECJ ruling, even though it was against French national interests. Without our EU membership and the ECJ ruling in the UK's favour, Britain would have had no leverage to force a sovereign French government to open up its market to British beef.

The EU tax row was a typical example of a great storm that should never have gathered force in a more rational world. Yet for a time it reached a pitch of passionate intensity over issues so complex that only technical experts could ever conceivably hope to understand them fully. For far too long, EU member states had tolerated a situation where citizens could evade tax by depositing cash in the bank of another member state. Images of German dentists driving to Luxembourg to deposit suitcases of

Deutschmarks in tax-free savings accounts were doubtless apocryphal (as of immigrants from the EU enjoying 'benefit tourism' at the British taxpayers' expense), but in Germany there were strong feelings, especially on the left, that tax evaders should no longer be allowed to get away with it. The Commission's original proposal was to impose a minimum withholding tax on all savings accounts throughout the EU. But of course if such a tax was to be effective, it would have to apply to the full range of savings instruments available to depositors or it would easily be avoidable. The City treated this as a threat to the very existence of the Eurobond market in London, which had migrated from New York as a result of an attempt by the US authorities to block a similar tax loophole in the 1970s.

Into this imbroglio Chancellor Brown now gleefully charged. According to him, the Commission proposal raised fundamental questions of national sovereignty over tax. This was despite the fact that tax had been identified as one of the main obstacles to a barrier-free single market in the much quoted Cecchini Report in the mid-1980s. Moreover, tax harmonisation was already a reality, with the rules for levying VAT governed by an EU directive, agreed by the Eurosceptic Norman Lamont when he was chancellor. At precisely the same time as Brown was defending national sovereignty on tax, one of his junior ministers, Dawn Primarolo, was chairing an EU group to look at how the problem of unfair tax competition could be tackled. Indeed, it is difficult to see in the longer run how social democrats can ensure that fair taxes are levied on transnational businesses and the mobile rich, and tax havens closed down, without collective action by the EU and other international fora.

Rational argument, however, was not allowed to get in the way of banging the sovereignty drum: Brown announced to an admiring British press that a withholding tax would never be levied on the City of London. The row this generated went on for months. In the end a sensible compromise was reached. Instead of imposing a uniform levy on all Eurobond holdings, Brown secured agreement to the key principle of 'exchange of information' between tax authorities. The Eurobond market did not migrate back to the USA or Zurich. Indeed, in time the EU successfully applied pressure on the Swiss to change radically their whole approach to banking secrecy.

In Brussels, Brown secured a sensible solution, but domestically he gave life to the proposition that the only successful way to conduct European policy was by 'standing up for British national interests'. Margaret Thatcher's handbag was rescued from the second-hand shop. Blair also then felt impelled to do his bit to demonstrate he was no pushover. The telling apotheosis of 'standing up for national interests' was the Labour government's long battle to oppose the granting of artists' rights to *droit de suite* (a percentage royalty) on secondary sales of their works, replicating for painters and sculptors the royalty rights that musicians and authors take for granted. One might have imagined that a modern social democratic government would be sympathetic to a policy that favoured the cultural sector, but this EU directive was vigorously opposed by the UK because of its allegedly fatal consequences for the prosperous London art market. Opposition occupied much prime-ministerial energy until a typical Brussels compromise was reached. Christie's and Sotheby's appeared to survive this regulatory hammer blow from Brussels with relative lack of difficulty, softened as it had been by much Blair expenditure of precious political capital. The irony was that the London art market was shortly afterwards to have major (and criminal) difficulties of its own over alleged price rigging. As was later to be seen in the financial markets, a far bigger threat to the market's position in London was posed by the ethical standards of its own participants than by the threat of EU regulation.

'Standing up for British interests' thereby became a self-conscious part of Britain's European policy. Of course in a diverse EU, national interests differ and every member state stands up for its own. But the UK does it like no other member state in a way that generates so much domestic hostility to the idea of Europe itself. This is mainly a reflection of the Eurosceptic British media, who in the aftermath of Blair's euro-changeover statement exploited every opportunity to make life as awkward as possible for him on Europe. Public support for Europe nose-dived. This had serious political consequences. Blair's euro policy was thrown off balance for the rest of the first term. Brown also realised the traction he could gain in the media by striking a Eurosceptic pose, reinforcing perceptions of him as the indispensable 'Iron Chancellor'. Initially No. 10 took this in its stride. After all, a chancellor who convinced the voters he was no pushover in Brussels would carry weight when he eventually came to make his 'favourable' euro assessment. But that assumed Brown was prepared to play Blair's euro game.

For the rest of his first term Blair retreated on Europe. He wanted the next election to be fought and decided on the central terrain of the economy and public services. The surest way of marginalising the Conservatives' populist appeals to anti-Europeanism was to emphasise the 'triple' lock on any British decision to join the euro – that it required the approval of the cabinet, Parliament and people in a referendum – and once again to put a clear distance between the eventual euro decision and the next general election. Blair firmly quashed speculation that the government would use a second election victory to launch an immediate drive for euro membership. Doubless Murdoch was pleased.

Step Change

This came at a moment when Britain was supposedly making a 'step change' in its European engagement. Colin Budd, back in charge of Europe in the Foreign Office, was the enthusiastic architect and driver of this initiative, which was so intense and, for a time, in part successful as to be labelled 'the new bilateralism' by European scholars.[3] Budd was the first official to recognise the importance of party-political networking in the EU context. From his position of civil service impartiality and neutrality, he whipped ministers and political appointees to be diligent attendees of meetings of the Party of European Socialists. He also argued for a vigorous programme of bilateral political contacts, because he rightly identified that it was crucial to build national links outside the pro-European and often pro-federalist 'Brussels bubble'. Paradoxically, this step change came at the same time as pressures mounted within the Conservative Party to sever their ties with the centre-right European People's Party.

One of the weaknesses of the British political system is that it is not easy to persuade British politicians to network across Europe. British national politics is very 'national'. Talented young Brits who go into a career in international business or management consultancy will spend much of their time abroad; however, this is the last thing any political aspirant should do in order to get selected as an MP. Also, the opportunities to gain a broader outlook do not widen significantly after election to Parliament. There is more chance (if one is a favourite of the whips) of serving on a Commonwealth delegation, or acting as an election monitor in some remote South Pacific island state, than of making regular trips to Berlin, Madrid, Paris and Rome. It does become easier to travel as a minister, especially as European and international business now affects most departments. However, there are not many real incentives for a minister to exercise a close grip on departmental EU business. Generally speaking, EU dossiers concern issues that take a long time to settle, in which a cumbersome process of patient negotiation eventually results in consensus. Whilst EU directives set crucial frameworks for policy, they are long term and indirect in their effects. This makes it difficult for those who play the short-termist musical chairs of British ministerial reshuffles to master or influence them or, for that matter, care.

Furthermore, the dominance of the Eurosceptic press in Britain imposes structural constraints on good Europeans. The way to rise up the ministerial ladder, and be perceived as doing a good job, is to avoid being caught in press controversy. Ambitious ministers steer clear, if they can, of what they see as potentially toxic issues – and there is nothing more toxic in British politics than a European row. As a result, officials tend to play the key role in shaping the government's European policy, whereas on 'nuts and bolts' issues the decisions are taken at the dozens of official working groups that meet in Brussels every working day. This only serves to heighten the democratic deficit between our national Parliament and the 'European system'. This distance from the EU is reinforced by over-reverence for the Westminster model on the part of MPs whose biggest ambition in life is to be part of it. This attitude of mind dampens any budding European enthusiasms and encourages an unwarranted attitude of superiority. I once heard a very senior Labour minister, who for the good of his reputation shall remain nameless, describe France and Germany as 'not really democracies, as we would understand it'.

In an attempt to overcome these multiple disincentives to European engagement, the Budd step change instituted centralised monitoring of European contacts – recording every meeting that ministers had with their opposite numbers in other member states. The minister for Europe in the Foreign Office was given responsibility for 'chivvying' ministers across Whitehall to take Europe seriously. For a time this achieved notable results. The minister for Europe who most successfully made this mission his very own was Keith Vaz. Keith himself proved to be a networker of great charm and style in the best Anglo-Indian tradition. I once accompanied him to Bratislava on a ministerial trip where we arrived by chartered jet: somehow Keith's private office had persuaded the FCO bureaucracy that the expense of travelling in style was necessary to impress our hosts. We were whisked off to see the Slovak Prime Minister. Keith was fulsome in his greetings, explaining how much importance Britain attached to Slovakia's forth-coming membership of the EU and how Tony Blair was personally committed to it – which was all true. At the end of this moving little introduction, he suddenly turned to me with a flourish saying, 'and Roger Liddle here, who works for Tony Blair in 10 Downing Street, whom I have *especially* brought with me, will now explain to you the Prime Minister's

European policy'. I have never before or since experienced a minister manage to avoid mastering the boring details of his brief with such panache. But in an important sense Keith was right: at that time and on that occasion, it was the demonstration of commitment that mattered, not the details of dozens of boring dossiers.

Plenty of dossiers did emerge, however, from 'step change', which bore a huge imprint of British influence. The first set concerned institutional reform: essentially the building blocks of Blair's vision for the future of the EU. The second set concerned the promotion of economic reform in Europe, which in terms of both substance and perception both Blair and Brown saw as essential to the success of the single currency and as vital preconditions for British membership. Succeeding chapters will assess how successful this strategy was. Any British government would have needed to determine its policies on these questions, but the priority that Blair gave to both these thrusts was in major part designed to achieve his third strategic goal: British membership of the euro, in which of course Blair was to fail.

Critics of Blair have argued that he was never really prepared to make the case. His big European speeches stand as a rejection of that claim. Some pro-Europeans may not have liked the way he made the European case, but argue it he did. His case for Europe was deeply political and significantly in advance of the usual 'jobs and growth' case that most British pro-Europeans make for the single market. The problem was not so much in what he said. Rather, Blair's problem lay in the lack of consistent follow-up to his pro-European interventions. He was hobbled by his inability to take forward the argument for the euro beyond the language of the October 1997 statement. As the political commentator Peter Riddell put it, 'it was always a case of tomorrow'.[4] Blair was not prepared to 'cross the Rubicon' of actively making the case for euro membership in advance of the promised Treasury assessment. The 'Britain in Europe' campaign was set up with stellar cross-party support. It achieved some notable successes, but the Treasury's insistence on control freakery on the one hand, and equivocation on the central issue on the other, doomed it to ultimate ineffectiveness. The anti-euro campaign groups had no such inhibitions.

The pressure generated by the anti-European media periodically forced Blair off the high-road pro-European message that his speeches were always intended to convey into a sub-Thatcherite posture of 'standing up for British interests'. For Blair this did not come naturally and he always avoided the worst excesses. For other ministers 'fighting Britain's corner' was always the easy option – the low road of European engagement. The truth is that a policy of noisily proclaiming a determination to stand up for national interests in practice undermines support for Europe in Britain. On the euro, the government's policy was supposedly, in its own words, to 'prepare and decide': those preparations had made miniscule progress as the time for making the assessment of the five tests drew near.

Blair ultimately has to take responsibility for this failure. He was not prepared to let loose an effective and well-financed pro-European campaign for which he could have undoubtedly raised the money. Nor did the government systematically attempt to counter the 'drip-drip' of misinformation with hard facts, for which he could also have mobilised the civil service machine. There was also an unwillingness to confront directly the press proprietors. He did not have the courage of Stanley Baldwin in 1930, who had famously attacked the press barons who were trying to undermine his leadership for exercising 'power without responsibility: the privilege of the harlot throughout the ages'.

There was also another crucial respect in which Blair underestimated his power. While Brown liked to give the impression of being all-powerful over the government's agenda, within the British system one man, the Prime Minister, could if he wished, at any moment of his choosing, announce a policy that trumped the Chancellor's. Brown would have only two choices: accept or resign. This was what Blair was to do to Brown, a little less than a year after the fudged euro-changeover statement, on the NHS in his famous 'Breakfast with Frost' interview. Blair, without consultation with his Chancellor, announced that Britain would match European levels of health funding. Blair always had this trump card in his hands. And in my judgement, he would always have got his way because, for Brown, the option of resignation was not at all attractive. While Brown might have remained a difficult force to be reckoned with on the backbenches, within the government his departure would have allowed someone else to emerge as the 'crown prince'. Brown was desperate for that not to happen and he could not afford to be seen by the party as a wrecker. What held Blair back on Europe and the euro must have been a deep insecurity: his unwillingness to confront the anti-European media, combined with an emotional gut instinct that, despite everything, he needed Brown in his government. He could not govern alone.

CHAPTER 7

Reforming the Club Rules

Most British pro-Europeans regard institutional questions as essentially a distraction from the positives that 'Europe delivers': the practical benefits of membership such as jobs and inward investment through the single market; free movement across borders; peace; the consolidation of democracy across Europe; and so on. Set against these real-world issues, institutional questions seem positively 'nerdish'. This attitude strikes a chord with the public. Most members of a club or society are pretty wary of the pedant, obsessive or bore who starts quoting clauses of the rule book: people do not join golf clubs to know the rules, but to play golf. Yet in political institutions rule books go to the heart of politics: who has power and what they can do with it.

The 'future of Europe' debate centres on the EU's competences (i.e. powers), institutions and decision-making processes. Most British prime ministers have tried to avoid it like the plague. It fatally undermined John Major. The Labour Party once vainly hoped that the Lisbon Treaty (finally ratified in 2009) had drawn a line under EU navel-gazing for a generation. David Cameron only got dragged back into it because of his obstreperous backbenchers. Tony Blair was different. He treated the 'future of Europe' debate as of vital importance in its own right, for the future success of a rapidly changing EU: an EU that was widening (through enlargement) and deepening (through the euro) at one and the same time. But also to end British semi-detachedness, Blair recognised that he would need to convince the electorate that there was no risk of closer European integration swallowing up British identity in a Brussels superstate. He was therefore attracted to the notion of defining a provisional *finalité* for the EU (the future was an open book), which would enable the EU to become more effective and gain greater legitimacy, at the same time as addressing domestic concerns about sovereignty, identity and democratic accountability. This proved to be ambition of a tall order.

Blair's Approach to the 'Future of Europe' Debate

The touchiness of these issues within Britain has been compounded by the way in which successive governments since the 1975 referendum have downplayed the essentially political nature of the European project. Europe has been a political project from the very first. The Coal and Steel Community was established in 1950 with a complex institutional structure precisely because its founding fathers saw it as a model for the step-by-step development of a deeper union. Nothing in the UK's 1972 Treaty of Accession changed the Community's essentially political nature: indeed, in the initial debate on Common Market membership in the 1960s, both Conservative and Labour pro-Europeans stressed the political benefits of membership, acknowledging that the economic arguments were more evenly balanced. Most, however, were coy about the pooling of sovereignty at the heart of European integration, thereby creating and perpetuating the myth that 'it was only a free-trade area that the British people voted to join'. The basic mission of the EU has always been to build a more united Europe. Blair accepted that and believed in it. He rejected, however, the didactic fallacy that if the EU is about more than a free-trade area, it is inevitably aiming for the polar opposite: a 'United States of Europe'. Rather, he saw the EU as *sui generis*: a unique attempt in world history to create a workable political entity where sovereign nations pool their sovereignty in certain domains in order to achieve together purposes that they cannot achieve nearly so well on their own. This involved a necessary pooling of sovereignty, but not a sacrifice of national identity, with the nation state remaining the main (but not exclusive) focus of democratic politics within the Union. As Blair himself put it:

> The basic ideology should be described in this way. Europe is the voluntary coming together of sovereign nations. Their will is to combine together in the institutions of Europe in order to further their common interests. In so far as it is necessary to achieve these interests, they pool their sovereignty. There is no arbitrary or fixed limit to what they do collectively; but whether they do it depends on their decision as group of nations. So whilst the origin of European power is the will of sovereign states, European power nonetheless exists and has its own authority and capability to act.[1]

Sovereign states *confer* specific powers on the Union: the Union does not exercise them in its own right. However, supranational institutions are essential to make sovereignty pooling workable. Who else could propose binding rules in the common European interest? Who else could police the rule book and stop member states free-riding on their partners' commitments? Blair's crucial insight was that the EU would always be a 'hybrid' of supranationalism and intergovernmentalism. Again, to quote Blair:

> The two are not in opposition to each other. It is the two together which are necessary for the unique union of nations that is Europe to function.[2]

For Blair, the key to the Union's democratic legitimacy was that the overall direction of the Union should clearly be in the hands of the member states comprising its membership. The nation state should remain at the centre of EU governance. This was for him a fundamental point, at least in the current phase of Europe's development: who could tell what challenges future generations of European leaders would face and how they would choose to respond to them? His big achievement in EU reform was to be the formalisation and strengthening of the role of the European Council as the top decision-making forum consisting of the leaders of the member states, with a newly established permanent president agreed in the Lisbon Treaty.

In Britain few people understand the real significance of what Blair did. Yet in Brussels, the Blair vision of European governance remains hotly contested. Classic exponents of the 'community method' still see the future 'government of Europe' as the Commission, with its president elected by and accountable to the European Parliament. Blair always saw the government of Europe as a *partnership* between the European Council and Commission, but with the Commission working to policy priorities set by the Council. Some criticise Blair's institutional legacy as the root of the EU's problems in developing an effective response to the eurocrisis. An alternative view is that without the strengthened European Council that Blair helped bring about it is difficult to see how the eurozone could have withstood the pressures of the crisis.

Blair's Commitment to Radical Institutional Reform

But Blair's concerns went wider than this. From the very start, he worried that the EU tried to do too much, over too wide an area, and did it badly, with an inability to make clear decisions. The European Council he first joined was a confused and unpredictable mix of chaos, drama and boredom, with no proper agenda, depending far too much on the qualities of who was in the chair, and 'conclusions' cobbled together, often at the last minute overnight, or in a disorderly drafting session at the end of meetings.

He also started with a low opinion of the Commission, having been forced to sit through Jacques Santer's mediocre performances at European Council meetings. Santer's successors, Romano Prodi and then José Manuel Barroso, both had their moments when improvement seemed possible, but Blair felt there was something about the institution that made it flawed, particularly the size of the college of commissioners and the indifferent quality of its membership. As for the European Parliament, in his view the great extension of its powers (which, at Robin Cook's instigation, he had agreed to in the Amsterdam treaty negotiations in 1997) had *not* brought Europe 'closer to the people': the high hopes of pro-Europeans that direct elections would have this effect had been comprehensively dashed. The Parliament came across to him as an undistinguished lobby group for its own aggrandisement, a group of 'failed MPs', the most vociferous of whom on the British side had been, in the past, among his most antediluvian 'Old Labour' opponents. This negativity softened a good deal over time, but it did not disappear.

Enlargement made institutional reform inevitable and urgent. The old habits of European summitry – deals stitched together in fireside chats – simply would not work in an EU of 25 members or more. An unreformed European Council would descend further into chaos and confusion: to remain effective, it had to become more formalised. Enlargement would also change the dynamic of the regular meetings of the Council of Ministers. The old ways of informal deals negotiated late at night behind closed doors simply would not work. In an unchanged Union, Blair calculated that the Commission would gain power as the key player able to position itself as the successful striker of compromise: the more unwieldy the Council, the stronger the Commission's relative position would become. At the same time the Parliament would be a likely gainer: it had more coherence – simply because it reached its decisions by majority. By contrast, an enlarged Council, having to reconcile the positions of numerous member states, would struggle to reach a common position, which it would then have difficulty defending in face of European Parliament pressure because its internal cohesion would be weaker. Without reform, a larger EU would mean an EU with the member states less in control.

Blair also feared that lack of progress on institutional reform might be used by the French as an excuse to delay enlargement. Traditionalists in the Quai d'Orsay, the French Foreign Office, saw enlargement as an existential threat to French influence, but here politics mattered. Jospin's Socialists in major part supported enlargement. Jacques Chirac as president was much more reluctant. His notorious outburst at one hapless east European prime minister: 'It would be better if you had the courtesy to remain silent!' was the fury of a man who knew enlargement would weaken France's position, but could do little about it.

The 'Brussels System'

Blair of course – and through no fault of his own – knew little of how the 'Brussels system' worked. Apart from questions of high politics, most decisions are the product of a complex three-way dynamic between Commission officials; specialist MEPs and their staff; and national civil servants from home departments and the member states' Brussels-based representations. While this triangle is marked by constant (and frequently infuriating) interinstitutional tension, its three sides also form an incestuous partnership. Commission officials generally are highly competent, often with a legal background, technically more expert than many UK civil servants because they move job less frequently, and myopically focused on the 'dossiers' under their management. Many still see their mission as building Europe through progressively extending the EU's reach. In the European Parliament, influential MEPs specialise in committee work, which, unlike in the House of Commons, gives them enormous leverage over the Parliament's eventual decisions in their area of specialism. The Parliament's initial response to Commission initiatives is framed by a *rapporteur* appointed from the relevant specialist committee, who generally works to achieve cross-party consensus. Controversial decisions are debated within the party groups where the commonest outcome is a compromise text negotiated between the centre-right EPP and socialist groups.

The Commission and Parliament are the most visible Brussels players; yet national civil servants also exert huge influence. Dozens of meetings of the Council working groups they attend take place in Brussels every week. The Commission canvasses its proposals with them in advance. Officials have wide discretion as long as they avoid political controversy. There is a built-in preference for opacity: as a technique for getting agreement, it generally works. The Brussels system provides national officials with an opportunity to achieve reforms through the EU that can be more difficult to achieve domestically. Take environmental standards: in the domestic system, objections from other departments would have to be overcome and legislative time found. In Brussels by contrast, consensus with colleagues from other member states can be easier to achieve because of a shared institutional and specialist interest.

This system has considerable strengths. New proposals are considered through successive iterations of a careful deliberative process. The meetings of national permanent representatives (COREPER) in Brussels are highly effective at resolving differences without having to involve ministers. The outcome generally reflects consensus not partisanship, but it is a consensus of insiders committed to progressing the business before them. It works with the grain of special interests whose voice has a major (perhaps too major a) say. The system neglects the question of whether what is proposed is an appropriate matter for the EU, and where the general public (i.e. non-specialist, non-departmental) interest lies. There is little real politics. It is a case of the technocracy knowing best what is in the EU public interest.

This style of decision-making is then replicated at member-state level. In the UK, EU policy-making throughout the Blair years was coordinated through the European secretariat in the Cabinet Office. The secretariat consisted of bright young officials who each maintained regular contact with the relevant officials handling EU business in their departments. As a result, No. 10 knew more about what was going on, often before departmental ministers did. Lead officials from departments met every Friday morning under the joint chairmanship of the head of the European secretariat and the UK permanent representative in Brussels to anticipate problems and smooth the flow of business. Unspoken assumptions were made about the national interest; on difficult issues, compromises were floated and discussed. There were occasional tensions, particularly with the Treasury, who institutionally behaved as though they were a law unto themselves. I observed with admiration as Brian Bender, David Bostock or Stephen Wall, as successive heads of the cabinet secretariat, conducted a civilised but sustained questioning of a senior departmental official on the demanding details of their brief, in which inch by inch they would gradually open up room for negotiating manoeuvre and compromise. When the 'line' was clarified, discussion would shift to how ministers should be 'handled'. Departments would 'flag up' any problems from their minister in taking the recommended advice. The head of secretariat might then seek to head off the difficulty by seeking a 'steer' from the prime minister in a minute which would then be put together with remarkable facility for the weekend box. If the prime minister ticked off the recommended course of action, the Downing Street steer would be quickly communicated to the problematic department the following Monday and normally that would be the end of the matter. If the prime minister raised a doubt, the head of secretariat would find a way of 'catching a quiet word'.

This was indeed a Rolls Royce operation and it was a privilege to see it at work. But it has one central weakness: the decision-making process lacks politics. In the Blair years European policy was in theory coordinated at ministerial level by a cabinet sub-committee chaired by the foreign secretary: in truth, little of value came out of these meetings. Few ministers were seriously engaged in thinking about the strategic direction of the government's European policy. The key players, the Prime Minister and Chancellor, never took part. Departments were often represented by ministers below full cabinet rank who tended to stick rigidly and without imagination to the departmental brief that officials had rehearsed many times before. From an official perspective, the role of the 'good minister' in European terms was to be an assiduous networker with ministerial colleagues from other member states. The record here was patchy. In the British game of ministerial snakes and ladders the frequency of moves on the board not only limits the effectiveness of individual ministers but dims their personal enthusiasm for European policy engagement, which involves sustained commitment simply to get up to speed.

In tandem, the complex triangles of the Brussels system and the closed processes for determining national policy contribute a good deal to the perception of opaqueness, technocracy and lack of genuine democratic accountability in the way the EU is run. For those involved, including the British 'Eurocracy', the system works. It is in their terms 'efficient', and they have every incentive – for the best of reasons in terms of protecting the national interest in their eyes – to keep matters that way. Yet how much was the existing institutional set-up a problem that itself needed reform?

The Blank Piece of Paper

The Amsterdam Treaty had been agreed in June 1997 before the Blair government had a chance to draw breath. Blair decided to launch on his own personal initiative an open-ended discussion on the 'future of Europe' at the June 1998 Cardiff European Council under the British presidency. Prior to the meeting, Martin Donnelly, then deputy head of the Cabinet Office European secretariat, and I were commissioned to write what in European circles is described a 'non-paper': that is, a policy contribution from within the machine that is not official policy. Blair asked his advisers to start with a blank sheet of paper and come up with new ideas for how

Europe should be run. Blair wanted, as we put it, to 'find a way of jumping ahead of the game and proposing something that takes us out of our traditional back marker position. But it has to be something that we can live with and sell politically here.' This included addressing 'sceptic concerns' about lack of accountability, over-intrusiveness, rigidity and loss of sovereignty; David Cameron may think he is attempting a renegotiation no government has tried before, but in essence he is not. Blair at that stage was looking for some 'magic bullet' that would reform Europe without triggering a full-blown exercise in treaty change. We proposed a new charter or declaration, which would set out a clear vision for Europe's future role but contain essential guarantees of national sovereignty. The open-ended federalist language of the 1950s about 'ever closer union' should be replaced with a modern statement of values and objectives, and offer some cutting edge on subsidiarity. The politics was to replicate in the EU what Blair had spectacularly achieved with the Labour Party through the symbolic reform of Clause Four. The idea of a non-legally binding 'Statement of Principles' caught on; it made its last outing in Blair's Warsaw speech in October 2000. Unfortunately by then the 'future of Europe' debate had moved on to a more classic agenda of treaty change.

'Bright Ideas We Can Always Choose to Ignore'

At the conclusion of the British presidency in June 1998, Blair ordered a major Whitehall review of European policy. Robert Cooper, the Foreign Office's in-house but highly independent intellectual, was commissioned to draft a think-piece. It emerged with a compelling clarity:

> How we shape European institutions will determine how far Europe (and with it Britain) succeeds in the next century. If we get the right institutions, we will get the right policies (as repeal of the Corn Laws followed the Great Reform Bill). If we continue with second class institutions – which is what we have now – Europe's potential may never be realised. Since the European Union is an important part of the governance of Britain this will damage Britain.
>
> The European Union should be a middle way between:
>
> - The nation state: in continuous conflict with its neighbours, too small for many of today's problems and too small to carry weight in today's world
> - A European state: too big, too clumsy, and too distant to respond to changes in society; inappropriate given the diversity of language and traditions in Europe

> We want a Europe that combines the advantages of the big state with those of the small.
>
> The problem with the European institutions is that we have given them wide-ranging powers – probably too wide-ranging – but none of us trust them. We deal with this problem by making sure the European Union is weak. Good management consist of giving organisations clear and limited tasks, giving them full authority to carry them out and making them bear the consequences of getting things wrong. In Europe, we have done exactly the opposite.

Cooper's remedy was with one hand to narrow the scope of the EU activity:

> Some of the areas where European action has been most popular are precisely those which the principle of subsidiarity would exclude: animal welfare, clean beaches, sex discrimination.

And instead of giving the Commission more powers, 'rather to give it less powers and make it more accountable for its exercise of them'.

This should be combined with a leap forward in the democratic accountability of the Commission. His preference was for direct election by all EU citizens of the Commission president. This should be accompanied by:

- more transparent EU decision-making;
- double majority voting in the Council (any proposal would have to achieve a majority of *both* member states on a one member, one vote basis and states that together constituted a majority of the EU population, in place of the complexities of qualified majority voting (QMV) weights);
- a smaller, streamlined Commission;
- abolition of the six-monthly rotating presidency;
- focusing the European Parliament on its investigatory and accountability roles.

Blair seriously toyed with the idea of making a directly elected Commission president the centrepiece of his reform policy. But the weight of Foreign Office opinion was firmly opposed and in the end, with the reluctant assent of his Downing Street advisers and a real tone of regret, Blair came down against. The elected Commission president proposal was 'an attractive idea that maybe my children's generation will implement', but it was not for now. (Interestingly, in a *The Times* interview in 2011, Blair reverted to the idea of a directly elected Commission president, which is now also the official policy of Germany's Christian Democratic Union.) He consistently wanted to 'think big', but even at his most powerful, it was somehow just too difficult to break out of the box of conventional positions and thinking. As Jonathan Powell sardonically remarked when No. 10 had dug itself into another policy hole, 'we can always commission Robert Cooper to come up with some bright ideas we like that we can then always decide to ignore'.

British Backing for 'More Europe'

Blair retreated at this stage from promoting a reform agenda of his own. He had a nagging doubt as to whether Britain had the credibility to take the lead in arguing for a radical shake-up, when, ten months before, his Labour government had ducked a decision on whether to join the euro. Might not our partners be actively suspicious of what might seem to them a typical British manoeuvre to roll back the power of Brussels? Blair would have preferred to fall in behind Helmut Kohl, who was exercised by the rise in German Euroscepticism and wanted to launch an initiative to curb the powers of the Commission and enforce subsidiarity, but Kohl was heavily defeated in the September 1998 federal election. His successor, the SPD's Gerhard Schroeder, was at that stage not the slightest bit interested in playing what he saw contemptuously as European word games.

Blair decided that the key priority for him in 1998 was to do more to demonstrate Britain's European commitment. He asked key members of the cabinet to bring forward ideas where 'more Europe' might be in the national interest. The Home Office proposed a more expansive Justice and Home Affairs agenda, which was worked up into a set of 'forward' British ideas for the Tampere Summit during the Finnish presidency in March 1999. However, the key contribution came from the defence secretary, George Robertson, one of the most underestimated members of Blair's cabinets, who with typical skill had won round the key figures in the military to the view that Britain should take an imaginative step forward on European defence. This was a genuinely bold move which Labour had resisted in the Amsterdam Treaty only a year before. Imagine then the surprise – and delight – of Blair's fellow heads of government when at the Portschaech informal summit in October 1998, under the Austrian presidency, Blair announced that the British government had abandoned its opposition to the creation of a European defence identity. His foreign affairs private secretary, Sir John Holmes, was duly dispatched to Paris to negotiate the terms of what would soon become the landmark St Malo

Declaration. This search for new areas where Britain could play a leading role in Europe, despite its absence from the euro, marks a clear contrast with Cameron's seeming indifference to the development of an inner core Europe with, in his eyes, Britain contentedly cast into some outer tier.

Europe Never Stands Still

The future of Europe burst again onto the scene as a result of a lecture by Joschka Fischer,[3] Germany's foreign minister and leader of the Greens in the SPD-led coalition. Its very title, *From Confederacy to Federation: Thoughts on the Finality of European Integration*, was sufficient in itself to send shivers down many a Eurosceptic spine, deliberately timed as it was to the emotionally poignant 50th anniversary of the Schuman Declaration. The reality was different. Fischer rejected a United States of Europe that would seek to erect the post-war German model of the federal republic on a European scale. The nation states of Europe would retain a much larger role than the German Länder. His vision was of a 'lean federation', which would be 'capable of action, fully sovereign yet based on self-confident nation states', with more open democracy at European level and a clearer division of competences between the EU and its nation states. Fischer proposed a 'full Parliamentarisation', by which he meant a European government accountable to a properly elected European Parliament, but left open whether the 'government' would be modelled on the existing Commission. He differed from traditional federalists in calling for the European Parliament to include a second chamber made up of national parliamentarians. He also supported the model of a directly elected president. Fischer spoke of a Europe 'established anew with a constitution' based around 'basic, human and civil rights, and equal division of powers between the European institutions, and a precise delineation between European and nation state level'. His emphasis on the constitutionalisation of rights and the importance of democratic transparency and accountability welded the spirit of the 1968 student rebellions onto the functionalist integrationism of the (mainly) Christian Democrat post-war founding fathers. In a final flourish that caused great consternation in the Foreign Office, he floated the idea of an 'avant garde' of member states that might wish to integrate further beyond his constitutionalised 'lean federation', thus reviving the concept of the infamous Lamers/Schauble paper (written in the mid-1990s by two German Christian Democrat integrationists of the old school) of a 'hard core, [...] oriented to greater integration and closer cooperation' in order 'to counteract the centrifugal forces generated by constant enlargement'. Fischer's 'avant garde' appeared a direct threat to Blair's ambition 'to lead in Europe'.

Suspicions grew stronger when a little more than a month later Jacques Chirac addressed the Bundestag.[4] Chirac floated the idea of a 'pioneer group' to complement Fischer's 'avant garde', to take forward deeper integration in areas such as defence, crime and, significantly, economic policy, as permitted for the first time by the new 'enhanced cooperation' provisions of the Amsterdam Treaty. Essentially his vision of Europe remained a Gaullist one, not surprisingly since he had first entered the French cabinet in 1967 as de Gaulle's minister of social affairs to begin a remarkable career of public office stretching over four decades. Chirac declared that neither France nor, in his view, Germany was 'envisaging the creation of a super European state which would supplant our national states and mark the end of their existence as players in international life'. The nation states 'will remain the first reference points'. Chirac wanted Europe to be a world power, naturally with France in a leading role, but without the constitutional trappings of a federation at European level such as elected presidents or parliamentary accountability. His view of Europe as a union of states was still heavily influenced by the Fouchet Plan which de Gaulle had failed to persuade the Six to accept in 1962.[5] However, in a radical departure from Gaullism, Chirac declared his support for a decision-making procedure 'in which majority voting is the rule and which reflects the relative weights of the member states'.

Chirac stopped short of describing his agenda as about drafting a European constitution, but he outlined a wide agenda of topics for examination which were certainly constitutional in their implications: simplification of the treaties; a better definition of the 'division of responsibilities' between the EU and its member states; a clarification of the 'nature' (that is, the legal and constitutional status) of the new Charter of Fundamental Rights; and a particular French concern, given rising political hostility to Turkish membership, the Union's ultimate geographical limits. He then suggested a remarkable innovation: a more open process of discussion on the future of Europe that might involve a committee of 'wise men' or more radically still a 'convention'. The device of a convention had been used in 1999 for the specific purpose of drafting the EU's Charter of Fundamental Rights, largely to involve human rights experts and lawyers. But a convention with a broader constitutional remit would allow ideas to be aired, and a measure of consensus to be established, without diplomats behind closed doors being able to squash them before they had seen the light of day.

These speeches initiated a top-level debate within Whitehall about how Britain should respond. At the time the Foreign Office was led by the brilliant, mercurial and delightfully cynical John Kerr. Kerr argued that this emerging constitutional debate was all a terrible distraction from the central European question facing the UK: our membership, or not, of the euro. Basically he recommended that Blair should strangle this emerging constitutional debate at birth. Britain should draw the line at whatever was agreed at the intergovernmental conference soon to be convened under the French presidency (at Nice) and not allow another process of European navel-gazing to begin. He warned of the politically destabilising consequences of the demands for a referendum that would inevitably arise on any major new EU treaty. His advice was not taken. Blair hesitated. His instinct was never to be a veto-player. More than that, he felt the larger issues that had been raised to be important; in his view, European integration had advanced so far, it was no longer possible to keep the constitutional genie in the bottle. Undeterred, Blair decided to make a major speech on the future of Europe in Warsaw in October 2000. Its quality was raised to a new level by the arrival in Downing Street of Stephen Wall as head of the European secretariat. Much has been written about Blair's difficult relationship with the senior civil service and there is no doubt that his cabinet secretaries did not feel that he had made the best use of their talents. But Wall was a class act and Blair came to know it and rely on him.

While the Warsaw speech was one of Blair's best in making the modern case for Europe, it studiously hedged its bets on the EU's constitutional future. Our partners were pleased by Blair's insistence that 'widening' did not rule out further 'deepening', contradicting the widespread fear that enlargement was a British Foreign Office plot to block a more integrated Europe. Yet his ideas for institutional change did not measure up to the challenge. A very British touch was the assertion that while the EU needed a 'constitutional debate', it did not necessarily need a constitution. Blair backed Joschka Fischer's earlier proposal for a new 'second chamber' made up of national Parliamentarians and he resuscitated the idea of a Statement of Principles to clarify the modern rationale for the EU, enshrine the central role of the nation state in its *finalité*, lay to rest British fears of 'ever closer union', and better define subsidiarity. The most striking phrase of the Warsaw speech was Blair's declaration that he wanted the EU to become 'a superpower, not a superstate', but the speech was distinctly short of concrete proposals to take forward European defence or build a stronger EU role in foreign policy. Blair was committed in theory but cautious in practice. Warsaw was enough, just, to keep him in the Fischer/Chirac league.

Then the Nice intergovernmental conference proved a disaster. The Foreign Office had been deeply concerned by Franco-German talk of 'avant gardes' and 'pioneer groups', fearing that pressure to make enhanced cooperation easier would result in the spectre of a two-tier Europe with Britain consigned to the outer edge. Blair, however, was unwilling to make a big issue of this. Wall's advice was that there was little risk of an inner core emerging because on no question of substance were France and Germany in agreement on what form deeper integration might take, and despite the eurocrisis since 2010 that remains largely true. The real disaster of Nice – and one that kept Blair out of bed for four successive nights – was an ugly row over the change in the balance of voting weights in the Council, and the related issue of a smaller Commission. On voting weights, France was reluctant to sacrifice its formal parity with Germany; and when that was settled a similar problem erupted between Belgium and the Netherlands. In addition there was the problem that Spain (and, by extension, Poland when they joined) was not prepared to see its voting weight reduced in line with its population share. Even more toxic was Chirac's insistence that the larger member states should be given 'compensation' for surrendering their second commissioner as a consequence of enlargement.[6] The 'smalls' were told in no uncertain terms that they should know their place. Chirac demanded that the size of the Commission be cut to make it more efficient, while insisting that all the 'bigs' maintained the right to permanent representation. The 'smalls' fought back that every member state should have its own commissioner. Chirac's bullying in the righteous cause of a more efficient Union failed to produce a sensible solution.

Blair saw these bitter arguments as infuriating distractions from the real challenges facing Europe, but he realised, once Nice had ended in such a hash, that a more fundamental examination of the future institutional shape of Europe would be inevitable. This paved the way for the establishment of the Convention on the Future of Europe at the Laeken summit under the Belgian presidency in December 2001. In the months before, the Foreign Office played its traditional backmarker role, but Blair's heart was not in it. Blair did not block Chirac's nomination of former French President Giscard d'Estaing as the Convention's president, although he might have backed the Dutch prime minister, Wim Kok, had he pushed his claim at the summit meeting. For all the initial Foreign Office doubts, Giscard was to prove a masterly choice. As for the Laeken Declaration itself establishing the Convention, Blair did secure helpful language. The Belgian prime minister, Guy Verhofstadt, went out of his way to accommodate British concerns. Laeken's language set a clear goal that 'within the Union, the European institutions must be brought closer to its citizens'. It acknowledged complaints of 'the Union [...] intervening in every detail in matters by their nature better left to Member States'; 'the Union [...] behaving too bureaucratically'; taking on 'too much in areas where its involvement is not always essential'. It sought 'guarantees (for the member states) that their spheres of competence will not be affected'; and for a bigger role for national parliaments 'in a new institution alongside the Council and European Parliament'. These sentiments were not a world away from those William Hague and David Cameron have more recently expressed. The difference is that Laeken set out clear ambitions for the EU in meeting the new economic, security, environmental and developmental challenges of globalisation. The Union was on course to begin its most profound constitutional debate hitherto.

CHAPTER 8

Reforming Member State Economies

One dimension of Labour's European policy on which Blair and Brown worked together in common cause was the battle for economic reform. This chapter explains why economic reform became such a high priority for New Labour. In practice, it became a 'sixth test' for Britain's euro membership: was Europe, and the eurozone, moving in a direction that New Labour would deign fit for Britain to join? How did this all come about?

Blair first put 'economic reform' on the EU agenda in launching Britain's EU presidency at Waterloo station at the end of 1997. Eyebrows were raised in diplomatic circles about the choice of venue. A small band of 'modernisers' saw Waterloo, then the terminus of the Channel Tunnel Eurostar, as a potent symbol of modern Britain strengthening its unbreakable Continental links. The more historically minded warned of French sensitivities about Wellington's famous victory: they were later to see a significant parallel in Blair's European diplomacy between his heavy courting of successive German chancellors and the late arrival of Marshal Blucher's Prussian divisions tipping the balance of the 1815 battle.

Malmö and the 'Problem' of the French Socialists

Within a few weeks of taking office Blair had burnished his credentials as the leader of modernisation and reform in Europe in a speech at Malmö to the Party of European Socialists. This caused a minor political sensation. Plenty on the European centre left were eager recipients of Blair's message. In Italy the Olive Tree Coalition was the kind of 'progressive alliance' to which Blair himself aspired in Britain, including centrist former Christian Democrats, of whom the prime minister, Romano Prodi, was one. In the Netherlands, the Dutch Labour Party (PvdA) under Prime Minister Wim Kok led the so-called 'Purple Coalition' with the Dutch liberals (the VVD), which to all appearances was successfully combining market liberalism with social justice. In the Nordic countries, social democracy was once again riding high after a series of economic crises in the early 1990s. The Nordic centre-left had boldly seized the mantle of reform after their old 'tax and spend' welfare model had run into problems. The Swedish social democrats, under the leadership of Goran Persson, put together a successful governing strategy based on open markets, tight fiscal discipline, welfare reforms, active labour market policies and 'social investment'. In Denmark, Paul Nyrup Rasmussen's labour market reforms pioneered 'flexi-security', which combined employer freedom to 'hire and fire' with generous social security for the temporarily unemployed on strict condition that they underwent retraining and searched for jobs. Across most of Europe the progressive left was in flux, open to new ideas, and recognised there was little future in an old class-based politics or simply defence of the traditional welfare state.

Yet for Blair, the Malmö conference was overshadowed by the surprise victory of the French left in the National Assembly elections the weekend before. Jospin's Parti Socialiste (PS) presented a clear and present danger to New Labour's claim to ideological hegemony in Europe. The PS had undergone no visible ideological renewal, and been through no 'Clause Four moment'. To Blair they felt very '1980s', as he would put it contemptuously. Brown and Blair disliked the PS pledge to return to full employment, which New Labour thought old-fashioned and hard to deliver without radical labour market reforms which the French left opposed. They feared that French demands for a European jobs plan would be a cover for a Europe-wide reflation, undermining New Labour's own commitment to economic discipline. Worst of all, the domestic centrepiece of their programme was a legally enforceable maximum 35-hour week, presented as a work-sharing policy to create new jobs, harking back to Leon Blum's 1936 Popular Front: it was the direct opposite of the labour market 'flexibility' to which New Labour was committed.

In government, the PS leadership were to prove far more pragmatic than their rhetoric. In Jospin, the Socialists had a leader of outstanding intellectual quality and personal decency who was no left-wing 'throw back'. Blair quickly realised this and sought to repair the relationship. The gesture was reciprocated in an invitation for Blair to address the French National Assembly, which he did – in French – the following spring. Yet the ideological tension between New Labour and the PS was plain for all to see. Right-wing deputies deliberately chose to receive Blair's speech much more enthusiastically than the left. However, Jospin eventually got his own back by producing the most memorable and effective critique of New Labour, when he succinctly described his own brand of modern social democracy as a belief in a 'market economy, not a market society'.

The Luxembourg Employment Strategy

Brown and Blair launched a determined 'push back' against the adoption of French economic ideas at EU level. By chance, this coincided with the Luxembourg presidency's efforts in the second half of 1997 to devise a European employment policy. The new EU competence on employment, agreed in the Amsterdam Treaty, arose from a Swedish initiative, where the social democratic government was anxious to reassure their Eurosceptic electorate that the EU was not biased against a Swedish 'full employment' vision of the welfare state. The Employment Pact, agreed under the Luxembourg presidency, was largely the work of Allan Larsson, the Commission's visionary director-general for employment. Larsson, a senior Swedish social democrat and former finance minister, was a passionate supporter of Nordic employment activation, not French-style work-sharing. The Pact set out ambitious guidelines for active labour market policies against which member states were to benchmark their national efforts. Working hours limitation was downplayed. In No. 10 this was seen as an early New Labour win in the ideological struggle for social democracy's soul, though in truth Labour could have learnt more itself from Dutch and Nordic experience.

The Pact's 'peer review' and 'benchmarking' approach caught a tide as a new form of European governance. It was judged more attractive and effective than laws and regulation, better reflecting Europe's diversity and enabling faster action than the cumbersome task of negotiating European directives and pursuing the long process of their transposition into national law. In the creative mind of one European thinktanker, Mark Leonard, this new mode of governance was dubbed the arrival of 'network Europe'[1] – a concept Prime Minister Cameron still thought worth plagiarising some 15 years later to differentiate his view of Europe from the spectre of 'centralisation'.

The Pursuit of Flexibility

The genesis of the employment guidelines crossed over with a larger economic debate about the single currency. For the euro to be successful, greater flexibility in labour, product and capital markets was deemed essential. Experts questioned whether the single currency could be sustainable if some euro members continued to follow down their historic path allowing unit labour costs to rise faster than Germany's. Italy, for example, had been a member of the ERM since it first came into operation in 1979, but the lira's rate of exchange with the Deutschmark had been realigned on many occasions. With the option of realignment ruled out in a single currency, and the absence of a 'transfer union', more flexible markets would be needed to adjust wages and prices internally and to prevent costs getting out of line.

Brown took up the argument for more flexible markets with great determination. In the 1998 British presidency he argued vigorously for the drive for more flexible markets to gain an equal status in economic policy coordination to the fiscal disciplines of the Stability and Growth Pact. The UK proposed that member states' progress towards structural reforms should be benchmarked in a common EU process. Farsighted as this now may seem, most of our partners were not impressed. Brown was seen as repeating the old Conservative refrain that 'Europe needs a Thatcher'. He was perceived as advocating the prescriptions of the controversial Organisation for Economic Co-operation and Development (OECD) 1994 *Jobs Study*,[2] which, at the risk of being simplistic, had argued that much of Europe needed to make Thatcher-style industrial relations reforms in order to improve economic performance. This concept of flexibility was, however, fundamentally different in nature to the Swedish activation policies advocated by Allan Larsson and the Commission. In Sweden's case, flexibility had proved compatible with the highest level of trade union density in the EU. Politically, Brown's approach to reform was as much anathema to German Christian Democrats as it was to the French Socialists. The Germans believed strongly in their model of co-determination. True, the German employers had started a major push for change and many deals on industrial restructuring and more flexible wage setting were to be agreed at plant level. But the German employers had no wish to engage in a frontal assault on the trade unions or to destroy their domestic structures of social partnership. In the face of German tepidness and French suspicion, Brown's efforts made limited progress. At the June European Council a 'Cardiff process' for benchmarking structural reforms was formally agreed as Britain held the presidency pen, but little real 'buy-in' from key member states had been achieved. Blair drew the conclusion that better ways of advancing economic reform had to be found.

The Schroeder Opportunity

The opportunity came with the SPD's decisive victory in the German federal election of October 1998. Schroeder had skilfully positioned himself as a man of the modern left, a German Blairite or so it seemed, to the extent one believes such terminology can cross the boundaries of national political culture. Schroeder labelled his political project the 'Neue Mitte', a clear plagiarisation of Blair's talk of the 'radical centre' and later the 'third way'. At one stage, in Schroeder's chancellery office, a copy of Tony Giddens' *The Third Way* was prominently on display on his desk with no other book in sight! For Blair the key question was whether Schroeder would embrace a reform agenda that would shake up German corporatism, renew Germany's economic dynamism and shift the negative perceptions of the Continental economy among opinion-formers in the UK. This mattered to Blair both as a modern social democrat and because the British Eurosceptic media constantly played upon negative perceptions of Germany to raise doubts about Britain joining the euro.

The issue for Blair was how to translate his ideological affinity with Schroeder into a common programme for Europe. A major stumbling block was Schroeder's disinterest in the EU when he initially came into office. This was in part an act of personal differentiation from Kohl. Schroeder saw himself as the first post-war chancellor who was not obsessed with German war guilt: he simply wanted Germany to be a normal country. The fact of course is that no holder of the great office of chancellor of the Federal Republic can disinterest themselves from Europe for very long. But the emotional commitment in him was skin deep. On the other hand, Schroeder and Blair did have in common a strong perception of themselves as modernisers and even outsiders in their own parties. Schroeder shared with Blair a genuine belief that the common challenge of globalisation required a new political response from the centre-left: the old verities were no longer relevant. On his first visit to London, Schroeder agreed to establish a joint working party that would set out common principles for modern social democratic governance. The outcome was the Blair–Schroeder Declaration of June 1999. While this document attracted reasonable notice in Britain, it caused a political sensation in Germany, in particular within Schroeder's own party, the SPD.

The Blair–Schroeder *papier* was 'New Labour' in argument and tone. All the New Labour themes were packaged together in a simple, uncompromising style. After the declaration was published, many of its critics assumed that the text had been drafted in London and forced down the throats of a reluctant Schroeder office by New Labour apparatchiks: flattering or alarming as this picture might seem, nothing could be further from the truth. The text was agreed in successive iterations of discussion between Peter Mandelson and Bodo Hombach, Schroeder's then Chancellery minister, who had been Schroeder's election strategist. Hombach was supported by Klaus Gretschmann, the Chancellery's newly appointed chief economic adviser, and Matthias Bucksteeg, a long-time political adviser to Hombach. On the British side, Peter was supported from the No. 10 Policy Unit by Geoffrey Norris and me.

On the German side, the politics of the whole exercise were complex. Schroeder, at the time he became German chancellor, was not even the SPD leader. Despite four successive defeats the SPD had only agreed to nominate Schroeder as their chancellor candidate at federal level because of his repeated success as an election winner in his home state of Lower Saxony. The highly charismatic but volatile figure of Oscar Lafontaine remained party chairman. He had been SPD chancellor candidate in 1990 when he had been subjected to a horrific knife attack: he returned to front-line national politics in 1995, defeating Rudolf Scharping for the party chairmanship. Schroeder appointed Lafontaine as finance minister, despite their disagreements over the SPD's political orientation and economic strategy, but the instability in this division of responsibility was fundamental. Lafontaine essentially bought into a Keynesian explanation of Germany's then high unemployment; Schroeder by contrast listened more to the business community and accepted the necessity for major structural reforms. It was a measure of Schroeder's political skills that, within five months of taking office, he had engineered a situation where in March 1999 Lafontaine spectacularly walked out of both the government and the party chairmanship. The Schroeder–Lafontaine clash was a titanic struggle for the soul of the SPD and the future of Germany – and the Blair–Schroeder Declaration played a role in it. Near the end of the process, the Chancellery in Bonn insisted on adding a more substantive economic section to the Declaration, drafted by Gretschmann, which basically set out the economic strategy Schroeder wanted Germany to pursue. Ed Balls was enthusiastically approving on Brown's behalf. In all likelihood this Chancellery edict contributed to Lafontaine's walk-out.

The collateral damage from the publication of the *papier*, however, went much wider. Having rid himself of Lafontaine, Schroeder had done little to prepare the ground for the huge controversy within the party that ensued. Inevitably Schroeder was forced into tactical retreat. Hombach was dispatched from the Chancellery to spend an unhappy two years as EU coordinator in the Balkans, before leaving politics to end up as chair of a leading German newspaper group. Gretschmann departed for comfortable exile in the EU Council secretariat in Brussels. Frank Steinmeyer, Schroeder's long-time chief of staff in Hanover, and later German foreign minister, took over full management of the Chancellery. His strategy was to lower the political temperature and restore normality. Nevertheless, the Blair–Schroeder Declaration had triggered a debate about modernisation in Germany that did not die away. It had broken the psychological barrier to discussion of reform within Germany's consensual political culture. After narrowly winning re-election in 2002, Schroeder came up with the radical Agenda 2010 package of welfare and labour market reforms. Schroeder never made the argument for his Agenda 2010 reforms in the high-ground way Blair would have done: he never argued that the reforms were the right thing to do for social democrats in their own terms, only that there was no alternative to change if the German welfare state was to remain sustainable. Yet while Blair's rhetoric of welfare reform may have been more compelling, Schroeder actually pushed reform through, achieving far more of significance on welfare reform than Blair ever did. However, in the end Lafontaine got his revenge. In 2005 he walked out of the SPD to join with the Left Party, the rump party of former German Communists from the East, in a new 'left alliance' (Die Linke). By doing so, he took just enough of the SPD's traditional voters with him in the West to deprive Schroeder of the chancellorship when he was narrowly defeated by Angela Merkel in the Bundestag election of that year.

These high dramas of German politics did little to change the European argument in Britain in the way Blair had hoped. The transformation of German economic prospects was dramatic but it came too late. As Blair and Brown limbered up to the euro assessment in the early months of 2003, German unemployment topped 5 million – only to fall by more than 2 million in the succeeding years. Until the middle of the last decade, the Eurosceptic commentariat continued to treat Germany as an economic 'basket case' from which a dynamic growing Britain should keep its distance. It goes without saying that they have never had the grace or intellectual honesty to admit how wrong they were. Instead, whereas ten years ago Germany was written off as a disaster because its alleged corporatism stood in the way of the flexibility that Britain enjoyed, now the Germans are damned for having pursued a ruthlessly successful mercantilism that has brought the euro sovereign debtors to their knees!

The Spanish Road to Lisbon

The major opportunity to Europeanise the economic reform agenda came with the Lisbon Strategy agreed by the European Council in March 2000. Lisbon was essentially a Portuguese presidency programme, following an initiative by the Spaniards, prompted by the UK Prime Minister and owing much to New Labour's influence and ideas. Early on, Blair decided to build a close partnership with José María Aznar, the centre-right prime minister of Spain since 1996. This caused much puzzlement and angst in the Blair entourage. As personalities they seemed as different as chalk and cheese: Aznar had a hard, unbending air about him, whereas Blair was full of boyish charm. Also, Aznar was a man of the right: not one of those nice centrist Christian Democrats from Benelux or Germany with whom a good social democrat might readily share a belief in democracy, human rights and the European social model. Beneath the surface Spanish politics were still defined by the Civil War and whether or not one's antecedents had stood for the Republic or Franco. Nevertheless, Blair was determined that these 'out-of-date taboos', as he saw them, should not stand in the way of a close alliance. It was to his first bilateral summit with Aznar in Madrid that Blair ventured, exhausted but triumphant, after the signing of the Good Friday Agreement in Belfast at Easter 1998. Blair's experiences with the Provisional Irish Republican Army (IRA) must have provided a lively topic of conversation, given the gravity of the ETA (Basque Euskadi Ta Askatasuna) terrorist threat in Spain.

However, the real bond that Aznar and Blair forged was that they both privately disliked a Europe dominated by France and Germany. Felipe González, Spain's legendary socialist prime minister until 1996, was happily content to sit at the feet of Chancellor Kohl, playing the role of his star pupil in support of European integration, while always maintaining a keen eye for Spanish national interests, when it came to EU cohesion funds, or opposition to CAP reform of 'Mediterranean products'! Aznar, equally competent as a master of playing hardball, wanted, however, to be counted in the big league and felt justified in this by Spain's apparently stellar record in economic convergence with its EU partners. To help break Franco-German dominance there was no better ally than Blair's Britain, ambitious also to 'lead' in Europe. Also, in terms of crude domestic politics, Aznar clearly hoped that some of the Blair stardust and charisma would brush off on him and damage his PSOE (Spanish Socialist Workers' Party) opponents. Over the succeeding years much effort was made to reassure our PSOE friends that we loved them too, but to little avail. Blair's willingness to go to the lengths of being a personal guest at the wedding of Aznar's daughter caused huge hurt to the PSOE's feelings, even if the electoral impact was marginal.

Aznar and Blair had to find issues on which they could work together. I was dispatched on an urgent mission to the Moncloa, the Spanish prime minister's office, to hammer out a common economic reform agenda with Aznar's advisers. These were intelligent, charming young technocrats, the new generation of modern Spain: as fervent economic modernisers, they were not that different in all frankness to the bright economists who worked for the PSOE. Their real enemies, in both cases, were the entrenched vested interests of Spain's crony capitalism on both sides of their tribal political divide. This pattern was fairly typical of southern Europe. One would often find the finest brains advising ministers, but with an incapacity to get a grip on the levers of power to push through necessary reforms on the ground.

As a first step, Britain and Spain began a series of bilateral conferences on labour market reform. Then in spring 1999 a wide-ranging joint declaration on economic reform was drafted. Aznar, when shown it, decided to suggest to António Guterres, the Portuguese prime minister, that Portugal should make economic reform the central theme of their EU presidency in the first half of 2000. In an example of Iberian solidarity across the party divide, the socialist Guterres responded with enthusiasm. This Aznar–Guterres accord marked for me the beginning of many trips to Lisbon for meetings with their newly appointed Portuguese presidency coordinator, the redoubtable Maria João Rodrigues. Maria had been plucked from academe to be Guterres' labour minister, but she clearly hadn't liked the experience very much. Facing stubborn resistance to change at home, she entered the European scene with the determination and courage of a modern Boadicea, armed with intellectual clarity, rigour and persistence, in the hope that the Lisbon strategy could be a game-changer in the reform debate and bring effective pressure to bear on member states, including her own. The Blair office helped her every inch of the way.

The Ideas Behind the Lisbon Strategy

At the time, the Lisbon strategy was seen as a great breakthrough. For the previous decade Europe's leaders had focused their attention on the launch of the single currency, with all the attendant requirements to meet (or fudge) the Maastricht Treaty's convergence requirements on inflation, deficits, debt and exchange rate stability. Lisbon marked a switch in political focus to the structural reforms necessary to raise Europe's growth and employment performance. The driving concept was for the EU to transform itself into a thriving and successful 'knowledge economy'. The concept of the knowledge economy was the intellectual fashion of the age. Sociological theorists saw it as the next transformatory stage of capitalism in post-mass-manufacturing societies. In a knowledge economy the future sources of competitive strength had changed from earlier stages of capitalist development: no longer was control over raw materials or mass productive power seen as the key to prosperity. The old Soviet vision of a planned industrial economy in which power stations and steel mills replaced the waste and human suffering of free-market capitalism was as redundant as the Communist system that fostered it. Rather the critical success factors in a knowledge economy would be the ability to develop human potential and society's capacities for innovation. The politics of production in the knowledge-economy era would focus on research, skills, the commercial exploitation of breakthroughs in technology, the fostering of fast-growing SMEs, knowledge-based innovation, creativity and culture.

The hallmarks of a successful knowledge economy were judged to be:

- an education system that offered opportunities to achieve high standards to the masses, and not just an elite, with multiple chances through life, not just a one-off opportunity as a young person;
- a dynamic higher education sector based on mass participation backed by generous public investment in research, and at the same time enterprising and engaged with the private sector;
- a successful innovation 'eco-system';
- labour market policies that promoted high-quality, adaptable skills and offered 'flexicurity' leading to much higher employment participation without gender, age or any other form of discrimination;
- a welfare system modernised to cope with 'new social risks';
- an open-market economy where new and growing business did not encounter barriers to their success in terms of unfair competition and obstacles (bureaucratic or oligopolistic) to market entry and enjoyed ready access to finance.

In this vision of 'silicon valley with a social conscience', Europe was judged to fall short in crucial areas: lack of focus on information technology and the importance of the digital revolution; too few fast-growing SMEs as a result of closed markets and inadequate availability of venture capital; indifferent public education with Europe slipping down the global league; high drop-out rates for post-16s; a higher education system that, outside a few elite institutions, was no longer world-class; poorly funded and unstrategic research; low employment participation, especially for women and older age groups; stark gender inequalities accentuated by poor childcare; unreformed welfare designed for male heads of household with jobs for life; and growing social exclusion and child poverty. Lisbon's aim was to remedy this charge sheet of failure.

Of course by no means all of Europe's member states were failures on all these counts. Indeed, some were outstanding successes. But despite the resilience of different 'varieties of capitalism' within Europe, the idea of Lisbon was to turn the EU into a laboratory of policy innovation where weaker countries learnt from best practice in their partners. The chosen means was a new mode of EU governance: the 'open method of coordination'. Building on the perceived success of the employment strategy, member states agreed to participate in a common process that involved benchmarking their national policies against an agreed set of EU targets and policy guidelines. Despite the fact that many areas included in the Lisbon strategy were matters of national competence, the member states did not see it as a competence grab by the European institutions, largely because its genesis lay very much with the member states themselves. Inside the Brussels bubble, Lisbon initially generated complaints about the sidelining of the 'community method'. That was its point. Except in areas where the member states had granted the EU exclusive competence (trade, competition, monetary policy for members of the euro) the EU legislative process had become a protracted bureaucratic exercise in negotiating harmonised common standards. The purpose of Lisbon was to promote much faster mutual learning from each other, while recognising the EU's inevitable diversity.

Was it wrong to involve the EU in policies of purely national competence? Some would argue that the OECD offers an adequate framework for cooperation amongst its sovereign members who want to learn from others' experience, based on authoritative data comparison and analysis: the PISA (Programme for International Student Assessment) studies of comparative educational standards are an excellent example. Yet EU members share much more than an intellectual interest in different policy approaches. A majority share a single currency. All have signed treaty obligations that require national economic policies to be seen as a common concern, and sensibly so, given the high degree of economic integration that exists. This is not legal pedantry. Whether or not the socio-economic models of EU member states function efficiently has significant spillover effects for their partners. Britain may be out of the euro, but we cannot insulate ourselves from the consequences of its flawed design, or the failings of structural reform in national economies, including our own.

The Lisbon Balance Sheet

It is now commonplace to dismiss the Lisbon strategy as an outright failure. Clearly it did not deliver its headline ambition: the EU did *not* become 'the most dynamic and socially inclusive economy in world by 2010'. Indeed the hype of that phrase now sounds ludicrous. The headline gap in output per head with the USA is still significant. The emerging economies are catching up with Europe at amazing speed, though the 'rise of the rest' and the 'decline of the West' is in terms of overall human welfare to be welcomed, not feared, as long as that decline is relative not absolute. Perhaps more seriously the outlook for future growth in Europe remains extremely problematic. In 2010, at the endpoint of the Lisbon strategy decade, the euro area was on the threshold of a grave and potentially existential sovereign debt crisis. Britain had seen the largest drop in output since the early 1920s and was about to enter its slowest ever period of recovery from recession. The European social model still had to face the twin long-term challenges of demography and global competitiveness, but from a much weaker position than the Lisbon strategy had envisaged.

Yet the Lisbon strategy had many strengths in its conception and some notable successes in its delivery. Lisbon was widely seen as a classic exercise in 'third way' triangulation. It contained a strong commitment to fiscal discipline combined with the need for structural reform and greater market flexibility. Some argue it bought into much, perhaps too much, of the market liberal agenda. Yet it had a distinctively social democratic stamp, not surprising in that 11 of the EU 15's heads of government came from the centre-left when Lisbon was launched. Its essence was an 'active government' agenda to improve supply-side performance, increase knowledge investment, raise labour market activation and tackle social exclusion. Its thrust was not sub-Thatcherite.

The unstated agenda was moving Europe towards the best of the governing principles of the reformed Nordic model, which since the mid-1990s had been uniquely successful in combining the goals of equity and efficiency, as André Sapir later argued.[3] Nor was the reformed Nordic model as statist and collectivist as many of its overseas admirers on the left believed. As Karl Aiginger explained, its success was built on an endorsement of an open competitive economy, a vibrant private sector and fiscal discipline as the essential framework for economic growth. The Nordics had, however, mastered how to use the power of an efficient state to enhance growth potential. During Sweden's tough but successful fiscal consolidation in the 1990s, public investment in knowledge – research, higher education and lifelong learning – had been increased, helping to sustain the country on a strong growth path. The Nordic countries generally boasted a flexible labour market that protected people not jobs. Employers faced few barriers to redundancy: active labour market policies retrained the unemployed and reconnected them with jobs. Families could rely on a strong universalist welfare state: this did require high levels of tax, but it proved sustainable because it guaranteed access to high-quality affordable services. The Nordics implemented a conscious strategy to raise employment participation rates through generous parental leave policies, the provision of affordable childcare and pension reform to encourage older people to stay in jobs. On the whole those policies commanded wide public consensus as well as improving the sustainability of welfare by broadening the tax base. Was it wrong to think that these strategies could be successfully universalised across Europe, given the shared ideal of a European social model?

Until the sovereign debt crisis broke, both the Continental 'core' economies and their Anglo neighbours made steady progress towards the Lisbon goals from widely different starting points. The 'leitmotif' of labour market policy in most member states became employment activation, not work-sharing on the French 35-hour week model. More countries, notably Germany, invested heavily in childcare and family-friendly policies. Female employment participation rose significantly in the Lisbon decade. Pension reforms were introduced, raising pension ages in line with improving life expectancy. Early retirement became less prevalent as the knee-jerk response to industrial restructuring. In the UK, the rougher edges of the Thatcherite labour market reforms were smoothed and a conscious effort was made to raise skills and educational levels, invest in research, improve work–life balance, and tackle poverty and social exclusion. Few national politicians would say 'we did this because of Lisbon'. However, Lisbon had a considerable influence on national policy-makers through framing the intellectual and policy debate in new and innovative ways.

Lisbon was wrong to put so much weight on the comparison between Europe and the USA: rather, it is comparative experience within Europe that has most to teach European countries. Europe's output gap with the USA remains a mix of what it has long been: fewer hours worked and significant differences in productivity per hour. It is not clear how much the fewer hours represent higher 'involuntary' unemployment in Europe and how much they represent different social choices. This is a difficult question to disentangle: do people in the USA work longer hours because they have the opportunity or because effectively they are forced to do so by lack of adequate social insurance and health care coverage? Are Europeans who retire earlier victims of 'involuntary unemployment' or choosing an easier, better lifestyle?

As for the differences in productivity per hour between Europe and America, some parts of Europe fare as well as the USA. Two factors are important in explaining higher US productivity overall. One is America's hegemony in information technology; European companies have been much less successful than American ones in developing and applying the IT revolution. A failure of Europe's single market may in part explain this: Europe became world leaders in mobile telephony as a result of the EU's rapid adoption of the global system for mobile communications (GSM) mobile standard in the late 1980s. Yet in the last two decades Europe has not succeeded in creating an effective single market in the new digital technologies, which has left the field open to dominance by US companies. The other factor in superior US productivity performance is retail. This is largely a result of a greater supply of land, laxer planning rules and greater prevalence of out-of-town, car-borne shopping. But does Europe want full 'Walmartisation' of its retail sector simply in order to match US productivity numbers? One doubts it.

Also we now know what we did not fully appreciate in 2000: US economic success have been a mirage for the vast majority of Americans. Ninety per cent of US productivity gains have been scooped up by the top 10 per cent. On most indices of quality of life and happiness, the top European nations still come out far better than the USA, never mind China or Brazil. As Jeffrey Sachs has argued, Europe can boast strong democracies without a US-style underclass. Europe has lower child mortality, higher life expectancy and a richer enjoyment of leisure than the United States.[4]

Lisbon's Flawed Politics

A larger failure of the Lisbon strategy was to grapple with the inherent problems in the EU's southern periphery that after 2010 was to find itself trapped in the vortex of the sovereign debt crisis. The Mediterranean member states were amongst the keenest proponents of Lisbon. Lisbon was after all a Portuguese initiative in response to a Spanish proposal. The Greeks and Italians were equally enthusiastic. Basically their political and civil service establishments supported the idea of Brussels prodding them into domestic actions that they knew would run into opposition from vested interests at home. But while their politicians talked a good game about their implementation of Lisbon, tough questions about rising labour costs, declining competitiveness and unsustainable property booms in these countries went unanswered; the real shame is that for much of the Lisbon decade these questions were not even properly and persistently asked by the European authorities.

Spain and Italy did attempt some liberalisation of their labour markets. But they left the 'core' highly protected, as the size of a secondary labour market of temporary jobs grew and grew. This dualism led to the wages of highly protected insiders rising much faster than productivity. At the same time generous pension arrangements for the same groups went unreformed, leading to big increases in inequalities between the generations. These problems of insider protection were exacerbated by widespread prevalence of restrictive practices that limit competition in diverse service sectors, from driving taxis to practising the law. Effective implementation of a more liberalising EU Services Directive might have helped create more pressure for domestic reform at an earlier stage, but the drive for that was weakened within the European Parliament in 2005. The Commission had limited success in pressing for 'flexi security' labour market reforms to lessen excessive insider protections. The southern periphery failed to invest sufficiently in active labour market policies to raise skills, particularly for young people. The former Flemish social democratic politician and academic Frank Vandenbroucke has tellingly pointed out that the member states worst affected by the eurocrisis are also those with the highest proportion of their workforce without skills in the whole EU 27.[5]

Lisbon also substantially ignored the tough challenges of public-sector reform. Protected public-sector employment has been both a source of fiscal pressure and a comparator for higher wages across the economy, contributing to lost competitiveness in tradable sectors. Italy has, for example, a big state in terms of public spending as a share of GDP, but by comparison with northern Europe the Italian state is staggeringly inefficient. It makes huge income transfers, but they fail miserably to narrow the gap between rich and poor, pre- and post-tax. In addition, far too little of the national budget is spent on knowledge investment: raising post-16 skills, modernising universities, and investing in research and innovation. Despite those failings, Italy retains huge competitive strengths in manufacturing and design. In Mediterranean countries the problem is essentially political: capture of the state by vested interests, to the detriment of future-oriented investments and the poor, and the inability of domestic politics to reform backward parts of their economies where a form of 'crony capitalism' persists.

In the euro's first decade, the bond markets gave national governments in the eurozone far too easy a ride: they were hopelessly quiescent in blithely assuming that the risks attached to each member state's sovereign bonds were roughly equal. This was a massive market failure. This lack of market pressure for reform was most damaging in the periphery countries: their public finances enjoyed the bonus of lower debt interest due to a fall in bond yields, but little incentive to pay down debt or make growth-enhancing social investments. European governance proved insufficiently robust to tackle these problems and address the competitive imbalances within the eurozone that began to emerge in the middle of the last decade. In retrospect, the big failure was in not differentiating more rigorously between the situation in different member states and not being able to apply some form of effective conditionality from the centre. The Commission had inadequate political sanctions or incentives to give its policy recommendations real bite. But since 2010, all has changed. Now extreme bond market pressures threaten countries caught in the vortex of the crisis, with a downward spiral of fiscal contraction and debt deflation that ignores the need for long-term public investments to tackle big competitive challenges. The sovereign debt crisis is both a major threat to the Union, but also offers a real opportunity for change. Reliance on markets alone to exert pressure for effective reform does not work.

Lisbon offered the Commission an opportunity for leadership, but it did not seize it. There was no Pascal Lamy who, as Jacques Delors' *chef de cabinet* throughout his Commission presidency, had totally dominated the the Berlaymont headquarters and enforced clear priorities. Germany became a big political problem. Schroeder agreed with the substance of the Lisbon themes but disliked the European process. He was only prepared to tolerate it if there was no suggestion of the Commission being empowered to tell Germany what to do. This instinctive hostility to the Commission became violent when in 2002, in advance of Schroeder's bid for re-election in September that year, the Commission issued an official warning to Germany on its fiscal projections. Schroeder saw this in terms of crude politics: Prodi siding with his German Christian Democrat opposition. The problem with Germany became compounded in 2003 when, together with the French, finance ministers famously set aside Commission recommendations for the enforcement of the Stability and Growth Pact. With the two largest founding member states in blatant defiance of the fiscal rules pact, it was little surprise that the Lisbon agenda achieved little political purchase.

The Commission dutifully prepared voluminous reports for the relevant meetings of the European Council. There was the usual 'tour de table' to discuss their conclusions. But increasingly while this proceeded, heads of government gossiped with each other in the margins of the Council room, or sloped off to make phone calls. In 2004–5, a serious attempt was made to revive Lisbon with the compelling Sapir report and the later Kok review and the launch of a revised Lisbon strategy by the incoming Barroso Commission. But the European Parliament weakened the thrust of what the Commission intended by complaining about the absence of sufficient emphasis on the social and environmental dimensions of the Lisbon strategy. The attempt to achieve renewed political momentum for economic reform fell foul of the bitter and symbolic row with the European Parliament over the Services Directive. Then the 'no' votes in the French and Dutch constitutional referenda were blamed on too much reform, not too little, and the attempt to generate a new impetus died. A dangerous mood of complacency about Europe's economic performance took hold.

CHAPTER 9

Drafting, Ditching and (90 per cent) Reviving Europe's Constitution

The Convention on the Future of Europe, established by the European Council in December 2001, was the most ambitious attempt to reshape the EU in the half-century since the Schuman Declaration. For a British government it represented the nearest thing there has ever been to an opportunity to forge a new relationship between Britain and the EU based on a fundamental renegotiation of its terms. And unlike the unilateral attempt that David Cameron launched with his January 2013 speech, it was a multilateral effort based on a set of reforming principles contained in the Laeken Declaration, which commanded wide-ranging support across the EU. But in its dual aim from Blair's perspective – to reform Europe and to reset the UK relationship – the endeavour failed. Indeed, by the end of the tortuous process, there were few firework displays anywhere in Europe to celebrate the ratification of the Lisbon Treaty in October 2009 to which Laeken had given birth. Rather, the mood was one of resigned determination never to let the messy process of fundamental treaty revision happen again. This, more than anything else, explains the shudders of horror that Cameron's 2013 speech sent down the spines of the chancelleries of Europe, not so much in reaction to its well-crafted content, with which many sympathised, but to the thought of another enforced trip down a troubled memory lane.

Why did the whole constitutional exercise end in such a *perception* of wholesale failure? The process was indeed messy: it took over eight years from the first discussions around the Laeken Declaration in 2001 to Lisbon's ratification in 2009. The French and Dutch referendum 'no' votes ditched the constitutional treaty in May/June 2005. It took two Irish referenda before its Lisbon replacement could be ratified. But the process was made unavoidable by a combination of the EU's biggest ever enlargement and the rapid but piecemeal expansion of EU activities since Maastricht. However, elevating the exercise to the level of 'drafting a constitution' was a mistake and I, for one, made it. The hope that a constitution would address intelligent Euroscepticism by convincingly defining the Union's nature, and limiting its reach, proved flawed. The constitution was intended to slay the Eurosceptic dragons of a Brussels superstate overwhelming national sovereignty, and a 'United States of Europe' swallowing up national identities. These hopes proved cruelly disappointed. What would anyway have been a difficult 'reform' debate, turned into a constitutional nightmare.

Contrary to what proponents of a constitution for Europe intended, the process legitimised fears that a superstate was in creation. In the UK, the Conservatives protested, misleadingly but effectively, that 'only states have constitutions'. On the French left, the process sparked a divisive (and otherwise avoidable) debate that, if this indeed was a constitution for Europe, it must contain stronger commitments to social rights. Once domestic political pressures forced Blair to concede a UK referendum in April 2004, breaking the deal he had done with Chirac, the French president followed suit. The French referendum on the constitutional treaty was then lost in June 2005. After much agonising among Europe's leaders, the failed constitutional treaty was recast by Merkel as a 'reform' treaty in the last month of Blair's premiership and the first of Sarkozy's presidency, on the clear understanding all round that (apart from in troublesome Ireland) referendums would not be placed in the way of its ratification. A line was eventually drawn under the constitutional argument, but only at an inevitable loss of Europe's credibility and legitimacy.

At the start, all appeared to be going swimmingly. The epicentre of the future of Europe debate shifted to the European Parliament building in Brussels where the Convention met under the incisive chairmanship of Giscard d'Estaing, the former French president. Tony Blair never went anywhere remotely near the Convention's 26 plenaries or the 50 meetings of its governing praesidium. But Blair was nevertheless a dominating presence in its deliberations: put bluntly, most *conventionnels* (as Giscard dubbed the delegates of various stripes from national governments and national parliaments, old member states and those soon to accede, as well as the Commission and European Parliament) recognised that they had to come up with a draft constitutional text that Blair would endorse. If he did, the common assumption was that this would become the backbone of a treaty that the UK would then ratify. In February 2002, when Giscard opened the Convention, this assumption appeared justified. In the wake of the 9/11 terrorist attacks, Blair's ratings as an international political superstar soared to the stratosphere. This was underlined, in scenes literally of Whitehall farce, by the Downing Street 'trilateral' (British, French,

German) dinner that Blair hosted after his post 9/11 visit to New York and Washington, which various other European leaders successfully gate-crashed. Blair's magnetism in Europe was at its peak.

Blair maintained a tight grip on Convention proceedings throughout through multiple channels of influence. Although the Foreign Office had formal responsibility, Stephen Wall masterminded the evolution of British positions from Downing Street. Stephen sent the Prime Minister a weekly report on the Convention's progress, supplemented by my own reflections on Convention meetings and networking contacts. These notes typically came back from a Chequers weekend with ticks, crosses, marginal notes and pretty clear instructions scrawled across the top of the page. The government's official representative was Peter Hain, minister for Europe after 2001. Hain started out political life as an anti-apartheid campaigner and Young Liberal activist; because of this, despite years of service with the Post Office workers' union, he was never fully trusted by Old Labour tribalists. Once an MP, Hain had aroused Brown's ire by voting against the deflationary Maastricht criteria. After 1997, he played a subtle role as an 'inside left' supporter of New Labour, basically loyal, but with an eye for the phrase that hinted at philosophical differences with prevailing orthodoxies. Hain proved an inspired choice for his European role: unfailingly energetic in the 'heavy lifting' of persuasion, working with our partners in a constructive, not hectoring way. From an initial wariness, I grew to like him enormously. Patricia Scotland was Hain's deputy. Her task in the Convention was to handle the more technical legal questions, particularly the consequences of enshrining the Charter of Fundamental Rights in the constitutional treaty. Patricia has all the virtues of the top-class barrister in politics – the capacity to master a complex brief the ability to make a case in compellingly simple language, and the skill to anticipate and answer opposing arguments in a respectful and charming way.

My main role in the Convention was to liaise with the Party of European Socialists (PES) members. Here the key contact was Giuliano Amato, former Italian prime minister, one of two vice presidents of the Convention, and the leader of its centre-left contingent. Amato combines a first-class intellect with the great subtlety necessary to survive the labyrinthine complexities of Italian politics. He once told me that the secret of his career was 'to be of the left, and not of the left, at one and the same time': in other words, to ensure the left always prefers you to the right, but keep enough freedom of manoeuvre to do deals with the centre! Amato wanted to keep Blair on board, but at the same time had to manage the federalist tendencies of many PES *conventionnels*. Amato always accepted what seemed like 75 per cent of what Blair wanted; on the other hand, he was adept at stretching the envelope of what Blair might live with. With the socialist *conventionnels*, Amato gradually coaxed his group towards a compromise. His speeches had a familiar structure: 'now of course we all want X; but what if we managed to achieve only Y; wouldn't that get us a lot of the way to where we want to be ...?' In the art of politics, it was a command performance.

Another crucial channel was the head of the Convention secretariat, John Kerr, whose retirement from the Foreign Office luckily coincided with the Convention's creation. Kerr was scrupulous in his loyalties to Giscard, but his presence at the centre of the Convention's work did ensure an open channel of communication about the direction of Giscard's thinking and the interplay of personalities and policies in the praesidium. Blair's personal relationship with Giscard d'Estaing was, however, crucial. In his efforts to strike a common bond (Downing Street joked that it would be based on a mutual suspicion of Jacques Chirac), Blair flattered Giscard by showing him the courtesy and respect due to one of Europe's great elder statesmen. For much of the Convention, Giscard studiously kept his counsel: he presided like a senior judge over a tribunal of enquiry, elderly but extremely alert, courteous in an old-fashioned, aristocratic manner, commanding and authoritative when there was any suggestion that the proceedings might go off the track, but offering only fleeting hints of his thinking in the sharp, even acerbic comments he occasionally made. However, as Giscard's thinking took a more formal shape, a great dinner was laid on for him in the spring of 2003 in Blair's Downing Street flat, with the government hospitality service providing the best 1964 Bordeaux it could find in its cellars. The dinner discussion was conducted in a spirit of great amity and ended in near unanimous accord. Giscard must have gone away thinking he had enough freedom of manoeuvre to strike a deal.

Yet unfortunately Giscard found the task of finding agreement within the Convention more difficult. Former presidents of France did not find the arts of compromise easy. As the Convention drew to its close, Giscard attempted to proceed by a mix of fiat and bounce, which did not recommend itself to fractious and self-opinionated *conventionnels*. The main points of reform he had agreed with Blair ran into serious trouble. For example, the 'smalls' among the member states rose up in arms against the creation of a full-time presidency of the Council and a slimmed down Commission on which the 'bigs' but not the 'smalls' would have guaranteed seats. The Spanish agitated about their loss of influence as a result of switching from QMV as presently weighted to a 'double majority' of states and populations. The Commission and European Parliament pushed for traditional federalist ideas such as majority voting in the Council as the general rule (including on foreign policy), the election of the Commission president by the European Parliament and the loosening of the requirement for treaty changes to be ratified by all member states. The national parliamentarians felt left out and increasingly squeezed between the aspirations of the Brussels bubble and the power plays of the member states. This led to a messy conclusion to the Convention's work in which lots of late additions to the text were made to buy off multiple discontents. 'Ever closer union' was reinstated as a treaty objective. Some grandiloquent absurdities crept into the Convention text such as flags and anthems and tactless (and unnecessary) references to the supremacy of European law, all of which were seized on as proof that a United States of Europe was in the making. Nevertheless, in typical EU style, out of chaos emerged at least a semblance of unity. Giscard's authority held sufficiently for him to declare a text as agreed before a plenary of the Convention, with only a handful of public dissentients. Peter Hain declared the British government as broadly satisfied with the text 'as basis for the treaty negotiations' that would then ensue. The body of delegates then moved to the reception area to drink a celebratory glass of champagne. Little did anyone realise at the time that it was to be more than six years before a treaty based on an amended version of the Convention text was finally to be ratified. But the world outside the Convention complicated the outcome and explained subsequent difficulties. First, a big problem for the treaty negotiations loomed: the last months of the Convention's work were dominated by European divisions over the Iraq War. Would differences between Britain, France and Germany over the constitution's text on foreign affairs and defence prove irreconcilable? Second, the UK politics of treaty ratification were to run out of Blair's control.

The Convention came up with its final text within a few days of the tragic suicide on 17 July of Dr David Kelly, a scientific weapons expert advising the Ministry of Defence's Defence Intelligence Service. Kelly's conversations with journalists had been the basis for inflated media reports implying that Blair had lied about the evidence of weapons of mass destruction in Iraq in order to justify Britain's part in the US-led invasion earlier that spring. This event, far more than any other, inflamed the controversy surrounding the Iraq policy itself. Month after month its consequences ate away at Blair's domestic authority. From that moment on, Blair was engaged in a 'life and death' struggle to save his reputation and his premiership – and he knew it. It deeply damaged his own confidence and morale. His ability to shape domestically Britain's European agenda became part of the collateral damage he had to be prepared to take in order to hang on to office. Yet despite the weakening of Blair's authority in Britain, and despite the unexpected bitterness of his falling out with Chirac and Schroeder over Iraq, Blair fought hard to prevent a temporary division becoming a permanent breach. Our partners judged that keeping Britain engaged was worth the effort: 'half a loaf' was better than none and in the end Blair delivered at least that.

Surmounting the Hurdle of Foreign Policy and Defence

In the Convention, foreign affairs and defence had fallen under the oversight of the Christian Democrat Jean-Luc Dehaene, the former Belgian prime minister whom John Major had vetoed as Commission president in 1994 on the grounds that he was a 'Belgian federalist'. In Foreign Office eyes, Dehaene was to live up to this reputation with his proposal to strengthen EU common foreign and security policy by amalgamating the functions of the existing commissioner for external affairs (then Chris Patten) with those of the Council's high representative (then Javier Solana) in order to create a new so-called 'double-hatted' post of European foreign minister. This sent tremors of fear through the UK system. From the institutional perspective of the Diplomatic Service, existing arrangements offered the best of both worlds. Where agreement between EU member states could be reached, the EU multiplied British influence. Where Britain had a distinctive position, it could still go its own way without EU let or hindrance. They saw 'European' foreign policy as the sum of the diplomatic efforts of its member states, not primarily an EU institutional function. The FCO framed its objections to the double-hatting proposal in terms of the new post-holder's accountability: in their view the European foreign minister would primarily be accountable to the Commission and, through the Commission, the European Parliament. To them this seemed an unacceptable attempt to bring foreign policy 'within the community method' and a bridge too far.

Blair took a more nuanced view. Blair wanted the EU to act together as a stronger force for good in the world, the 'superpower, not superstate' ambition of his Warsaw speech. He had recoiled at Europe's helplessness in the face of the Bosnia and Rwanda genocides. Fortified by the success of Kosovo, in which German military forces had for the first time joined in a military operation outside Germany's borders since World War II, and inspired by the initial spirit of European solidarity with America over the 9/11 attacks, Blair felt his instincts for a stronger Europe were justified by events. Yet as divisions over Iraq policy intensified, he became torn. He was keen to ensure that Europe did the right thing, as he saw it. Blair felt personally betrayed by Chirac and Schroeder. It was not that they disagreed with US policy – Blair did not object to that. Indeed he campaigned hard for Schroeder's narrow victory in the September 2002 Bundestag election on the basis that Germany was perfectly entitled to take a different view of the Iraq question. What in his view was outrageous was their active conniving to undermine the policy, going to the lengths of uniting with Putin to oppose their closest NATO allies and EU partners. Blair felt that Chirac was jealous of his personal international standing and wanted to pull him down a peg. Iraq also presented France with a golden opportunity to rebuild close links with Germany which Blair had deliberately attempted to weaken. What Blair found difficult to accept was the strength of Chirac's genuine conviction, based on considerable Middle East knowledge, that the Iraq invasion was wholly misguided and would turn out to have disastrous results.

Nevertheless, Blair remained totally convinced that Europe's external effectiveness, including European defence, needed to be much stronger. He had little time for the 'Eurosceptic Atlanticists' of the British right-wing commentariat who argued that the failure of France and Germany to back US policy on Iraq demonstrated that the EU was a waste of time. The EU majority, especially after enlargement, could be relied upon to oppose crude anti-Americanism. Also, despite Iraq, Blair stuck to his gut conviction that an essential precondition of a stronger European voice in the world was an effective trilateralism between Britain, France and Germany: trilateral intergovernmentalism had to be made to work again, as it had in Blair's first term, when Cook as foreign secretary had built a close partnership with his French and German counterparts, Hubert Védrine and Joschka Fischer.

Blair accepted Dehaene's proposal that a more effective European foreign policy needed a stronger coordinating figure and endorsed the concept of double-hatting. Whilst Blair shared the Foreign Office view that big questions of foreign policy should not be decided by the Commission, he acknowledged the importance of the Commission support role, given its control over EU policy instruments such as budgetary assistance and trade, which were significant in the Western Balkans and Middle East and in sustaining the Palestinian Authority. The new European foreign minister needed control over the necessary resources to pursue an effective policy: diplomatic staff, financial resources, civilian capabilities and, with European defence, the potential for military intervention. Blair's bottom line was that the primary accountability of the new European foreign minister should be to the member states, not the Commission. Dehaene cleverly met Blair's point by the bold stroke of proposing that the foreign minister would become the permanent chair of the Foreign Ministers' Council to whom she or he would be accountable. It was a neat solution.

Blair, however, continued to oppose majority voting on key foreign policy issues. Giscard pressed him hard on this but he would only agree to the extension of QMV on so-called 'implementing' decisions. On the fundamentals of foreign policy, as opposed, say, to financial regulation, QMV was not in his view an appropriate device to resolve differences. Britain had to maintain its foreign policy independence even if the price was European ineffectiveness. I challenged him on this. Did he accept the logic that tiny Latvia could block an EU agreement with Russia, or an obstreperous Cyprus a deal with Turkey? Yes, he did. Nor did he think that the UN model offered a way forward for the EU where big member states would retain the veto, but others did not.

In the final months of the Convention, however, the French and Germans suddenly put forward a proposal designed, it seemed, to circumvent Blair's insistence on unanimity. This was for the inclusion in the treaty of the possibility of 'permanent structured cooperation on defence' between a willing group of member states 'whose military capabilities fulfil higher criteria and which have made more binding commitments to one another', without other member states being able to block the move: in other words, a European defence inner core could be established, without British assent or the power to block, which could in theory pursue a policy inimical to the transatlantic alliance. What made this seem even worse was a meeting on 29 April 2003, hosted by the Belgian prime minister, Guy Verhofstadt, with Chirac, Schroeder and Luxembourg's prime minister, Jean-Claude Juncker, which resolved to establish a distinct European defence headquarters at Tervuren just outside Brussels, within a few kilometres of NATO headquarters. This gathering was a somewhat unconvincing quartet: their original intention had been to commit the 'founding six' to this idea, but Italy and the Netherlands refused to play ball. The gesture was largely symbolic as any move to create a stronger European defence without the commitment of British armed forces was hardly credible. Yet the symbolism of what was dubbed the 'chocolate soldier' summit aroused real fears in Downing Street. It was interpreted as a calculated manoeuvre by Chirac to drive Europe and America apart, undermine NATO and destroy Blair's transatlantic bridge.

Blair's instinctive pro-Europeanism overcame his initial anger. He was determined Iraq would not lead to a permanent breach with France and Germany. He had after all launched the European defence initiative at St Malo, on the working assumption that its purpose was to give Europe the capacity to act where the Americans did not wish to do so. So Blair bit his tongue; he passed up the opportunity to rubbish the French and German actions, which would have won him lots of plaudits in the British media. Instead, he sought to rebuild the trilateralism that had prevailed prior to Iraq. After months of diplomatic bridge-building, a trilateral summit was held in Berlin on 20 September 2003. Blair listened with great patience to Chirac's lengthy analysis of what was wrong with British and American policy in Iraq. The truth is that Chirac's warnings about what would happen in Iraq after the invasion proved powerful and prescient, of which Blair can now hardly be unaware. But despite these tensions, the three agreed on a united policy for the forthcoming constitutional treaty. Britain would support inclusion in the treaty of the possibility of permanent structured cooperation on defence. France and Germany for their part would agree to language that made clear that European defence cooperation would always be compatible with their NATO commitments, not in opposition to them. Over the succeeding months Stephen Wall was charged with agreeing suitable language with his French and German counterparts to embody these commitments in the treaty text. Blair made clear that as far as he was concerned, this was the deal-breaker on which the fate of the new treaty hung. After much difficulty, particularly on the specifics of a separate European defence headquarters, satisfactory texts were negotiated and the constitutional/Lisbon Treaty went ahead. Yet it was also an example of Blair's far-sighted commitment to Britain as a leading player in the EU. The agreement paved the way for France's return to the NATO command structures in the first year of the Sarkozy presidency and the British–French defence treaty signed in 2010, which the Cameron government has sought to build upon. In the midst of the Iraq debacle, an important step forward for Europe had been taken.

Domestic Politics of Treaty Ratification

Britain's European policy (with the partial exception of the euro) had been largely driven from No. 10 since Blair became prime minister. In the period from the conclusion of the Convention in the summer of 2003 until the British presidency in the second half of 2005, it ran out of his control. In the aftermath of Iraq, Blair's domestic authority weakened and on Europe the foreign secretary, Jack Straw, became a significant player. The appointment of Jack Straw as foreign secretary in May 2001 was inauspicious for the European cause. Straw had risen to Labour prominence in the 1970s as special adviser to Barbara Castle (whose Blackburn seat Straw went on to inherit) and Peter Shore. Castle and Shore can both lay claim to a much-admired place in Labour's pantheon of heroines and heroes, but they were both consistently diehard anti-marketeers. Of course, in 2001 that was all a long time ago and the world had changed. Straw had become in favour of British membership of the EU, but he was always a 'pragmatic European', not a 'true believer' like Blair. Straw accepted the EU as an important reality of modern life: significant economically for jobs in Britain, and useful politically as a means of maximising British influence, but he was no enthusiast. He had a bullish and exaggerated view of Britain's independent standing and influence in the world: for him, our permanent seat in the Security Council marked us out from other nations. Second, unlike Tony Blair, he was a deeply committed Westminster parliamentarian. His love of Parliament gave him an acute sensitivity to where he thought Parliament's sovereignty and status might be unduly under threat. Third, although Straw was an effective minister – diligent, affable, full of common sense, well liked by his civil servants, and unpretentious with a sharp eye for the absurdities of political and ministerial life – he was also a very 'political' politician. The title of his autobiography, *Last Man Standing*, advertises his self-regard as a great political survivor, which indeed he was: he had an acute sense of the way the political wind was blowing and tacked accordingly.

Since Straw's appointment in 2001, Peter Hain, his minister of Europe, had been the government's representative on the Convention. I doubt that initially Straw was heartbroken over this: he would have seen his job as concentrating on the big challenges of foreign policy, not attending what he would have dismissed as a talking shop in Brussels. Like senior officials in the Foreign Office, he underestimated Giscard's determination to come up with a definitive text that would set tight parameters for the intergovernmental treaty revision to follow. But Straw may have become less comfortable when he saw Hain working to a No. 10 agenda, a situation that became even more apparent when Hain left the Foreign Office and was appointed to the cabinet as Welsh secretary in October 2002, but continued to serve as the government representative until the Convention's conclusion the following summer. Straw's discomfort at his exclusion may have become all the greater when his opposite numbers in France and Germany, Dominique de Villepin and Joschka Fischer, appointed themselves as their national representatives to the Convention around the same time.

Straw's marginalisation on the 'future of Europe' ended when the Convention finished its work. Hain's involvement ceased. Until the summer of 2003, the public debate on Europe had almost exclusively focused on the euro. However, once Gordon Brown made clear that euro entry was at least on hold for the indefinite future, the anti-European media shifted its attentions to the proposed European constitution. Blair was distracted. That same July he delivered a barnstorming speech to the US Congress setting his vision of America and Europe working together to make the world a freer, better place. In Tokyo he was due to deliver another passionate commitment to Britain's eventual membership of the single currency, demonstrating that despite Brown's negative assessment, he had not given up the fight. News of the death of Dr Kelly reached him on the plane journey from Washington to Tokyo. The impact of the speech was totally lost in the horrors of the Kelly suicide. Blair's leadership entered its worst period of turbulence since he had been elected nine years before.

The famed New Labour communications machine was by then in meltdown: Alastair Campbell had been fighting an increasingly desperate battle with the BBC to force them to disown the broadcast of their *Today* reporter, Andrew Gilligan, which was the basis for wider media claims that Downing Street had 'sexed up' the intelligence dossiers justifying the Iraq invasion. On 27 June, Alastair, in an act of typical guts and bravado, had invited himself into the Channel 4 studio for an extraordinary interview with Jon Snow. The battle with the BBC had become all-consuming. Within three weeks it was to become an issue of who bore at least partial responsibility for Kelly's suicide. By the end of July, Alastair had announced that he was bringing forward his intended departure from No. 10 to the following month.

At the same time, pressures on Blair from within the PLP were mounting: the Iraq rebellion against a three-line whip had been the largest ever in Labour history. Discontent with Blair's leadership now focused on planned public service reforms (foundation hospitals and university tuition fees), which was in part fomented by close allies of Gordon Brown – or at least that was how No. 10 saw it. There were pressures from within the No. 10 court for Blair to soft pedal his reform policies and revamp his team of advisers. Blair turned once again to Mandelson to lead the efforts to rescue his leadership and premiership, starting with restoring some stability to his No. 10 operation, although not all elements of the Downing Street machine were easily reconciled to Mandelson's new role. The house still felt divided against itself. Mandelson, with the help of John Birt, Jeremy Heywood and Jonathan Powell, was preoccupied with a major reorganisation of the No. 10 office following Alastair's departure. Blair himself worked out a new political strategy. His immediate priority was to demonstrate he could win the battles in the Commons on public service reform; this was essential to his leadership credibility, even though at that stage it looked perfectly possible that he would face defeat. At the same time he had to manage the continuous media and political fallout from Lord Hutton's public inquiry into the circumstances of Kelly's death. If either went wrong, his premiership would in all likelihood be in mortal danger.

This context had major consequences for Blair's European strategy. The chances of the centre of government working out and implementing an effective strategy for the handling of Europe's draft constitutional treaty were not good. No systematic attempt was made to sell the outcome of the Convention as a good one for Britain. In the consequent vacuum, confusion took hold as to what the whole Convention exercise had been about. Peter Hain's unfortunate belittling phrase that the Convention was merely a 'tidying up exercise' was contrasted with the Convention's conceit that it had been engaged in drafting a constitution in the spirit of the American founding fathers. It could be one thing or the other but not both. In truth it was neither, but the essential points about the exercise's whole reforming purpose were completely lost. The EU was not about to become a state, and it was acknowledged in the treaty that it never would. In normal circumstances Blair might have made a major speech after his return from holiday in late August, setting out the government's position on the Convention text and framing the debate positively for the treaty negotiations to follow. But understandably this was not high enough in his priorities and did not happen.

Jack Straw and the Foreign Office stepped in to manage the next steps. Straw's first instinct was to set up a political 'us and them' battle with the rest of Europe that Britain could win. So Hain's warm words about the general acceptability of the Convention text were downplayed: instead, British objections to the draft text were highlighted. These were then presented publicly as 'red lines' that the British government would not cross. Many of the changes that the British proclaimed to be 'red lines' were essentially questions of drafting. For example, the European foreign minister was to be downgraded to the title of high representative. That did not imply anything of significance for the nature of the job and its powers: it was all symbolism. Similarly, the British demanded changes to the treaty draft on the clauses concerning the supremacy of European law and the coordination of economic policies. Again, little of substance would change as a result of this redrafting: its purpose was to soften the wording to be less explicit about the powers of the EU. An opt-out from the Charter of Fundamental Rights was demanded, but the legal significance of what it was that we were opting out from, never mind whether the opt-out had any practical legal effect, was unclear. And so on. I watched this exercise with dismay. In the short term it somewhat eased the political pressure on the government because Britain put forward a negotiating position that was patriotically presented as 'standing up for British interests' against the allegedly federalist and centralising instincts of our partners. Yet it painted a picture of what had been proposed that was a distortion of the truth and failed to engage in serious debate about what kind of institutional change was needed in Europe and why. Of course there were foolishnesses and conceits in the draft the Convention had presented: for example, the clauses on flags and anthems were gratuitous and absurd. However, the whole emphasis on 'red lines' and 'standing up for national interests' presented Europe as a threat: in anything but the short run, it fuelled the Eurosceptic frenzy.

A taste of what was to come was the *Sun* front page on 10 September 2003. It printed a photo of Blair in an undertaker's hat beneath the headline: 'Last rites: Blundertaker Blair is set to bury the nation.' It became clear that the Murdoch press, plus the *Mail* and the *Telegraph*, were going to mount a press campaign for a referendum on the new constitutional treaty. Infuriatingly, it was the word 'constitution' together with the emergence of a new Conservative leader, that put wind in their sails. With

Michael Howard's replacement of Iain Duncan Smith as Conservative leader, the anti-Europeans gained an effective spokesperson for the referendum cause. Straw believed that to limit the political damage Labour should match Howard's referendum commitment. In a roundabout way Straw raised the possibility with Blair at a meeting at Chequers in the autumn: he rambled round the course at some length and it was only after a while that it became clear where his tortuous line of reasoning was leading. Blair exploded.

> Jack, are you seriously proposing a referendum on a treaty of this nature, less important in substance than either the Single European Act or Maastricht, both of which had been ratified by Parliament? Do you really see yourself campaigning up and down the streets on the housing estates, to get our people out to vote for the creation of a double-hatted foreign minister, high representative or whatever it is you want the post was to be called?

This agitated but reasonably good-humoured torrent of dismissiveness spilled out from the Prime Minister's lips for a good 15 minutes. Yet Jack Straw was to get his way the following April. How did this remarkable about-turn happen?

In part it was the 'force majeure' of electoral politics. For most politicians, the imperative of winning the next general election trumps all else. It was argued that the promise of a referendum was the only way to avoid the treaty becoming a damaging election issue. Yet what was the evidence that a failed Conservative campaign that had seemed obsessed with Europe in 2001 would be more successful in 2005 when the issue of British membership of the euro was no longer 'live'? In 2005 the Conservatives would have more resonant tunes to play on immigration, crime and tax. In theory, though, if ratification were postponed until after the general election, the Conservative promise of a referendum might garner them some extra votes, even if it was implausible that the number would be decisive. But why could ratification not, as Blair preferred, be pushed through Parliament before the general election? In the Commons the government could be confident of a huge majority, even though the Liberal Democrats, who were supporters of the treaty, feebly promised to back a referendum. In the Lords, where the government did not have a majority, the situation was less clear. However, the Lib Dem peers would have been much divided on the merits of a referendum. Yet there would also have been a large group of cross-benchers and Conservative pro-

Europeans who would have opposed a referendum as well. The whips misleadingly advised Blair that ratification might fail in the Lords.

In my view, Blair's eventual decision to support a referendum was a tragic and classic example of Jim Bulpitt's dictum of *Primat der Innenpolitik* in the politics of Britain and Europe. As part of his strategy for political survival, Blair opened secret discussions with John Prescott and Gordon Brown about the possibility that he might retire as prime minister in the summer of 2004. Prescott and Brown attempted to recruit Mandelson to support this plan on the promise that he might be appointed European commissioner or return to the cabinet. In all the available accounts it is unclear how far Blair genuinely contemplated departure and what conditions of support he sought to attach to it. His personal morale was at a low ebb for the first half of 2004 and at its lowest in April when he finally gave in to Jack Straw's pressure to support a referendum.

Blair may have feared that Straw might form an alliance with Brown to constrain his room for negotiating manoeuvre in the run-up to the Dublin summit in June 2004, which was to settle the constitutional treaty. The Foreign Office had prepared a draft joint minute with this aim in mind, which was forwarded to the Treasury, but Brown, to his credit, hesitated and refused to play ball. Had this happened, the episode would have been the Labour equivalent of the 'Madrid memorandum' on joining the ERM which Howe, Hurd and Lawson sent to the Prime Minister on the eve of the summit and which was so central to the weakening of Margaret Thatcher's political position in 1989. Second, there was much gossip in No. 10 about Murdoch's role. Murdoch was greatly exercised by the constitutional treaty: in simple terms, he wanted a weaker Europe and a stronger America, with Britain firmly in the American camp, a legitimately arguable position but not one Blair himself endorsed. Murdoch supported Brown's stance on the euro but greatly admired Blair for the leadership which, in his view, he had shown on Iraq. It is entirely plausible that Blair reasoned that the Murdoch newspapers would stand behind him against any leadership coup by his Chancellor and support him in the next general election, as long as Blair backed a referendum on the constitutional treaty. This was exactly parallel to the position Murdoch had taken on the euro prior to 1997.

For one reason or another, the referendum pledge was made. In front of his staff, Blair put on a bravura performance: he had always wanted a referendum to resolve the European issue and, now that the euro was on hold, this was his great chance to do it! But he was so inwardly unconfident about it that he failed to discuss his decision with Mandelson, his closest confidant and adviser, before he made it. He then claimed, typically, that it was all due to a briefing by David Hill, Alastair Campbell's replacement, that he had never authorised, but it was now too late to squash. It was also apparent that he almost instantly began to regret his decision: it was the most painful moment in seven and half years of working for him.

Like many European policy decisions taken for purely domestic reasons, the referendum decision had profound European consequences. Blair's about-turn in practice scuppered the constitutional treaty, even before its detail was finalised. Blair had made a pledge to Chirac and Schroeder not to call a referendum: he broke it and, what's worse, he did so without telling them in advance. Chirac felt Blair had made him look foolish. So he too switched his position to support a referendum. And that French referendum was famously lost in May 2005, enabling Blair to escape his commitment to hold one in the UK. For Jack Straw and many in the Labour cabinet, this was almost the perfect outcome, with the promise of a referendum having 'shot the Tory fox' on Europe prior to the 2005 election and the French 'no' vote offering Britain its 'get out of jail free' card to avoid holding a referendum in Britain. Straw rushed to pronounce the constitutional treaty 'dead' and claimed it was perfectly possible for the EU 'to live with Nice' – that is, the institutional arrangements put in place by the Nice Treaty in 2001. In 2005 Blair allowed Straw his moment of temporary triumph, but wisely kept his own counsel. By then as prime minister he had gained a deep enough understanding of the EU to know perfectly well that the French 'no', although poignant with significance for Europe's future direction and legitimacy, was very unlikely to be the end of the road. Blair never danced on the grave of the constitutional treaty. Rather, once Blair had established, as he anticipated, that Angela Merkel, the narrow victor in the German elections that September, would not relent on the need for a new treaty, Jack Straw had by accident or design been removed from the Foreign Office before the time came round to revive it and the detailed Lisbon negotiations took place.

Some readers may find this focus on the Convention and its aftermath disproportionate. Wasn't it the case that the whole exercise achieved nothing, because the constitutional treaty that flowed from it failed to be ratified? Yet the great bulk of the Convention draft formed 90 per cent of the constitutional treaty text that then found its way into the Reform (renamed Lisbon) Treaty for which the German presidency agreed a precise negotiating mandate at Blair's final European Council in June 2007.

Essentially, the Germans did a 'scissors and paste' job on the old constitutional text: abandoning that treaty's attempt at elegance and coherence in its structure, they chopped up its clauses and inserted them as amendments to the relevant sections of the existing treaties. The really significant change was the dropping of the presentation of the new treaty as a *constitution* for Europe. This was of course more than symbolically significant: it was a blow to federalist pretensions. As a result, the newly elected President Sarkozy felt able to argue that France's previous commitment to a referendum was no longer valid. This time, Tony Blair and Gordon Brown followed Sarkozy's lead. In Britain, the Conservative Party and anti-European media reacted with furious indignation. But the truth is that their campaign for a referendum on Lisbon completely failed to catch fire. Once Gordon Brown had secured the premiership, he pushed ratification through Parliament with relative ease, as anyone with any political judgement should have anticipated. With Blair out of the way, and no prospect that the European question could any longer be used to play on internal divisions within Labour's ranks, the Eurosceptics proved a broken reed.

In some respects it was a tragedy that Blair never had the chance to make the public case for what many on the Continent complained was a British text. The constitutional principle on which the European treaties were now explicitly based was that the EU was a union of sovereign states who had conferred specific competences on the Union: anything not specifically conferred remained fully under national control. There was no automatic escalator to a federal Europe; every decision to pool sovereignty had to be taken by deliberate unanimous decision. The goal of 'ever closer union' was thus constrained. Furthermore, the power of the member states within the EU's decision-making structures had been greatly strengthened. National parliaments gained a new right to intervene on proposed legislation that in their view offended the principle of subsidiarity: a reform that might be built on in future changes.

The European Council, the body containing all heads of government, became a formal institution of the Union for the first time with its own full-time president. Blair rightly attached enormous importance to this: as long as this position held, it meant that the EU would never evolve into a classic federation. The elevation of the European Council's role thwarted the long-time federalist ambition to turn the Commission into the 'government' of Europe, accountable to both the directly elected European Parliament and the Council of Ministers, acting purely as a legislative senate of the member states. Yet the Lisbon Treaty was also a pro-European text in that it accepted the need for 'more Europe', where the case for sovereignty pooling could be made, as Blair believed in justice and home affairs, and (with safeguards) in foreign policy and defence. The treaty also improved the quality and effectiveness of European decision-making, by slimming down the size of the Commission, accepting the principle of majority voting in the Council as the norm (again with a limited number of 'unanimity' provisions retained) and introducing the new simplified 'double majority' system. Greater democratic legitimacy was secured by putting the elected heads of government clearly in the EU driving seat and on legislation, giving the Parliament for the first time equality of decision-making power with the Council. The preambular aims and values, spelt out for the EU in the Lisbon text, set as one of its objects a 'highly competitive social market economy', to which only the most ideological of neo-liberal free marketeers would object. And the Charter of Fundamental Rights (for all the misleading furore it caused with British business) simply codified the values and rights that already existed in EU law and practice.

Eurosceptics argued that the treaty gave the EU more the appurtenances of a state, whereas they wanted to reduce it to the mechanics of a free-trade area. They objected to 'more Brussels', when they wanted 'less', and argued that an opportunity for the repatriation of powers had been missed. On one point they were right. While the treaty made clear that Europe's exclusive competences were very limited (essentially to trade, competition and fishing for non-euro members), a major failing of the Convention was that it had not had time to review in detail the reach of EU policies and whether they remained appropriate for the modern age. Had Blair still been dominant, this would have been his logical follow-up to the agreement on the constitutional treaty. In building and making the British case for Europe, the political fall-out from the Iraq War turned what had started out as a chance for real reform into another depressing missed opportunity.

CHAPTER 10

Blocked on the Euro

The story of Blair's failure on the euro has frequently been told but rarely analysed. Instead of offering another blow-by-blow account of this well-known Blair–Brown difference of view, this chapter will concentrate on analysis. Why was it that Blair, the man who was bold or reckless enough, depending on one's perspective, to lead Britain to war in Iraq, could not achieve his settled determination to take Britain into the euro? Why in 2003 did Brown decide euro entry would be a mistake, and was he right?

Going for the Euro

As the 2001 general election approached, Blair felt his first-term record lacked real, lasting achievement. It did have transformatory reforms to its credit, on constitutional reform and the national minimum wage in particular, but what weighed with Blair was his failure, as he saw it, to leave a personal mark, apart from (and it is a substantial, historic 'apart from') the Good Friday Agreement in Northern Ireland. The second term, he decided, should be about 'building a legacy'. Two areas of ambition appealed: the euro and public service reform. He had no settled political strategy for achieving either as the 2001 campaign was to show.

Blair insisted that public service reform should be the centrepiece of Labour's manifesto launch, but he failed to offer adequate definition. Loose talk of bringing in the private sector sounded like an 'agenda for privatisation' to many Labour and trade union activists. Offering choice and opportunity to families who could not afford to opt out or go private might have been a better pitch, as would tackling the gross inequalities in state provision that defenders of uniform public services tend to ignore. But Blair was pitching to the aspirational centre ground to achieve a mandate for a radical shake-up: it strengthened him with voters, but weakened his position in the party. Brown quickly seized the opportunity to exploit this.

On the euro, the 2001 manifesto confined itself to a single defensive sentence: 'no membership of the single currency without the consent of the

British people in a referendum'. These 16 words contrasted with the euro's more forward-leaning treatment in 1997 and in the 2001 document, a 400-word mini-essay on the key national priority of agriculture and fishing! Blair's personally drafted preface was hardly more revealing. 'British ideas leading a reformed and enlarged Europe' was one of ten goals he set for 2020. This muted clarion call was then elaborated in the single prime-ministerial sentence: 'We will engage fully in Europe, help enlarge the European Union, and insist that the British people have the final say on *any* [my emphasis] proposal to join the euro.' Maybe this coyness reflected tactical prudence, when everyone knew the Conservatives under William Hague would base their campaign on 'ten days to save the pound'. Maybe it reflected fear of press hostility. For whatever reason, the language of the 2001 manifesto on the euro revealed a telling lack of confidence and consensus in the Labour election team, even though Blair had settled in his own mind that euro membership would be a central objective of his second term.

Part of Blair railed against his own feebleness. He chose to deliver at Edinburgh a bravura pro-European speech based on a splendid draft that David Marquand had provided. Blair also decided that he would brief the *Financial Times* on his true intentions. In the middle of the campaign, Anji Hunter summoned the *Financial Times*' political editor, Philip Stephens, to a hotel off the M4 where the prime minister conveyed his determination to take Britain into the euro if re-elected. However, the front page splash the following day caused such a furore in the Brown camp that Alastair Campbell dismissed the story as a rogue briefing, doubtless by some overenthusiastic pro-European adviser from No. 10.

With the election won, however, it soon became clear within Downing Street that Blair was serious about the euro. Peter Hyman, the strategic communications director, who in the Blair court counted very much as 'family', started to draft a referendum 'war book' on how the case for the euro could best be made. A little later, Jonathan Powell pulled together a group to think through the mechanics of a referendum campaign with Pat McFadden coordinating the plans. After his 2001 summer holiday, Blair worked on a pro-euro speech for the TUC Congress on 11 September. But before he got up to speak, the twin towers of the World Trade Centre in New York had collapsed; little though anyone realised it at the time, Al-Qaeda was to change the politics of the euro in profound ways.

The Impact of 9/11 and Iraq on the Politics of the Euro

Blair thrived in foreign crises. His great qualities – clarity of thinking, decisiveness, courage in the face of high risk and persuasiveness – all displayed themselves to great advantage. In the first term, he had handled a succession of foreign crises well – most notably Kosovo, but also the 1997 Iraq bombings, Bosnia, Sierra Leone and Macedonia. The serving chief of the defence staff, General Sir Charles Guthrie (now Lord Guthrie of Craigiebank), greatly admired Blair's leadership qualities, particularly in Sierra Leone, where Blair authorised a risky hostage rescue, which Guthrie had had to warn Blair could well go horribly wrong. Guthrie prophetically warned me just before his retirement in 2001 that his biggest fear for Blair was that his boldness would lead him to enter a war that turned into a political disaster.

For Blair, the 9/11 attacks changed world history. Blair believed that the West had a new enemy in Al-Qaeda that could not be deterred or defeated by conventional military means alone. Also, in the USA itself, 9/11 risked reinforcing dangerous trends towards unilateralism. Countering both these threats required, in his view, a new global alliance to defeat terror and persuade America they did not stand alone. Blair believed he could make a unique personal contribution in forging that alliance. His extraordinarily powerful speech to Labour's September 2001 Conference painted a picture of Britain at the centre of the world stage, as a moral force combating evil and fighting injustice, in the best traditions of progressive internationalism. He had no truck with the old imperialist condescension that freedom, democracy and human rights were not the universal aspiration of all mankind. He rejected the appeasing mentality of the establishment mindset during the Bosnia and Rwanda massacres of the 1990s, which was wary of intervention in faraway countries of which we know little. Blair combined the passion of a Gladstone in his rejection of the Bulgarian horrors of the 1870s with the commitment of a Bevin and a Gaitskell in the immediate post-1945 world to stand courageously alongside America in freedom's battle anew.

This was the authentic Tony Blair. But it was also clear that he loved it, behaving with new confidence like a man liberated from the dreary torments of everyday political life, not least having to negotiate with a truculent chancellor. The new foreign policy challenge also fitted his political aim of repositioning Labour as a party that could be trusted with the nation's defences. The unilateralism and pacifism that had contributed directly to Labour's catastrophic defeats in the 1980s he would consign to the dustbin of history. Moreover, Blair insisted he would 'never be a Harold Wilson'. On Afghanistan and Iraq, he was not prepared to follow Wilson's Vietnam example of supporting US policy with words, but not with British troops. The apotheosis of Blair's determination on this point was reached in March 2003, when the Americans suggested that, to ease Blair's domestic problems, British troops should not take part in the Iraq invasion but only join peacekeeping operations under UN authority once Saddam had been deposed. Such a move would have knocked the ground from under the protesters who argued that Britain was supporting an illegal invasion under international law. Blair turned down the suggestion point blank even though Mandelson urged him not to dismiss it.

In truth, the iron had entered his soul. No one could have been more convinced of the righteousness of his Iraq policy. On the day of the massive marches against the Iraq invasion, Blair made a courageous (indeed magnificent) speech at the Scottish Labour Conference in Glasgow, which, in the sheer moral force of its argument, won over many sceptics in the hall. Yet simultaneously Blair may more cynically have believed this was his 'Falklands moment': that a clear and famous military victory would transform his standing at home within the cabinet, party and country. In Downing Street those closest to Blair talked up the possibility of a 'Baghdad bounce': a surge in the opinion polls that would greatly strengthen Blair's personal authority. What might he use that authority for? The house gossip was to push through sweeping public service reforms, lead Britain into the euro and, if necessary, change his chancellor.

This was not to be. Any Baghdad bounce was shortlived. It was also clear that Iraq had decisively weakened Blair's hand on Europe *before* the invasion took place. In his September 2002 Labour Conference speech, Blair made the bold claim that Europe and the euro is 'our destiny'. The public breach with France and Germany over Iraq completely undermined his own argument. How could Europe and the euro be our destiny if on such a central question of war and peace we could not bury our differences with our major Continental partners and arrive at a common position? The harsh truth is that as the legitimate war on terror transmuted itself into the Bush administration's determination to settle scores with Saddam Hussein, where the link between Al-Qaeda terrorism and regime change in Iraq was at best tenuous, Blair of his own free will lashed himself to the mast of US policy, without making any serious attempt first to agree a common European position. The parameters of such a position were clear: support for UN weapons inspectors to return to Iraq; sufficient time for them to establish whether Saddam still possessed weapons of mass destruction; a conditional commitment to back US military action if Saddam failed to cooperate; an insistence that if the Bush administration wanted Europe's moral and practical support for eventual military intervention, the Americans had to put real pressure on the Israelis to negotiate a Middle East peace settlement. The Bush administration would doubtless have regarded any such position as time-wasting and wishy-washy. But with hindsight, it made supreme sense, and (who knows) the threat of having no European allies may have altered the course of US policy. Blair may legitimately have thought that US unilateralism posed a real danger to the world: if Britain had not stood with our US ally, who else would? But did it make sense to tie Britain to a US commitment to regime change and a military plan that, like the railway timetables of World War I, made war inevitable unless either Saddam caved in or his regime collapsed from within?

Of course the allure of partnership with Washington was strong. The drama of Blair's personal partnership with Bush was played out on a global stage. The prospect of trilateral summits with Chirac and Schroeder, followed by endless arguments with our EU partners over the details of texts in Brussels, was a lot less glamorous. But a joint mission to Washington of Blair, Chirac and Schroeder would have been a game-changing demonstration of Blair's wish for Europe to become a 'superpower, not a superstate'. It would have shown how Blair's 'transatlantic bridge' was capable of carrying two-way traffic. Clem Attlee's famous trip to Washington in 1951 to warn President Truman not to use atomic weapons in Korea comes to mind. 'Whose finger on the trigger?' became one of Labour's biggest rallying cries to get out the vote in the November general election that year.[1] Blair badly weakened his own case for Europe just as the moment of Britain's fateful euro decision was to be reached.

Politically Blair was weakened too. To carry Parliament and the public with him on Iraq, he used up most of that political capital that he had so painstakingly conserved in his first term, in Roy Jenkins' memorable phrase, 'like a man carrying a priceless vase of Chinese porcelain across a slippery floor'. Iraq deeply divided the constituency of progressive opinion that a euro referendum would have needed to rally. The pro-European Liberal Democrats were united in their hostility. The pro-European Ken Clarke was one of the few Conservatives to vote against the war. Within Labour ranks, Robin Cook, who had by then made himself the party's most prominent pro-European and strongest advocate of the euro, resigned from the cabinet over Iraq. As for the wider opinion-forming community on which Blair would have depended to get a fair hearing for the pro-European case in a referendum campaign, many in the world of centre-left commentators and current affairs broadcasters now harboured an undying hostility to Blair's alliance with Bush. The big tent and the progressive alliance lay in tatters. And of course there was no chance that Blair's allies in the right-wing media on Iraq would come to his rescue on the euro. The whole episode was for them proof of what they had felt all along: that Europe was a waste of time. From 2001 to 2003, the pro-European constituency was torn apart; it has been an enfeebled force ever since.

For the first time since 1994, Blair's Labour leadership looked fragile. As the moment approached when he would need to face down Brown on the euro, he needed Brown's support more than ever before in order to sustain his Iraq policy in a divided party. Brown's natural instincts were to support Blair's pro-Americanism: that in itself was not problematic, as they were both deeply in hock to an Atlanticist world view. Some voices in Brown's circle, and among his new anti-Blairite, anti-public service reform allies in the PLP, urged a more oppositional course. After weeks of invisibility, Brown broke his silence. The effect of his intervention showed his new power. Blair's premiership could hardly have survived an opportunistic refusal by Brown to back Blair's Iraq policy. Equally, Blair could no longer convince Brown that he would seriously look for a new chancellor if Brown refused to go along with his desire to join the euro. Their relationship had reached a stalemate where neither could defy the other.

Brown's Motives for Rejecting the Euro

This in itself does not explain why Brown turned against the euro, only why he got his way. In the summer of 2001, no one in No. 10, almost certainly including the Prime Minister, had much of an idea what the eventual attitude of the Chancellor would be. Two ministerial autobiographies convey something of the flavour. Jack Straw describes the conversation he had with Blair on his appointment as foreign secretary in 2001.[2] Blair quite rightly raised the euro, given Straw's past history as an anti-European:

> 'There's just one thing we do need to be clear if you are going to be Foreign Secretary,' Tony added. 'The euro. If Cabinet recommends we go in, I have to know you'll be onside.'

The future Foreign Secretary then adds a comment of his own, very much in character:

> the man's not daft I thought to myself. Close though we were, Tony knew that we came at the issues of the EU and the euro from different positions. I'd long believed the euro was fundamentally flawed. The five tests had been a relief.

He went on of Brown:

> It was obvious that since he'd not only set the exam paper but would be sitting it and marking it too, this was the one test in his life he'd be determined to fail. [There was] no risk that Gordon would ever bring proposals to cabinet to join. I nodded assent to Tony, shook his hands and went out very happy to begin another extraordinary chapter in my life.

This cynicism by Straw about Brown's likely behaviour was not, however, shared by Peter Hain who paid a call on the Chancellor that same summer on his appointment as minister of Europe:

> His clear dilemma – the thing that was haunting him – was that if the wrong decision was made at the wrong time, then Labour's hard won reputation for a strong economy and rising living standards could be destroyed by a shockwave, taking us back in the public's mind to 'Old Labour' economic incompetence. He then added as if trying to convince me: 'Look, I'm committed to the single currency. It's something I believe in and in the right economic circumstances it's going to be good for Britain, no question about that. But this decision can't just be made on the basis of setting a deadline and then going for it.' [...] he then went into a semi-academic analysis of the dilemmas involved.[3]

The Hain account sounds authentic as matters stood in 2001, but the uncertainty continued as the deadline for the assessment approached. The normally open channels of communication between officials in the European secretariat and the Treasury elicited little. The official Treasury line was that it all depended on the outcome of the five tests. The Treasury went to huge lengths, at great public expense, to underline the comprehensive nature, objectivity and unprecedented detail of its euro assessment, for which a wide range of high-quality academic studies were commissioned. Yet no one in No. 10 thought the outcome would be an outstanding examplar of evidence-based policy-making. Blair knew that Brown's judgement would mainly be informed by how he saw the politics of euro membership, which would include of course the euro's economic impact, but also the chances of winning a referendum and the political ramifications for the next election. Underlying all of this, how would the outcome help promote the Brown succession in the shortest possible order, and lay the ground for a successful Brown premiership? This was the nature of the frank conversation Blair wanted with Brown, but by all accounts Brown refused to engage. When the assessment findings were eventually presented in a series of secretive Downing Street seminars in early 2003, Blair found the intellectual pretensions and professed objectivity of the whole process an irritating charade.

In the run up to the assessment, Brown himself gave off mixed signals. Some convinced themselves that Brown's insistence on the rigour of the assessment was all part of a clever public relations strategy to make an eventual recommendation in favour of the euro convincing and persuasive. A procession of strong single currency supporters lobbied him: Brown assured them his mind was not closed, that he remained a strong supporter of the euro in principle, but that the economic conditions for Britain's entry had to be right. A casual reading of the press conveyed a somewhat different impression. Treasury-inspired briefing was uniformly negative. Every opportunity was taken to flatter UK economic performance as against the euro area's, often in a misleading way. Briefings stressed the high hurdles that the assessment had to pass: the evidence in favour had to be 'clear and unambiguous', a single phrase picked out for special commendation from the October 1997 statement. The tight circle of Brown's briefers left little doubt that the assessment would be 'rigorous', independent of prime-ministerial interference and, by implication, negative.

Yet the idea that there was not a balance of considerations to be taken into account was patently absurd. As any sensible euro supporter acknowledged (and Jeremy Heywood had put to the Prime Minister at a much earlier stage), there was bound to be some economic upheaval in switching from the UK's existing macroeconomic regime, based on a domestic inflation target to a monetary policy regime run for the whole euro area by the ECB. The real question was the size of the upheaval, and whether it could be managed, as against the long-term costs and benefits of membership of the single currency. Ed Balls, now firmly esconced as the Treasury's chief economic adviser, appeared to recognise that point. His Cairncross lecture in 2002 warned of the risks of politics driving major economic decisions, quoting the British membership of the ERM as an example.[4]

From External Anchor to Domestic Rules

There had been an intellectual shift in Brown's thinking. In the 1992 election, the commitment to the ERM and support for Britain's eventual membership of the single currency had been seen as the external guarantee or anchor of Labour's prudence and anti-inflationary rigour. Following the ERM debacle, Gordon Brown shifted emphasis to an internal anchor based on pre-commitment to domestic policy rules. Prior to 1997, Labour committed both to an inflation target and monetary policy decisions being made independently of ministers. (Immediately after the 1997 election, Brown made the Bank of England fully independent.) As for fiscal policy, Brown committed Labour to the 'golden rule' of public finance by which current spending would be balanced by current revenues over the economic cycle. Brown pledged that Labour would 'borrow only to invest' and to limit the stock of public debt to 40 per cent of GDP. A new fiscal code would bind a Labour Treasury. In 1997 the credibility of these rules was reinforced by a commitment to stick to the Conservatives' spending plans for Labour's first two years in office – effectively a two-year spending freeze – and not to raise the standard and top rates of income tax for the whole Parliament.

Labour's new commitments to inflation targeting and binding fiscal rules were never presented as an alternative to single currency membership. Indeed, they were essential preparations for it: an independent Central Bank, low and stable inflation, and a fiscal deficit below 3 per cent of GDP were prerequisites for meeting the Maastricht criteria. On the single currency, Brown's new macroeconomic rules looked an intellectually robust each-way bet. However, this new emphasis on *domestic* rules meant that Labour's pro-Europeanism moved from being central to its economic credibility to a much more general aspiration.

The Apparent Success of the New Domestic 'Macro' Framework

From 1997 to 2003 the performance of Brown's new domestic macro regime exceeded all expectations. The spike in inflation when Labour first came to power was curbed by immediate interest rate rises. The new monetary policy framework came through the Russian and Asian debt crises with flying colours. Senior officials in both the Treasury and Bank bought into the new regime with enthusiasm. For Britain this was indeed a golden economic policy experience by comparison with post-war 'boom and bust'. The typical pattern had been for rising wages and prices, a deteriorating balance of payments and sterling weakness to force the authorities to slam on the economic brakes, causing significant costs in lost output, higher unemployment and macroeconomic instability that held back business investment. Brown's rules appeared to have solved Britain's eternal problem of how to achieve expansion without inflation. Although senior figures in the Treasury baulked at the surrender of power over interest rates to their Threadneedle Street rival, they treated the central questions of macroeconomics as though they were essentially solved. They switched their focus to the supply-side challenges, seizing the opportunity of buoyant tax receipts and a powerful chancellor to extend their reforming reach across Whitehall. For each Budget and Autumn Statement, Treasury officials beavered away at fresh initiatives, confident they could make an impact in raising Britain's long-term growth potential.

As time went on, the Bank, its status boosted by its newly granted monetary policy independence, indulged in an orgy of self-congratulation as it forecast the UK economy could look forward to its 'nice' decade of 'non-inflationary consistent expansion'. Mervyn King summed up the new consensus in his 2003 Leicester speech:

> The macroeceonomic framework in this country is sound and proven. And the real benefit from Britain's new-found position of macro-economic stability is that it provides an opportunity to improve our supply side performance [...] such improvements are in the long run both more important and more glamorous than the rather dull and repetitive role of the Bank of England in trying to maintain macro-economic stability.

In this self-confident atmosphere, there was no institutional pressure from the domestic economic policy-making establishment to join the single currency. From the 1950s, the Bank and Treasury as institutions had always feared that they would end up clear losers as power and legitimacy were transferred to Brussels and Frankfurt. Some accepted its inevitability, if 'needs must'. Robin Leigh-Pemberton as Bank governor had been notably sympathetic to the single currency project, as his stance on the Delors Committee had shown. His successors, Eddie George and Mervyn King, now saw no need to follow in his footsteps. Similarly at the Treasury, Nigel Wicks had played a key role in shaping EMU in the 1990s, but on his retirement as second permanent secretary in June 2000 there was no voice in the Treasury with his experience, weight or sympathy on matters

European. The views on the euro of Brown's appointments as permanent secretaries – Andrew Turnbull, Gus O'Donnell and Nick McPherson – ranged from the neutral to the sceptical. There seemed no reason impelling the policy establishment to contemplate a radical transfer of their own power. Instead, the success of the new domestic framework armed the euro's sceptics with a powerful new line of argument: why risk joining a European single currency when Britain's economy was performing so strongly? It was no longer the case that Britain needed an external 'anchor of stability' to correct abject domestic policy failures, in response to which British backers of the ERM and single currency had originally framed their arguments. Why should Britain chance its arm on a project that might in reality be a cause of instability in the economy, not the stability Britain had once found so elusive? Gordon Brown's chancellorship raised the self-confidence of Britain's economic policy establishment in the Bank and Treasury to levels they had only briefly known in the post-war period, in the first half of the 1960s under Maudling and in the second half of the 1980s under Lawson. But then, as before, hubris led to nemesis and it was all to go badly wrong.

The key intellectual influence in shaping Labour's new macroeconomic framework had been Ed Balls, the outstanding *Financial Times* economics journalist who had been appointed Gordon Brown's economic adviser in 1993. Before he was approached to work as a Brown adviser, Balls had published a Fabian pamphlet in 1992 that was sceptical of the single currency. The pamphlet had a dramatic title: *Euro-Monetarism: Why Britain Was Ensnared and How It Should Escape*. However, its actual content was more measured:

> Monetary union, *in the manner and timetable envisaged in the treaty*, is an economically and politically misconceived project [...] The goal of a single currency is *not inherently misconceived* [...] The risk is that EMU, *any time soon*, would risk destroying rather than cementing European political ties. (My emphases in italics)

The context for Balls' pamphlet was the ERM debacle. As an avowed pro-European, Balls made clear he did not have an overriding sovereignty objection to sacrificing the pound. Rather his concern was that, in the absence of sufficient convergence between participating countries, without adequate labour market flexibility and without a centralised budget stabiliser, the monetary union project was badly flawed. By 2003, the UK economy was certainly more convergent than it had been in 1997, and a lot,

lot further than it had been in 1992, though there was still room for legitimate debate on whether it was convergent enough. But the flaws in the wider euro project remained unaddressed.

There was, however, a flaw, or at least a tension, in Balls' logic too. A clear implication of his argument was that Britain should only contemplate single currency membership when its economy was broadly convergent. On the other hand, if the project was in principle desirable but in practice flawed, the only credible way that a Labour government could correct these flaws in design was by becoming a member as soon as was practical. In 2003 the politics of reforming the euro looked ripe for British membership and influence. The French and German governments had just opted to toss aside the rules of the Stability and Growth Pact, creating an opening for Britain, had we joined, to press for radical reforms in the EMU design. At the same time the Lisbon agenda of economic reform needed the new impetus that British euro membership could have given it.

The Politics of the Euro Decision

The lukewarmness of the economic policy establishment reinforced Gordon Brown's innate caution. By July 2002, Brown had become the longest serving (and seemingly then, most successful) chancellor of the Exchequer in Britain's post-war history. This was the foundation of his personal political standing. Prior to Iraq, he was widely seen alongside Blair as Labour's most powerful electoral asset. Post Iraq, many felt he no longer needed to share the accolade with a weakened prime minister. Brown felt he was on the threshold of No. 10. According to Mandelson, when Brown in May 1994 had painfully decided not to enter the contest to be John Smith's successor, his clear understanding of the so-called 'Granita pact' was that Blair had promised to serve no more than ten years as Labour leader. In the first months of 2003 when the conclusions of his euro assessment were presented to Blair, Brown's assumed handover date was less than 18 months away.

The superficial 'politics' of this conjuncture might have suggested that Brown should offer Blair firm support on the euro in return for a clear commitment that Blair would retire as prime minister after a successful euro referendum. But that raised a number of crucial 'what ifs'. What if a referendum were to go wrong from the government's perspective and the British people voted 'no'? That, after all, was what the crude numbers from the polling suggested. Even if one thought credible the careful analyses of public opinion that Britain in Europe had undertaken indicating that a referendum was nevertheless potentially winnable, there could be no guarantee. Blair was always convinced that if the referendum could be turned into a basic ‘yes’ or ‘no’ choice, the ‘yes’ side would win. However, in any euro campaign, there would be powerful voices arguing that Britain could perfectly easily stay in the EU, but out of the euro. Many mainstream Conservatives would happily place themselves on that comfortable ground. So also did the former Labour foreign secretary and SDP leader, David Owen, a public figure whose independence and standing with the public Blair and Brown still feared. A lost referendum would change the political weather in unforeseen ways. It would not be a happy beginning to a Brown premiership.

But what if one assumed, as was more likely, that a firm Brown/Blair ‘yes’ recommendation would carry the day. It would be backed by most credible business leaders, the Liberal Democrats and the Conservative former ‘big beasts’ who still carried much public respect. Blair would retire from the premiership with his glorious legacy. But how solid and secure would be the Brown inheritance? There was always a risk that a narrow ‘yes’ vote would not settle the political argument: the Conservative opposition might make the case that every economic problem the British economy encountered thenceforth was a direct result of joining the euro.

It is now largely forgotten that the thrust of the euro assessment was extremely positive about the long-term benefits of membership. To quote from the assessment itself:

> EMU membership could significantly raise UK output and lead to a lasting increase in jobs in the long term [. . .] the UK could enjoy a significant boost to trade with the euro area by up to 50 per cent over 30 years [. . .] and UK national income could rise by between 5 and 9 per cent [. . .] a boost to potential output of around a quarter percentage point a year, sustained over a 30 year period.[5]

To put this in perspective, the growth stimulus to the UK provided by deeper economic integration as a result of adopting the euro was estimated over the next three decades to offset the additional public spending costs of an ageing population in terms of pressure on pensions, the NHS and social care, as well as allow for a substantial increase in infrastructure spending. The long-term benefits of euro membership in enabling Britain to meet the challenges of demography and globalisation were deemed substantial. It could be a historic error to throw them away for short-term tactical reasons.

However, in the political mind the short term always looms larger. In the economic circumstances of 2003, a decision to join the euro involved UK acceptance of a somewhat looser monetary policy and a somewhat tighter fiscal policy. Since the launch of the euro, Bank of England interest rates had been consistently higher than those set by the ECB. By 2003 the nominal interest rate differential had narrowed to a much smaller 1.25 percentage points, whereas it had been as high as 4 per cent in 1999. It was still likely that, once membership was certain, the interest rates prevailing in the UK would fall by 1 per cent or so.[6] The likely result of this monetary easing would be threefold. First, there would be a stimulus to the housing market. Second, there would be a boost to domestic consumption as falling mortgage rates increased disposable incomes, only partially offset by falling interest-rate income for savers. Third, a modest depreciation of sterling to a more realistic 'right' rate for entry was likely to stimulate exports but also push up the cost of imports and the domestic price level. Some of these effects would be politically beneficial – more manufacturing jobs and lower mortgage costs. This monetary stimulus would, however, ratchet up inflationary pressure in an economy in 2003 operating at or near capacity. Of course it was questionable whether any negative effects would be much noticed by the time of a general election in 2005.

A bigger worry for Brown, however, was that monetary loosening would sooner or later need to be offset by fiscal tightening. The markets would almost certainly expect this. The Commission might also recommend it in full public gaze to bring the UK into line with the rules of the Growth and Stability Pact (though France and Germany had just decided to set them aside). Various figures were bandied about as to the scale of the fiscal tightening that would be necessary. In a March 2002 Fabian pamphlet, Janet Bush and Larry Elliot, opponents of euro entry, highlighted this uncertainty:

> Nor does it endear the British electorate to the Euro for Gordon Brown to be told in January 2002 that if we joined he would have to cut public spending by anything between £10bn (the Treasury's interpretation of the Commission's ruling) or £22bn (the estimate published by NIESR) to come into line with the Eurozone's fiscal rules.

To put this in perspective, the numbers in contention here were of the order of 1–2 per cent of GDP, a quarter or a fifth of the scale of the fiscal consolidation that George Osborne announced in October 2010. Any tax rise was, however, seen as politically toxic. Brown had already taken the risky step of raising national insurance contributions in his 2002 budget, as a tax increase to pay for increased 'investment' in the NHS. A tax increase to pay for joining the euro did not sound the most attractive political proposition in the run-up to a general election!

Nor was it appealing for Brown to contemplate adjustments to his ambitious spending plans with the next spending review pencilled in for completion in the summer of 2004. In the 2001 election, Brown had established the political dividing line as 'Tory cuts versus Labour investment'. It was on this basis that he intended to fight the 2005 election. At the very moment he was gearing up for this campaign, he did not want to embark on either slowing the rate of increase in public spending or raising taxes as a result of euro membership. This mattered in the party too. The personal political damage from any sense that he had mismanaged Britain's entry to the euro could be deeply damaging.

A political way could probably have been found through these dilemmas. Immediate tax rises could simply have been avoided. The 2004 Red Book could have projected increased fiscal revenues or tighter spending plans for the three years ahead that would not have been implemented until after the 2005 election. Commission warnings that the Stability and Growth Pact rules were in danger of being breached could have been kicked into the long grass. For all that, why take the political risks of joining the euro when there was no compelling impulsion to do so?

By the end of 2002, it was clear to me that the euro was not going to happen under Tony Blair's premiership. It was a very difficult period in which one of the central ambitions of Blairism bit the dust. Of course one had to recognise that Brown's decision was justifiable in its own partial terms. Convergence was not fully complete. Changing the macroeconomic policy regime would have involved potentially tricky adjustments. While Brown's decision was devastating in terms of missing the historic opportunity to secure Britain's long-term position at the heart of the EU, it was an understandable piece of risk aversion from the perspective of Labour's re-election chances.

Mandelson fought a strong rearguard action to soften the impact of Brown's decision on Blair's personal reputation, but it was impossible to reverse the basic decision. Blair himself vetoed Brown's wish to announce the euro decision as part of his March budget. For Blair this would have been a humiliation. Instead the assessment was distributed round the cabinet and discussed with each minister in a series of bilaterals: that exercise demonstrated to Brown the degree of enthusiasm for euro membership that many colleagues shared. The assessment itself was rewritten under Jeremy Heywood's supervision to bring out more strongly the potential positive benefits of single currency membership, for which there was plenty of evidence in the detailed research that the Treasury had undertaken. Blair himself held out the possibility of reopening the assessment the following year, with much talk of how action could be taken quickly to overcome the obstacles to convergence, such as much-needed reforms to the UK housing market. Legislation to allow a euro referendum would, it was announced, proceed that parliamentary session. A 'roadshow' in which Brown and Blair together would sell the benefits of the euro was promised, though even at the time few believed it would actually happen. As always, the optimist in Blair tried to convince others that the battle was not lost. Indeed he may have convinced himself of this until the tragedy of David Kelly's suicide made him rethink the politics of the possible. The ever-loyal Peter Hyman pleaded with me to show faith and go out spreading a message of hope to the media, ambassadors and our EU partners. One tried one's best, but with little conviction and to little avail: Brown had administered a hammer blow to Blair's European credibility.

Could Blair Have Done the Euro without Brown?

One of the great historical questions about the Blair governments will be why, if Blair was serious about the euro (and indeed public service reform) and thought Brown was such an obstacle in his path, he did not remove him as chancellor. After all, previous prime ministers had not hesitated to make a sacrifice of their chancellors. When Peter Thorneycroft stood in the way of Macmillan's desire to reflate the economy in 1958, Macmillan effectively forced his resignation, which he famously dismissed as a 'little local difficulty'. Similarly when Nigel Lawson put huge pressure on Margaret Thatcher to join the ERM, she created the conditions in which he resigned in 1989. Macmillan was ruthless in sacking Selwyn Lloyd when he outlived his usefulness in 1962; Wilson demoted Callaghan to the Home Office in the wake of the 1967 devaluation; and John Major sacked Norman Lamont in 1993 when he simply became too unpopular, making him pay the political price for the ERM debacle.

Why did Blair never move against Brown? The answer lies mainly in the complex personal relationship between the two men and Blair's own acceptance of implicit limits to his quasi-presidential powers. This question is as relevant to their disputes about public service reform as to the euro. The difference between the two issues is that on public services, Labour's internal politics posed a real constraint on Blair's freedom of manoeuvre, whereas on the euro they did not. Within the PLP the old Common Market Safeguards group of anti-Europeans was reduced to a tiny rump. There still remained a 'soft left' constituency of generally pro-European, but on the euro genuinely more sceptical, Keynesians, also well represented in the public-sector trade unions. While previously this group had been concerned that adherence to the Maastricht criteria would impose unacceptably tough fiscal discipline, the views of its leading exponents, such as the Bristol MP, Roger Berry, were softening.

Blair's first cabinet, while not brimming with single currency enthusiasts, harboured few out and out opponents. Blair was later to bring into the cabinet a new generation of firm pro-Europeans, such as Stephen Byers, Charles Clarke, Patricia Hewitt, Tessa Jowell and Peter Mandelson (twice temporarily). Not all the cabinet members who became labelled as Blairites were keen supporters of the euro: David Blunkett, Alan Milburn and John Reid fell in that category, but they were not going to resign over the issue. Only a handful of the cabinet were thought of as strongly committed personal supporters of Gordon Brown, such as, at various stages, Nick Brown, Alistair Darling and Andrew Smith. Why then did Blair allow Brown's veto to prevail?

For all his increasing frustrations with Brown, Blair could not envisage the possibility of any other relationship at the centre of power that would give his government the necessary dynamism and strength to meet the challenges of office. In a series of intimate dinners before 1997, Roy Jenkins had warned Blair about his over-dependence on Brown. Jenkins, as a senior figure in the Wilson cabinets, as well as a historian and biographer, had an acute understanding of the dynamics of the power relationships at the top of governments. Wilson had retreated into weakness and isolation as prime minister and Labour leader, essentially because he could not build sufficient mutual trust with his most senior colleagues: this had had a devastating impact on his effectiveness as a political leader. Jenkins contrasted Wilson's weakness with Attlee, where he also had a unique insight because his father, Arthur Jenkins, had been one of Attlee's closest confidants and parliamentary private secretary. Attlee had survived as prime minister, despite all his government's many tribulations, only because among Labour's 'Big Five' (the other three being Stafford Cripps, Hugh Dalton and Herbert Morrison), Ernie Bevin was always prepared to give unstinting support to Attlee's leadership, even when Attlee had been woefully ineffective, which from time to time he was. The others at various times were part of conspiracies to remove him.

Jenkins warned Blair that he could not rely on Brown as Attlee had relied on Bevin. In the last analysis, Brown wanted his job. Jenkins' advice to Blair was that he should seek to construct other alliances at the top on which he could at all times depend: John Prescott was the obvious ally to cultivate. Blair followed Jenkins' advice and worked hard to strengthen his relationship with his deputy: Prescott in return offered Blair great loyalty, which was crucial in sustaining Blair's leadership. Prescott had great strengths of character and authentic appeal which outweighed his flaws. While he lacked the intellectual self-confidence to stand up to Brown's force of argument, he had a sharp political eye for Brown's manoeuvres and an acute ear for the drift of opinion within the party.

The other potential big player was Robin Cook. Cook was viewed with general suspicion in Blair–Brown circles. Cook's relationship with Brown was much more complex and difficult than Blair's, with an intense personal suspicion and rivalry, lost in the mists of 1970s Scottish Labour politics (though shortly before Cook's untimely death in 2006 they had an apparent reconciliation). On the single currency, prior to 1997 Cook was thought to harbour classic 'left' objections to the supposed 'monetarist' and deflationary implications of the concept, which Blair and Brown most definitely did not share. Brown was determined to keep Cook out of any economic role.

Cook remained an outlier on the single currency for a little while after Labour came into government. On my first substantive encounter with him as foreign secretary, in an hour-long private conversation soon after the 1997 election in the magnificence of the foreign secretary's office overlooking St James' Park, Cook argued that he did not see how Labour could support a single currency project, in the design of which the European Central Bank had been given such a narrow counterinflationary remit. I responded that if that genuinely was his view, he could never support membership because essentially he was arguing for prior treaty change, which would be quite impossible for Britain to negotiate. Cook, however, countered that the French Socialists, who had just won the national assembly elections in June 1997, took the same view as he did. He expected the Jospin government to be pressing for a postponement of the single currency start date. I questioned this. Historically the whole strategy of Mitterrandism, when faced with tough economic choices, had been to commit to Europe and accept 'half a loaf' as better than none: as long as France was seen as an equal partner with Germany in shaping the future of Europe, they would find a way of persuading themselves that they could seek to reform the single currency from within. This is indeed what happened.

Within months, however, Cook became a strongly pro-European foreign secretary, by far the best of Blair's premiership. For him, Europe was a great discovery: he suddenly realised that he fundamentally shared the values of many of his closest EU counterparts like Hubert Védrine and Joschka Fischer, the French and German foreign ministers. He soon came to accept a commitment to the success of the euro as part of the package of being a committed pro-European and by the middle of the first term was keen to play a bigger role in advocating the euro. He became a true Mitterrandist himself.

Despite this, Blair continued to keep Cook at a distance. He then inexplicably removed him from the Foreign Office to become leader of the House of Commons in 2001. This was, at first sight, a very odd decision given Blair's intention to take Britain into the euro in his second term. If the euro was indeed Blair's overriding objective, a clever move might have been to swap jobs between Brown and Cook, making Cook his chancellor and Brown his foreign secretary. Cook may well have been angling for this and some voices in Downing Street argued for it. Brown would then have been confronted with a choice of petulant resignation or of serving as foreign secretary bound in to Blair's euro policy, with his replacement as chancellor making a more sympathetic judgement of the five tests.

For Blair, such a move would obviously have carried high political risks. If Brown had refused the foreign secretaryship and resigned, the potential for a damaging party split would have opened up: but the Labour Party does not like disloyalty and it seems unlikely that it would have been rewarded. If Brown had wanted to maintain his position as 'crown prince', the best bet would have been to stay in the cabinet, perform well as foreign secretary and see whether his successor as chancellor could live up to Brown's 'golden' record. Jim Callaghan had after all won the premiership from the position of foreign secretary, having been, in his case, a 'failed' chancellor.

Blair had no personal stomach for such a bold gambit. As Peter Mandelson put it at the time: 'he just couldn't face it. Can you ever imagine Tony in a room on his own with Gordon, having the nerve to tell him he was moving him on?' For all the increasing tensions in their relationship,

Blair still respected Brown's economic judgement, and who else could he have appointed to the Exchequer? Blair discounted Cook because he did not see him as 'New Labour' in his attitudes. Jack Straw could be an adequate foreign secretary, who would essentially do Blair's bidding, but not a chancellor. Alan Milburn was beginning to perform strongly as health secretary but in 2001 would have been a risk. At a later stage Charles Clarke was intellectually and politically up to the job, but he only gained sufficient prominence in the second term at a time when the Blair hegemony was already under siege: in 2006 he was being groomed for the Foreign Office when he ended up being forced out of the home secretaryship in a typical 'non-scandal' about the failure to deport foreign prisoners serving sentences in British jails.

The underlying assumption of Blair's single currency policy was that, in the end, Brown would offer strong support. Blair assumed that in a stand-off between them, he could eventually get his way. After all, in the leadership campaign in 1994, it was Brown who had blinked. He did not anticipate how the balance of power in their relationship would shift against him because of Iraq. In Blair's judgement, Brown's support was a *sine qua non*. This was not simply because Brown was then a highly credible chancellor whose judgement would carry weight with the public. For all the horrible and growing tensions in their relationship, there was also a fundamental dependency: he saw no other way New Labour could govern. Nothing else can explain the great conundrum of Blair's premiership that his autobiography, *A Journey*, fails to unravel: if Gordon Brown was such a dreadful person unfit to be prime minister, how was it that our hero, Tony Blair, allowed a situation to occur in which that eventuality became inevitable?

CHAPTER 11

A Glass Half Empty

There is a clear consensus on New Labour's European record: it was considerably more successful at promoting Britain in Brussels than Europe in Britain. Some go further. The failure to join the euro may be seen as either a disappointment or a stroke of good luck, but the Blair–Brown record of European engagement showed that Britain could sustain its position as a leading player in the EU without being a euro member.

Eurosceptics argue that this semblance of British influence was bought at too high a price in terms of accommodation to a Brussels 'integrationist' agenda. But the counterfactual to those who assert they would have vetoed the new treaties Labour ratified (Amsterdam, Nice and Lisbon) is that an institutional crisis of a far deeper kind would have gripped the EU as it sought to cope with the pressures of enlargement and interdependence, by means of rules devised for another age. The eventual outcome of such a crisis might well have been the emergence of an EU inner core from which Britain either was excluded or excluded itself. How one would view such an eventuality depends on whether one thinks that membership of an effectively functioning EU, in which Britain is a leading player, is in the national interest, and whether one believes a proud nation like Britain can happily get what it wants out of the EU from a second-rank status in an outer tier.

An equally pertinent question is whether New Labour's success in increasing British clout in Brussels was sustainable in the medium to longer term, given Britain's continued semi-detachment from the idea of Europe, a semi-detachment not just of wider public opinion, but shared by its political and opinion-forming class. Indeed, the tragic paradox of New Labour is that the tactical arguments it used at home to defend its European policy may well have strengthened the myths that underlie British semi-detachment. Just think of the promotion of economic reform based on the alleged (and now seemingly dubious) superiority of Britain's economic record under Blair and Brown by comparison with our EU partners. Or the arguments for Blair's progressive internationalism, based (for the most part, when it was effective) on united EU positions, but publicly celebrated as a demonstration of continuing pride in British leadership in the world and the US special relationship. Or the knee-jerk reaction when any EU issue created awkward headlines that Britain should demonstrate the value of its EU membership by vigorously defending 'UK national interests' *against* our partners.

The Labour government never summoned up the courage to invite the British people to make a clear and decisive pro-European choice. That was not for lack of intent on Blair's part. At times he wobbled and wavered, but by the second term he was absolutely set on making membership of the euro a central plank of his legacy. Alongside that, he hoped to present, as the outcome of the Convention, a coherent vision for Europe's future which was much more than a free-trade area, but never going to become a United States of Europe: a unique constitutional 'hybrid' of pragmatic sovereignty pooling in which distinct national identities flourished and the member states continued to play the central leading role.

The current conventional wisdom is that Brown did the right thing in blocking Blair's euro ambitions. But it is worth pausing to question that received wisdom. Is it not possible that, in years to come, scholars will look back on the events of 2003–4 and conclude that this was another episode in the long catalogue of missed opportunities for Britain and Europe?

The Positive Case for New Labour's Record

New Labour was the first government that made Britain count in Brussels for a sustained 13-year period, with only a short hiatus around the Iraq invasion. There had been similar successes before, but they were episodic and brief: Heath's 1973 honeymoon; Thatcher's highpoint of influence from the Single European Act in 1985 to her 1988 Bruges speech; and the 'heart of Europe' first phase of the Major premiership from November 1990 to the June 1992 Danish referendum 'no'. By contrast, Labour's 'constructive engagement' over 13 years bore fruit in British influence over a whole range of issues:

- consistently backing enlargement;
- signing up for three successful EU treaty revisions at Amsterdam (1998), Nice (2001) and Lisbon (2007), widely regarded as 'British texts';
- shaping the Lisbon strategy of economic reform;
- deepening the single market with the opening up of telecoms, energy and wholesale financial markets, at the time regarded as crucial gains for

the UK (but marking the last hurrah of the Delors/Cockfield pro-liberalisation consensus);
- initiating European security and defence policy (the ESDP), where the 1998 St Malo Declaration paved the way for Europe to act together militarily where the USA did not wish to take part;
- strengthening Europe's capacities to combat cross-border crime and illegal migration, the so-called Justice and Home Affairs (JHA) agenda, while legally affirming the UK's rights to operate its own border controls;
- putting the EU at the forefront of global efforts to tackle climate change and meet the Millennium goals for international development;
- achieving a gradualist, but nonetheless substantial, reform of the common agricultural policy (CAP), with capped and reducing 'direct payments' to farmers largely replacing (over-)production subsidies, with a switch in spend to rural development;
- leading under Brown the EU's, and, more remarkably, the eurozone's response to the immediate aftermath of the global financial crisis in September 2008.

In this period, the EU changed profoundly: on the one hand, its legitimacy declined with the rise of populist anti-European parties across the Continent; on the other, there occurred major widening and deepening of European integration and rapid EU institutional development. The big internal changes were underway before Blair took office as a result of the political momentum behind the single currency and eastern enlargement. Blair never sought to block progress on the first and was a consistent 'speeder-up' of the second, but he and Brown deserve credit for trying to shape Europe's responses in terms of the broader structural context of globalisation and the twin challenges to the European social model of competitiveness and demography.

New Labour were active drivers of the EU's increased 'reach'. In response to new fears about the rise of xenophobia, the EU extended its competences in the fields of equalities and human rights. Given worrying developments in some more fragile EU democracies, this may prove highly significant. The economic reform agenda 'Europeanised' – but did not attempt to harmonise – issues as diverse as active labour market policies, social inclusion strategies, child and pensioner poverty, pension reform, education and training, research and innovation, information technology diffusion, entrepreneurship and small business growth. Concerns about climate change brought energy security and carbon reduction to the top of the EU agenda, in contrast to the 1970s oil crises when energy had been largely kept off it. The growing porousness of national borders led to the European arrest warrant, common asylum rules, the strengthening of Europol and a whole range of JHA activity. There were the first tentative steps towards building a capacity for independent European military and humanitarian intervention – a turning point in the history of the Atlantic alliance. These developments all reflected Blair's approach to the EU. He had no instinctive objection to 'more Europe'. His attitude was 'if it works, let's do it': Europe would justify itself by results.

When David Cameron succeeded to the premiership in 2010, the EU had become a far different and more complex polity than when he first joined government as a special adviser in 1992. Institutionally, the following changes were highly significant:

- In the first month of Blair's premiership, the office of EU high representative was established in the person of Javier Solana; this has now grown into a 'double-hatted' role of as yet unfulfilled potential, where the high representative chairs the Foreign Ministers' Council, serves as a vice president of the Commission, and heads a new Community institution, the External Action Service – the EU's fledgling diplomatic corps.
- The European Council has become an official institution in its own right with a permanent president, with his own staff and coordinating role. Herman Van Rompuy, its first president, increased the frequency of European Council summits, building its role as the EU's main governing institution and streamlining its operation.
- Co-decision between the European Parliament and Council has become the rule: as a result, there is now much less scope for a single member state to obstruct a compromise that a majority in the Council and European Parliament favours.

The Academic Judgement

Yet the overall judgement on the Blair record must remain qualified. Academic specialists in European policy have drawn attention to its patchiness. Bulmer characterises Labour's European policy as one of 'utilitarian supranationalism'.[1] Essentially Labour embraced European policy solutions only as long as domestic Eurosceptic pressures could be kept firmly under wraps. James and Oppermann see an 'inconsistent record of engagement and leadership'[2] on three of the biggest issues on the Blair agenda:

- The European defence initiative is seen as the clearest legacy of 'leadership', ending decades of British objection to the EU taking on a military role in potential competition with NATO.
- Blair's legacy on the euro was essentially one of 'deferral', eventually reinforcing the perception that Britain would remain a permanent 'out'.
- On treaty change, there was 'obfuscation'; Britain signed up, but only because our partners watered down their ambitions to accommodate UK 'red lines'. Few positive arguments for treaty reform were made; the government preferred to minimise what change meant, as in Peter Hain's infamous description of the Convention's draft constitutional treaty as no more than 'a tidying up exercise'.

As one British Europeanist, Julie Smith, put it: 'however deeply committed the Prime Minister and his colleagues were to the European Union, they were ultimately more committed to ensuring that the Labour party remained in power nationally'.[3] Welcome to the world of politics!

Blair's View of his Legacy

Tony Blair's own account in *A Journey* makes pretty clear that he does not think much of his own European legacy. Of course that is never explicitly said, but it is the only conclusion that can be drawn from the fact that he devotes a mere 12 pages of his 700-page memoir to Europe. Blair's assessment is tagged on to an account of the row over the EU budget in Blair's second presidency of the EU in the second half of 2005, after his third election victory and more than eight years after he had first come to power.[4] The 2005 budget deal is now heavily criticised by the Conservatives as 'surrendering' a hefty chunk of Britain's budget rebate, but Blair rightly defends his settlement as a wise act of statesmanship: sticking to the existing rebate formula would have led to an indefensible outcome where, without reform, the Poles (and other new members), with a standard of living less than a third of the UK's, would have ended up as net contributors to the British rebate. Britain, as a leading advocate of enlargement, had to pay its proportionate share of the costs, particularly as France and Italy were set to become net contributors on a similar scale to the UK.

Blair's compromise predictably provoked a fierce row with Brown. It was no surprise that any chancellor of the Exchequer would resist an extra budgetary burden but, as putative 'prime minister-elect', Brown also had political reasons to be seen to be 'standing up for British interests'.[5] It was the one time in his premiership when Blair courageously stood up to Brown on Europe, which perhaps explains why he chose in his memoir to make it the peg for the principal discussion of his European policy – which of course is, in its own way, an unintended revelation of its own! When it comes to the euro, Blair skips over his record in a few short paragraphs.[6] The euro was the big battle against Brown that *A Journey*'s great hero lost.

Was Blair Ever Serious about the Euro?

In the historiography of the Blair governments, which is still to be written, some of his defenders will argue that he was never fully serious about the euro: his personal commitment was heavily conditional and Labour's public position on the single currency was always qualified. They will say that Blair might have done well to stick to that position, and maybe claim that he largely did. It was the fault of pro-European Blairites that unrealistic expectations were raised. Blair himself sidesteps this question in his memoirs, simply making the observation that, while the political case for joining was overwhelming, the euro is essentially an economic project. As the economics for Britain were shown not to stack up, that was the end of the matter.

This is a disingenuous account. In March 2003, Blair initially refused to accept the findings of the euro assessment as presented by Gordon Brown and demanded Brown's resignation.[7] Even when Blair backed down (and it must be remembered that the invasion of Iraq was underway at the time and, literally days before, over a hundred Labour MPs had revealed the vulnerability of his premiership by voting against Blair's decision to go to war), he made strenuous and partially successful efforts to soften the negativity of the assessment and hold the door open for a second assessment 12 months later.[8] It is understandable that Blair would now prefer the world to think that he believed the economics of Britain's euro entry were flawed in 2003, but it was not in accordance with his behaviour at the time.

Blair always intended the euro to be his legacy. Until the summer of 2003, joining the euro was one of the central motifs of his premiership. Rather like the motifs of a Wagner opera, it swelled, faded and then swelled again during that period, before dying away on an intensely dramatic note – the horror of the tragic suicide of Dr David Kelly. But until then, it was continuously present. Of course Blair believed the economics of euro entry mattered. His working assumption was that, together with Brown, they would make a political judgement on the best economic moment to call a referendum and campaign for a 'yes' vote. The Treasury's assessment of the 'five tests' would provide the economic rationale and technical justification for what essentially would be a political decision; no one in No. 10 imagined that, in itself, the assessment would be decisive. The truth is that Blair was not persuaded of the Treasury case; he was simply out-manoeuvred by Brown – for a whole complex of reasons, only some of which related to the euro itself.

Blair's argument in his memoirs that, on the euro, the economics had to exercise a veto over the politics is a curious one for someone with Blair's bold geopolitical vision. It ignores the reality that the economic costs and benefits of such a decision are in truth difficult to assess, especially the 'dynamics' in the longer run (as James Meade and Donald McDougall told Hugh Gaitskell in 1961, when Common Market membership first came up). Also, to put the economics first turns political judgement on its head. No one (or at least, very few) asked whether the economics favoured Britain's decision not to conclude a peace deal with Hitler in 1940; sustain a huge defence budget throughout the Attlee government, and, for decades after, maintain a costly independent deterrent; and, one might even add, during the Blair government send British troops to Iraq and Afghanistan. In all these big political decisions, the economics were undoubtedly debatable, but the politics were judged to matter much more. The interesting question is why Labour chose to apply a different test to the major long-term issue of Britain's power and influence in Europe.

'Leading in Europe' Outside the Euro?

In the aftermath of his euro failure, Blair may have half persuaded himself that Britain could continue to 'lead in Europe'[9] from the outside. Sir John Grant, one of a long line of distinguished British diplomats who served as Britain's permanent representative in Brussels, certainly endorsed this view. He interpreted Blair's victory in backing Barroso over Verhofstadt in the choice of Commission president in 2004, against the forcefully expressed wishes of the French President and German Chancellor, as a striking demonstration of Britain's continuing capacity for leadership. Absence from the euro notwithstanding, the swansong of Blair's premiership became a textbook example of British influence and leadership. By mid-2004, Blair had signed up for a Constitutional Treaty, which on the Continent was widely regarded as a British text. In summer 2005 he lifted the spirits of Europe after the referendum 'no' votes in France and the Netherlands with his powerful speech to the European Parliament in June 2005 and his remarkably successful British presidency, settling the EU budget. In partnership with the new German chancellor, Angela Merkel, he set Europe new ambitions to play a leading role in energy and climate change. At the Gleneagles G7 he led a united Europe in setting a new priority for Africa and the millennium development goals. At his last European Council as UK prime minister, he settled the detailed outline of what became the Lisbon Treaty. So did these successes show that it was wrong to believe that membership of the euro was the *sine qua non* of British leadership in Europe?

The argument made at the time was that enlargement represented a bigger structural shift in favour of British interests than any damage to them as a result of loss of influence through not being in the euro. Certainly Blair had done his damnedest to promote rapid enlargement. In the midst of the Kosovo conflict, Blair promised Romania and Bulgaria membership, well ahead of their readiness for it. He pressed successfully for a 'big bang' accession by the EU 10 in 2004, when the official consensus favoured a more gradual 'flotilla' approach. And he held open the door for Turkey, despite the determination of Continental centre-right governments after 2005 to kick Turkey's application into the long grass. However, unlike some in the Foreign Office, Blair did not see enlargement as a Machiavellian Anglo-Saxon plot to weaken integration. He always argued that simultaneous widening and deepening would be required:[10] without reform and deeper integration, enlargement would paralyse EU decision-making.[11] His position on enlargement was quite different to the Conservatives, who supported enlargement but never accepted the necessity of any further integrative moves.

Enlargement has undoubtedly been a centripetal force greatly increasing the Union's diversity and weakening Franco-German dominance, thereby creating a more comfortable environment for Britain. In some respects enlargement moved the EU 'in a British direction'. The post-communist new members were wholly Atlanticist in outlook, though their enthusiasm for overseas military adventures dimmed as time and grief wore on. Within the Brussels institutions, the old integrationist consensus showed signs of fracture, particularly in the European Parliament and its dominant group, the centre-right EPP, which had been more successful than the socialists in accepting affiliates from the new member states. In the first years after the EU 10 enlargement in 2004, senior Commission officials reported with some shock that the commissioners from the new member states were instinctively hostile to tax and social harmonisation. The newcomers saw this as a protectionist attack by the old EU 15 on the new EU 10's competitiveness.

The British assumed too readily, however, that the 'new Europe' that Donald Rumsfeld famously praised would be the UK's automatic allies. The member states of central and south-eastern Europe depend on annual EU Structural Fund and CAP transfers of up to 4 per cent of their GDP; they are highly suspicious of British leadership curbing the EU budget, at the same time as protecting what seems to them a wholly inexplicable and unjustifiable UK rebate. Here, post-2010, David Cameron was to fall into a trap Blair avoided.

The British also misunderstood the extent to which the central and eastern Europeans see their fundamental national interests as bound up with European integration. Although there is an undercurrent of Euro-sceptic resistance to any suggestion of Brussels diktat or centralisation (understandable in an eastern Europe that so recently gained its freedom and independence from the Soviet Union), economically Poland and the other central European countries have bet their future on European integration. This is a historic reconciliation with Germany, as remarkable as the Franco–German reconciliation in the previous generation. Economically, German markets and German inward investment are crucial to their economic advance. Britain is a bit player by comparison. Since 2010 the eurocrisis has made some central Europeans nervous about rushing into euro membership, but it has also strengthened their idea of themselves as 'pre-ins' who want the eurozone's new rules to be open to influence by those still outside. The euro is where in the medium term they see their future. There is no natural affinity between them and longer-term euro-outs, such as Britain and possibly Denmark and Sweden.

While on balance enlargement has helped Britain, it has not solved the British problem. In one crucial respect its consequences intensified British Euroscepticism in a totally unanticipated way. So wholehearted was Blair's commitment to enlargement that in 2004 he waived the seven-year derogation Britain could have used to delay the 'free movement of labour' for new EU citizens. Hundreds of thousands of east Europeans have taken advantage of their right to live and work in Britain, with profound social and political consequences for immigration and its salience as a political issue.[12] This had a bigger impact on domestic politics than any other European decision Blair took. His critics are right that inadequate preparation was made for coping with the social consequences of this migration 'shock', but it is depressing that the entire British political class has run away from explaining the benefits of the eastern migration to our economy and society. At the 2010 general election, the British electorate exacted their revenge on Labour and it has since been a major factor in the strength of the UK Independence Party (UKIP). The strength of grassroots feeling on the migrant question calls into question the political viability in Britain of what had hitherto been a strong cross-party consensus in favour of an 'open Europe' vision for the EU's future. This weakens our capacity for leadership on the single market at the same time that our politics has become more hostile to Britain playing as big a role in shaping the future of Europe as France and Germany.

Labour's Failure to Sell Europe in Britain

By the end of the Labour government, the long-term basis of popular support for our EU membership had weakened; by 2010 the European cause was more unpopular than it had been in the mid-1990s, with increased support for outright withdrawal, a trend that was magnified by the eurocrisis. In the Labour period there was also substantial erosion, even disintegration, of the pro-European interest in the British polity. This erosion had started in the late 1980s when Conservative divisions over Europe first emerged. Yet in 1997 a strong pro-European consensus still extended across the leadership of big business, the trade unions and our major political parties from Major and Clarke, through Ashdown and Campbell, to Blair and Brown. The strength of this consensus was remarkable by comparison with the partisan disagreements that had prevailed from the 1950s to the 1980s. The euro was acknowledged to be a difficult issue for Britain, but, despite the Maastricht opt-out, polling in the 1990s suggested that a big majority of the public accepted that Britain would become a member some day. Yet Labour failed to take advantage of the high-level consensus that existed in 1997 and immediately thereafter. Although Blair made a number of fine speeches on his pro-European mission, none of these translated into a consistent effort on the part of the government as a whole to make a strong pro-European case. The big choice was never put to the people as it would have been in Labour's first term. The forces of pro-Europeanism felt badly let down and have since scattered to the winds. Pro-Europeans judge this failure in terms of a massive missed opportunity, a disillusion that is felt more acutely today as the fires of Euroscepticism in the British polity burn ever more fiercely.

One example of how Labour failed to make the best case is the Lisbon economic reform agenda, which became a powerful symbol of Blair and Brown's engagement in Europe yet ended up doing little to help the pro-European argument. This outcome was largely the government's own fault, because of the way in which it chose to present the issues at stake. Britain was repeatedly held up as the exemplar of a reformed model to which (the rest of) 'Europe' should aspire. Britain, it was claimed, unlike the poor benighted Continentals, had become a flexible market economy, capable of steady growth and rising employment. This was contrasted with a Continental 'other' of slow growth, high unemployment and 'unreformed' economies. The government's discourse accentuated the perception that 'Europe' was a 'problem' for Britain. This message was gleefully echoed by the Eurosceptic media, who added their own distinctive twist. How could it make any sense for Britain to join the euro when it meant locking Britain permanently inside a failing European economy?

How did this happen? In part Europe was a victim of New Labour's addiction to 'spin'. Comparison with an allegedly failing, unreformed Europe was a good way of communicating the successes of Labour's own domestic record, backing New Labour's claim to economic competence, which was rightly seen as fundamental to sustaining New Labour's electoral appeal. However, the motivation was not simply partisan. New Labour wanted to paint a picture of a Britain that internationally was no longer in decline. To justify this claim the USA was repeatedly held up as the lodestar, as against a Continental Europe painted as an inward-looking trade bloc with fundamental problems. These claims were tendentious at best:

- In the five years prior to the 2003 euro assessment, nine of the EU 15 grew faster than Britain.[13]
- Four months after the 2003 euro assessment, Gordon Brown made the claim that 'European inflexibilities continue to widen the productivity gap with America.'[14] On the measure of productivity *per hour* worked, the EU average was 8 per cent below the USA, but in five EU member states (Germany, the Netherlands, Ireland, France and Belgium)

productivity *per hour* was actually higher than America's. Britain's was below the EU average.

- Another well-publicised Brown claim was that 'global Europe cannot afford the social model which means that 40 per cent of Europe's unemployed, in contrast to 5 per cent of America's, are long term unemployed.'[15] The facts showed that at this time some 23 per cent of Britain's unemployed were long-term unemployed, a higher figure than in Denmark, Sweden, Austria and Finland.

In EU terms, Britain's performance was 'middle of the pack' rather than 'top of the league'.

This need not have been the nature of the British reform discourse. Blair and Brown could have made a different, more pro-European argument that their aspiration for Britain was the best of a reformed European social model. They could have said that this was how they wanted Britain to move on from Thatcherism – not to turn the clock back to the statist, corporatist social democracy of the 1970s, but to achieve the transformation of Britain into a modern European social market economy. They could have pointed to the individual successes of European countries that they wanted Britain to emulate: for example, the Netherlands in flexicurity; Germany on skills; Sweden on family-friendly employment policies; Denmark on childcare. This would not have been to minimise the case for reform in Europe, but it would have badged reform as an essentially European ambition – a Britain that in its commitment fairness, social mobility and a modern welfare state, was different in emphasis to the USA. But it was not to be.

Why was this course not taken? Part of the explanation must lie in the myths that constrained New Labour's thinking: the myth of Britain's uniqueness and exceptionalism as a nation with little to learn from its Continental neighbours; the myth that our mission in Europe could only be defined by a Thatcherite mission to drive forward the single market; the myth that globalisation entailed acceptance of an Anglo-American view of capitalism and that all other alternative forms of capitalism would end up conforming to its hegemonic precepts. This was the discourse that international business based in Britain apparently wanted to hear and one that the Eurosceptic press were only too happy to convey. These myths and constraints narrowed the space available for a rational and balanced view of the European reform project. But the fact is that reform was necessary and Europe would now be the better for it if Blair's ambitions for economic reform had been more successfully fulfilled.

'Failure' on the Euro

It seems incontestable that Labour could have fought and won a euro referendum in its first term. Blair and Brown both started out instinctively well disposed to a bold move, but for a complex of reasons – mostly their own fault – they failed to get their act together and strike while the iron was hot. When it got to the point of decision in 2003, an agreed strategy for advance had by then become impossible. This was not only because their relationship had soured, and Blair's own position had become vulnerable as a result of Iraq. The case for the euro had become a victim of Labour's seeming economic success. Gordon Brown had managed the economy successfully for six years. There was no 'killer' argument that membership of the euro was economically necessary for that success to continue. Instead, a bundle of 'known unknowns' posed political and economic risk.

Was Blair at fault in seeming to define his European ambition in terms of euro membership? Given the disasters of the post-2010 eurocrisis, many might think so. But are they right? From the perspective of the second half of the 1990s, it is difficult to see in what other terms the big strategic question facing Britain about its relationship with Europe could have been put. To have declared that Britain would continue to exercise its Maastricht single currency opt-out for the foreseeable future would have been a curious way of demonstrating renewed British 'engagement' in the EU. The political consequences of a definitive 'no, never, not at any price' for Britain's long-term position would have been severe. In the light of Major's Maastricht legacy, seriously keeping open the option of joining the euro was the only European hand a pro-European Labour Party could play.

The conventional wisdom today is that, on the euro, Brown secured for Britain a desperately lucky escape. But conventional wisdom is always worth questioning. The euro was rejected in 2003 on what we now know to be the false premise that Brown's domestic macroeconomic framework was working well and was intrinsically superior. We now know change was necessary. The argument that the British economy would have fared even worse inside the euro is at least worth challenging. Living within the euro would have forced a tighter fiscal policy on Britain. It would have confronted the government at an earlier stage with the need for housing and financial market reforms. It should have led to a lower exchange rate for sterling on joining the euro, which would have slowed the precipitous decline of UK manufacturing. Since the banking crisis, the much vaunted freedom to devalue has been of little apparent value in helping Britain cope with its economic consequences. On the other hand, Britain has demonstrated that, more than many of our EU partners, we have the labour market flexibility to live within a single currency regime.

A Flawed Domestic Policy Regime

The flaws in Brown's seemingly robust and disciplined macro framework of policy did not come home to the public until five years after the abandonment of Blair's euro ambition. The golden rule of fiscal policy had proved bendable to the point of absurdity, as the government kept altering the definition of the economic cycle over which current spending and revenues were supposed to be kept in balance. Between 2003 and 2008, the government consistently ran budget deficits at around 3 per cent of GDP at a time of steady economic growth. True, Labour was in part 'borrowing to invest', as public infrastructure, particularly schools, hospitals and urban regeneration, had been badly neglected in the previous 30 years. Yet, setting aside the borrowing needed for capital investment, the government was also running a current deficit, when at a time of steady growth it should have been accumulating surpluses under the golden rule. At the same time, the fragility of the tax base was disguised by booming revenues from the banking and housing bubble, allowing Brown rashly to cut the main income tax rate from 22 pence to 20 pence in the March 2007 budget and weaken the tax base further.

The larger flaw in the New Labour economic policy regime was the way the Bank of England interpreted its independent remit as tightly focused on the government's inflation target. It proved comprehensively incapable of constraining the unsustainable asset price boom and massive build-up of private debt in the UK economy that accentuated the severity of the banking crisis. As the academic Helen Thompson pointed out:

> we must also recognise the specific nature of the acute problems the UK economy faces [. . .] comparing the UK with the other G7 economies plus Spain, total debt in the UK financial services sector in 2011 was around 100% higher as a percentage of GDP than the next highest state and much higher than most of the others, including the US with which the UK is often compared as an 'Anglo-liberal economy'.[16]

The consensus is now to blame this on a failure of financial regulation. Certainly the prevailing 'light-touch' philosophy legitimised irresponsible risk-taking, gross excesses of reward and, worst of all, a grave moral failure on the part of those in senior positions running our financial institutions. Yet the banking crisis was also a fundamental failure of an economic policy regime in which the authorities, with a myopic focus on inflation, appeared oblivious to the risks posed to economic and financial stability. And this in turn reflected a failure of theory and understanding. The economics profession in the main appeared blinded by the mathematical elegance of 'rational expectations' theorists and forgot the intuition of earlier generations that capitalism is a creative, dynamic force that has tendencies to catastrophic instability inherent within it.

The euro assessment correctly identified the housing market as one area where the UK economy was prone to dangerous instability. Brown and Blair agreed in 2003 that if Britain was to join the euro, major housing market reforms were inevitable. In practice, when euro membership fell by the wayside, the radical reforms were not implemented. As in the case of the government's fiscal stance, if membership of the euro had forced UK policy-makers to address the housing bubble at an earlier stage, some of the depths of the later crisis might have been avoided.

The years after 2003 represented a massive failure of economic policy for which senior officials in both the Bank of England and Treasury cannot escape their proper share of responsibility. The Coalition argued tendentiously in government after 2010 that 'Ed Balls should apologise for all his mistakes'. This highly personalised attack is a childish and absurdly agency-centred view of what went wrong: the fault lay in virtually the whole of the British economic policy establishment. There has been very little sign of critical self-examination, still less any public admission of responsibility.

How Much Is the 'Freedom to Devalue' Now Worth?

Would the UK economy have been in a worse position to face up to the 2008 banking crisis had we joined the euro in 2003? Consider the counterfactual. The flexibility of Britain's labour markets has made the UK one of the economies in Europe most capable of coping with economic shocks; the degree of labour market flexibility was shown by the unexpectedly muted rise in unemployment in response to the collapse in economic output in 2008.

Opponents of the single currency point out that within the euro the sterling depreciation of 2008 would not have been possible: we would have been locked into an unrealistically high exchange rate. Of course an exchange rate correction should have taken place as part of the preparations for euro membership. At that point an adjustment in the real exchange rate before euro entry might have made a lasting improvement to our competitiveness. But since 2008 the much vaunted 'freedom to devalue' has done little to improve Britain's trading performance. As long as Britain is outside the euro, business will organise its supply chains to hedge currency risk. The consequence is that devaluation increases the supply costs of imports as much as it makes exporting more profitable.

Nor has the 'freedom to devalue' avoided the need for a brutal fiscal adjustment in the UK. Within the euro, there would have been no way of avoiding the necessity for this huge adjustment if bond market confidence in UK government debt was to be maintained – or else Britain could have found itself in the position of Ireland, Spain or Italy. The crisis has once again shown the limitations of national sovereignty over fiscal policy. In the 1970s, the Labour government learnt very painfully that the scope for nation state Keynesianism was pretty limited. Post-2010, the same painful lesson has had to be learned.

Outside the euro, Britain has surrendered its ability to exercise decisive influence over the economic policies of the area that accounts for nearly 50 per cent of our trade. We have had to live with the mistakes of the eurozone's collective austerity without having any power to change them. That in itself is a considerable loss of British sovereignty.

Of Course the Euro was Flawed As Well

Blair always believed that if Britain was to play a leading role in Europe, at some stage Britain had to join the euro. But at the point of decision in 2003, there was no knock-out argument for membership that could be made. Coincidentally this was also a period of great complacency on the Continent about the euro and its future, with mutual self-congratulation all round. As prime minister, Blair felt instinctively that at some stage the good times could not continue and there would be some kind of 'crunch' that would trigger the need for more integration. He certainly did not foresee how precisely the problems would arise: no one did. But he did not expect that the governance arrangements that had been agreed at the euro's launch in the late 1990s would prove adequate and sufficient for all time. Like most European leaders he felt instinctively that the euro arrangements were flawed. There was widespread acceptance that unreformed labour markets were likely to prove problematic and would lead to labour costs getting out of line between countries. Also, tighter fiscal coordination would at some stage be needed and single representation of the euro area in bodies like the IMF was much discussed. My own recollection of Blair's conversations with European leaders is that the eventual need for future integration in the euro area was accepted as inevitable, but for understandable reasons very few leaders speculated about these issues in public.

A typical exception was the deeply reflective, free-thinking intellectual Romano Prodi – the former prime minister of Italy who became Commission president. In December 2001, he told the *Financial Times*:

> I am sure the euro will oblige us to introduce a new set of economic policy instruments. It is politically impossible to propose that now. But some day there will be a crisis and new instruments will be created.

Blair grasped that the euro was an existential issue for the countries who were its members: it was central to their economic future. So if its future ever became in doubt, it would be the dominating issue in European politics and Britain would suffer a loss of influence if we were not a member at the time. He also thought that the political commitment to do whatever would be necessary to save the situation would be huge. Blair would instinctively have preferred Britain to be at the table when the problems occurred, but he had no inkling of when that would be or what precise form the crisis would take. In the early to mid-2000s, Britain was enjoying a fools' paradise as much as the euro members were.

A Labour government, under Blair or Brown, would not have accepted the marginalisation of Britain in the European debate that has occurred under the Coalition. In my view, Labour in government would not in principle have ruled out UK financial involvement in the rescue packages, particularly in bank recapitalisation and restructuring, because our own interests are vitally affected. Nor would Labour in government have stood aside from negotiations on the fiscal compact and banking union. But none of this can disguise the fact that outside the euro Britain is not the leading player Blair would have wished it to be.

What Does the Euro Decision Mean for the Labour Government's Place in History?

The attraction of Blair had always been that he was no ordinary centre-left politician. As a social democrat I was proud of a Labour government that was redistributing the increment of economic growth through 'tax and spend' to tackle poverty, invest in the public realm and overcome supply-side underperformance. But this in essence was the old politics of the Westminster model – winning a majority in the House of Commons to pull the levers of the British central state in order to improve ordinary people's lives and extend opportunities. This model of politics had worked well in the age of Attlee with a relatively closed economy and much more rigidly class-bound society, but was not well attuned to the trends in our society to class de-alignment, individualism, multiculturalism, diversity, complexity and interdependence. Blair was the first Labour prime minister who appeared to recognise the need to find a political response to these trends in his pursuit of a new 'non-class-based' model of progressive politics, his acceptance (however grudgingly) of the case for radical constitutional reform and his commitment to put Europe at the centre of his politics.

The euro was important to the achievement of the 'new politics'. First, a successful referendum campaign would have weakened a divided Conservative Party and curbed the power and pretensions of Britain's right-wing press. Second, it would have rallied a broad range of progressive opinion beyond the traditional reaches of the Labour Party itself. Third, it would have been a decisive blow to the centralised Westminster model: the single currency would have brought Britain firmly and decisively into the world of multi-level governance where power flows up and down.

Sovereignty should not be seen as a theoretical legal concept. It means the 'power to act', and the power of the markets in practice means that the theoretical sovereignty offered by maintaining our own currency is worth very little. The mission of social democrats should be to work across countries to find new institutional means of fettering the power of markets. The euro has deep flaws but it offers a structure on which in future social democracy can build.

As Andrew Gamble put it in a Fabian pamphlet in 2002:[17]

> Nation states by themselves can exercise little effective sovereignty within this new world order. If they are to avoid competitive deregulation and preserve the social democratic gains of the second half of the twentieth century they need to come together to establish new democratic forms of cooperation.

Gamble saw the debate about the euro as a political argument about the social democratic response to globalisation:

> How we should respond to it and how we can avoid experiencing it as a malign fate over which we have no control. We have to extend democracy and

> cooperation and solidarity beyond the national level. The big question was 'How can self government be best secured in the present global economy?'

These were the big reasons for me why membership of the euro was of such fundamental importance. For all the euro's flaws, it was about getting our country and our politics to recognise that we lived in a new kind of world in which politics had to organise itself quite differently if it was to remain meaningful and relevant. This was a test that was far bigger than any of the five economic tests set for British entry. It was the test that New Labour decisively failed.

Act Three: Cameron's Gamble

It is a policy he never wanted, on an issue the public doesn't care about, at a time when no decision is required. As an act of statesmanship, it is a serviceable piece of party management.

Janan Ganesh, the *Financial Times* political columnist, summing up David Cameron's January 2013 speech on Europe[1]

CHAPTER 12

The Unexpected Return of Europe to British Politics

Europe burst again onto the British political scene with unexpected suddenness and intensity some 18 months after the 2010 general election. No one anticipated this. When the Conservative–Lib Dem Coalition was formed, it seemed that a new, if weak, pro-European consensus had been consolidated. The game-changer was the eurocrisis, which laid bare the deep structural tensions over Europe within British politics, and particularly the Conservative Party. The result was the increasing incoherence of the government's European policy as it strove both to promote Britain's national interests in the resolution of the eurocrisis and to manage the growing Conservative demands for an in/out referendum. Events have once again placed the European question at the epicentre of British politics.

The Coalition's New European Consensus

After Blair's failure on the euro, and through the tribulations of the Brown interlude, Europe faded as a major domestic issue. The Conservative demand for a referendum on the Lisbon Treaty never really took off, once Gordon Brown had disappointed his once fawning Eurosceptic admirers by pushing ahead with its parliamentary ratification. The formation of the Coalition appeared in itself to represent a settling of old scores on the European question. In 13 years of opposition, the Conservatives had struck highly Eurosceptic positions, opposing every single new treaty Labour had signed. On the single currency, the party was now committed 'never' to join, though by 2010 this was no longer as extreme a position as it would have once appeared, as no party looked likely to advocate British membership of the euro in the foreseeable future. As Britain's banking and fiscal crises deepened, there was no pressure within any of the parties, or from British business and the trade unions, to reopen the euro issue; ironically, the scale of Britain's economic woes was judged to rule out euro entry, as had the perceived successes of the New Labour record some years before! Once the eurocrisis gathered strength, the risks of being 'locked in' to the euro, as the sovereign debtors clearly were, appeared horrendous: keeping the pound, with the freedom to devalue it, was still thought to provide an essential escape hatch, not that many in the sovereign debtor countries visibly contemplated or wished for the restoration of their own national currency.

On the other hand, in 2010 there were no significant voices in the leaderships of any of the three main parties publicly questioning Britain's EU membership. The Conservatives still stood on the ground defined by both parts of the slogan that William Hague had coined in 1999: 'in Europe, not run by Europe'. No one disputed that there existed within their ranks what was typically dismissed as an anti-European fringe. Also, the cabinet itself contained a significant number who identified themselves as hard-core sceptics: James Forsyth, the well-respected *Spectator* columnist, estimated in 2012 that nine Conservative cabinet members were 'relaxed' about the possibility of UK withdrawal.[1] Cameron himself was more ambiguous: before the election, he had been forthright that the Conservatives could only present a different, more sympathetic image to the public if 'they stopped banging on about Europe'. To prove the point, he appointed Ken Clarke, the Conservatives' most prominent pro-European veteran, as his first justice secretary. By contrast, the 'bangers-on' were portrayed as powerless throwbacks to a bygone era, rather like the elements of the Labour left that had never reconciled themselves to Blairism. This comparison was, however, seriously misleading. As a political ideology, state socialism was well and truly bankrupt after the collapse of communism; it belonged to history. The left imagined wrongly that the 2008 financial crisis would do the same for neo-liberalism, demonstrating as it did the capacity of markets to undergo systemic failure. However, the transformation of the crisis from one of the markets into a crisis of the state, as public debt mounted in its wake, saved the day for neo-liberalism. Its counterpart, the continuing strength inside the Conservative Party of various brands of visceral anti-Europeanism and believers in 'off-shore' Britain, only became apparent in the Coalition's second year of office.

The Conservatives' minority partners, the Liberal Democrats, were by contrast a party for whom pro-Europeanism was embedded in their DNA. In the 1950s, the surviving remnants of the once great Liberal Party of Gladstone, Asquith and Lloyd George had been the first to commit to Europe. That European inheritance was reinforced by the Alliance with the breakaway Social Democrats in the early 1980s, for whom anti-Europeanism was symbolic of Labour's wider retreat from the centre ground. Despite this proud heritage, the Lib Dem passion for Europe had, by the new century, somewhat dimmed. In 1997, under Paddy Ashdown's leadership, the party made a significant breakthrough in parliamentary representation under Britain's 'first-past-the-post' voting system, by forming a tacit 'progressive alliance' with New Labour and winning the largest number of seats held by a third party since 1929. The party gained seats against the Conservatives in parts of the nation beyond even New Labour's reach: non-industrial Scotland, the West Country, the south coast and in comfortable suburbs populated by academics and public service professionals. To retain their seats, the new generation of Lib Dem MPs depended on constituency hard work and a broad non-ideological appeal: where Euroscepticism was rife, especially in the West Country, constituency opportunism trumped pro-Europeanism, with support for a referendum on Europe seen as an easy cop-out in retaining Eurosceptic support. On the other hand, the party leadership remained committed Europeans. The Lib Dem leadership contest in 2007 was between Nick Clegg and Chris Huhne, both of whom had served as MEPs and had been strong supporters of Britain's euro membership. Both also represented new departures for the party in another way, inheriting Westminster seats from Lib Dem MPs who had stood down, in itself an indicator of the party's stronger parliamentary base. In 2010, they both joined a Conservative-led cabinet, the first peacetime Liberal ministers since forgotten figures such as Sir John Simon, Sir Herbert Samuel and Leslie Hore-Belisha served in the national governments of the 1930s.

The Coalition professed a keenness to be constructive EU partners, with a noticeably emollient tone struck by Prime Minister Cameron, Chancellor Osborne and Foreign Secretary Hague. Like previous British governments the Coalition prioritised alliances with other 'northern liberal' member states to deepen the single market and support enlargement. In foreign policy, William Hague worked with his European counterparts, acknowledging that Britain gained global leverage if common positions could be agreed: for all his deep reservations he did not block the creation of the new External Action Service, brought into being by the Lisbon Treaty. Cameron struck a tougher note than his Labour predecessors on the EU budget, though his obduracy was shared by the growing ranks of net contributors amongst our EU partners and resonated with public opinion in a period of austerity. Similarly, the government resisted any extension of the social dimension, but again this mattered less in a centre-right-dominated EU. The Coalition contributed to the sharp EU policy shift away from the Keynesianism of the 2009 G20 summit in London (which, under the leadership of Brown, Merkel and Sarkozy had supported) in favour of front-loaded fiscal retrenchment. However, in showing little imagination about the long-term damage to growth prospects that 'collective austerity' might cause, they were not alone among our EU partners.

As a result, the UK Coalition was initially given the benefit of the doubt in the rest of the EU. British commentators discerned the pragmatic style of a Baldwin or a Macmillan, coming to terms with the realities of power, for which the creation of the Coalition with the Liberal Democrats provided a convenient cover. Two early decisions in particular went down positively on the Continent. First, on EU financial regulation, the new government supported Alistair Darling's backing for the establishment of three new regulatory agencies at EU level. In the new post-crisis environment David Lidington, the Europe minister, made clear to the City at Mansion House on 25 May 2011 that 'there can be no question of things simply returning, somehow, to the way they were for the financial services sector before 2008'. He went on: 'we must be relentless in dispelling the myth of Anglo-Saxon isolationism and a default laissez-faire approach to regulation' and 'not to fuel the arguments of our detractors who are very quick to claim that the UK prefers to compete only through a light touch regulatory environment'.

Second, the Coalition signed a path-breaking bilateral defence treaty with France, originally a Gordon Brown initiative. This could in future pave the way for wider European defence cooperation as public spending cuts bite into national capabilities, though the Coalition emphasised its commitment to bilateral cooperation rather than embracing an explicit EU defence agenda. Yet there was no British withdrawal from the fledgling European Defence Agency at which, before the election, the Conservatives had hinted. Pro-European optimists interpreted the early phases of the Coalition's European policy as representing a historically consistent pursuit of UK national interests.

The Lingering Influence of the Tory Eurosceptics

The one awkwardness was Cameron's refusal to reverse his decision to withdraw Conservative MEPs from the Christian Democrat (EPP) group in the European Parliament. Instead they formed a new grouping of anti-integrationist European Democrats, along with the populist right-wing Polish Law and Justice Party and other MEPs from mainly small East European parties, some of whom had unsavoury anti-semitic, homophobic and even neo-Nazi form. Not only did Cameron's decision greatly upset Angela Merkel, who set great store by the development of pan-European political links between 'respectable' centre-right parties with a pro-EU, pro-social market orientation, but Cameron also excluded himself from the influential meetings of EPP leaders that always precede European Councils. Cameron had made the pledge to pull the British Conservatives out of the EPP under duress in the 2005 Conservative leadership election in order to win over a crucial handful of Eurosceptic MPs who had been supporters of Liam Fox (Cameron's short-lived first defence secretary). Tellingly Cameron refused to reverse this decision, despite the very real loss of credibility and influence it caused.

Cameron was sensitive to how far the Coalition disappointed Conservative Eurosceptics. Lisbon had been finally ratified by all 27 member states six months before the 2010 election, scuppering the firm Conservative pledge to hold a referendum on its ratification. President Václav Klaus of the Czech Republic ignored the pleas of British Eurosceptics to delay his signature, despite Cameron's well-publicised personal appeal to him. Yet Klaus' firm rejection of his entreaties must have been a genuine relief. Among his fellow modernisers, the party's past obsession with Europe was seen as reinforcing the Conservatives' problematic image as out of touch with the electorate's real concerns, notwithstanding opinion polls that suggested British voters would have rejected Lisbon by a large margin. Conservatives rested on William Hague's enigmatic promise that if Lisbon was ratified before the Conservatives came to office, the new government 'would not let matters rest there'. The Conservative manifesto had pledged to 'repatriate' limited powers from Brussels, but the Coalition agreement abandoned this pledge. Instead the Coalition merely committed to examine the 'balance of competences' between Britain and the EU, a process which started in 2013 and has as yet to yield the 'red meat' that would satisfy Eurosceptics. Eurosceptics must have known that, before the election in 2010, allies of David Cameron and William Hague were briefing that the commitment to repatriation of powers would not be an 'early priority' for fear of setting off an immediate confrontation with our EU partners.

The Coalition's major concession to Eurosceptic opinion was the passage into law of the European Union Act 2011, introducing a so-called 'referendum lock' on any future transfers of power to Brussels. The Act reflected the prevailing received wisdom, shared by the leadership of all three main parties, that the Lisbon Treaty should draw a firm line under further institutional navel-gazing. Brussels already had more than enough powers and certainly did not need more! The Act specifies in great detail the potential transfers of powers to Brussels that must be subject to a referendum, some of which would seem trivial and obscure to all but the most EU-obsessed. A referendum would be required not just to ratify new treaties, but also for decisions on future transfers of power provided for within treaties already ratified by Parliament. At first sight the Act's practical effect was highly restrictive in preventing British agreement to 'more Europe', even if the proposed transfer of power was minor and clearly in the national interest. No government of any stripe would risk a referendum it might lose, unless the issue at stake was seen to be fundamental, and possibly not even then. However, the Act contained a little-noticed qualification: it did not require referendums on extensions of EU competence per se, only on those extensions that resulted in a transfer of power *from* the UK *to* Brussels. It was left to ministers to judge whether any particular measure represented a transfer of power, though that ministerial decision would be subject to judicial review. It also emerged in the passage of the bill through Parliament that, as no Parliament can bind its successor, any future government could push a ratification measure through Parliament without a referendum, provided that the ratification measure contained a clause specifying that the provisions of the EU Act 2011 would not in this case apply. Throughout the passage of the bill, ministers pooh-poohed the suggestion that any further transfer of sovereignty might at some stage become an unavoidable necessity. The growing crisis in the eurozone soon brought the realism of that 'thus far and no further' judgement into question.

The Initial British Response to the Eurocrisis

The crisis clearly demanded integrationist responses that no one had contemplated before. The government initially argued that, as Britain was not in the euro and had no intention of joining, consequent treaty changes necessary to strengthen euro area governance were not transfers of power from the UK to Brussels. Yet for British Eurosceptics, the need for British assent to treaty change presented a heaven-sent opportunity to force on our EU partners the new relationship with Europe that they hankered after. Also, a more tightly integrated eurozone clearly represented a change in the *power relationship* within the EU between euro-outs and euro-ins, even if in legal terms it did not represent a formal transfer of powers.

First in the queue for treaty change was the establishment of a permanent bail-out fund: the European Stability Mechanism. Further down the track was talk of treaty change to secure greater fiscal integration (what became the fiscal compact of December 2011), banking union, possibly a eurozone budget to act as an economic stabiliser, perhaps some form of debt mutualisation, and an even more ambitious project of political union to strengthen the democratic accountability of the integrative moves underway. Yet this largely remained 'talk'. Member state governments were much more circumspect.

The eurocrisis gave British Euroscepticism a huge boost. For the pundits opposed to the euro, the crisis proved they had been right all along. Former chancellors of the Exchequer Nigel Lawson and Norman Lamont, who had been single currency sceptics from the late 1980s, trumpeted their sense of personal vindication. Supporters of Gordon Brown defended his battered reputation on the basis that his most important decision had been to keep Britain out of the euro. Yet the crisis also exposed Euroscepticism's inner dilemmas, even contradictions. After years of campaigning against the euro's unworkability, Eurosceptics now had to decide whether it would be better to hasten (in their eyes) the euro's inevitable demise, or help our European partners to remedy its 'design flaws'. This tension was brought out early on in the evidence that Sir Martin Jacomb, a highly respected City grandee, gave the House of Lords European Select Committee in October 2010. 'Our national policy ought to be to encourage the dismantling of the eurozone,' Sir Martin opined.[2] His views may seem extreme to some: yet they are logically consistent if one believes that exchange rate flexibility is a fundamental requirement for the successful management of a national economy. Sir Martin is no anti-European fanatic: he acknowledges the considerable benefits of the single market. His line of thinking struck a chord with many Conservatives, including London's mayor, Boris Johnson, who believed the euro was fundamentally misconceived on economic and democratic grounds. In their hearts they would have liked to see it fail: if only it could somehow disappear without inflicting pain on those outside!

Conservative ministers found themselves impaled on the horns of a considerable dilemma. Whatever their private views on the euro, the immediate economic consequences for Britain of its break-up would be very serious. Much as break-up might emotionally be their desired outcome, hard realities suggested it was not in the British or Conservative interest. The Coalition's economic strategy was predicated on rebalancing the British economy away from the excesses of debt-financed consumption in both the public and private sectors towards exports and investment. For this rebalancing to succeed, the economy of the eurozone needed to be buoyant and prosperous, as it represented getting on for half of Britain's export trade. Supporters of British membership of the euro were proved right in one of their main arguments: Britain could not escape the consequences of the euro by not being a member.

The Eurozone's 'Remorseless Logic' of Integration

Nevertheless, it must have caused a turn in some Eurosceptic stomachs when the chancellor of the Exchequer, George Osborne, declared in a speech in Paris in January 2011: 'Britain of course is not a member of the euro. But Britain wants the euro to be a complete success and we will support you in achieving that.' Equally, many British Eurosceptics would have been, to say the least, surprised when they read in the *Financial Times* in July 2011[3] of the Chancellor's strong backing for greater fiscal integration in the eurozone. In what he memorably described as the 'remorseless logic' of a single currency, Osborne carefully chose a phrase that indicated British distance from and distaste for the single currency project, but the 'spin' could not disguise the realpolitik of the Chancellor's policy: Britain would support the eurozone in taking whatever integrative steps it needed to save the euro. In a reversal of British foreign policy for the previous half century, and some would say centuries, Britain would support a more politically integrated Continent of which she would not be part.

The breathtaking significance of this historic policy shift was lost in the immediate political turmoil. The drama of the eurocrisis offered the Coalition politically convenient cover for Britain's continuing economic difficulties. The eurozone 'headwinds' became the Chancellor's favourite explanation for failing to deliver on his forecasts of economic growth and debt reduction, obscuring the fact that, over the two and a half years from mid-2010, growth in the eurozone had in fact been stronger than in the UK, with France and Germany making a far more robust recovery from the 2008 crisis than Britain. Nonetheless, the Chancellor was able to point to the Office of Budget Responsibility's judgement that 'weaker than expected growth can be more than accounted for by over-optimism regarding net trade'. This of course could have been as much due to domestic supply-side weakness and the failure of sterling depreciation to boost UK international competitiveness as to the problems of the euro area.

The Chancellor's decision to put so much stress on the 'remorseless logic' of eurozone integration also served a wider political purpose. He was setting up a binary choice to justify the Conservative's European strategy: on the one hand, the inevitability of economic and political integration within the eurozone to a depth that would make membership impossible to contemplate for any British government; on the other, the UK could remain in a looser EU outside a federalised inner core. A two-tier Europe was inevitably emerging which would require a thorough institutional rethink for all EU members, and through which Britain could negotiate a new relationship and a new settlement.

For all the political convenience of the eurozone's difficulties, however, the crisis aggravated the government's internal political problems. It undermined public support for EU membership; earlier generations had in part been persuaded that Britain had no alternative but to join Europe because the Continental record on economic growth in the 1950s, 1960s and 1970s had far outshone our own. Now the public saw on their television screens constant witness to a failing and divided Europe: the absence of any single clear step towards crisis resolution, the endless succession of summits in Brussels which never appeared to do enough, banking collapse in Ireland, the political crisis in Italy, civil disturbance in Greece and Spain – all played out before a gloating British media, conveying an image of chaos, confusion and deep woe. Understandably, the public were horrified and it was no surprise that support for EU withdrawal in opinion polls rose. However, the significance of this public shift should not be exaggerated. During the early 1980s recession, there had been a similar period when a clear poll majority favoured withdrawal. For all the bad headline numbers about Europe, only 8 per cent of the British public think of Europe as an important issue for them.[4] It was not public opinion that changed Cameron's European policy.

The Renewed Rumblings of Euroscepticism

The eurocrisis activated a rumbling volcano in an unmodernised Conservative Party which erupted on a Commons backbench motion calling for an in/out referendum in October 2011. The Prime Minister and Chancellor made a tactical mistake by heavily whipping Conservative MPs to oppose the motion, inflaming what otherwise might have been a low-profile backbench debate. Labour, after some initial hesitation, also opposed the motion, which was defeated by the impressive margin of 483 to 111. However, 81 Conservative backbenchers defied a three-line whip, a larger rebellion than any there had been on Maastricht in the early 1990s. The rebel ranks extended well beyond the anti-European 'last ditchers', including backbenchers from the 2010 intake, traditionally loyalist in the hope of future office. Some acted from high motives of conviction, others from the low calculation of pleasing constituency activists, whose role in their political futures would become crucial in a review of constituency boundaries that was then anticipated with much trepidation. However, the size of the rebellion showed that many backbench Conservatives believed the momentum behind a referendum was unstoppable and that the leadership would eventually be forced to bend to it, and that, if it did not, regime change would be in prospect.

The structural factors in this upsurge of militant Conservative Euroscepticism were in existence well before the eurocrisis. Conservative MPs owe their position to a 'selectorate' of activists, much less representative of 'middle Britain' than in earlier decades. Party membership has collapsed from the millions of the 1950s to a couple of hundred thousand today. Those who remain are predominantly elderly, noncosmopolitan in outlook, and out of touch with the social currents of modern Britain. This explains why in 2013 gay marriage was to arouse seething discontents among Conservatives, while public opinion appeared relaxed. Similarly, for Conservative activists Europe *is* a key issue facing the country, whereas for most of a highly sceptical public it is low in their priorities.

How much this represents a change from the past is uncertain. The party base was probably never as enthusiastic about Europe as its leadership became in the 1960s and 1970s. Yet at that time a tradition of deference, and a high premium on loyalty to the party's leaders, was sufficient to keep doubters quiet. There was of course then an older generation emotionally scarred by wartime enmities and deeply attached to the Empire and Commonwealth, but they did not represent the 'future'. Many of the ambitious rising stars in the first generation of affluence were classless 'modernisers' who identified strongly with Europe and saw Labour's opposition as symptomatic of the party's backward-looking class consciousness and union ties. By contrast, since the fall of Thatcher the ambitious have found it virtually impossible to win a Conservative selection without striking a Eurosceptic posture. Hostility to Europe unites old-fashioned xenophobes, romantics with a backward-looking idea of

'Englishness' and libertarian hyper-globalisers who see EU rules as holding Britain back. The 'party in the media' exerts a major influence on party activists: it has consistently preached an ideological Thatcherism in which hostility to Europe has played a crucial part. At the same time, since 1992 the party's leaders have commanded less loyalty and respect because they have been less electorally successful, in part because that very same 'party in the media' has severely constrained their freedom to 'modernise' and move onto the electoral centre ground.

David Cameron claimed to be different. His project of modernisation played on media symbols of a new Conservatism. He talked sympathetically about poverty and inequality. He famously made a trip to the North Pole to demonstrate environmental Blue/Green commitment. His 'hug a hoodie' speech was intended to demonstrate a sharp break with the 'hang 'em and flog 'em' approach to law and order. Yet on Europe Cameron avoided any direct challenge to the mindset of both his activists and the party in the media: there was nothing to compare with his courageous commitment to homosexual equality. On Europe no one quite knew where he stood. He had never been a pro-European enthusiast – that mood had passed by the time he joined Conservative Central Office shortly after Thatcher's Bruges speech. As a special adviser he worked for leading Eurosceptics, in Norman Lamont and Michael Howard. His period in business at Carlton Communications exposed him to the hyper-globalist assumptions of the younger generation making their fortunes in the City. When he became Conservative leader, he courted Murdoch far more assiduously than Blair ever did. Yet for all that, it is difficult to believe that someone of his comfortable stockbroker background in the Berkshire countryside would see his place in history as taking Britain out of Europe.

Cameron must have been aware of the risk he was running inside the Conservative Party: that, at some point, Europe would come back to haunt his leadership. But, prior to 2010, his short-termist public relations mindset led him to take the risk of assuming nothing dramatic was in prospect that would change the weak pro-European consensus that had been established after Blair's failure on the euro. Despite his evident admiration for Blair, he did not make Europe his 'Clause Four', deliberately engineering a battle within his party to rid it of its most damaging shibboleth that weakened its credibility as a party of government.

Cameron entered office with little political capital in the bank. He had made strenuous efforts to get a new, more socially diverse generation of candidates selected, with mixed results in terms of their underlying ideological beliefs and prejudices. But this was accompanied by what one can only describe as a class prejudice, inside the Conservative Party of all places, on the part of the provincial Poujadistes who were vocal on the backbenches against the public school, cosmopolitan, socially liberal 'Cameroons'. In the 2010 campaign, for all his strength of personality and presentational skills, and Brown's weaknesses, the Conservatives failed to win an overall majority. Their share of the vote on 36 per cent was some 6–8 per cent lower than the 42–44 per cent share the Conservatives consistently won under Thatcher and Major. As soon as the 2010 result was clear, Cameron moved swiftly, without wider consultation in the party, to enter into a five-year Coalition agreement with the Liberal Democrats. This was not the only option available: an alternative would have been to form a minority government as the largest party and call another election in six months. True, the state of the economy needed a strong and stable government: but there was the precedent of Harold Wilson who had formed a minority government in similarly grave economic circumstances in February 1974 and went on to win a small overall majority that October. While many Conservatives were excited by the party's long-awaited return to power, few at the grassroots accepted the leadership's argument that the government of the country was strengthened by the very act of forming the Coalition. And Cameron, unlike Clegg for the Liberal Democrats, did nothing to consult the Conservative grassroots and bind them in.

Conservative activists regard post-1960s Liberals with a mixture of fear and loathing. Since the Orpington by-election in March 1962 which marked the revival of the Liberals as a third force in British politics, they have been the 'yellow peril', far more menacing to the Conservative activist base than the 'socialists', particularly in the Conservative heartlands of semi-rural and small-town constituencies, and in the home counties and West Country, where Labour historically mounted a weak challenge. The Liberals had form in opposing the Conservatives on the issues closest to their innermost convictions: immigration, law and order, family values, and of course Europe. The Coalition was not a marriage made in heaven as far as the Conservative base was concerned: the sooner it could be terminated the better, and on what more emotionally resonant issue than Europe. A sizeable section of Conservative MPs sympathised with these views.

Conservative negativity towards the Coalition was strengthened by UKIP's rise. Paradoxically the UKIP surge was a different side of the same coin as the Lib Dems becoming a party of government. As the Lib Dems surrendered their role as the third-party receptacle for mid-term protest votes, UKIP gained a considerable mid-term boost, increasing the likelihood of their success not just in European Parliamentary elections, where in 2009 they won second place in the national vote, but also in parliamentary by-elections and local council contests, arousing strong feelings of angst at the Conservative grassroots. In the eyes of the party base, the absence of sufficiently strong Conservative policies was blamed; the promise of an in/out referendum seemed the obvious panacea. It would help the Conservatives ward off not only the undoubted UKIP threat in European elections, but also the more considerable risk of vital votes in Conservative marginals draining away in a general election. The gut instinct of the depleted Tory base is that UKIP is made up of natural allies and friends who should return to their true home. Since 2010, when UKIP under its charismatic leader, Nigel Farage, branched out from its anti-European core to campaign on issues like immigration, welfare and gay marriage, these instincts have strengthened. Philip Stephens argued astutely that what was happening at the Conservative base in British politics had crucial similarities to the rise of the Tea Party at the Republican base since Obama's election as US president in 2008.[5]

Growing Ambiguity and Confusion in Britain's Response to the Eurocrisis

The Coalition's handling of the eurocrisis ceased to be sure-footed once the Eurosceptic volcano erupted. The ambiguity about how best to defend UK national interests became starker. Initially ministers were categorical that rescuing the eurozone was a vital national priority. Logically this implied maximum engagement in sorting out the euro's problems and remedying its design flaws. The first dent in this commitment came on the question of financial support for the eurozone. At the emergency summit on the Greek crisis held the weekend after the 2010 general election, Alistair Darling, Labour's outgoing chancellor, had agreed to two rescue funds being set up: an intergovernmental European Financial Stability Facility (EFSF) with 500 billion euro subscribed by eurozone members only; and the European Financial Stability Mechanism (EFSM), a smaller 60 billion euro EU 27 fund for which the UK would be liable for its proportionate share. Conservatives criticised Darling on the grounds that it was wrong in principle for British taxpayers to contribute to the costs of the euro rescue.

As the eurocrisis deepened, David Cameron set as his first main negotiating objective winding up the EFSM and any consequent British liability.

In autumn 2010, Germany pressed for a minor treaty change to allow the establishment of a permanent European Stability Mechanism to replace the EFSF on a proper legal basis, in order to satisfy the requirements of the German Constitutional Court. Cameron agreed with Angela Merkel to support this treaty change on condition that the British liability under the EFSM was wound up. At the time, this played well with Eurosceptics on the government backbenches and in the media. But was this gesture of distancing really in the UK *national* interest, as opposed to what suited the internal politics of the Conservative Party?

Arguably Cameron's policy minimised British influence over our partners' economic and financial policies at the very moment that influence needed to be maximised. The Chancellor of the Exchequer had quickly and correctly spotted that resolution of the eurozone crisis required rapid restructuring and recapitalisation of the Continental banks. Not only was this essential to eventual economic recovery, there was a clear and specific UK national interest given the large potential exposure of UK banks to Continental defaults. In Paris in January 2011 (18 months before the European Council eventually backed the principle of a banking union), Osborne urged immediate action: 'We really do not want to be back here a year from now in January 2012 still discussing the future of the euro.' In the Irish rescue in early 2011, he offered bilateral loans to the Republic – interestingly on the same scale of support Britain would have had to make had we been members of the euro. Osborne argued that Ireland was a special case, given the especially close linkages between the British and Irish banks, but massive interdependencies also existed between British and Spanish banks. Had the UK put itself at the forefront of calls for a Spanish rescue, the UK could have used the political leverage thereby won to press for quick and decisive action to break the link between Spain's bankrupt banks and their indebted sovereign.

Eurosceptics mock the idea of 'influence': if the European Union is a Continental conspiracy against the British national interest, what is the point? Yet even if one partly accepted this conspiracy theory, there would still be a powerful case for maintaining the maximum armlock on our partners when vital British interests are judged at stake. Yet the Coalition's policy of distancing weakened that armlock just when it was most required. Of course given Britain's own deficit and debt problems, it is reasonable to ask whether the UK could afford to get involved. The question was implicitly answered by the Chancellor every time he boasted of the UK's exceptionally strong creditworthiness in the UK bond markets. Britain was already involved through our IMF obligations. Britain could have been a more active and influential partner in the eurozone rescue but, for reasons of domestic politics, chose not to be. British policy came to be looked upon contemptuously by our Continental partners. Tightfistedness on solidarity with our partners in trouble was coupled with hectoring imprecations to take faster steps to economic and political integration. In almost the same breath, the government made clear that these integrative steps would involve unacceptable sacrifices of national sovereignty that Britain could never make, but it was assumed that our Continental partners would readily see no alternative but to accept. The Coalition's policy combined condescension with every offer of support, short of actual practical help.

Cameron's Non-Veto in Brussels

With Britain's Continental relationships fast deteriorating, relations plunged to new lows at the December 2011 European Council when David Cameron vetoed Germany's proposal for a treaty-based fiscal compact. By no stretch of the imagination could this be the action of a British government giving top priority to saving the euro. The German government saw this new treaty as crucial to persuading their electorate that solidarity would not be a bottomless pit. Cameron's veto did not stop the treaty going ahead, leading only to its not being agreed under full EU auspices. Twenty-five of the EU 27 partners signed a separate intergovernmental treaty, but making full use of the European institutions to implement its provisions.

This so-called 'veto' temporarily did wonders for the Prime Minister's ratings in the Conservative Party and country, but at the price of severe damage to our national interests. The tighter fiscal integration, which the Chancellor and Prime Minister had so strenuously urged on our partners, went ahead anyway on an intergovernmental treaty basis. Britain voluntarily surrendered its seat at the table on key questions of European economic policy and no longer attended eurozone summits, unlike other euro-outs. As a euro-out, we would have been spared implementing the treaty's full fiscal rigours (though why Cameron and Osborne should have objected on economic grounds to its content was difficult to comprehend, given their commitment to austerity). Britain's 'non-veto' took us out of the negotiating room when any question of future implementation or revision arises. Instead of demonstrating the power of the British veto, the episode showed the threat of its use to be of little practical effect: in any future clash of interests, our partners could simply press ahead outside the existing EU structures and we would be powerless to stop them. British threats of taking our partners to the ECJ for making use of the European institutions proved pure bluster. The ECJ later made clear that it saw no objection to future separate intergovernmental treaties, outside the Lisbon Treaty framework, which allowed EU member states to make use of the EU institutions in their implementation, as long as the terms of any such treaty did not conflict with existing EU treaty obligations. A new principle for treaty ratification of revolutionary significance in EU terms was also introduced, to which any previous British government would have objected. The treaty would come into full effect once 11 of the 17 euro member signatories had ratified it, breaking the principle that all must first ratify before a treaty comes into effect. The veto was a humiliating surrender of influence for no discernible national gain.

If the balance of national interest was so clearly against a veto, why then did Cameron do what he did? The Prime Minister probably decided that he could not face the prospect of having to take a Bill ratifying the fiscal treaty through the House of Commons. Had he done so, his rebellious Eurosceptics would have tried to attach to it a requirement for an in/out referendum. Cameron saw ahead of him the prospect of months of divisive debate and destructive argument, with the Labour opposition seeking as much tactical advantage as it could. Better therefore to wash his hands of the awful prospect.

The Prime Minister's public argument for his veto was different. He claimed that our EU partners had failed to agree essential safeguards that he had sought for UK national interests if there was to be deeper eurozone integration. In an episode clouded by obfuscation, Cameron tabled a last-minute paper at the European Council, demanding safeguards on financial services regulation as the price of UK assent to the fiscal compact. His manoeuvre was badly flawed procedurally and in substance. The document was sprung on the Council late at night, without delegations being briefed in advance, with the consequence that heads of government were mystified by the purpose and content of the British demands. The substance of the paper was a toxic combination of the complex and alarming: complex in that the subject matter concerned highly technical details of financial regulation on which heads of government would require official briefs; alarming in that the first word at the top of the paper, almost in red flashing lights, was 'unanimity'. It came across as the British seeking to obtain a veto over key questions concerning the City of London. This was a complete non-starter with our partners. Once any member state had restored the right of veto on a matter of vital national interest to them, the wholesale unravelling of the single market would be in prospect. The Prime Minister was either extremely naive in behaving as he did, or cynically calculating, because he knew his demands would not be met and he wanted a plausible excuse for justifying his veto to the UK media.

Defending Britain's Position in a New Outer Tier

Nonetheless, the issue of potential discrimination by a block of euro-ins against the euro-outs that Cameron had identified is a real potential concern. If a two-tier EU is in the making, how does the outer tier protect itself against (possibly unwitting) discrimination by a eurozone inner core adopting common policy positions, when the eurozone bloc constitutes a qualified majority in the whole EU 28 Council of Ministers? Euro-outs could find their influence reduced in practice to a Norway or a Switzerland. These fears may be more theoretical than real. As of writing, there is no certainty that an inner core will develop with full decision-making powers and a wide remit on any clear timescale. Eurosceptics assume an outcome that fits their world view, not one that is inevitable. As Osborne's endless repetition of the mantra of the 'remorseless logic' of eurozone integration showed, British Eurosceptics want to promote the notion of a strengthening inner-core Europe as a self-fulfilling prophecy, in order to justify the renegotiation of a new looser relationship between Britain and the EU.

Three realities call this 'remorseless logic' into question. First, on most questions to do with the single market, Germany has more in common with euro-outsiders, such as Britain and Sweden, than it traditionally has had with southern member states within the euro – and would not want to see that 'northern' influence reduced. The eurozone is by no means a united block. Second, Germany has bent over backwards to reassure east European euro-outs such as Poland that their fears of relegation to second-class status are groundless, and that they will not be excluded from economic policy decisions because they are not yet members of the euro, as they still intend to be. There is no common interest among the euro-outs. Third, although the French are the strongest advocates of building an architecture of eurozone governance, they are unwilling to see wide-ranging treaty changes that would result in irresistible pressure for a French referendum. This opposition to fundamental treaty change is widely shared – for example by the Dutch, who are more sympathetic than any other euro member to British concerns about the general direction of the EU.

Nevertheless, in the single financial market the UK has a legitimate concern. Here the strengthening of macroprudential economic governance and financial regulation necessary to prevent any repetition of the eurocrisis may genuinely come in conflict with a level playing field for the whole EU. The potential tension is more complex and highly charged by the City of London's success as the financial centre of the EU (and the main trading centre of euro-denominated financial assets) and the reality of Britain's position outside the euro. In Eurosceptic eyes, this issue is often emotively framed as jealous continentals, envious of the City's predominance, set on imposing new regulations with a rapacious intent to siphon off for themselves the rich pickings of London's financial sector. One must not of course be naive: the French authorities would undoubtedly like to see Paris grow as a financial centre and the number of French citizens working in the City of London (and earning high salaries) rankles a good deal with some in France. But the City equally has powerful cards up its sleeve. The European business community holds the City's skills in high regard; its success has been an example of successful specialisation within the single market, where financial integration proceeded apace both as a result of EU liberalisation, particularly in wholesale markets, and the creation of the euro itself. Before the banking crisis, the historical record shows that the British government was rarely, if ever, outflanked in a vote on financial services regulation in the Council of Ministers.

Yet both a political and a technical problem has emerged. The technical issue is a genuine dilemma in devising nondiscriminatory regulatory policies that ensure financial stability within a single currency area if its main financial centre is outside. Prior to the banking crisis, everyone imagined financial deregulation could proceed apace within the single market, with home-based national regulation of financial institutions being sufficient. This judgement proved catastrophically wrong. Largely unregulated cross-border financial flows fuelled the imbalances that underlay the eurocrisis and inflated the bubbles that burst with such damaging consequences in Spain and Ireland, and, of course, outside the euro area in the UK. The ECB, as the new eurozone regulator, may well insist that certain aspects of financial trading, which could pose systemic risk within the euro area, have to be under its direct regulatory jurisdiction (that is, not in the City of London).

This is compounded by a political problem of much greater magnitude. The British, as the leading exponents of the light-touch approach, are widely held to be responsible for the failures of regulation that led to the financial crisis. The political argument is made, particularly on the left, that the eurozone debt crisis is as much a failure of inadequate financial market regulation as of any design flaws in the euro. The European political zeitgeist is therefore to be tough – hence symbolic gestures such as tight regulation of bankers' bonuses. London must either assent to tighter EU regulation or lose the privilege of being the financial centre of the eurozone. But the gap between rhetoric and reality is huge and in many respects the debate on regulation is far more advanced and radical in London than it is in Brussels.

The UK made these potential conflicts much worse by standing aside from the project of banking union in June 2012. The British government argued that because banking union was about rescuing the euro, Britain should have nothing to do with it. As Cameron said, 'we have to stand behind our own banks, but I don't want British taxpayers guaranteeing eurozone banks.'[6] Yet the stated objective of the banking union is to create 'a single financial union'. Once the ECB becomes in practice the single supervisor for the eurozone's banks, the drive to create this single financial union will be its central concern, with deep implications for the City of London and the regulation of the single financial market. The instant rejection of possible British membership of a banking union appeared an ideological prejudice, not a rational and balanced calculation of national interests. Euro-outs were not automatically by definition excluded. The Swedes did explore the possibility of joining, but they failed to gain adequate assurances that they would have a proper say in ECB regulatory decisions, because of the ECB's insistence that non-members of the euro cannot have a decisive say in its governance. If Britain had joined Sweden in pressing for inclusion, this might have made a crucial difference and led to a different outcome.

In December 2012, Britain won important concessions to protect its position as a euro-out. A new voting regime was agreed for the London-based European Banking Authority (EBA), the regulatory coordinator established for the whole EU in the wake of the 2008 banking crisis, whereby a double majority of both euro-ins and euro-outs has to be secured for new regulations. However, the protection looks fragile. The EBA will remain a weakly resourced body by comparison with the ECB once it becomes the single eurozone supervisor. Other euro-outs may well follow a German rather than British lead. Significantly, the arrangement is time limited; it comes to an end when four member states or fewer remain outside the euro. The eurozone was not prepared to concede a permanent British veto over financial regulatory decisions for the very good reason that it cannot cede control to a non-euro member of the powers necessary to ensure the eurozone's future financial stability. But the question of the banking union and the whole future of the City of London had by then become a sideshow in far more profound domestic political drama.

CHAPTER 13

Renegotiation and Referendum

The European Council in June 2012 proved the decisive moment in bringing to a head the Conservative divisions over Europe. In the previous eight months the eurocrisis had grown in intensity. November 2011 had seen the establishment of two technocratic governments in Greece and Italy, under Lucas Papademos and Mario Monti, basically because politics as normal was not able to face up to the austerity measures necessary to secure the second Greek bail-out and restore bond market confidence in Italy. These developments were accompanied by a deepening crisis in Spain as the newly elected Mariano Rajoy government implemented budget cuts that caused unemployment to soar and raised fresh uncertainties over Spanish bank solvency. The realisation took hold that the eurozone could not continue with a series of piecemeal responses to the crisis but needed a comprehensive strategy. Hence President Van Rompuy's report to the Council, *Towards a Genuine Economic and Monetary Union*, set out in broad terms the steps necessary to achieve an integrated financial framework, an integrated budgetary framework, an integrated economic policy framework and strengthened democratic legitimacy and accountability. The outcome was agreement in principle to establish a banking union and draw up a 'specific and time-bound road map' of wider change. Monti also succeeded in a late-night coup in overcoming Merkel's resistance to wider use of the ESM bail-out fund. The Council concluded that the ESM could intervene in bond markets to support eurozone members as long as they were meeting their commitments under the fiscal compact (which would help Italy) and to recapitalise banks directly (which would help Spain). In the minds of Eurosceptics, these developments signalled decisive steps to eurozone integration: the historic opportunity for a major EU-wide treaty renegotiation that they had been aiming for now appeared in clear prospect.

As the Prime Minister arrived in Brussels, over 100 Conservative backbenchers signed a letter calling for a clear commitment to an in/out referendum. As its instigator, John Baron MP, put it, 'the heart and soul of the Conservative Party now believes it is time to consult the British people'. At his summit press conference Cameron cavalierly dismissed these backbench demands. He argued that the issue of Europe could not be reduced to the simplicities of an in/out choice; as a 'pragmatic Eurosceptic', what people want is a 'government that stands up for and fights for Britain in Europe and gets what we want'. That statement was a long way from offering the British people a vote on whether to leave.

The following day Liam Fox (the former defence secretary, by then languishing on the backbenches) called for an immediate in/out referendum, adding that for him 'life outside [the EU] holds no terror'. In an atmosphere of growing Conservative hysteria, Cameron penned a rushed article for the *Sunday Telegraph* which for the first time made the admission that, for him, 'the two words referendum and Europe go together'. In his report back to the Commons the following Monday, Cameron spoke in more measured and ambiguous terms of the need for a 'fresh settlement' with 'fresh consent'. He pronounced that 'far from there being too little Europe there is too much of it'. He argued that 'whole swathes of legislation covering social issues, working time and home affairs should be scrapped'. To advance this agenda of renegotiation he spoke of opportunities, 'more to come, probably future treaties where we can take forward our interests'. His proposed fresh settlement would require the 'full-hearted consent' of the people, though the statement still contained no specific and binding commitment to an in/out referendum. The Labour leader, Ed Miliband, mocked to great effect Cameron's shifts of position on a referendum as 'no, yes, maybe'.

The Prime Minister spent the rest of the year promising to set out his policy in more detail in a major speech which he first said he would deliver in the autumn. Eventually, after repeated postponements, he delivered it in January 2013. The long delay suggested a huge reluctance on his part to commit to an in/out referendum, but by the final months of 2012 it was clear that the task of his speech was to make the best of a bad job, which at Bloomberg he sought to do.

Cameron's Bloomberg Speech

The Cameron speech made one announcement of seismic political significance:

> The next Conservative Manifesto in 2015 will ask for a mandate from the British people for a Conservative government to negotiate a new settlement with our European partners in the next Parliament [...]

> And when we have negotiated that new settlement, we will give the British people a referendum with a very simple in or out choice. To stay in the EU on these new terms; or come out altogether. It will be an in/out referendum [...]
>
> We will complete this negotiation and hold this referendum within the first half of the next parliament.

That is, at the latest, by the end of 2017.

Yet paradoxically the speech was couched in more positive terms about Britain's membership of the EU than anything delivered by a Conservative leader since John Major's 'heart of Europe' address in Bonn in 1990. The peroration hit emotional highs worthy of one of Tony Blair's better efforts:

> When the referendum comes, let me say now that if we can negotiate such an arrangement I will campaign for it with all my heart and soul.
>
> I believe something very deeply. That Britain's national interest is best served in a flexible, adaptable and open European Union and that such a European Union is best with Britain in it [...]
>
> Over the coming weeks, months and years, I will not rest until this debate is won [...]

Blair himself professed that he agreed with 90 per cent of its language: the problem was the 10 per cent that committed a future Conservative government to an unworkable strategy of renegotiation and referendum.

The bulk of the speech was a characteristically British argument that, while the EU had massive historical achievements to its credit, it now needed to change and reform. Cameron's 'vision for a new European Union, fit for the twenty-first century' was built on 'five principles'. (For the historically minded, a familiar reworking of a conditional commitment, recalling the 'five conditions' Labour set for Common Market membership in the early 1960s, and the 'five tests' for British membership of the single currency.) These principles were well honed to appeal to Continental centre-right and business opinion:

1 *Competitiveness*. Completing the single market should be 'our driving mission'. The EU should urgently address 'the sclerotoic, ineffective decision-making that is holding us back'.
2 *Flexibility*. 'We must not be weighed down by a one size fits all approach that implies all countries want the same level of integration.' The 'essential foundation' of the EU is the 'single market rather than

the single currency'. In place of ever-closer union, the British had a vision of 'flexibility and cooperation [... that] is just as valid'.

3 *Power must be able to flow back to member states.* 'Let us not be misled by the fallacy that a deep and workable single market requires everything to be harmonised [...] Countries are different. They make different choices [...] We need to examine whether the balance is right in so many areas where the European Union has legislated including on the environment, social affairs and crime.'

4 *Democratic accountability.* 'We need to have a bigger and more significant role for national parliaments [...] in the way the EU does business.'

5 *Fairness.* 'Whatever new arrangements are enacted for the eurozone they must work fairly for those inside it and out.' That is why 'Britain has been so concerned to promote and defend the single market as the eurozone crisis rewrites the rules on fiscal coordination and banking union.'

For all the careful argument and high-flown rhetoric, Cameron would have preferred not to have made this speech. Eighteen months earlier he had imposed a three-line whip against demands for an in/out referendum. His speech once again put the European question at the forefront of British politics: quite the opposite of what, as a Conservative moderniser, he originally wanted. Cameron's defence was that a referendum was now inevitable:

> Public disillusionment [in Britain] with the EU is at an all time high [...] People feel the EU is heading in a direction they never signed up for [...] They resent interference [...] by what they see as unnecessary rules and regulations [...] They feel the EU is heading for a level of political integration that is far outside Britain's comfort zone.
>
> I believe in confronting this issue – shaping it, leading the debate [...] not simply hoping a difficult situation will go away.

But crucially that confrontation was some years away. 'Such a momentous decision about the future of our country' could not be made 'while the EU is in flux and we don't know what the future holds'. And his road map was far from clear:

> To make the changes needed for the long term future of the euro and to entrench the diverse, competitive, democratically accountable Europe that we seek [...] *the best way* to do this will be in a new Treaty.

His strong preference was:

> to enact these changes for the entire EU, not just for Britain. But if there is no appetite for a treaty for us all, then of course Britain should be ready to address the changes we need in a negotiation with our European partners.

The multilateral way forward was the preference, but the unilateral demand was not ruled out. The nature of the reforms in the EU that a future majority Conservative government would seek is extremely ill-defined and Cameron's 'bottom line' for any negotiations is totally unclear. He temporarily closed down active rebellion on Europe, but for the Eurosceptics in his party, once the short-term fix of winning the promise of an in/out referendum had worn off, they would come back to 'bang on' about little else.

The short-term nature of Cameron's triumph became evident after the May 2013 local elections in which UKIP scored 23 per cent. Most electoral analysts are agreed that Europe is only one factor in the UKIP insurgency: immigration and dislike of the political establishment in all parties are more potent. But Conservative backbenchers are not so sanguine: they reacted to UKIP's strong performance by demanding immediate legislation for a referendum. As the Liberal Democrats would not agree to such a proposal being included in the Coalition legislative programme, Cameron announced that the Conservatives would impose a three-line whip in support of a private members' bill legislating for a referendum in 2017. Yet for voters who are anti-Europe above all else, UKIP will always offer a clarity that Cameron cannot match. It may be that Cameron's in/out pledge will prevent UKIP gaining some Conservative votes they would otherwise obtain in marginal constituencies. But the major challenge to unity will be the next Conservative manifesto; if Eurosceptics press publicly for a much harder bottom line for the negotiations, this might be dismissed out of hand by some EU partners, strengthening the major anxieties about the possibility of EU exit already being expressed by pro-Europeans and the business community. UKIP may offer not to stand against Conservative MPs who make an unconditional pledge to support EU withdrawal. There is also the likelihood of further damaging dissension if those with an eye on the future Conservative leadership toughen up their rhetoric. The party's image of competence could be damaged if in the election Europe makes it look badly split.

The strength of Cameron's speech is that its sentiments chime with probably where the centre ground of British public opinion lies: the sense that there is something fundamentally amiss with the EU that needs to change, but that if that change can be brought about, the best option for Britain is to stay. The post-speech polling suggested that the speech has somewhat enthused disillusioned Conservatives, but there was scant evidence that the promise of a referendum would in itself switch Labour and Liberal Democrat voters in a Conservative direction. Paradoxically the generally pro-EU tone of the speech, alongside the public debate that it generated, significantly strengthened public support for staying in Europe, though some polls still showed a small majority for withdrawal. The pro-European tone of Cameron's Bloomberg speech sounded genuine. But there was also a cynical logic to it, in attempting to minimise the damage to business confidence that Cameron must have known his speech would cause. Even if Cameron was confident when he made the speech that his new strategy of renegotiation and referendum could be made to work, he must be conscious of the inevitable uncertainty that his announcement of an in/out referendum five years in advance of it being called must have for investor confidence in Britain and possibly the strength of sterling. Even if one believes that in the past such scares have been exaggerated, as they clearly were by the advocates of Britain's membership of the euro a decade before, the added uncertainty cannot help the recovery. For all Cameron's protestations about the vital importance of our membership of the single market, it is his new policy that is calling this membership into question. For all Cameron's fine words, it was a bad day for Britain.

The Imponderables of the Cameron Renegotiation: The 2015 General Election Result?

The strategy of renegotiation and referendum is subject to a number of obvious imponderables. The first is whether the Conservatives win an overall majority at the 2015 general election and will therefore be in a position to deliver their referendum pledge. The second is whether Labour will match the referendum promise. Whilst the 2015 election outcome is unusually unpredictable, given the fragility of the economic recovery, the five-year decline in living standards that the majority of the working population experienced from 2008, the general disillusion with politics, and the vagaries of Britain's voting system, a Conservative failure to win an overall majority may not be the end of the renegotiation venture. If the parliamentary outcome results in a renewal of the Coalition between the Conservatives and the Liberal Democrats, it is difficult to believe that the Lib Dems would have the power to block a renegotiation/referendum commitment. The Lib Dems might, however, act as an effective countervailing force to the Eurosceptics in preventing the government setting too high a bar for defining a renegotiation success, as their influence over the 2013 balance of competences review already suggests.

As for Labour, Ed Miliband adopted a courageous stance in opposing the Conservative referendum commitment on the grounds of the economic uncertainty that it generated. Miliband argued that the pledge was only made for the basest reasons of party management rather than to advance Britain's national interests. Yet, in a public display of lack of confidence in its own convictions, the party briefed that it had not definitively ruled out an in/out referendum. This reflected an internal party perception of strong electoral and media pressures to match the Conservative referendum offer at some future stage, particularly if Labour's opinion poll lead started to narrow. A switch to support for a referendum would face Labour with awkward dilemmas, apart from the personal blow to the Labour leader's credibility. Would Labour be offering an in/out referendum on the status quo, ignoring the Conservative promise to negotiate a better deal for Britain within the EU? Labour has spoken of an agenda of EU reform that it would pursue with our partners. The essence of the difference between Labour 'reform' and Conservative 'renegotiation' is that the former is a multilateral endeavour, working with our partners, whereas the bottom line of the latter is a set of unilateral demands for change in Britain's relationship with Europe. As long as Labour sticks to the reform/renegotiation distinction, it would be difficult for the party to devise a renegotiation strategy of its own. Again, as with the Conservatives, there is no clarity on whether Labour's emphasis would be put on policy reforms that can be agreed without treaty change, or on institutional changes that would require treaty change and be much more difficult to achieve.

A switch to a commitment to an early in/out referendum could be presented by Labour as a move to end economic uncertainty and 'clear the air'. This assumes such a referendum would be won. But the stakes for a Labour government would be huge. On the assumption that the Conservatives have re-entered opposition and chosen a new post-Cameron leader, the likelihood is that they would have drifted decisively into the anti-European camp. This would heighten the risk of an 'out' vote, which would for certain badly weaken, and possibly destroy, a Labour government. A referendum 'out' vote would not end uncertainty; rather, it would heighten it. For an 'out' vote would be the start of a long and complex negotiation of British withdrawal, in which there would be no certainty for investors about the future of Britain's position inside the single market. There would be little incentive to invest in Britain while this uncertainty persisted, and the outcome would be problematic. Would it satisfy the anti-Europeans if Britain opted to be like Norway – remain a member of the single market but fully accept all its rules and regulations with no say over their content? How disadvantageous would be the terms of any UK–EU trade deal that might conceivably be on offer? The economic dislocation would be considerable.

Similarly, a referendum 'yes' vote would not clear the air. Both Labour and the Liberal Democrats have announced that they will not repeal the EU Act 2011 which mandates a referendum on any further transfer of powers to Brussels. Even if Labour were to win a referendum on membership shortly after 2015, our EU partners may decide for reasons of their own to launch negotiations for a new treaty at a later date that would require a *further* referendum, with more uncertainty generated about Britain's long-term position in Europe. The first referendum would have settled nothing.

The Second Imponderable: Is a Major New EU Treaty Likely within the 2017 Timescale?

The second imponderable is whether there will in fact be a major treaty negotiation within the Cameron timescale. Clearly the possibility of a new treaty for the whole EU makes renegotiation a more credible venture. Without it, a package of unilateral UK demands comes across as a thinly disguised ultimatum to our partners that, unless they prove accommodating, Britain may end up leaving the EU.

Views on the likelihood of a process of full-blown treaty change have waxed and waned. At one point there was a general assumption that the process would be launched after the 2014 European Parliament elections: there would be a convention in 2015–16 and an intergovernmental negotiation in 2016–17, broadly compatible with the timetable Cameron announced. It was always assumed that the pressure for this would come from Germany. In principle, the Christian Democratic Union of Germany (CDU) supports a radical leap forward in political integration, creating a federal European finance ministry, and a directly elected EU president. Committed federalists like the German finance minister, Wolfgang Schauble, have long had a strong preference for a more formalised and integrated inner core Europe based on the euro, of which Schauble, to be fair, always argued Britain should be part. Yet Chancellor Merkel is more cautious. Following the September 2013 election outcome, a 'grand coalition' with the Social Democrats may be more integrationist than the previous government, but if there is German backing for treaty change, it will be limited in scope.

Yet it is not just a German decision: Germany is the most important member state by far, but its position is not hegemonic. In Brussels, José Manuel Barroso, the Commission president, wants to bequeath a comprehensive plan for treaty revision before he leaves office in 2014. President Van Rompuy is more circumspect: he knows the majority view of the European Council is opposed, including, crucially, France. The Lisbon Treaty experience demonstrated how difficult it could be to secure quick ratification of a new treaty by all 28 EU members; it would be foolhardy to embark on such an enterprise, until either bond market confidence in the solidity of the new euro framework had been restored, or a new treaty became the only possible means of saving the euro. Van Rompuy's whole approach has been to frame proposals for strengthening eurozone governance within the existing treaty framework.

The long-term weakness of this approach is that it cannot deal with the democratic accountability deficit that further fiscal centralisation would exacerbate. Van Rompuy is not oblivious to these arguments; as a classic Belgian integrationist, he recognises the intractability of some of the institutional issues. Equally, the German Constitutional Court may at some stage insist on treaty change. The Court has no 'in principle' objection to further European integration per se, but what it finds unacceptable is the idea of further integration that takes power away from the Bundestag, without establishing new forms of proper democratic accountability at European level. There are no easy answers to the dilemmas raised.

There is a huge question as to whether a common institutional structure for the whole EU, with its EU 28 Commission and EU 28 Parliament, can survive unchanged in the longer term if the eurozone integrates in a more formal way. Legally the currency of the EU is the euro, and all member states, other than the UK and Denmark, have an obligation to join when they meet the criteria for membership. In principle, a two-tier Europe divided between euro-outs and euro-ins is a passing phase in the long and gradual process of EU integration. Yet this view may not prove tenable: the experience of Greece joining when it was clearly not ready has proved a terrible warning. 'Unreadiness' for some euro-outs may begin to look like a semi-permanent state, creating a fundamental euro-in/euro-out divide.

There has been talk of a new forum for national parliamentarians to exert a stronger say over EU-wide fiscal decisions, though this has met resistance from the European Parliament. Even bigger and more problematic is the issue of how a European Commission and Parliament representing all 28 member states can legitimately make fiscal and banking decisions for a 17-member eurozone, given that the issues at stake go to the heart of national sovereignty on taxation, spending and borrowing. No one has yet has come up with convincing answers to these difficult conundrums, and are not likely to within the Cameron timescale.

Much depends on whether the eurocrisis re-emerges in its full intensity. Has ECB President Mario Draghi's pledge in July 2012 to do 'whatever it takes' to save the euro done enough, underlined as it was by one of the most effective asides ever delivered: 'and be in no doubt, we mean it'? There are major doubts. Some fear the eurozone might become subject to grave social unrest and political instability, as the strains show in debtor countries forced to bear a huge burden of adjustment. One future trajectory of eurozone policy envisages Germany agreeing reluctantly to extend and maybe partially to write off debts to make the position of Greece, Ireland, Portugal and Spain fiscally sustainable. In return for this relief from their past mistakes, and possibly for financial assistance to support their reform efforts, the debtors would accept tough new limitations on their sovereignty that could take the form of legally binding contracts between debtor countries and the EU authorities. Yet there is no certainty that this will require treaty change. If the sacrifice of sovereignty was voluntarily agreed by member states in receipt of assistance, this would avoid full pooling of sovereignty all round. Further decisive steps towards banking union, including the partial mutualisation of responsibility for bank restructuring and recapitalisation, and some form of deposit guarantee, do require treaty change in German eyes, but not according to others. Therefore any resulting change might well sharply limit the scope for comprehensive treaty revision.

President Hollande would clearly prefer to avoid treaty change that involves any risk of a referendum in France. The Constitutional Treaty referendum in 2005 was a particularly searing experience for the French Socialists, who ended up badly split. However, France's own economic prospects are uncertain: a market loss of confidence in French sovereign debt at some stage is not impossible. This could result in some new 'grand bargain', where the Germans agree to a measure of debt mutualisation through Eurobonds in order to bolster France's bond market defences, in return for France assenting to eurozone pooling of sovereignty over fiscal policy. However, such a turn of events would be so difficult politically in France as only to occur as a last resort.

There is a strong lobby in the European Parliament and Commission that wants a new, 'more federal' treaty, which would permit, for example, the issuing of Eurobonds, but it is not clear whether the integrationist group is prepared to face up to its own logic and the need to strengthen democratic accountability in a eurozone inner core. Prospects for a new comprehensive treaty within this timescale depend on the interaction between markets on the one hand and social and political developments on the other. At some stage the institutional issues will have to be addressed, but not necessarily on the Cameron timetable.

If there is no comprehensive treaty, Cameron would be left with two options for renegotiation. One would be to request the opening of an intergovernmental conference that would exclusively concern itself with negotiating a new settlement for Britain. That decision would be taken by majority vote in the European Council. A bloc of member states might oppose such a decision, but while a minority could not stop negotiations with Britain being opened, as the outcome would in the end be subject to unanimity, the process could be especially fraught. The second option would be to conduct a renegotiation that did not involve formal treaty change (or perhaps only one or two very specific changes under the simplified revision procedure), but instead consist of an agreement to amend certain EU laws, as well as reform EU policies and working practices through various protocols and declarations. Angela Merkel and other EU leaders may well be willing to go down this road, as the price of keeping Britain in the EU. This would follow the precedent Harold Wilson's 'renegotiation' set in 1974–5.[2] David Cameron may be able to pull off the same trick. It would leave him searching for the symbolic gesture that would signify real change – the equivalent of Wilson's success in increasing quotas for cheap New Zealand lamb and butter!

The Third Imponderable: Is a Successful UK Renegotiation Feasible?

The third imponderable about renegotiation is how high, or more pertinently how low, Cameron sets the bar for success. The answer depends ultimately on the internal politics of the Conservative Party. From one view, no feasible version of renegotiation achievable with our partners would unite the Conservative Party. Yet, a more limited renegotiation could be presented to the British public as a success and provide the basis for a victorious vote to remain in the EU in an in/out referendum. With a Conservative prime minister advocating continued British membership, supported by the leadership of Labour and the Liberal Democrats, an in/out referendum would have a better chance of being won than many Eurosceptics currently believe. But there would be a major political cost to the Conservatives in terms of party unity. A Europe referendum could even prove the trigger for a major realignment of British politics.

Most member states want to keep Britain in the EU. The Dutch would regard a British departure from the EU as a major blow to their national interests: they were always the strongest supporters of Britain's membership of the Common Market, when for a decade in the 1960s de Gaulle successfully kept Britain out. The other 'northern liberals' share the Dutch view; with all of them, Cameron's speech struck a chord, particularly his emphasis on deepening the single market, curbing the extended reach of Brussels and strengthening national parliaments. The Germans regard the British as firm allies for an economically open and outward-looking EU. There is a likemindedness between British Conservatives and German Christian Democrats in wanting to curb the Commission, enforce subsidiarity and strip down the 'acquis'. Yet Germany's overriding national interests remain in its alliance with France and the new member states to its east under the umbrella of the EU. German sympathy has clear limits. It is a mistake to interpret ties of sentiment as a willingness to cut a special deal in the form of a new treaty specifically defining a new settlement between Britain and the EU.

Some east Europeans – the Czechs, Hungarians and Baltics – are wary of deeper EU integration and, along with the Poles, have traditionally been strongly Atlanticist in outlook. However, Cameron's negativity on the EU budget has damaged the alliances Britain had previously built up. Similarly, in the Blair years the Italians and Spanish looked to Britain as an alternative to Franco-German domination, but then they assumed Britain would become their partner in the euro. Now the future of their economy and society is bound up in a project from which the British appear ever more distant. The French are pulled in opposite directions; their strong ambitions for Europe to be 'a force for good' in the world role depend on a shared British commitment. Yet again their top national priority is the success of the euro. Cameron's renegotiation agenda is for them destructive of their concept of the progressive construction of Europe. French critics of any special deal for the UK will argue that it represents a set of demands to protect UK special interests, such as the City of London, and to enable Britain to compete in the single market without having to adhere to a set of common rules.

Some aspects of renegotiation will be relatively easy. Our partners are alive to the new issues that might arise in future as a result of a more integrated eurozone acting as a cohesive voting bloc within the Council. They will offer legally enforceable guarantees of fair treatment to avert the potential for discrimination against the UK and other euro-outs. But the best guarantee of Britain's position within the single market is not words written on paper, but a renewed momentum behind the project. That first requires a resolution of the eurocrisis; second, a strengthened Commission with the single market as its core mission; and third, broad political support among member states. Renegotiation cannot substitute for active EU engagement by the UK, and UK backing for a strong Commission. Nor can the UK strengthen its single-market cause by seeking special protections for key UK interests, such as the reintroduction of the 'Luxembourg compromise' or the negotiation of an emergency brake on financial regulation. Special deals for the UK of this kind are likely to be non-starters.

Our partners see Britain as already enjoying major EU opt-outs: from the single currency, the Schengen agreement on open internal borders and the potential opt-out from Justice and Home Affairs legislation in 2014. This has caused genuine puzzlement to our partners. Britain's own police and intelligence chiefs have been clear that exercising the opt-out risks Britain's security. Since 9/11, senior British personnel have played a leading role in building up European cooperation and capabilities. Although Britain wants to opt back in to key measures, there is no guarantee that the process will be smooth and all member states will agree.

Beyond that, our partners are puzzled by the nature of the 'new settlement' Cameron proposes. How radical a change is the Prime Minister actually seeking? Is it right to assume that one clear Cameron objective is to reintroduce some equivalent of the Social Chapter opt-outs that John Major secured at Maastricht? Does the government want directives such as those on parental leave, agency workers, information and consultation, and maybe working time, either to be modified for the whole EU or no longer to apply in the UK? Is the government's objection simply to social measures being ones of EU competence, in which case equivalent domestic legislation might be introduced, or is it that all the social protections that the EU currently offers working people are unnecessary burdens on business that should be scrapped? The Conservatives have remained studiously vague.

Social opt-outs may be the minimum or maximum change that the government is seeking: this is unclear. However, an opt-out agenda will lead to problems, possibly big ones. How would it be possible for the UK to uphold the single market, never mind pursue an agenda to deepen and extend its impact, while negotiating an 'à la carte' Europe at the same time? If, for example, Peugeot and Fiat are already having difficulty competing against Volkswagen, why should our partners in France and Italy agree to arrangements that would allow British-based manufacturers to scrap regulation, cut costs and gain an unfair competitive advantage as they will see it? Many on the Continent think that as a euro-out Britain already enjoys the unfair advantage of a sterling depreciation. What many Conservatives demand on deregulation for the UK would be completely unacceptable.

The Limitations of Cameron's Single-Market Vision for Europe

Cameron's Bloomberg speech puts the single market at the centre of his case for Europe:

> At the heart of the European Union must be, as it is now, the single market. Britain is at the heart of that single market and must remain so. [...] Our participation in the single market and our ability to help set its rules is the principal reason for our membership of the EU.

The single market is both the core of his argument for renegotiation and at the same time for Britain's continued membership.

Eurosceptics believe renegotiation is necessary because European law and regulation has overreached itself. In accepting the case for renegotiation, Cameron implicitly backs the misleading and ahistorical assertion that 'Europe is no longer the free-trade area that in 1975 the British people voted to join.' Yet, in his view, the single market cannot be sacrificed. So what is his renegotiation about?

Boris Johnson, London's mayor, talks of a Europe 'pared down to the single market'. George Eustice MP, a leading member of the Fresh Start Group, talks of a relationship with Europe limited to 'trade and cooperation'. Yet the single market is much more than a free-trade area, which David Cameron acknowledges, but many Eurosceptics refuse to accept. In addition to the absence of tariffs and quotas at the border, it involves the removal of barriers to trade that exist *behind* borders by setting common regulatory standards without which there can be no free flow of goods and services. These common regulatory standards cover a wide range of issues such as consumer rights, environmental standards, health and safety rules under which goods can be made and services offered, drug testing, food safety, packaging, waste disposal, and a host of other matters. It is quite unclear whether Eurosceptics see a Europe pared down to the single market as including these rules and protections. Some talk as if the single market were separate from the regulations that are at its heart.

Cameron is here setting up an argument that he can never honestly win. The single market cannot logically be separated from the body of EU regulation that makes it possible. Without that single body of regulation, the itch to regulate would not disappear; rather, there would be 28 different sets of national regulation which businesses operating in the EU would have to work within. That would not contribute to a decreasing regulatory burden on business.

There is more than a grain of truth in Cameron's argument when he says:

> let us not be misled by the fallacy that a deep and workable single market requires everything to be harmonised, to hanker after some unattainable and infinitely level playing field. Countries are different [. . .] they make different choices.

The original objective of the single-market programme was to secure a level playing field across a broad range of economic sectors without the need for 'heavy' harmonisation. 'Mutual recognition' was supposed to square this circle, but member states have in practice been very reluctant to accept mutual recognition without insistence on a comprehensive set of minimum standards. Two major examples where 'mutual recognition' has applied were wholesale financial services and professional qualifications. In wholesale financial services, mutual recognition resulted in the absence of adequate cross-border regulatory standards and supervision. The fact that regulation remained nationally based undoubtedly contributed to the severity of the banking crisis. Britain is held primarily responsible because the UK had been the strongest opponent of Brussels intrusion in the City and the most vocal advocate of light-touch regulation.

In the case of mutual recognition of professional qualifications, this measure of liberalisation proved highly effective. It facilitated the free movement of labour from central and eastern Europe after the 2004 enlargement. For advocates of labour market flexibility, as most British Conservatives claim to be, their support for mutual recognition facilitating the free movement of labour has been muted. The British public's sharp reaction to the realities of EU migration demonstrates how public opinion wants any market opening to be accompanied by common rules and policies to safeguard the public interest. But in this case there proved to be inadequate rules to prevent wage undercutting by unscrupulous employers. Countries like the UK that want to extend market opening to new unregulated spheres need to accompany their demands for liberalisation with support for common standards of public interest regulation. Otherwise their demands will not get very far politically. The alternative of restricting the principle of 'free movement' will fall on even deafer ears.

The Monti report for the European Commission in 2010 made a powerful case for a renewed drive to complete the single market. It accepted this would not happen without additional social protections on free movement. The British government enthusiastically endorsed the overall thrust of the Monti report, while rejecting the additional regulatory safeguards proposed. Cameron argued in his speech:

> the single market remains incomplete in services, energy and digital – the very sectors that are the engines of a modern economy – it is only half the success it could be.

Yet the reason for this is precisely that different countries have made their own choices in terms of balancing a free market with their own rules and regulations to protect what they see as their public interest. So far there has been a failure of will at EU level to establish a level playing field. The British consensus on the future of the single market is not in the right place to deliver the economic benefits from the deepening Britain desires. Completion of the EU single market depends on an acceptance of additional EU regulation: no liberalisation is possible without new EU rules to protect the public interest.

Of course no one would argue that the way the EU presently makes laws and regulations is perfect. The acquis of European legislation and regulation should constantly be reviewed to establish its continuing relevance. In managing the single market, the Commission should give greater weight to the economic effects of national differences in regulation, not pursue harmonisation for its own sake. But this is a reform agenda for the whole EU, not an agenda for special opt-outs for Britain.

The status quo on the single market is of course highly beneficial to the UK. The biggest benefits have arisen from the encouragement given to inward investors to base activities in the UK, precisely because Britain offers unimpeded access to the European single market. This is the one consistent industrial policy that Britain has pursued with notable success since the abandonment of state activism in the Thatcherite 1980s. Inward investment has come to the UK from all over the world, including the rest of the EU, the USA, Japan, Korea and latterly India, China and the Gulf. It has benefited many different parts of the economy. Two of the most notable examples are the revival of the UK-based car industry and the presence of foreign banks located in the City of London. Of course Britain's access to the single market is not the only reason businesses base themselves here: labour market flexibility and the availability of top talent, alongside the attractions of British and London life, have been important magnets too. However, access to the single market has been a vital element in the mix.

Contrary to Eurosceptic assertions, the pull of the single market has not diminished with the growing importance of trade outside Europe. The single market offers businesses a rich and large home market, in which they can innovate and identify successful market niches for growth, which provide a base for their competitive success in global markets. The process of European enlargement has enabled European businesses steadily to improve the competitiveness of their supply chains. When one adds in all the economic benefits to the UK of EU membership, including the attraction of inward investment and the free movement of labour, as well as the growth in trade from being part of the world's most powerful trade bloc, the CBI puts the total benefit at 4.5 per cent annually of UK GDP.[3]

Yet for all the truth of these arguments, pro-Europeans would be foolish to rest on the single-market status quo as the knock-down argument for a positive 'yes' vote in an in/out referendum. The single market has been crucial for inward investment, the revival of British manufacturing and the success of the City. But there are far fewer jobs in manufacturing than when the 1975 referendum was won. A lot of the domestic economy now consists of smaller firms operating in the service sector. While polling of employers in the firms still suggests that support for EU membership remains strong, the perception of unwanted EU regulation for which they see few offsetting benefits looms large in their consciousness.

Moreover, pro-Europeans cannot expect big business to be as powerful a factor in putting the case for Europe as it was in 1975. Much of UK manufacturing is now owned by overseas investors who may be more reluctant to engage in a UK domestic political debate. The largest British registered companies tend to be hyper-global, such as BP and Rio Tinto, without much real activity of their own based in Britain. And larger firms that remain domestically owned often do business in sectors such as retail, where experience in the single market has been mixed. The single market remains central to the case for Europe, but it would be a mistake to think that it will convince the public on its own.

Will Cameron be Prepared to Pay the Political Price of a Referendum Victory?

One optimistic pro-European interpretation of Cameron's speech is that he has left himself the room for manoeuvre to secure the 'yes' victory he wants. An informed but dispassionate US-based observer, Jacob Funk Kirkegard, put this possibility rather well:

> Cameron may be playing a much more cautious game, one that ends up with Britain staying in the EU but Cameron supporting the cause after he has won some concessions that will not be unreasonable.

In the Bloomberg speech Kirkegard detected 'no red lines', 'no explicit negotiating demands'; to him Cameron appeared to be setting 'a pretty low bar for what he will accept as a new arrangement'.[4] The outcome Kirkegard envisages would certainly offer the Cameron premiership a tempting place in history.

If this is so, the major issue for Cameron would not be winning the referendum but whether he could contain a Conservative rebellion against a renegotiation outcome that would have the potential to split his party and weaken its future electoral prospects. He could follow Harold Wilson's course and hope to maintain party unity by permitting 'an agreement to differ' in his Cabinet and wider party. However, a referendum might lead to the defection of a whole group of activists and MPs to UKIP. How many, and how significant a breakaway this would be, is uncertain. The key issue would be how much of the Conservative cabinet Cameron could carry in selling what could only be a relative success. Unfortunately, the outcome of the renegotiation will coincide with the time when Conservative minds will be turning to the Cameron succession. This makes the whole outcome highly problematic.

The obvious tactical course for leadership aspirants would be to oppose Cameron's terms, but in as loyalist a way as possible, on a platform of maintaining party unity, but with an eye to an appeal to Eurosceptics in a future leadership election. But it would require great political skill to argue for coming 'out' in the referendum and then present oneself as a credible Conservative leader who accepted a positive referendum outcome. It might not restore unity. The 1975 referendum settled nothing in the Labour Party: by 1981 the party had committed itself to a policy of unconditional EU withdrawal without a referendum.

There is possibly space within the Conservative party for a future leader who would support a Cameron advocacy of a vote to stay 'in' on the basis that this is a decisive moment in the modernisation of the Conservative party and an opportunity to close a troubled historical chapter that began with the Thatcher leadership challenge in 1990. Such a future leader would not fear some defections to UKIP, possibly even cabinet resignations, if Cameron were to insist on collective responsibility; in private this might be highly welcome. Such a moderniser would be seizing a historic opportunity, but it would be one that would carry high risks.

For the determined Eurosceptic the likely terms of renegotiation that Cameron would recommend would be a massive disappointment, if not a betrayal. After a referendum 'yes' vote, anti-Europeans would have to decide whether they had any future within the Conservative Party. They would be forced to calculate whether this could be the occasion for a permanent split in the Conservative Party on the issue of Europe. It could be another 1846, 1886 or 1916–18 in British politics. If Cameron faces the historic choice between winning a referendum and splitting his party, what course will he follow? Who knows?

CHAPTER 14

A Progressive Alternative

The British case for Europe is normally made in terms of a narrow economic calculus of our national interests in the single market. These arguments remain valid, but they do not stir the soul. Rather the argument for Europe should be an integral part of the argument for a progressive alternative for Britain. As part of making a historic break with over three decades of neo-liberal political economy, Britain should take a decisive 'European turn'. Pro-Europeans should argue for a recast vision of a united Europe as a vital means of advancing our core values and essential interests in a world undergoing the most profound transformations in terms not just of the balance of power, but of technology and the possibilities of human existence.

The first step is to build a coalition of support for a continent-wide 'post-Keynesian new deal' to set Europe on a new path to sustainable and inclusive prosperity. We should decisively reject for Britain the illusions in the modern world of a 'nation state social democracy' as well as the risks of an off-shore competition state. We should build on the emerging but fragile cross-party consensus that our society needs a more responsible capitalism and underpin it with new EU norms and standards. We should take a lead in pressing for the difficult reforms needed to revitalise the 'European social model', not seek its residualisation.

To enable Europe to face up to the challenges of the world's growing multipolarity, Britain should take a lead in building, within EU structures, an inner core European Security and Defence Union. That is, an ESDU to match EMU as a project of integration necessary for our times, but offsetting the (perhaps exaggerated) risks of an inner core eurozone permanently relegating Britain to a second division outer tier.

Progressives need to be advocates of a bold programme of democratic reforms for the EU to reconnect the British people with the idea of Europe, and European citizens as a whole with reformed EU institutions. Part of this step change in accountability we British can implement straight away for ourselves: part will have to await the eventual negotiation of a new major EU reform treaty.

Progressives should not accept the current conventional wisdom that Britain can never join the euro. *If* (and this is still uncertain) a successful 'Mark Two' euro emerges from the eurocrisis, the debate about British membership should reopen. In these circumstances, progressives should not be content with Britain's unsatisfactory status quo as a euro-out where we have little influence on many key economic decisions impacting on Britain's future.

For Europe to evolve as progressives wish, there will eventually need to be radical treaty change. Progressives should not be frightened of putting such a treaty to a referendum that offers a clear in/out choice based on a positive vision for a British European future. Labour should seek to unite the progressive forces in British politics among Liberal Democrats, Greens, the churches and single-issue campaign groups around a common platform that puts a renewed European commitment at the centre of its political strategy and appeal. By contrast, an early in/out referendum on the present basis of British membership is high risk, is a craven appeasement of populist anti-Europeanism and solves little for the longer term.

A Post-Keynesian 'New Deal' for Sustainable and Inclusive Recovery in Britain and all Europe

Britain cannot separate itself from the economic consequences of the euro simply by not being part of it. The big long-term challenges for Britain and the eurozone are very similar. So are the immediate economic priorities: how to return economies mired in debt to sustainable growth. Recovery in Britain and the eurozone are deeply intertwined.

The Conservative-led Coalition, like the eurozone, put its faith in public austerity which they assumed would automatically rebalance the economy away from debt and consumption towards private-sector investment and exports. That programme stalled because their calculations did not sufficiently take into account the impact of fiscal consolidation on growth at a time when private sector de-leveraging and the impact of the eurozone crisis on trade exerted a heavy drag on the economy. Even as growth has resumed, there is little evidence that much rebalancing has taken place. The Conservatives misread the lessons of the Howe budget in 1981, which raised taxes and cut public spending in the teeth of recession, famously defying the advice of 300 economists, but was later seen as courageous statesmanship triggering economic recovery. But 1981 was different: fiscal tightening then facilitated genuine monetary loosening with lower interest rates and a sterling depreciation. In 2010, interest rates were already at rock bottom. While unorthodox monetary policies such as quantitative easing were attempted, their uncertain impact recalled Keynes' pithy dismissal of monetary policy in the 1930s depression, as 'pushing on a piece of string'.

Labour's call for a domestic stimulus, on the other hand, forgot the lessons of the mid-1970s when a Labour government was forced to abandon Keynesian policies and seek IMF support. Then the Labour left argued for an 'alternative strategy' to the 'cuts' Labour was forced to pursue, but, to make it work, they frankly acknowledged the need for import controls, stricter exchange controls and central economic planning. They understood that in a highly interdependent economy like the UK, nation state Keynesianism expands demand for imports, leading to a balance of payments and sterling crisis. A Europe-wide economic boost, that by definition also increases demand for British exports, is a more viable and attractive option.

The strongest argument for a Europe-wide plan is that it has worked before. At the London G20 in 2009, Britain, France and Germany showed the intellectual flexibility to act decisively in coordination with the USA to counteract the risks of a global economic slump. Yet once the eurocrisis took hold, fiscal discipline became for Germany the guarantee (in truth, a fragile one) that German taxpayers would not be held liable for other countries' debts. Tough requirements on sovereign debtors to tackle the structural deficits in their public finances became a firm condition of collective help. The fiscal compact constitutionalised a balanced budget objective for all members of the euro, although the Commission interprets the rules flexibly to take account of the economic cycle. In August 2012, Mario Draghi's pledge to 'do whatever it takes' to save the euro insured member states against speculative bond market attack and lowered the crippling bond yields some were facing, but it did not alter the eurozone's contractionary course.

Germany's response to the eurocrisis has been wrong on three fundamental points:

- There was too much initial focus on the moral failures of fiscal deficits, with insufficient attention to banking system excesses across all Europe.
- The unsustainable imbalances within the eurozone built up during the fool's paradise of the euro's first decade arose in part because of failures

to control public spending, curb irresponsible wage rises, make labour markets more flexible and tackle crony capitalism (all regrettably true), but also because huge balance-of-payment surpluses in northern Europe were rashly reinvested across borders through the single market's integrated but inadequately supervised banking system.
- While unsustainable fiscal deficits had to be corrected, however painful the consequences, the speed of the planned consolidation created a downward spiral of collective austerity as a result of the multiplier effects within countries and the spillovers into other countries.

Recognition that fiscal consolidation could be pushed too far and too fast came too late to prevent the emergence of a major social and political crisis in southern Europe. The long-term survival of the euro requires radical reforms to correct this flawed rescue. Without them, there will be little hope of light at the end of a long and dark tunnel. The British government should urge our European partners to:

- allow the ECB to intervene to reduce the crippling interest rates that businesses in indebted countries face;
- recapitalise Continental banks on a pan-European basis, with some degree of mutualisation of the bad debt problem;
- encourage higher wages in surplus countries;
- allow more time for debtors to achieve their fiscal targets;
- most difficult of all, negotiate debt write-offs to make fiscal sustainability achievable, in return for step-by-step structural reforms.

Because the health of the eurozone is critical to British recovery, Britain should place no ideological barriers of its own in the way of these efforts. We should reconsider the decision not to join the banking union; we should be partners in the necessary pan-European restructuring of Europe's banking system.

The Five Giant Challenges We Share in Common

The crisis, however, is much deeper than fiscal indiscipline, banking excess and unmitigated austerity. European societies, including Britain, face profound structural challenges. These existed before the crisis broke. Austerity is both intensifying them and obscuring our failure in addressing them. They are the five giants that threaten modern European civilisation.

The first is *global competition*: the rapid entry into the global labour pool of the emerging economies and the rise of Asia as the workshop of the world, combined with an unprecedented pace of technological change. The old European growth formula of productivity catch-up with the USA, the driver of the post-war '*trente glorieuses*', is no longer a sufficient option: surplus capital has available more attractive locations. While Europe as a whole will still be net gainers from the 'convergence machine' of EU enlargement, the most developed EU countries have no alternative but to pursue a high road to competitiveness based on knowledge and innovation. Yet Europe and Britain's record in education, research and innovation is at best patchy, as is our ability to foster dynamic, growing businesses that turn innovation into commercial success and well-deserved profit. This needs dramatic change.

The second is *demography*: the remarkable advances in life expectancy are not being matched by social reforms and lifestyle changes to make our welfare states sustainable. The rising costs of ageing are squeezing out the social investments necessary to facilitate the knowledge-based growth model. The good times for the retirees of the post-war baby boom are not matched by sufficient social support for young people and the successful nurturing of children. Progressives cannot be supporters of a welfare state status quo. There has to be a new accommodation with the facts of demography, a rewriting of the intergenerational compact, and a willingness to tackle lifestyle challenges such as obesity in which the single-market regulation of consumer industries plays a crucial role.

The third is *migration*: Europe, as an ageing society with falling indigenous birth rates, needs migration, but it induces deep social tensions in European societies. Europe is proud of its many distinct cultural identities and rejects an American model of assimilation, but a complacent multiculturalism that creates ghettos of the mind, as well as place, is no answer either. Europe needs to develop models of social integration that are based on clear citizenship rights and obligations (like language learning) and be seen to promote fairness on welfare entitlements and access to affordable housing, yet make no compromises on equality and equal opportunities in combating racism and xenophobia. Enlargement should not be seen as a migration threat, but an opportunity to establish a mutually beneficial circular flow of European citizens as countries become more prosperous.

The fourth is *climate change*: the recession has temporarily displaced this existential challenge, but it has not gone away. The profound transition that needs to take place in our energy supplies, our economies and the way we live has barely begun. The challenge is not just one of investment in low-carbon energy, renewables and transport infrastructure. Europe has to reformulate its failing Emissions Trading Scheme, develop a common policy for gas, and face up to the political and social challenges of higher energy prices. Europe's nation states are too small to manage these structural changes in underlying competitive conditions on their own.

The fifth is *inequality*: there are deepening inequalities in many European societies as a result of widening gaps between the 'winners' and 'losers' from globalisation. Unemployment rates among low-skilled young people have risen to crisis proportions. A tiny minority at the top scoop a larger share of rewards. In some countries there is a crisis of living standards for the so-called 'squeezed middle'. A new politics of fairer distribution needs to be argued for and a new politics of production defined that promotes better-paid, higher-quality jobs. Europe's clout is needed to clamp down on tax evasion and ensure fair trade.

Europe does not need a Keynesian stimulus that would only return it to an old, failing growth model. It needs a recovery plan that, at the same time as reviving demand, also tackles the five giants of Europe's underlying structural weaknesses in order to put us on a new path to more sustainable and inclusive growth. To slay these five giants requires a commitment to a *high investment decade* across Europe in, for example:

- cooperative breakthrough research (Europe has to pool its efforts more to match the USA and China);
- the creation of digital infrastructure;
- modernisation and reform of higher education as a driver of both greater equal opportunity and knowledge-based innovation to match the best in America and Asia;
- European energy grids, with new sources of renewable wind and solar energy in the south 'keeping the lights on' in the north;
- rail and urban transport infrastructure to reduce radically air transport, urban car use and carbon emissions;
- an innovation-centred approach to the ageing society to activate older people and raise their quality of life, as well as transform traditional (and increasingly unaffordable) health services.

Without public intervention, the level of investment required will not be forthcoming. However, the aim is not a bigger role for the state, but a private-sector-led *innovation economy*. Given the problems of the banking system in large parts of Europe, which may take years to remediate, a network has to be created of regionally based, publicly backed business banks and venture capital institutions to offer access to finance for growing firms. But it also needs a creative approach to regulation at EU level that will stimulate new industries and new consumer demands.

This should be accompanied by a programme of *social investment* in:

- comprehensive childcare and support for parenting, to raise employment rates and help overcome inherited disadvantage;
- a job and training guarantee for all young, unemployed people;
- a European qualification 'kite mark' to enable any young European to access an apprenticeship to a German standard;
- intensive language teaching as a right and responsibility for all EU migrants;
- investment in social housing in areas where migration has led to housing stress.

Member states need the freedom and capacity to 'borrow to invest' in programmes that genuinely tackle the five giants and raise Europe's growth potential. But there cannot be a general license for a return to fiscal indiscipline. Apart from projects that qualify under this European recovery plan, governments should commit to stick within existing spending constraints. This means further public-sector pay restraint, firm limits on discretionary spend, and welfare improvements which are either financed by switching priorities or explicit tax increases. Each member state's investment programme would need to be verified independently at EU level and approved collectively for financing under a mutual debt guarantee. For member states that face severe spending constraints, assistance should be mobilised through existing European instruments: the European Investment Bank, the new EU project bonds, EU budget co-financing and EU investment guarantees. What is now required is the will to mobilise these instruments on a substantial scale.

A 'British Turn' to a More European Model of Responsible Capitalism

The EU does not impose a rigid socio-economic framework on its members. It allows within it several models of capitalism to flourish, most famously the Rhineland model of coordinated capitalism, characterised traditionally by close relationships between the social partners, long-term commitment by employers to develop the skills of the workforce and locally based relationship banking. At various points in our post-war history, the argument has been made that Britain should model itself more on Germany. Scholars of the 'varieties of capitalism' warn against the notion that EU member states can pick and choose aspects of each others' social model, each of which has features that are path-dependent and culturally embedded. Nevertheless, change and convergence is possible over time. For example, from the late 1990s all welfare states moved towards more active policies to promote high employment participation.

In the case of the UK, our political economy underwent several changes of course in the post-war era. The Attlee government's model of state control to ensure fair shares for all gradually gave way to a failed attempt to construct a British model of coordinated capitalism from the late 1950s to the late 1970s. The election of Margaret Thatcher marked a sharp turning point in ending the post-war consensus. New Labour accepted important aspects of the Thatcher model, in particular labour market flexibility and disregard for inequalities at the top, but it manipulated the central levers of the state to redistribute the fruits of growth in order to improve public services, invest in the supply-side weaknesses of the economy and tackle poverty. The Achilles heel of this new Anglo-social model was the fragility of the tax revenues used to finance increased public spending, which proved overdependent on financial sector excess and a classic asset price bubble.

Since 2008, the British economy has been awkwardly positioned between, on the one hand, a return to neo-liberalism and, on the other, a tentative search for a new model to rebalance the British economy. The Coalition's response to deep fiscal crisis has in many respects been classically neo-liberal: drastic spending cuts, reduction in corporate and top tax rates, business deregulation and marketisation of public services. Yet Britain has also seen tentative moves towards much tougher banking regulation, a more activist and devolved industrial policy, a more robust approach to corporate tax avoidance, a strong prioritisation of apprenticeships, an attempt to incentivise long-term investment in infrastructure, and widespread recognition of the need for a less short-termist business culture. For the first time since the 1970s, the political space has been created for an incoming government to consolidate a shift towards a new British model of responsible capitalism.

Reforms in EU law and regulation should play a central role in underpinning this shift:

- There should be a deepening of the single market, with no 'race to the bottom' in social rights and a strategic industrial policy vision for key sectors crucial to Europe's success in global competition.
- A tough approach to financial regulation will be required, which recognises the vital role of banks in financing innovation and business growth, but safeguards financial stability and limits the risk to taxpayers in any future financial crisis, while fostering the new banking culture that many in the City recognise is needed.
- A coordinated EU attack must be made on tax evasion and avoidance, using the combined power of the EU to ensure that the mobile super-rich and international businesses contribute fairly to the tax revenues necessary to finance a modern welfare state. This would include action to close down tax havens and prevent companies from 'profit shifting'. A harmonised corporate tax base across the EU with minimum corporate tax rates would put a floor under a potential 'race to the bottom'.
- A reformed EU regional policy is required to provide a stable, long-term framework for addressing regional inequalities within member states. The disbursement of structural funds should be conditional on policy reforms. The funds should focus on promoting new sources of growth, tackling long-term and youth unemployment, and in sectors that are victims of trade or technology shocks, offering adjustment assistance for employee retraining and relocation, and attracting alternative new businesses. Re-nationalisation of the structural funds is not sensible; under single-market rules, every form of domestic regional support then becomes a questionable 'state aid'.
- A new policy for free movement of labour should be adopted, which maintains the fundamental right of free movement but ensures migrant workers are paid the prevailing 'rate for the job' and unscrupulous employers are not able to undercut wages. Meanwhile, the standards of UK apprenticeships should be brought up to the best in the EU.
- An EU carbon tax, or a minimum carbon price floor, should replace the presently failing Emissions Trading Scheme and provide real incentives for member states to meet their carbon emission targets. The proceeds would be used for a dual hypothecated purpose: to finance low-carbon investments that the market will not itself undertake; and to provide resources for tackling poverty, as higher fuel prices hit the poor hardest.

With such a portfolio of radical policies, the EU could make major strides to a socially just, environmentally sustainable and globally competitive capitalism.

A United Europe, with a European Security and Defence Union at Its Core, to Maximise Our Strength, Defend Our Interests and Promote Our Values

The United States National Intelligence Council (NIC) in their report on Global Trends 2030 forecast that by that date, 'Asia will have surpassed Europe and America combined in terms of global power based on GDP, population size, military spending and technological investment'. Europe as a whole will be dwarfed not just by the rise of China and India. The NIC analysis expects that by 2030 a range of middle-tier countries – what they call the 'next eleven' – such as Colombia, Indonesia, South Africa, Mexico and Turkey, will together have greater global power than the whole EU. Under the Obama administration, a profound reassessment of the USA's role in the world is underway. After military failure in Iraq and Afghanistan, the USA has hesitated in the face of appalling slaughter to get involved in the Syrian civil war. US attention has switched to the Pacific and the potential Chinese threat. America faces the prospect of a decade of defence cuts.

These hard facts underline what David Marquand has provocatively called the *End of the West*.[1] Marquand is surely right, not just in terms of the dramatic power shifts that are taking place, but also in the decline of the 'idea of the West' as the dominant force in world history, in terms of economic power, military might, and ideological unity in pursuit of freedom and democracy, however flawed in practice that idea proved. Today, the passionate Atlanticism of Blair's 'we will always be with you' speech to the US Congress in July 2003 feels out of sync with current world trends.

Where does this leave Britain? In truth, we are struggling to come to terms with the reality of a changing world. The UK presently accounts for less than 3 per cent of global GDP: a position in rapid relative decline, as the British economy stagnates and the emerging world bounds ahead. Gordon Brown incessantly boasted that Britain was the fourth largest economy in the world: his implicit message was that Britain alone still counts. Already France, China and Brazil have overtaken the UK in size. Forecasts suggest that by 2020 Britain will have slipped to 13th place in the global rankings. Cameron, in a style reminiscent of Brown, boasts that Britain still has the fourth largest defence budget in the world. But for how much longer can this last, given the weakness of the British economy, and the planned trajectory of decline in UK defence spending? Britain's situation may increasingly resemble the imperial overstretch of the post-war years. As America turns inwards and towards the Pacific, where else are we to seek allies who basically share our outlook on the world than amongst our partners in the EU?

However, Europe's record of acting in a united way has been disappointing. A pragmatic approach to the pooling of sovereignty is now needed to replace Europe's clumsy and ineffectual intergovernmentalism. At present, the only area where Europe effectively negotiates as one is trade, with the result that the trade commissioner is put under constant pressure to achieve multiple objectives in trade negotiations from human rights and the advancement of democracy to closer political cooperation. This does not make practical sense. There is a huge trade agenda for the EU to pursue, but Europe could mobilise its soft power more if it genuinely pooled its efforts in other spheres. For example, the EU and its member states are collectively the largest donors to Africa with the common aim of promoting better governance and human development. Yet Europe by its divisions has allowed China to become the dominating influence in many African countries. The pooling of sovereignty over external action does not involve cumbersome bureaucracy or detailed regulation; it simply requires political will. Trade provides an ideal model. The trade commissioner regularly reports back to EU trade ministers on the progress of negotiations and acts within a mandate that they determine. The Commission's trade officials report back to officials from their member states every single week. EU positions are decided by majority vote. This is not a transfer of power to Brussels: it is the only means to regain power that Europe's member states have already lost.

Additionally, an inner core, with Britain and France in the lead, should form a European Security and Defence Union, which the Lisbon Treaty provisions on 'permanent structured defence cooperation' allow. Such a move is not anti-NATO; indeed, one of its main purposes would be to demonstrate to the USA Europe's seriousness of intent in fulfilling its wider global responsibilities. Like the single currency, membership would not be automatic for all EU members, but should only be open to member states prepared to make specific defence and security commitments. These would focus on defence spending, its composition, its quality and a readiness to pool defence industry resources and procurement decisions. 'European defence' has so far only gone a little way in the necessary direction. The next step would be common defence procurement to ensure interoperability, achieve major cost savings and fill major capability gaps. This requires a new willingness of imagination to pool sovereignty over force planning and equipment decisions. European nations have now to abandon the myth that any single European country can afford to develop all-round capabilities of their own.

The ESDU should only be open to member states prepared to commit their armed forces to operations outside EU territory. This would obviously exclude countries like Ireland and Austria who remain sensitive about their status as 'neutrals', but it would not necessarily exclude non-NATO members such as Finland and Sweden if they wished to join. Britain, France, Italy and Poland would be natural core members of such a union alongside our traditional smaller NATO allies. There remains a big question mark over Germany. Many argue that Germany, understandably in the light of history, has become a pacific central European power, now concerned above all with stability and security to her east, rather than being willing to develop an outward-looking and if necessary interventionist projection of an EU role. Chancellor Schroeder took a huge risk in deploying German troops in the Kosovo crisis, but since then German foreign and defence policy has appeared in retreat. Germany will only settle this national debate when other EU partners demonstrate a willingness to move ahead. This is the historic role that Britain and France should now play.

An Agenda for Democratic Reform of the EU

British politicians have a tendency to bemoan the EU's lack of democratic legitimacy, while at the same time coming up with few ideas of their own for democratic reform. Eurosceptics on the right of the spectrum tend towards the view that the EU would be more legitimate if only it did less. If only it could be pared back to the historical myth of the 'free-trade area we first joined', then the EU's democratic problem would disappear, because in their eyes markets are self-governing agents of human prosperity and welfare in which politics should have little place. By definition, there would be little need for more democracy. Yet this benign view of markets is, to say the least, contentious. Any realist also knows that continued British membership of the EU involves – at the minimum – acceptance of the considerable body of better European law that governs the single market.

For the making of these laws, any democrat would insist on some system of accountability being in place, as the EU presently has.

This highlights the deeper problem that parliamentary sovereigntists have long had with the EU. Parliament imposes limits to its own sovereignty when it legislates for British membership of any international organisation that imposes rules on its members; but as Enoch Powell most effectively pointed out for the first time in the 1960s, there was a unique problem with Parliament's assent to EEC membership. The act of joining represented a *pre-commitment* that future laws agreed under the provisions of the EU treaties, of which Parliament, by definition, could have had no knowledge when it voted for UK accession, would have direct legal force without Parliament having to agree them first.

At the time the government made a two-fold response to this Powellite critique. First, Britain joined the EU as a result of an Act of Parliament. Parliament could always choose to repeal that Act at any future point. So the democratic legitimacy of the applicability of EU law in the UK flowed from a decision of Parliament that was not irreversible.

Second, as the explanatory leaflet that the government circulated to every household at the time of the 1975 referendum stated: 'No important new policy can be decided by Brussels or anywhere else, without the consent of a British Minister answerable to a British government and a British Parliament.' Ministers honestly believed this statement was accurate at the time it was made. Their interpretation of the 'Luxembourg compromise' (endorsed by Pompidou and Heath at their first summit) was that majority voting did not apply on any issue that an individual member state declared of national sensitivity and importance. However, Enoch Powell has had the better of this particular argument:

- The Luxembourg compromise was effectively disapplied at the time of the 1985 Single European Act. Although there have been very few occasions on which the UK has been formally outvoted, the dynamic of QMV inevitably forces member states to make compromises they might not otherwise have made.
- 'Co-decision' now applies over most EU decisions, which means that the Council of Ministers and European Parliament have both to reach agreement on each and every measure, further attenuating the power of any single member state.
- Because the processes of EU law and policy-making within the Council have traditionally been seen as a process of diplomatic negotiation, no

> democratic decision-making, standards of transparency and accountability have historically been poor. A national parliament less in hock to the government whips than the House of Commons would have exerted more grip over European policy-making by debating policy issues in advance of their resolution in a Brussels ministerial Council and defining the negotiating envelope within which ministers and officials had to work in Brussels. But of course the Whitehall machine, through the executive's control of Parliament, has fought tenaciously to retain secrecy and its freedom of manoeuvre.

For pro-Europeans, the solution to this dilemma has traditionally been strengthening the powers of the European Parliament. The European Parliament is a much-maligned institution, which in many respects works well. Legislation is thoroughly scrutinised. MEPs exert real influence in policy areas in which they specialise, unlike members of many national parliaments. It has opened up the EU legislative process to lobbies, interest groups and non-governmental organisations whose views have a legitimate right to be taken into account. It has forced administrative reforms on the Commission which they would otherwise have been reluctant to implement. It has opened up politics beyond the 'establishment' closed shop: in the UK, the Greens and UKIP have both gained a voice for their legitimate points of view that they would never otherwise have obtained without the introduction of proportional representation in European Parliament elections.

However, the greatly strengthened role of the European Parliament has not, so far at least, brought Europe closer to the people. Turnout in European elections has declined since direct elections were first introduced in 1979. Politics in most EU member states remains a largely national and (in countries such as Belgium, Germany and Spain) sub-national business. MEPs are seen as aspirant politicos who failed to make it into national politics. European elections are generally a set of national opinion polls on the standing of national parties in each member state, not the expression of a general will about what kind of Europe voters across Europe want to see. The offer of a clear choice between competing candidacies for the president of the Commission may help change that perception, but in itself one has to be sceptical. The hope must be that the seriousness and scale of the eurocrisis, and the existential threat it poses to the post-war achievements of European integration, is in itself creating the European 'demos' which has so far been lacking.

Tony Blair advocated a different view of how to make the EU more politically legitimate. The strengthening of the European Council would demonstrate visibly that the member states were in charge. By definition this was a 'big member state' solution to the legitimacy question: Luxembourgers cannot have imagined that they were 'in charge' in Europe simply because of Jean-Claude Juncker's visibility on the European scene (though to be fair, he did an excellent job of trying!). For Blair, the democratically elected heads of government were the 'government of Europe', not the Commission, which in his view was as much answerable to the European Council as it was to the European Parliament.

In democratic terms, the Blair proposition has two flaws. First, if the European Council is indeed the main source of democratic legitimacy in the Union, there is no way voters could express their discontent with the way Europe is being governed by collectively 'throwing the rascals out'. The eurocrisis has probably brought home to the public that the European Council, with its incessant meetings and dramas, is in charge of whatever strategy Europe has. If they do not much like its direction, the only way they can make a change is by voting out their own head of government. Much as European voters have resorted to this, the curse of incumbency has made little appreciable impact on Europe's trajectory. This reinforces the dangerous perception that in the European Council only one vote counts – that of the eurozone paymaster, Germany.

The second, more subtle flaw is that the periodic meetings of the European Council could by their nature only concern themselves with the big strategic choices facing Europe. There is no way the European Council can exert much real grip over the workings of the Brussels system – essentially the sprawling, entrenched networks of Council working groups, European Parliament committees and conciliation meetings, consisting of Commission officials, national departmental officials, officials from each member state's Brussels representation, specialist MEPs and their advisers, who together shape the vast output of Brussels decision-making.

An agenda for democratic reform of the EU is therefore complex and multi-faceted:

- *First, the ministerial accountability to the House of Commons for the European policy decisions that ministers take on the British people's behalf must be 'for real'.*

The cabinet should be reorganised to create a secretary of state for Europe. As a result, official coordinating machinery for European business in

Whitehall and Brussels would acquire for the first time a senior political head. The new secretary of state would spend part of their time in Brussels representing the UK at Ministerial Council meetings and in key negotiations with the European Parliament. The rest would be spent in Westminster, answerable to Parliament on a regular basis for the government's European policy. A new Joint Committee of both Houses might be established to grill the secretary of state on a weekly basis on their conduct of European business, as happens in Denmark and Finland. This new secretary of state would be answerable directly to the prime minister for the government's overall European policy. While the foreign secretary and chancellor would remain the lead British members of the Foreign and Finance Ministers' Council, the new secretary of state would have the right to attend all Councils, as priorities dictate, alongside a minister from the relevant department. This change would give much greater visibility to European affairs in our national parliamentary life and, in a helpful way, 'politicise' decision-making in Brussels. The downside would be that it might make decisions and agreements harder to reach, but that loss of efficiency would be worth it in order to secure greater visibility, transparency and accountability.

- *Second, the scrutiny committees of national parliaments should have greater powers, not just over proposed new legislation, but to review the existing 'EU acquis'.*

Eurosceptics are right to complain that once a new EU law is agreed, it becomes extremely difficult to change, despite the fact that the circumstances that first justified it may have changed. Europe needs to acquire a new mechanism to review the existing acquis and offer a 'reverse gear'. The Commission has its own programme of work to review the continued relevance of existing EU law and propose simplification, but the Commission cannot be the right body to review its own life's work. A new agency that is independent of the Commission is needed at EU level – a 'Standing Commission to Review EU Law and Regulation' – to challenge established assumptions and ways of working. This Standing Commission should report on a regular basis to COSAC, the coordinating body of national parliament scrutiny committees. As COSAC speaks for national parliaments, its voice should serve as a strong countervailing force to the Commission and European Parliament. It should gain the right to initiate legislative and regulatory reform.

- *Third, a big effort should be made to reconnect national parliamentarians with the governance of the EU.*

EU and national affairs are not separate spheres in which EU institutions settle questions that are EU competences and our national institutions concentrate on purely national affairs. Constitutionalists and political scientists may at times think like that, but it is not how real politics works. The interdependence between national and European politics should be acknowledged in the way the EU functions. There is an urgent need to connect national MPs with Europe.

An annual Congress of National Parliamentarians should debate the 'State of the Union'. This was proposed by Giscard in the Convention on the Future of Europe in 2003. It failed to find sufficient support then, but, since the onset of the eurocrisis, consciousness has increased dramatically of the crucial role that Europe plays in our national politics and of the need for national parliamentarians to have their say. At the same time, within the eurozone, the finance committees of national parliaments need to have a formal voice in the annual interpretation of the fiscal rules that will be of crucial significance in setting national budgets.

Furthermore, the idea first proposed by Joschka Fischer in 2000, for a new small second chamber made up of senior national parliamentarians, should be revived. Its purpose would be to enforce the principles of subsidiarity and proportionality in EU legislation and policy-making. It is difficult to constitutionalise competences at different levels of government without giving huge powers of decision to some form of Supreme Court. The only practical alternative is to set up an effective political body which takes decisions on a pragmatic case-by-case basis.

- *Fourth, the separate posts of president of the Commission and president of the European Council should be amalgamated and a new single president of Europe be directly elected.*

The EU needs to make a real democratic breakthrough. In a Europe which is more confederal than federal, the heads of national governments must continue to play a key role in setting the Union's strategy, but not at the expense of sidelining the Commission, the Union's executive arm, uniquely charged with acting in the European interest. Yet the Commission itself urgently needs to be smaller and more streamlined in order to avoid a proliferation of second-order activity. The principle that every member state should have its own commissioner should be pulled off its semi-sacred plinth. It is inefficient and contradicts the principle that the Commission's purpose is to act in the European interest, not represent the interests of individual member states.

A smaller, more effective Commission should have three distinct lines of accountability. First, it should report bi-monthly to the heads of government in the European Council, where every member state is represented. At that meeting every head of government should have the right to raise what to them is an issue of vital national importance, which in the old system their commissioner might have done. Europe's 'government' would then follow the model of the ECB's Governing Council: it would be an amalgam of a small, independent, full-time executive and the lead representative from each member state. Second, the Commission should also be accountable to the European Parliament. Third, the president would chair both the Commission and the European Council, but the legitimacy of the post would flow from the fact that she or he would be directly elected.

Cynics will say that the EU would end up with Beppe Grillo or David Beckham as its president. But such cynicism underestimates the maturity of Europe's citizens. Also, it would be legitimate to require candidates first to demonstrate a certain threshold of support in the European Parliament. In addition, an electoral college system, similar to the USA, would require candidates to demonstrate solid support across a wide range of member states, not just to rely on heavily concentrated support in a populous handful.

Critics will say such a system would never work because of the absence of a European demos. This condemns politics to be forever national and never genuinely European. The eurocrisis may well be changing this. The historical example of the creation of India as a functioning democracy in 1947, with no history of its own as a single country, hundreds of languages and widespread illiteracy, is also instructive. A democratically elected president would mean an election in which real choices would be offered about the future of the EU. It would become a crucial riposte to all those who argue that Brussels is a remote bureaucracy that is out of control. It would be the making of a genuinely European politics.

British Membership of a Mark Two Euro?

The current conventional wisdom is that the euro has proved a disastrous mistake and therefore Britain was right to have stayed out; that the integration necessary for the euro to survive involves sacrifices of sovereignty that Britain could never accept; and that a new relationship can now be put in place between Britain and the rest of the EU where Britain continues to benefit from its membership of the single market without having to be a full part of an entity that is on its way to a more federally integrated inner core EU.

The history of conventional wisdoms is that they can be very strongly held at the time, but can often turn out to be disastrously wrong. Think of the conventional wisdom a decade ago that financial regulation should be 'light touch', or that Gordon Brown had successfully abolished boom and bust. Or the assumption in the late 1980s that Thatcher and Lawson had solved the underlying supply-side problems of the British economy, or, little more than a decade before, that the only way for governments to handle the question of trade union power was by consensus. Conventional wisdoms are frequently wrong.

On UK macroeconomic policy the Treasury has always asserted, with extreme confidence, that the framework for managing the British economy that is current at the time is the only possible one to follow, until the point when it is suddenly forced by events to change course. It exerts these U-turns with such speed and confidence that, while luckless chancellors suffer long-term reputational damage, the institution and its officials survive unscathed. Yet over the decades it has combined supreme arrogance with a record of successive economic failure. There is no certainty that the current negative conventional wisdom on the euro will be proved wrong. In my view, on the basis of British economic history, there is a very reasonable chance that it will!

Of course, there is a respectable school of thought that, had we been members of the euro in 2008, the havoc wreaked on our economy by the banking crisis would have shifted from the disastrous to the catastrophic. Bond market investors at least viewed Britain as a safe haven in contrast with the default risk attached to bond markets in the eurozone. Had Britain been a member of the euro, given the fact that our public-sector deficit was higher than any member state other than Greece, and that the UK debt-to-GDP ratio of public and private debt combined was higher than all but Ireland's, Britain might well have become the victim of a confidence crisis on the scale of other sovereign debtors. This could have forced the government into an even sharper fiscal consolidation, with more deeply damaging effects on growth and with knock-on effects for our fragile banks of more bad loans and defaults. There are some questionable assumptions here, but one has to recognise the strength with which the view is held that the euro is not for Britain.

On the other hand, these arguments are all about the past. Does the same judgement apply to the future? UK interest rates are now on a par with the ECB's. Britain enjoys an exceptionally flexible labour market; employment has risen impressively as output has stagnated. The counterpart is falling real wages for the vast majority of employees, but that shows that the UK has been capable of an internal devaluation that allows members of a single currency to respond to shocks. The problems of sustainable convergence that were central to Gordon Brown's analysis of the five tests do not look as considerable today. Were confidence to return to the euro on a secure basis, then being outside might become a more uncomfortable place. The story of the coming decade *could* be one of British economic weakness as against a eurozone gradually overcoming its problems. That is not a forecast. It is too early to tell. The euro still has many challenges to overcome.

This pragmatism is not, however, shared by the Coalition. Their view is that if a eurozone Mark Two emerges with its original design flaws corrected, it would represent such a degree of integration that Britain could never accept the sacrifice of sovereignty involved. But that assumes we have much 'real' sovereignty in the first place. George Osborne asserted in 2010 that unless Britain followed his path of fiscal austerity, we would end up in the same position as Greece. That is not the statement of a chancellor who believes we can have real sovereignty of decision in the economic policies we follow. And of course he is largely right. There may have been more scope for nation state Keynesianism than Osborne admitted, but in practice it would have been pretty limited. Different political choices on tax and spending could have been made, but within a broadly similar fiscal framework.

What sacrifices of sovereignty would membership of a redesigned eurozone Mark Two in practice involve? Eurosceptics believe Britain would have to commit to a version of fiscal federalism where national budgets are decided in Brussels. For them it would be impossible for a British government ever to accept such constraints on sovereignty. But then there are some glib and rather shaky assumptions being made here. There can be no loss of sovereignty in sticking to rules that a sovereign government and parliament has willingly signed up for. The problem the eurozone faced in its first decade is that its members signed up to rules that they did not stick to and, in Greece's case, explicitly lied about. It cannot be regarded as a loss of sovereignty to be expected to mean what you say and to demonstrate to your partners the integrity of your own actions. So, for example, disclosure of full information about national budgets, including the assumptions on which forecasts are made, cannot be regarded as unreasonable. And it is also reasonable for this information to be disclosed in advance of the public announcement of the budget to the national parliament so that checks can be made that the information is consistent with the commitments that the member state has already signed up to make.

The relevant question is whether any loss of sovereignty would be acceptable because it would be outweighed by potential gains. The loss might be thought unacceptable if every item of the national budget were to be subject to Commission scrutiny and diktat. If the Commission were to tell us what the level of national 'tax and spend' should be, that might also be unacceptable. That is something on which voters make a broad judgement in general elections. But if the only sacrifice of sovereignty is that the level of the UK deficit has to be consistent with fiscal rules we have agreed to, then that is a different matter. Indeed, there is a powerful argument that if a government pre-commits to follow certain fiscal rules, and hands the discretion for monitoring its compliance with these rules to an independent body (which in this case would be the European authorities), it gains additional credibility. Real investment is encouraged because there is a greater prospect of economic stability and interest rates are lower because the 'risk premium' lenders require is lower.

The question is whether the fiscal rules to which euro membership would mean commitment are ones that the UK could in theory be prepared to live with. Critics will argue that the fiscal compact and the stricter rules of economic governance agreed in 2011 and 2012 would commit Britain to a balanced budget and an automatic annual reduction in its debt-to-GDP ratio that defies economic rationality. Yet the Commission is already showing flexibility in the application of the deficit and debt rules to take the economic cycle into account. The prudent course for Britain is to keep its options open.

Conclusion
Britain's Unresolved Choice

Many pro-Europeans will disagree with parts of the previous chapter, maybe the whole of it. That is not surprising: it represents a very individual take on the kind of European policy a progressive British government might pursue. This conclusion focuses on the common ground on which the British case for membership of the EU should be made.

Too often when the British case for the EU is made, it is coupled with a strong rhetoric on the need for reform which carries with it a heavy implication of negativity. Pro-Europeans have to be careful not to overdo the argument for reform of the EU to the point where the public sees little point in being a member. The traditional pro-European discourse in the UK concentrates on standing up for British jobs and British interests. Of course, every other member state stands up vigorously for its own. But ever since Margaret Thatcher in the early 1980s achieved a long-term settlement of the evident unfairness of the British budgetary contribution to the then EEC, an adversarial 'standing up for Britain' has been the almost automatic posture of most British politicians when faced with a European problem. This discourse treats the EU as at best a necessary evil, but basically an unwanted intrusion in our national life, far removed from the British people's instinctively generous internationalist commitment.

In most areas of the public realm, there is much that needs reform. However, the rhetoric of EU reform often embraces a contradictory mishmash of proposals: typically, for cuts and reforms in the EU budget and legislative acquis; for more proportionality and subsidiarity in EU decision-making; for less bureaucracy, faster decision-making and an attack on 'waste'; and for a bigger role for national parliaments in how decisions are made. Advocates of reform often fail to make clear whether they are calling for less Europe, or a different type of Europe; how calls for a more deeply integrated single market are in practice consistent with less regulation and more subsidiarity; how they reconcile their demands for a Europe that is more liberal in terms of trade with one that is less liberal when it comes to free movement of people; how they square faster, more efficient decision-making in Brussels with more veto powers for 28 national parliaments.

Pro-Europeans have to acknowledge more openly the reality of the EU: business proceeds by slowly establishing consensus. It is much more a confederation than a federation. The EU status quo represents the outcome of hundreds of historic compromises between member states, the UK included, that are therefore difficult to unravel and reopen. If one finds this situation impossible to bear, there are only two options: either to leave and lose the advantages of membership, or to support moves towards greater pooling of sovereignty that would facilitate more decisive change and push Europe forward towards a more federal structure. This is an uncomfortable choice that British pro-Europeans are keen to avoid, so muddle persists and Europe remains a convenient whipping boy for point-scoring national politicians.

At the root of our problem in arguing why Europe matters is the blinkered perpetuation of a nation state mindset inside the Westminster-centric bubble of our political class that appears oblivious to the degree of interdependence in the modern world. This interdependence is broad and deep: it covers the central questions of economics, tax, security, migration, crime, pollution, and standard and quality of life that are at the heart of the concerns of all our citizens. On Europe, British politics too often tries to ignore the facts of life: interdependence is closer and stronger with our near neighbours in the rest of Europe than anywhere else in the world. It is the facts of interdependence, not the existence of the EU, that limit our sovereignty. It is the failure to build effective means to reassert the beyond-the-border sovereignty we have lost, not the existence of the EU, that erodes trust in politics. Building a more democratic and effective EU should be part of a modern concept of multi-tier governance in an increasingly interdependent world: a political and constitutional vision that embraces a reformed, less centralised and less instinctively centralising Westminster model, and a revitalised and genuinely devolved regional and local politics with real power of decision. The case for Europe should be presented as part and parcel of a new way of thinking about politics and government that is essential to restoring the popular belief in the capacity of politics to change people's lives for the better.

The Questionable Assumption of a 'Looser Relationship'

The British political class now appears to take for granted that there is too much Europe, when the real need is for intelligent debate about where Europe needs to do more and where it could do less. It is simply assumed that those who argue for more Europe are by definition 'pro-integration' and therefore are to be damned as closet federalists who will never be satisfied until there is a United States of Europe. Ever since the 1950s, the British political class has been deeply attached to this assumption of federalist inevitability as the justification for their view of British exceptionalism. In the 2010s it has been assumed that this is the direction that the eurozone is taking as the only means to correct its original huge design flaws. The presumed loss of national economic sovereignty in making the euro work means Britain could never join. On this logic, Britain is approaching a decisive point in its relations with Europe that can only mean that in future Britain can only survive in some form of looser relationship with our EU partners. The old aspiration to end Britain's semi-detachedness is no longer a viable option and can be dispatched to the lost world of Blairite illusions.

Yet there are many questionable assumptions in this thinking. To support more EU integration, where a pragmatic case can be made, is not to be in favour of a United States of Europe in which national identities would be lost and nation states submerged. The British totally exaggerate the federalist momentum on the Continent. Throughout the eurocrisis, member states' determination to do whatever is necessary for the euro to survive has gone alongside a deep attachment to the nation state and extreme caution about bold federalist ideas. There is no certainty – indeed a likelihood of the opposite – that a 'United States of the Eurozone' will emerge. There will certainly be more pragmatic steps towards deeper integration: further moves on banking union and debt restructuring; the development of binding fiscal rules, and the processes to enforce them; maybe even a eurozone budget with limited power to tax and borrow at eurozone level. The *gouvernement économique* of the eurozone, which started with the establishment of the euro group in 1998, will have advanced significantly. The ECB has transformed its role. The ESM has been established to offer support to eurozone debtors in market difficulties on the basis of conditionality. The Commission has gained more rigorous monitoring powers over national government budgets. Yet for all these governance changes, the essential nature of both the eurozone and the EU as a unique hybrid of intergovernmentalism and supranationalism has not fundamentally altered. The member states will still play the decisive role in its governance. We will have seen a pragmatic pooling of sovereignty in response to unforeseen challenges, not the final leap to a federal Europe.

This gives Britain more options to remain a leading partner in the EU than many of its political class want to assume. The choice for Britain is not only between the permanent semi-detachedness of David Cameron's 'in' or the uncomfortable isolation of becoming an 'out'. Britain can and should be the champion of a more progressive Europe.

The Emphasis on 'Jobs and Growth' is Necessary but not Sufficient

Today when the case for Europe is made, it is invariably in terms of British jobs and growth, in which the centrality of UK access to the single market is key. These points have to be hammered home. It would be madness to put at risk the 4.5 per cent of GDP by which the CBI reckons that our membership annually benefits us. It is also crucial to the pro-European argument that these points are not misleadingly oversold.

Eurosceptics are right that if Britain left the EU, our trade with the Continental mainland would not grind to a halt overnight; it would remain substantial. Overseas companies based in Britain because of our membership of the single market would not suddenly withdraw; they would continue to work the investment they have 'sunk' here while its profitability lasted and at least until new investment decisions have to be made. On the other hand, it is highly likely that exports would be put at some significant disadvantage, that new inward investment would be discouraged, and that our global trading clout would be reduced.

Britain could in principle avoid these disadvantages by being prepared to join Norway in the associate status of the European Economic Area (or, like Switzerland, negotiating complex trade deals with the EU). There are, however, strong disadvantages in such arrangements from a Eurosceptic perspective. We do not thereby avoid European regulation, or making contributions to the EU budget. The only difference from the present is that we would have no say over the rules to be applied to us. The problem of Brussels interference would remain as significant as at present, according to one's perspective, people think it to be, and the problem of democratic legitimacy would grow.

Fully outside the EU, the UK-based car industry, for example, one of our principal manufacturing successes since the 1980s, would face a 10 per cent tariff on its output destined for the EU, unless a free-trade deal between the EU and UK could be negotiated. Those who think that EU countries would be prepared to grant UK exports unrestricted access could be in for an unpleasant surprise. Why should France, Germany and Italy tolerate a situation in which British-based companies could gain competitive advantage through ignoring EU regulation and cutting costs, and at the same time enjoy the benefit of an independent currency that can freely depreciate against the euro? The idea that they would grant the UK access in order that they themselves can keep free access to the UK market ignores the simple fact that British trade represents some 8 per cent of our EU partners' exports, while EU trade represents over 40 per cent of British exports. There would be huge difficulties, on the other hand, for a British government in imposing tariffs on imports from the Continent. Given the integration of supply chains across national borders that currently exists in Europe, there would be howls of protest that UK tariffs would raise the cost of essential inputs to UK production. A protectionist policy would also raise prices for UK consumers and in the end make British-based companies more inefficient. The risk that something like this might occur would be a major deterrent to new inward investment. Similarly, it is difficult to see how, in the medium term, the City of London could continue to prosper as the financial centre of the EU single market from outside the EU.

The EU's Contribution to Our Social Well-Being

Yet as a positive case for Europe, these arguments sound too defensive. A narrow calculus of self-interest about Britain's membership of the single market is fully justifiable and necessary, but not sufficient. As Jacques Delors famously said, 'who falls in love with a market?' British pro-Europeans too readily go along with the Eurosceptic criticism of an over-regulated EU, without defending the common social and environmental standards that make the crucial difference between our European 'civilisation' and a global race to the bottom. This is coupled with a failure to acknowledge the common values that Europeans share about how our societies should be shaped and how the world could be more justly ordered.

The EU's contribution to our social well-being goes largely undefended. The debate about British membership divides between, on the one hand, supporters of the single market, who argue that, inside it, the 'burden' of EU regulation should be reduced, and on the other, proponents of an 'offshore Britain' freed of the EU's regulatory constraints. It is time for this debate to be reframed.

As a result of the way pro-Europeans have allowed the debate about the EU to be distorted, the British public is dimly aware of how much the EU has changed their quality of life for the better. How many people in Britain know that it is only because of the EU that workers are entitled to four weeks' paid annual holiday; that part-time and agency workers enjoy equal rights on a proportionate basis to full-time employees; that equal pay and anti-discrimination rights have their foundations in EU law; that the EU has mandated national action to clean up rivers and beaches of pollution and sewerage; that drinking water has to reach high standards of purity; that rubbish can no longer be disposed of in open cast tips; that products cannot be legally sold unless they are accurately labelled; that consumers have clear rights of redress, for example for flights that are cancelled or long delayed – and there are many other examples of this kind.

For Eurosceptics, however, the regulatory reach of the EU is what they most dislike. For them, it is more than an irritant that when shown to be imperfect should be modified; it represents an unacceptable constraint on the government's freedom of action and an anti-democratic obstacle to change. In the first two years after the formation of the Coalition, it was widely reported that Steve Hilton, the Prime Minister's long-term friend and guru, and for that period Downing Street strategy chief, railed against the obstruction that EU law put in the way of the deregulatory reforms that he wanted the government to espouse. To his way of thinking, the key to the revival of enterprise and growth in the UK was a massive programme of employment and business deregulation to which Britain's legal obligations as a result of EU membership stood obstinately in the way. Similarly, his concept of the 'big society' – in his eyes, the replacement of state-run, top-down public services by community-based self-help was hampered by EU rules on protected labour rights and the transfer of undertakings.

These criticisms of EU laws and regulation ignore the fact that British ministers had in the past assented to them, many under previous Conservative governments. Yet from the mid-1990s onwards, neo-liberals and an increasing number of 'hyper-globalisers' were no longer prepared to accept that the price of market opening was regulation at a European level. They increasingly saw the EU as standing in the way of their vision of how Britain could compete and succeed in the face of the bright new opportunities and fresh competitive challenges posed by rapid globalisation and the rise of Asia's economic power.

The Illusions of an Offshore Competition State

The logic of this Eurosceptic position is an 'offshore Britain' freed of EU constraints. Some of its proponents would like to hang on to as much access to the European single market as proves negotiable, but they put their main focus on the new world of opportunity they see opening up 'beyond the oceans'. They see themselves as the new Elizabethans, defeating the threat to English freedom in a myth that likens the EU and the euro to the Spanish Armada, and venturing outwards to build a new trading empire (though hopefully this time not based on the modern equivalents of piracy and slavery). To some, this vision may appear intellectually coherent, but what is its evidential base? The main arguments are flawed:

- The choice between a European and global strategy for British business success is simply false. For many businesses it is the depth and critical mass of the single market that is their home market and gives them the competitive strength to compete overseas.
- Why have the French, Germans and Swedes been more successful than British companies in penetrating emerging markets, if the problem for the UK is EU regulation? For they also face it and it does not seem an insuperable problem for them. Is it seriously being argued that the French, German and Swedish culture of regulatory enforcement is less stringent, lighter touch, less bureaucratic and less legalistic than the UK's?
- Can Britain's supply-side weaknesses and problems of competitiveness and growth really be attributed to over-regulation by the EU? On comparative indices of competitiveness, Britain has one of the most flexible labour markets in the world. It is one of the easiest places in the EU to set up business. Most of the available evidence suggests that the main barriers to business growth in the UK are factors such as: limited access to finance for firms with real growth potential, widely attributed to the short-termist failings of our financial system; inadequate supply of intermediate skills; inability to transfer world-class research into commercially viable innovation; and failings of infrastructure in terms of digital, energy and transport investment. It is only by a long stretch of the imagination that any of these failings can be put down to the EU. Indeed, the fact that many of our EU partners, particularly in northern Europe, are better than the UK at doing many of these things suggests that it is not membership of the EU that is holding us back.

Some may counter that Britain's failings in successfully pursuing a high road to competitiveness are so culturally embedded as to be impossible to overcome. Then the only viable course for Britain is to follow the low road of competing with Asia and other emerging economies on the basis of cheap labour and unregulated flexibility. But is that really feasible? How much would labour costs have to fall for Britain to compete on price with Asia? And is it not a counsel of despair?

The flaws in this narrow Eurosceptic vision for Britain's future as an offshore haven of deregulation and free enterprise need to be ruthlessly exposed. How many millions of our citizens does it condemn to lifetimes of low-skilled, low-paid work so that a lucky few can make their fortunes across the seas? Far from turning Britain into a Hong Kong next to mainland China, there is an alternative: to address our inherent competitive weaknesses by moving towards a more Continental model of capitalism for which a revitalised EU membership can play an important underpinning role.

The Search for a New Growth British Model Requires a Stronger European Commitment

Historians warn us to be wary of the language of 'turning points' and we should be cautious as a result. Yet 'turning point' is a ready description of the situation facing the UK in the aftershocks of the 2008 crisis of the world banking system and the rapidly changing global balance of power. It requires a rethinking of what Alan Milward, the pre-eminent historian of Britain's post-war relationship with Europe, described as our 'national strategy'.[1] Cameron is right in one sense. The moment is opportune for a full reassessment of Britain's relations with Europe and our global role of a seriousness that has not been seen since the Macmillan government reviewed Britain's position in the aftermath of Suez. There are some uncomfortable parallels between Britain's situation today and the late 1950s. The Macmillan government came to realise then that the economic model on which Britain's post-war recovery had been based was, at best, time limited and in need of fundamental rethinking. At the end of the 1950s, the protected markets of the Commonwealth and sterling area were fast eroding. Strong German export performance was driving British goods out of expanding European markets. And British industry was in need of 'modernisation'.

The 2008 financial crisis has similarly raised fundamental questions about the balance and competitiveness of the British economy, and a sustainable growth model for the future. Britain faces huge economic problems in the present decade for which our EU membership should be part of the solution. At the minimum, Britain needs a prospering single market and eurozone to support the export drive on which a new wave of private-sector-led growth depends. More boldly, it needs to be part of a wider transition by the whole European economy to a new model of global competitiveness based on knowledge and innovation, ecological sustainability and social inclusiveness. Britain simply cannot afford to take delight in the EU's troubles, or stand apart with insouciant indifference. It is not only the eurozone that is struggling to cope with a badly damaged model of political economy. Britain is living through a debt crisis of its own making, the result of the catastrophic failure of a model of consumption-led, debt-driven growth, brought to its knees by overconfidence in Anglo-American financial capitalism. The Anglo-American economic and social paradigm that held sway from the 1980s onwards needs to undergo fundamental adjustment in the wake of the 2008 crisis. The necessary rebalancing of the British economy will prove unachievable without it and our membership of the EU can play a vital role.

One might have imagined that the contrast with the relative success of the renewed and reformed models of Germany, Sweden, Austria, Finland and the Netherlands (all members of the euro apart from Sweden) might have something to teach the British – but seemingly not. Britons today need to ask themselves basic questions about our country's future, which are highly relevant to whether we view our long term as in Europe. Do we share the same broad ideas about how our economy should be run as our European partners on issues like the responsibilities of business to society, the regulation of mergers and takeovers, as well as financial markets, stakeholder versus shareholder capitalism, and the long-term commitment of investors to companies and companies to their employees? Are Britain's preferences on these issues so different from the Continent's – and if they were different and more Anglo-American in the 1980s and 1990s, in the light of the crisis should Britain now be changing its disposition towards a more European view? Similarly, given increasing post-crisis public concerns about fairness, what do Britons think of as an acceptable degree of inequality in society and the legitimate role of the state? Is our view fundamentally at odds with how our European partners look at questions of social justice and social cohesion? Is there some special exceptionalism in our conception of the modern welfare state and the obligations of citizens which marks us off as different from our Continental neighbours?

The Modern Case for a More United Europe

The original goal of the European project was a united Europe that would never again suffer the disasters of the twentieth century's two world wars. In terms of the European continent, it has been a spectacular success, fully justifying the award of the Nobel Prize to the European Union in 2012. However, the political vision of the founding fathers was always more than peace: it was also about the political power that unity could bring. This was a major animating motive on the part of the prime ministers who led Britain into the European Community. Macmillan, Wilson and Heath all shared with France's General de Gaulle the ambition that Europe should be a powerful actor on the world stage. The problem was that their conception of a united Europe's relationship with the USA crucially differed.

There is no better statement of this political, not economic, vision for Europe than in the speech Labour's foreign secretary, George Brown, made in presenting Britain's second application for membership in 1967. Brown argued not on grounds of economics, where 'the balance of economic advantage is a fine one'. The most decisive consideration for Britain was 'the ability to assert a European influence on events [that] could only grow out of economic strength [. . .] if that unity could be achieved, then Europe would maintain a commanding position in the international markets of the world'. But the aim was not simply 'material prosperity: it should lead to a greater political purpose for Europe, in short as a power for peace'.[2]

For decades in Britain that spirit of European ambition has been lost. In truth, as a force for good in the world, the EU has so far been a disappointment. This judgement may underplay the force of 'soft power' which, as Joseph Nye reminded us, those of us with a 'great power' history or mindset have a tendency to do. The EU is far from powerless: it gradually acquired key external competences where its internal competence had been established. Starting with the decision of the Six to form a Customs Union, the Commission acquired exclusive competence to negotiate external trade agreements. Europe, despite the problem of its agricultural protectionism, became the driving force behind the global free-trade agreements that have been the motor of globalisation. Equally, the deepening of the single market has given Europe major clout over global standards of regulation from transport to food standards to financial regulation. China's compliance with the REACH directive (the registration, evaluation, authorisation and restriction of chemicals) regulating the chemical inputs into manufacturing processes is a typical example of Europe's soft power.

In parallel, EU intergovernmental cooperation has gradually deepened in foreign policy, disaster relief, migration, international development, terrorism and (as a result of Tony Blair's initiative) defence. This deepening of cooperation has been accompanied by significant institutional changes. Yet the EU has always appeared to punch below its collective weight. The story is one of divided counsels towards Putin's Russia, unseemly national competition for contracts in dealings with China, ineffectiveness in managing aid, inability to counter growing Chinese influence in Africa, weakness in the EU neighbourhood and irrelevance in the Middle East.

Yet fundamental structural factors may now be forcing change. Britain and France have moved significantly closer together. From the late 1950s, Britain and France – as Europe's leading military powers – failed to resolve their differences of outlook towards their shared alliance with the USA. If one thinks of Blair and Iraq, one can imagine the voice of de Gaulle arguing from his grave that the veto he wielded on British membership in January 1963, had been justified by events on the grounds that Britain could never truly be a European power. Yet paradoxically the British and French divisions over Iraq appear to have been cathartic in bringing the two countries closer together – exactly the opposite consequence of their divisions over Suez 50 years earlier. President Sarkozy's symbolic decision to return France to membership of NATO's joint military command, the UK–France 2010 Defence Treaty, the 2011 joint operation in Libya and British support for President Hollande's military operation in Mali in 2012 have all been signs of a changed relationship. This transformation could now go much further.

At the same time, the USA is making its own profound reassessment of its global position. The USA under the Obama administration has grown increasingly impatient of Europe's inability to step up to the plate. The 'special relationship' looks set to diminish, while Britain's relationship with its closest neighbours in Europe remains as ambivalent as ever. Yet the global pressures that call for an ambitious foreign policy have not gone away. In the last decade we have seen increasing US disengagement from Europe, an economic revolution in China, the rise of the BRICs, the emergence of resource scarcity and conflict, not to mention turmoil in North Africa, the Middle East and the so-called Af-Pak region. Once wary of European defence cooperation, the USA now wants the EU to get its act together. But Britain remains hesitant. In his speech to the 2012 Democratic Convention, Bill Clinton argued that 'basic arithmetic' is the only way to defeat the Tea Party dogma that lower taxes are the answer to America's every problem. In order to drive home the twenty-first-century realities of Britain 'standing alone' in our rapidly changing world, Eurosceptics need to learn some basic arithmetic too. Britain's membership of the EU brings hard advantages in terms of international clout, trade, inward investment and the fight against cross-border crime and terrorism.

Britain needs an effective EU to multiply its own reduced capacities for influence in a globalising world. Instinctively we may still prefer to shelter behind the unparalleled military might of the USA, but the last decade has demonstrated the limits of what military power can alone achieve. If we agree with our European partners that climate change poses an existential threat to our way of life, is it such a leap in the dark to be prepared to work closely with those who hold similar beliefs so that we can act more effectively in the here and now? Similarly, when it comes to questions such as nuclear proliferation, the abuse of human rights, the threat of terrorism, who are the best people to work with who share these concerns? The EU offers a stronger collective voice on global issues and could offer a lot more – on a broad range of progressive opinion it cares deeply about: world poverty, climate change, fair trade, human rights, gender equality, the horrors of people's lives in 'failing states', etc. The early socialists dreamed of world government: in a world increasing nationalisms, the EU remains a unique symbol of hope in demonstrating that 'pooled sovereignty' – a polity 'beyond the nation state' – can be made work.

There is still an element of idealism about Europe of which it should be possible to convince the British people. As Cameron acknowledges:

> what Churchill described as the twin marauders of war and tyranny have been almost entirely banished from our continent. Today hundreds of millions dwell in freedom, from the Baltic to the Adriatic, from the Western approaches to the Aegean.

Perhaps as we stand at the centenary of the start of World War I, the pictures of Kohl and Mitterrand holding hands at Verdun mean little to younger generations. But Kohl himself expressed it more graphically when he received the Freedom of the City of London in 1998 and described Europe's transformation in his own lifetime:

> As a teenager growing up in Ludwigshaven on the Rhine at the end of the Second World War, three zones of occupation divided my city. I needed an identity permit to cross from one to the other. Now whenever one visits on a fine summer evening, the heart of Europe's great cities, the Spanish Steps in Rome, Trafalgar Square in London, the Brandenburg Gate in Berlin, you see crowds of young people from all nationalities mingling together, at peace with each other, enjoying themselves. I would not have regarded this as remotely within the bounds of possibility when I was a boy.

With the Cold War's end and the Soviet Union's collapse, there was an inevitable tendency to take all this for granted. The peace project had been achieved. But this is no longer certain. Europe is in crisis and no one knows quite where it will all end. Europe is more than a market: it is a vital part of our civilisation and contentment. Its populist opponents are marshalling their forces at its gates and some of the defenders have little spirit for the fight to come. Can this really be the moment for Britain to leave?

APPENDIX

A Timeline of UK–European Relations

1945 – Victory in Europe Day

World War II comes to an end on 8 May.

1946 – 'Speech to the academic youth'

In a speech at the University of Zurich, Winston Churchill calls for the establishment of a 'kind of United States of Europe'. He had spoken of a Council of Europe as early as 1943 in a radio broadcast.

1948 – Plans for a peaceful Europe

The future structure of the Council of Europe is discussed at a Congress of several hundred leading political figures at The Hague, the Netherlands. There are two schools of competing thought: some favour a classical international organisation with representatives of governments, while others prefer a political forum with parliamentarians.

1949 – Treaty of London: establishment of the Council of Europe

The Council of Europe is founded on 5 May by the Treaty of London (The Statute of the Council of Europe) signed by ten states: Belgium, Denmark, France, Ireland, Italy, Luxembourg, the Netherlands, Norway, Sweden and the United Kingdom. Both the federal and the intergovernmental approaches discussed at the Hague Congress are combined through the creation of the Committee of Ministers and the Parliamentary Assembly under the Statute of the Council of Europe. This dual intergovernmental and interparliamentary structure is later copied by the North Atlantic Treaty Organization, which is founded later that year, the European Communities and the Organization for Security and Co-operation in Europe (OSCE).

1950 – The Schuman Declaration

French Foreign Minister Robert Schuman announces a plan for France and West Germany to pool coal and steel production and invites other states to join them. His plan is based on the idea that European unity is the key to peace. Solidarity in production, he says, would make war between France and Germany 'not merely unthinkable but materially impossible'.

1951 – Treaty of Paris establishes European Coal and Steel Community

The Treaty of Paris is signed by the 'Original Six' (Belgium, France, West Germany, Italy, Luxembourg, the Netherlands), establishing the European Coal and Steel Community (ECSC). They set up a High Authority to manage the coal and steel industries, a European Court of Justice (ECJ) and a Common Assembly – a precursor of the European parliament. The Dutch, supported by the Germans, also insist on the creation of a Council of Ministers made up of ministers from member states to counterbalance the supranational High Authority. The first president of the High Authority is Jean Monnet, the inspiration behind the Schuman Declaration. The ECSC brings its member states together as equals, cooperating within shared institutions.

1952 – The rise and fall of the European Defence Community

At the height of the Cold War, the USA insists that Europe must contribute more to its own defence and that West Germany must re-arm. In 1952 the six ECSC members agree to create a European Defence Community which envisages German soldiers joining a European army, but the French parliament delays ratification and ultimately rejects the idea in 1954.

1955 – The Messina Conference

The Messina Conference of the foreign ministers of the six member states of the ECSC in June agrees to encourage free trade between member states through the removal of tariffs and quotas, leading to the Treaty of Rome and the formation of the European Economic Community (EEC) in 1957 and Euratom in 1958.

1956 – The Suez Crisis

Following Egyptian President Gamal Abdel Nasser's decision to nationalise the Suez Canal, Britain, France and Israel invade Egypt. The USSR threatens a nuclear attack against the Anglo-French-Israeli allies in response. A lack of support from their fellow NATO member the USA forces the allies to withdraw. The crisis demonstrates how Europe's dependence upon the USA is not reliable and, as a result, interest in the idea of a European Defence Community to make Europe a 'Third Force' in the Cold War is reinvigorated, helping to lead to the formation of the EEC in 1957. The conflict also highlights the decline of the UK as an international power. Prime Minister Anthony Eden had assumed the USA would automatically endorse military action taken by its closest ally, Britain, but instead was forced to bow to American diplomatic and financial pressure to withdraw from the conflict, resigning from office shortly thereafter. With growing differences between the UK and the rest of the Commonwealth, most of whom refuse to give military aid to the UK on the basis that Suez is not in their economic or political interests, Eden's successor, Harold Macmillan, greatly accelerates decolonisation as British foreign-policy thinking increasingly turns away from acting as a great imperial power.

1957 – The Treaty of Rome, a first step towards the Common Market

The six members of the ECSC sign the Treaty of Rome, setting up the EEC and the European Atomic Energy Community (EAEC or Euratom). The EEC aims to create a Common Market, a customs union plus free movement of capital and labour. To please France it also promises subsidies to farmers. Euratom's goal is the joint development of nuclear energy.

1958 – The first European Commission takes office

The first session of the European Parliamentary Assembly is held in Strasbourg, France. Robert Schuman is elected president of the Assembly. The EEC quickly establishes itself as the most important of the European communities. It has a commission, a council of ministers, and an advisory parliamentary assembly whose members are drawn from national parliaments.

1960 – European Free Trade Association launches another kind of Europe

As British decolonisation progresses, the UK's relationship with the Commonwealth is in transition. In reaction to the creation of the EEC, the UK government brings together Austria, Denmark, Norway, Portugal, Sweden and Switzerland to form the European Free Trade Association (EFTA) as an alternative to the EEC. Like the EEC, the EFTA aims to establish free trade, but it opposes uniform external tariffs and sees no need for supranational institutions.

1961 – The UK, Denmark and Ireland apply to join the EEC

The decision to apply for UK membership of the EEC is taken by the Conservative government of Harold Macmillan and negotiated by Edward Heath as Lord Privy Seal. However, the request is vetoed in 1963 by French President Charles de Gaulle, who is concerned about the UK's close ties with the USA, saying that the British government lacks commitment to European integration.

1962 – Hugh Gaitskell speech to the Labour Party Conference

The EEC adopts regulations providing for a Common Market in agriculture so that everybody now has enough to eat – and soon there is even surplus agricultural produce – along with financial regulation and rules governing competition.

In a speech to the Labour Party Conference in October 1962, party leader Hugh Gaitskell claims that the UK's participation in a Federal Europe would mean 'the end of a thousand years of history'. Gaitskell's speech alienates some of his pro-European supporters, ultimately starting a long process of Labour division over Europe leading in 1981 to the Limehouse Declaration where the so-called 'Gang of Four' – Roy Jenkins, David Owen, Bill Rodgers and Shirley Williams – signal their intent to leave the Labour Party and form a Council for Social Democracy, which later becomes the basis for the British SDP.

1967 – The treaty creating a single Council and a Commission for the three communities comes into effect

After initially hesitating over the issue, Harold Wilson's Labour government in May 1967 lodged the UK's second application to join the European Community. Like the first, though, it is vetoed by de Gaulle in November that year.

The Merger Treaty uniting the three communities (ECSC, EEC, Euratom) into a single EEC enters into force.

1970 – The Werner Report

The Werner Report sets out a path towards Economic and Monetary Union (EMU).

1972 – The 'snake in the tunnel'

The European Commission (EC) launches its first attempt to harmonise exchange rates: participating governments are required to confine the fluctuations of their currencies within a range of +/– 2.25 per cent against each other. Countries that struggle to do so can request aid in the form of loans. The new system is referred to as the 'snake in the tunnel'.

1973 – The UK, Denmark and Ireland join the European Community

Following his victory in the 1970 election (and helped by de Gaulle's fall from power in 1969), the new Conservative Prime Minister Edward Heath negotiates Britain's admission to the EC in 1973, alongside Denmark and Ireland. The three new member states along with Norway had failed to join ten years earlier because of General de Gaulle's veto on UK membership. This time all, except Norway, whose electorate voted against joining in a referendum, sign an accession treaty in 1972. Denmark and Ireland hold successful referendums. The Conservative government does not hold a referendum. The Labour Party in opposition continues to be deeply divided on the issue, risking a major split. Labour leader Harold Wilson shows political astuteness in devising a position that both sides of the party could agree on, opposing the terms negotiated by Heath but not membership in principle. Labour's 1974 manifesto includes a pledge to renegotiate terms for Britain's membership and then hold a referendum on whether to stay in the EC on the new terms.

Labour's referendum proposal leads the anti-EEC Conservative politician Enoch Powell to advocate voting for Labour in the February 1974 election, a move thought to have influenced Labour's return to government.

1973 – Oil crisis

In October 1973 OPEC declares an oil embargo in response to US and Western European support for Israel in the Yom Kippur War, drastically forcing up oil prices. The Copenhagen meeting of European leaders of state and governments in December 1973 fails to agree a common energy policy. Progress on monetary union is stalled. While agreement is reached on the establishment of a Regional Development Fund, the resources allocated to it are much less than the Commission had hoped.

1974 – James Callaghan's statement to the Council

Incoming UK Foreign Secretary James Callaghan makes a statement to the Council on the new Labour government's policy on the Community in which he calls for 'fairer methods of financing the Community budget', major changes in the Common Agricultural Policy (CAP) and solutions to monetary problems.

The Community's heads of state or government decide to hold meetings three times a year as the European Council, agree direct elections to the European Parliament, resolve to set up the European Regional Development Fund and work to establish economic and monetary union.

1975 – UK–EU referendum

Following Labour's return to power in February 1974, the UK government attempts to renegotiate Britain's membership of the EC. The discussions focus primarily on Britain's net budgetary contribution to the EC. As one of the less prosperous member states and a small agricultural producer heavily dependent on imports, Britain suffers doubly from the dominance of agricultural spending in the EC budget and agricultural import taxes as a source of EC revenues. During the renegotiations, other member states concede, as a partial offset, on the initiative of George Thomson, Labour's first commissioner, the establishment of a significant European Regional Development Fund (ERDF), from which Britain would be a major net beneficiary. The UK referendum splits Harold Wilson's Labour government, but 67.2 per cent of the public vote in favour of the UK remaining a member.

1978 – The road to the euro begins with the European Monetary System

The establishment of the European monetary system (EMS), including the exchange rate mechanism (ERM), begins. The EMS introduces the European currency unit (Ecu) and the ERM, providing the basis for creating a single European currency in the future (i.e. the euro). All members, apart from the UK, join the ERM.

1979 – First direct elections to the European Parliament

In a statement at a press conference at the EEC Summit in Dublin, UK Prime Minister Margaret Thatcher says of her efforts to renegotiate Britain's EEC budget contribution, 'We are not asking for a penny piece of Community money for Britain. *What we are asking is for a very large amount of our own money back*, over and above what we contribute to the Community, which is covered by our receipts from the Community.'

The 1979 Labour manifesto declares that a Labour government would 'oppose any move towards turning the Community into a federation'.

In June, direct elections to the European Parliament are held for the first time (until this point, members of the Parliament were appointed by national parliaments).

1981 – Greece becomes the EEC's tenth member

1983 – Labour Party drops its opposition to the European Communities

After Labour's heavy general election defeat under Michael Foot on a manifesto that had proposed EU withdrawal, under the new leadership of Neil Kinnock the Labour Party gradually moves away from its opposition to the European Communities.

1984 – The UK rebate

The European Council agrees to grant a rebate to the UK after Prime Minister Margaret Thatcher threatens to halt payments. The agreement reflects the fact that the EU's CAP subsidies were of much less benefit to the UK (at the time the EU's second poorest EEC member) than other countries because the UK has a relatively small farming sector as a proportion of gross domestic product (GDP).

1985 – European Council agrees to amend the Treaty of Rome and to revitalise integration by drawing up a Single European Act

Jacques Delors becomes president of the EC, upon which he proposes that the EC should, by the end of 1992, remove a series of barriers to free trade and free movement of capital and labour, creating a 'single market', believing the single-market programme will revive European integration by spilling over from the economic into the political arena. This is widely seen as a necessity if Europe is to compete with the USA. In February 1986 the Single European Act (SEA) is adopted, setting out a timetable for the completion of the Common Market by 1 January 1993. National vetoes are abolished by introducing qualified majority voting (QMV) in the Council of Ministers for areas relating to the single market (based on 'four freedoms' allowing goods, services, people and capital to move freely throughout the EC). The legislative power of the European Parliament is increased and the basis for a European foreign policy is laid. The SEA is the first commitment by member states to create a 'European Union'.

1986 – Portugal and Spain join the EEC

Spain and Portugal join the Community. The European flag, adopted by Community institutions, is flown for the first time in front of the Berlaymont building, headquarters of the Commission in Brussels.

1987

Turkey and Morocco formally apply to join. Morocco's bid is set aside as it is not geographically part of Europe, but accession talks begin with Turkey.

1988 – Jacques Delors' speech to the Trades Union Congress

Following a speech by Jacques Delors, then president of the Commission, at the Trades Union Congress (TUC) conference, the Eurosceptic inclination in the Labour Party as a whole becomes less pronounced. In the context of Margaret Thatcher's anti-trade union Conservative premiership, Delors' advocacy of a 'social Europe' becomes attractive to many within Labour.

Separately, market liberalisation is seen to work to the benefit of the more developed northern European member states, so the poorer southern states demand compensation. This comes in the form of agreement to double the allocations for structural funds paid to poorer regions.

1989 – German reunification

In December 1989, UK Prime Minister Margaret Thatcher opines that she does not want the reunification of Germany, fearing a united Germany would dominate Europe and complaining that 'We defeated the Germans twice! And now they're back!' Thatcher and French President François Mitterrand discuss the reunification of Germany. Mitterrand recognises that reunification is inevitable and adjusts his views accordingly. Unlike Thatcher, he is optimistic that participation in a single currency and other European institutions will prevent a united Germany from becoming a threat to European peace.

1990 – The UK joins the ERM and the fall of Thatcher

Although Britain had not joined the ERM, the Treasury, under Conservative Chancellor Nigel Lawson – then a believer in a fixed exchange rate and admirer of the low inflationary record of West Germany, which he attributed to the strength of the Deutschmark and the management of the Bundesbank – follows a policy of 'shadowing' the Deutschmark from early 1987 to March 1988. In 1989 matters come to a head in a clash between Lawson and Margaret Thatcher's economic adviser Alan Walters, when Walters claims that the ERM is 'half baked'. This leads to Lawson resigning as chancellor to be replaced by John Major, who persuades Thatcher to join the ERM.

By September 1990 opinion polls report that Labour has a 14 per cent lead over the Conservatives, and by November the Conservatives had been trailing Labour for 18 months. In late October 1990, Prime Minister Thatcher reacts strongly against Jacques Delors' plans for a single currency in the House of Commons, famously declaring that her response to such a vision would be 'No. No. No.' Negative poll ratings, together with Thatcher's combative personality and willingness to override colleagues' opinions, magnify discontent within the Conservative Party. On 1 November 1990, Geoffrey Howe resigns from his position as deputy prime minister. In his resignation speech, Howe comments that Thatcher's European stance 'is rather like sending your opening batsmen to the crease, only for them to find, the moment that the first balls are bowled, that their bats have been broken before the game by the team captain.' Howe's dramatic speech reinforces the change in the general perception of Thatcher from the 'Iron Lady' to a divisive and confrontational figure. Within a week, the pro-European former cabinet minister Michael Heseltine announces that he will challenge her for the leadership of the party. Although Thatcher wins the first ballot, Heseltine attracts sufficient support to force a second ballot. Thatcher initially states that she intends to 'fight on and fight to win' the second ballot, but consultation with her cabinet persuades her to withdraw and she is replaced as prime minister and party leader by her chancellor, John Major.

1991 – Maastricht turns the Community into a Union

The Maastricht Treaty (Treaty on European Union) is agreed, leading to creation of the euro and the 'pillar' structure of the EU: the European Community pillar, the Common Foreign and Security Policy (CFSP) pillar, and the Justice and Home Affairs (JHA) pillar. Maastricht also introduces the concept of EU citizenship, which gives Europeans the right to live and vote in elections in any EU country. The UK negotiates an opt-out on both monetary union and the chapter on social policy, with Prime Minister John Major famously claiming to have negotiated 'game, set and match for Britain'. Nevertheless, 22 back-bench MPs belonging to his governing Conservative Party refuse to support the Major government in a series of votes in the House of Commons on the issue of the ratification of the treaty in 1992–3. The rebellion has the support of former Prime Minister Lady Thatcher and Lord Tebbit. Thatcher declares in a speech in the House of Lords that she 'could never have signed that treaty' and that it is 'a recipe for national suicide'. The Conservative government has only a small majority of 18, thus giving the relatively small number of rebels disproportionate influence, so in 1995 Prime Minister Major calls an early leadership election in an attempt to re-impose his authority on the party. He wins; however, the infighting does not stop and the Conservatives are heavily defeated in the general election of May 1997.

1992 – Black Wednesday: the UK is forced out of the ERM

The ERM was intended to stabilise currency values in a fixed exchange rate regime ahead of creating a single currency. In the summer of 1992, sterling comes under severe market pressure, and the UK government raises base rates in an effort to prompt currency traders to buy British pounds. Traders keep selling, however, forcing the government to pull the pound out of the ERM.

1993 – Maastricht Treaty comes into effect

In a referendum in June 1992, Denmark votes against ratification of the Maastricht Treaty and only accepts it in a second vote in May 1993, after receiving an opt-out on monetary union like the UK. In France, the treaty squeezes home by just 50.4 per cent 'for' to 49.7 per cent 'against'. There is also evidence of public discontent in other countries including Germany and the UK.

The United Kingdom Independence Party, advocating the UK's complete withdrawal from the EU, is founded in 1993 but has only very limited success initially.

1994 – Tony Blair elected as UK Labour Party leader

Following John Smith's sudden death, Tony Blair wins the Labour leadership contest. His close friend Gordon Brown decides not to run.

1995 – Borders come down

Austria, Finland and Sweden join the EU, bringing membership to 15.

The Schengen Agreement comes into force between Belgium, France, Germany, Luxembourg, the Netherlands, Portugal and Spain, lifting border controls on persons. The UK and Ireland stay out of the agreement for administrative reasons, as well as fears of terrorism and illegal immigration.

1997 – The Amsterdam Treaty is signed

The Treaty of Amsterdam, officially the Treaty of Amsterdam amending the Treaty of the EU, strengthens a series of employment and social protection policies and the social chapter of the Maastricht Treaty becomes an official part of EU law. The Schengen Agreement is incorporated in EU law, although Ireland and the UK maintain their opt-outs. The Stability and Growth Pact is also agreed, defining rules and penalties for the member states that form the eurozone to ensure that each member state keeps the amount they spend and borrow under control in order to help create stable conditions for the new currency.

Separately, the Referendum Party is founded to fight the 1997 general election, calling for a referendum on aspects of the UK's relationship with the EU. It briefly holds a seat in the House of Commons after George Gardiner, the Conservative MP for Reigate, switches party in March 1997, but although the party polls 810,000 votes to finish fourth in the general election, it does not win a seat in the House of Commons.

1998 – The ECB is established

The European Central Bank (ECB) is established in Frankfurt, Germany.

1999 – Crisis at the Commission: fraud and resignation

The entire Commission led by Jacques Santer resigns following a report by the Committee of Independent Experts on allegations of fraud, mismanagement and nepotism. In September, Romano Prodi becomes the new president of the Commission, promising radical change in the way it is run. Only a handful of the old commissioners are reappointed.

Separately, three years after the worldwide export of British beef is banned in 1996 amid fears over the threat of bovine spongiform encephalopathy (BSE), or 'mad cow disease', tensions rise as France and West Germany refuse to lift their ban on British beef. The EU begins legal action against France and later West Germany for their failure to lift their bans, but the ban is not fully lifted until 2006.

2000 – Charter of Fundamental Rights of the EU

Denmark votes against joining the single currency.

The formal proclamation is made of the Charter of Fundamental Rights of the EU, a non-legally binding declaration drafted by a group of legal experts which sets out the civil, political, economic and social rights of European citizens and all persons resident in the EU.

2001 – Treaty of Nice

The Treaty of Nice is signed, reforming the institutional structure of EU decision-making processes to allow for eastward expansion. Ireland votes against enacting the treaty in a referendum.

Speaking on what the Conservatives dub 'Keep the Pound Day', Conservative Party leader William Hague warns that a Labour election victory would spell the end of parliamentary democracy in the UK, claiming Labour would start the process of joining the euro the day after an election victory and insisting that there were just '12 days to save the pound'. Shortly thereafter a poll for the *Daily Telegraph* finds that 66 per cent of voters consider Hague to be 'a bit of a wally' and 70 per cent of voters believe he would 'say almost anything to win votes'. After the party's electoral defeat, new Conservative Party leader Iain Duncan Smith attempts to disaffiliate the Conservative Party from the federalist European People's Party (EPP) group in the European Parliament, instead seeking to merge his party with the Eurosceptic Union for a Europe of Nations (UEN) group. Conservative MEPs veto the move because of the presence within the UEN of representatives of neo-fascist parties.

11 September 2001 marks the beginning of the 'war on terror'. EU countries begin to work much more closely together to fight terrorism.

2002 – Introduction of the euro currency

Euro notes and coins enter circulation in the 12 participating member states: Austria, Belgium, Finland, France, West Germany, Greece, Ireland, Italy, Luxembourg, the Netherlands, Portugal and Spain. Sweden, Denmark and the UK stay out.

In a second referendum, the Irish people vote in favour of the Treaty of Nice.

A minority of Labour parliamentarians form the 'Labour Against the Euro' group, opposing prospective British membership of the single currency.

2003 – Gordon Brown's five economic tests

In 1997, Chancellor of the Exchequer Gordon Brown announces that the Treasury will set five economic tests to ascertain whether the economic case has been made for the UK to join the European single currency. In June 2003 the Treasury announces that the tests have not been passed.

On 19 March 2003, coalition forces from the USA, UK, Australia and Poland launch an invasion of Iraq. The invasion strains the relationship between the UK and other European states, particularly France. In a dispute which becomes popularly known as 'le row', French President Jacques Chirac is angered with the so-called 'Letter of Eight' supporting the war, signed by several of the new accession states to the EU, which UK Prime Minister Tony Blair had backed, following President Chirac's statement that he would veto a UN resolution authorising the use of force in Iraq.

The first European troops are deployed to take over from a NATO mission in FYR Macedonia under the European Security and Defence Policy (ESDP), following its creation in 1999.

2004 – No votes plunge the EU constitution into crisis

In the EU's biggest enlargement to date, ten new countries join – Cyprus, Czech Republic, Estonia, Hungary, Latvia, Lithuania, Malta, Poland, Slovak Republic and Slovenia.

With the Treaty of Paris due to expire after 50 years, the heads of state and government and EU foreign ministers sign the treaty establishing a Constitution for Europe (TCE). Its goals are to simplify the EU treaties to make the EU more easily understood by its citizens and to help it work efficiently after enlargement. In May 2005, French voters reject ratification of the treaty with Dutch voters doing the same in June. As the constitution cannot come into effect unless it is ratified by all 25 member states, many commentators declare it dead. The EU continues to function on the basis of its existing treaties.

The 2004 European elections provide the UK Independence Party's (UKIP's) first major electoral victory, coming third and getting 12 MEPs elected.

2006 – David Cameron's first Party Conference speech as leader of the Conservative Party

Many commentators believe the Conservative obsession with Europe to be an important reason why the party lost the general elections of 2001 and 2005. They argue that the UK electorate is more influenced by domestic issues than by European affairs. In his first Party Conference speech as leader of the opposition Conservative Party, David Cameron calls for his party to stop 'banging on about Europe', conceding that by doing so, the party had alienated voters.

2007 – New candidates admitted

Bulgaria and Romania join the EU, bringing membership to 27.

The Constitutional Treaty is renamed the Lisbon Treaty, with much of the original innovations of the constitution carried over, but some of the more symbolic aspects, such as the EU anthem, dropped. New UK Prime Minister Gordon Brown misses the televised ceremony of the leaders signing the Lisbon Treaty, but presses ahead with its parliamentary ratification, refusing to concede the referendum that Tony Blair has reluctantly offered on the Constitutional Treaty in 2004.

2008 – Beginnings of the eurocrisis

A major financial crisis hits the global economy in September 2008.

In June, Irish voters reject ratification of the Lisbon Treaty.

2009 – The Lisbon Treaty enters into force

Having received guarantees in areas such as military neutrality and ethical issues, Irish voters elect to ratify the Lisbon Treaty at a second referendum. In November, the Czech Republic becomes the last EU member to sign the treaty after securing an opt-out from the Charter of Fundamental Rights, which the treaty made legally binding. The Lisbon Treaty enters into force in December. The following year, two new posts created by the Lisbon Treaty are filled: the UK's Baroness Catherine Ashton (Labour) is appointed high representative of the Union for foreign affairs and security policy and Belgium's Herman Van Rompuy is appointed permanent president of the European Council.

UKIP's European election results improved in the 2009 UK European election, coming in second above the incumbent Labour Party.

Despite a promise by his predecessor, Michael Howard, that the Conservative Party would remain in the EPP group so as to maintain influence in the European Parliament, new Conservative Party leader David Cameron pledges to remove the party from the EPP group and instead launches a new political group, the European Conservatives and Reformists (ECR) group, along with the controversial Polish party Law and Justice (PiS) as well as the Civic Democratic Party (ODS) of the Czech Republic.

2011 – Cameron clashes with EU leaders

Following the formation of the Conservative–Liberal Democrat Coalition in 2010, David Cameron clashes with EU leaders over plans for a new fiscal compact treaty, saying the reforms were not in the UK's interests. His so-called veto failed to stop a new treaty being agreed outside the formal EU framework.

2012 – Cameron announces plans for an EU referendum

Two days after refusing the prospect of holding a referendum on the UK's relationship with the EU, Prime Minister David Cameron, under pressure from Eurosceptic members of the Conservative Party, signals that the Conservatives intend to include a referendum in their manifesto ahead of the next general election, but leaves obscure whether a referendum would pose the 'in/out' question sought by many.

2013 – Cameron's Bloomberg speech

In January 2013, Cameron changes his position again by agreeing to hold an in/out referendum should the Conservative Party win the next UK general election. The move is seen as an attempt to calm Eurosceptic rebellion within his party.

A new campaign group, comprising 20 Labour MPs, called 'Labour for a Referendum', is launched to put pressure on the Labour leader to offer an in/out vote on Europe.

Notes

Preface

1. Cameron, D. *We Stand for Social Responsibility*, Speech to Conservative Party Conference, 1 October 2006, available at http://www.conservatives.com/News/Speeches/2006/10/Cameron_We_stand_for_social_responsibility.aspx, consulted 19.07.13.
2. Wall, S. *The Official History of Britain and the European Community, Vol. II: From Rejection to Referendum, 1963–1975*, Routledge, 2012, p. 166.
3. Giddens, A. *Turbulent and Mighty Continent: What Future for Europe?*, Polity Press, 2013.
4. Colley, L. *Britons: Forging the Nation*, Vintage, 1996.

A Drama in Three Acts

1. Young, H. *This Blessed Plot: Britain and Europe from Churchill to Blair*, Methuen, 1998.
2. Blair, T. Speech to the Royal Institution of International Affairs, 5 April 1995.
3. Cameron, D. *EU Speech at Bloomberg*, Speech at Bloomberg's London Office, City Gate House, 23 January 2013, available at https://www.gov.uk/government/speeches/eu-speech-at-bloomberg, consulted 06.08.13.
4. Blair, T. *Britain's Role in Europe*, Speech at European Research Institute University of Birmingham, 23 November 2001, available at http://tna.europarchive.org/20050302152644/http://www.strategy-unit.gov.uk/output/Page1673.asp, consulted 31.07.12.
5. Campbell, J. *Roy Jenkins: A Biography*, International Affairs, 1983.
6. George, S. *An Awkward Partner: Britain in the European Community*, Oxford, 1998.
7. Charlton, M. *The Price of Victory*, BBC Books, 1983, p. 307.
8. EU. *Eurobarometer*, Spring, 1997, Section 4.2, available at http://ec.europa.eu/public_opinion/archives/eb/eb47/eb47_en.pdf, consulted 22.07.13; also EU. *Eurobarometer*, Spring, 2010, Section 2.1, available at http://ec.europa.eu/public_opinion/archives/eb/eb73/eb73_first_en.pdf, consulted 22.07.13.

9. Stephens, P. 'Britain would have fared better in the euro', *Financial Times*, 14 February 2011.
10. Blair, T. and Chirac, J. *Joint Declaration on European Defence*, British–French Summit, St Malo, 3–4 December 1998, available at http://www.iss.europa.eu/uploads/media/cp047e.pdf, consulted 22.07.13.
11. Cameron, *We Stand for Social Responsibility*.
12. Giles, C. and Parker, G. 'Osborne urges eurozone to "get a grip"', *Financial Times*, 20 July 2011.
13. Bale, T. *The Conservative Party from Thatcher to Cameron*, Polity, 2010.

The Prelude

1. Gamble, A. 'The European issue in British politics', in D. Baker and D. Seawright (eds), *Britain For and Against Europe: British Politics and the Question of European Integration*, Clarendon Press, 1998.
2. YouGov. 'If there was a referendum on Britain's membership of the European Union, how would you vote?', September 2010–January 2013, available at http://d25d2506sfb94s.cloudfront.net/cumulus_uploads/document/brs76vk9v0/YG-Archives-Pol-Trackers-Europe-210113.pdf, consulted 22.07.13.
3. Churchill, W. 'Speech at a Conservative Mass Meeting, Llandudno, 9 October 1948', in R. Churchill (ed.), *Europe Unite – Speeches: 1947 and 1948 by Winston Churchill*, Cassell, 1950, pp. 417–418.
4. Blair, T. Speech at Lord Mayor's Banquet, London, 10 November 1997.
5. Cameron, D. 'Foreign Policy in the National Interest', Speech at Lord Mayor's Banquet, London, 14 November 2011, available at http://www.number10.gov.uk/news/lord-mayors-banquet, consulted 26.07.13.
6. *Hansard*. HL Deb Series 5, vol. 515, 11 May 1953, available at http://hansard.millbanksystems.com/sittings/1953/may/11, consulted 21.10.13.
7. Clarke, P. *The Last Thousand Days of the British Empire: Churchill, Roosevelt, and the Birth of the Pax Americana*, Bloomsbury, 2009.
8. Young, *This Blessed Plot*, p. 83.
9. Gaitskell, H. 'The end of a thousand years of history (Brighton, 3 October 1962)', in B. MacArthur (ed.), *The Penguin Book of Twentieth Century Speeches*, Penguin, 1999, pp. 319–321.
10. Fowler, N. *A Political Suicide: The Conservatives' Voyage into the Wilderness*, Politico's, 2008.

Act One: Missed Opportunity

1. Wall, S. *A Stranger in Europe*, Oxford, 2008, p. 205.

CHAPTER 1 The Conservative Legacy

1. Macmillan, H. 'The wind of change', in B. MacArthur (ed.) *The Penguin Book of Twentieth Century Speeches*, Penguin, 1999; Thorpe, D. R. *Supermac: The Life of Harold Macmillan*, Chatto and Windus, 2010, pp. 432, 458.
2. Owen, G. *From Empire to Europe,* HarperCollins, 1999, pp. 28–29, 30–53, 258–259, 447–449.
3. Macmillan supported the EFTA policy as a means to 'association with Europe without injury' by aiming 'to harmonise the interests of Britain, the Commonwealth, and Europe' through technical and diplomatic discussion rather than public high politics; see *Hansard*, HoC, 26 November 1956, col. 39–42; Camps, M. *Britain and the European Community*, Oxford, 1964, pp. 106–108.
4. Camps, *Britain and the European Community*, p. 102.
5. T234/100, Harold Macmillan to Sir Edward Bridges, 1 February 1956; and Macmillan, H. *Riding the Storm 1956–59*, Macmillan, 1971, p. 74.
6. Kaiser, W. *Using Europe, Abusing the Europeans*, Macmillan, 1996, p. 219.
7. Dale, I. (ed.) *Conservative Party General Election Manifestos 1900–1997*, Routledge, 1999, pp. 130, 137–138.
8. Dumbrell, J. and Schaefer, A. *America's Special Relationships*, Routledge, 2009, p. 49.
9. Kaiser, *Using Europe, Abusing the Europeans*, pp. 136–142, 146, 218–220.
10. Ellison, J. *Threatening Europe: Britain and the Creation of the European Community*, Macmillan, 2000, p. 148; Young, *This Blessed Plot*, p. 125.
11. Camps, *Britain and the European Community*, pp. 106–108; Kaiser, *Using Europe, Abusing the Europeans*, p. 146.
12. Dumbrell and Schaefer, *America's Special Relationships*, p. 115.
13. Milward, A. S. *The European Rescue of the Nation-State,* Routledge, 2000, pp. 1–20, 345–424.
14. Kaiser, *Using Europe, Abusing the Europeans*, pp. 150–151.
15. Gamble, A. *Between Europe and America*, Palgrave Macmillan, 2003, pp. 115–116, 145–146; Gamble, A. 'Two faces of neo-liberalism', in R. Robinson (ed.), *The Neo-Liberal Revolution*, Palgrave Macmillan, 2006.
16. Riddell, P. *The Thatcher Government*, Blackwell, 1985, pp. 211–215.
17. Wall, *The Official History of Britain and the European Community, Vol. II*, p. 38.
18. Dyson, K. and Featherstone, K. *The Road to Maastricht*, Oxford, 2003, pp. 534, 569; Grant, C. *Delors: Inside the House that Jacques Built*, Nicholas Brealey, 1994, p. 89.
19. Wall, *The Official History of Britain and the European Community, Vol. II*, p. 38.
20. Young, *This Blessed Plot*, p. 330.

21. Grant, *Delors*, pp. 88–90.
22. Burgess, M. and Lee, A. 'The United Kingdom', in J. Lodge (ed.), *The 1989 Election of the European Parliament*, Macmillan Press, 1990, p. 197.
23. Burgess and Lee, 'The United Kingdom', p. 199.
24. Fowler, *A Political Suicide*, p. 169.
25. Dyson and Featherstone, *The Road to Maastricht*, pp. 534, 602.
26. Grant, *Delors*, p. 89.
27. George, *An Awkward Partner*; Dyson and Featherstone, *The Road to Maastricht*, pp. 334–343; Bache, I. and Nugent, N. 'Europe', in A. Seldon (ed.), *Blair's Britain 1997-2007*, Cambridge, 2007, pp. 530–531; Wall, *The Official History of Britain and the European Community, Vol. II* , pp. 177, 211.
28. Ellison, *Threatening Europe*, pp. 130, 238; Milward, A. S. *The Rise and Fall of a National Strategy: The UK and The European Community: Volume 1*, Routledge, 2002, p. 268; Kaiser, *Using Europe, Abusing the Europeans*, p. 133.

CHAPTER 2 Europe and the Failure of Labour Revisionism

1. MacArthur (ed.), *The Penguin Book of Twentieth Century Speeches*, pp. 319–321.
2. 'The new hope for Britain' (1983) in I. Dale (ed.), *Labour Party General Election Manifestos 1900–1997*, Politico's and Routledge, 2000, pp. 241–288.
3. Broad, R. *Labour's European Dilemmas*, Palgrave, 2001, pp. 22–23, 27–28; Camps, M. *Britain and the European Community 1955-63*, Princeton, 1964, pp. 446–447; Gamble, *Between Europe and America*, p. 29; Dale (ed.), *Labour Party General Election Manifestos 1900–1997*, pp. 47, 55, 280–281.
4. For contemporary examples see, 'Let us win through together' (1950) in Dale (ed.) *Labour Party General Election Manifestos 1900–1997*, pp. 71, 81–82, 99–101.
5. Donoghue, B. and Jones, G. *Herbet Morrison: Portrait of a Politician*, Phoenix, 1973, p. 481.
6. Bullock, A. *Ernest Bevin: Foreign Secretary, 1945–1951*, Heinemann, 1983, pp. 768–773.
7. Bullock, *Ernest Bevin*, pp. 768–773; Chace, J. *Acheson*, New York, 1998, pp. 250–251; Turner, M. J. *Britain and the World in the Twentieth Century: Ever Decreasing Circles*, Continuum, 2010, p. 43.
8. Healey, D. *European Unity: A Statement by the National Executive Committee of the British Labour Party*, London, 1950.
9. Pimlott, B. (ed.), *The Political Diary of Hugh Dalton*, Jonathan Cape, 1986, p. 476.
10. Williams, P. (ed.), *The Diary of Hugh Gaitskell*, Jonathan Cape, 1983, Appendix III.
11. Gaitskell, H. *Speech to the Labour Party Conference*, Speech to Labour Party Conference, Brighton, 1962, available at http://www.cvce.eu/obj/speech_by_

hugh_gaitskell_3_october_1962-en-05f2996b-000b-4576-8b42-8069033a16f9.html, consulted 03.09.12; MacArthur (ed.), *The Penguin Book of Twentieth Century Speeches,* pp. 319–321.
12. Castle, B. *The Castle Diaries 1964–1976*, Macmillan, 1990, p. 245.
13. Morgan, K. O. *Keir Hardie*, Littlehampton, 1984, pp. 163–170.
14. Morgan, *Keir Hardie*, pp. 40, 180, 182.
15. Morgan, *Keir Hardie*, p. 181; Cole, G. D. H. *A History of the Labour Party from 1914,* Routledge, 1948, p. 20.
16. Weiler, P. *Ernest Bevin*, Manchester, 1993, p. 90; Estorick, E. *Stafford Cripps: A Biography,* London, 1994, p. 144.
17. Attlee, C. *Labour's Peace Aims*, London, 1939.
18. MacArthur (ed.), *The Penguin Book of Twentieth Century Speeches*, pp. 319–321.
19. Memorandum by Rt Hon. Hugh Gaitskell to President Kennedy, 11 December 1962.
20. Sassoon, D. *One Hundred Years of Socialism: The West European Left in the Twentieth Century*, The New Press, 1996.
21. Sassoon, *One Hundred Years of Socialism*, p. 231.
22. Speech to SPD Congress in Hamburg, 1950; Sassoon, *One Hundred Years of Socialism*, p. 218.
23. Potthoff, H. and Miller, S. *The Social Democratic Party of Germany 1848–2005*, Dietz-Verlag, 2006.
24. Shanks, M. *The Stagnant Society: A Warning*, Penguin, 1961.
25. Crosland, C. A. R. *The Future of Socialism*, Camelot, 1956.
26. Sassoon, *One Hundred Years of Socialism*, p. 231.
27. Williams, P. *Hugh Gaitskell: A Political Biography*, Jonathan Cape, 1979, p. 736.
28. Pimlott, B. *Harold Wilson*, HarperCollins, 1992, pp. 577–579.
29. Pimlott, *Harold Wilson*, p. 224.
30. Brivati, B. *Hugh Gaitskell*, Richard Cohen, 1996, pp. 371–375; Williams, *Hugh Gaitskell*, pp. 610–612, 624–628; Pimlott, *Harold Wilson*, pp. 244–245.
31. Bell, P. *The Labour Party in Opposition: 1970–1974*, Routledge, 2004, p. 77.
32. Jenkins, R. *A Life at the Centre (Politico's Great Statesmen)*, Politico's, 2006.
33. Radice, G. *Friends & Rivals*, Little Brown, 2002, p. 194.

CHAPTER 3 Labour's Turn to Europe

1. 'The way forward', in A. Wood (ed.), *The Times Guide to the European Parliament 1984*, Times Books, 1984, pp. 268–273.
2. Stuart, M. *John Smith: A Life*, Politico's, 2005, p. 64.
3. Broad, R. *Labour's European Dilemmas*, Palgrave, 2001, p. 171.
4. Thatcher, M. *Speech to the College of Europe*, Speech at the College of Europe, Bruges, 20 September 1988, available at http://www.margaretthatcher.org/document/107332, consulted 10.08.12.

5. Radice, G. *The New Germans*, Michael Joseph, 1995; Hutton, W. *The State We're In*, Jonathan Cape, 1995.
6. Young, *This Blessed Plot*, p. 482.
7. Broad, *Labour's European Dilemmas*, p. 191.
8. Nairn, T. *The Left against Europe*, Penguin, 1973.
9. Richards, S. *Whatever it Takes*, HarperCollins, 2010, p. 53.
10. Young, *This Blessed Plot*, p. 482.
11. Major, J. *The Autobiography*, HarperCollins, 1999, pp. 603–604, 610, 685, 698.
12. Broad, *Labour's European Dilemmas*, p. 186.
13. Gifford, C. *The Making of Eurosceptic Britain: Identity and Economy in a Post-imperial State*, Ashgate, 2008, p. 135.
14. 'It's the Sun wot won it', *Sun*, 11 April 1992.
15. 'Why I love the pound', *Sun*, 17 April 1997.
16. 'The Sun backs Blair: Give change a chance', *Sun*, 18 March 1997.
17. Mandelson, P. and Liddle, R. *The Blair Revolution: Can New Labour Deliver?*, Faber and Faber, 1996.
18. Blair, T. Speech to Labour Party Conference Blackpool, 1994, available at http://www.britishpoliticalspeech.org/speech-archive.htm?speech=200, consulted 20.09.12.
19. Blair, T. Speech to Labour Party Conference Brighton, 1995, available at http://www.britishpoliticalspeech.org/speech-archive.htm?speech=201, consulted 20.09.12.
20. Blair, T. Speech to Labour Party Conference Blackpool, 1996, available at http://www.britishpoliticalspeech.org/speech-archive.htm?speech=202, consulted 20.09.12.

CHAPTER 4 In Power without a Policy

1. Wall, *A Stranger in Europe*, p. 163.

CHAPTER 5 Policy-Making at the Red Lion

1. *Hansard*, HoC, Columns 179–196, 23 February 1999, available at http://www.publications.parliament.uk/pa/cm199899/cmhansrd/vo990223/debtext/90223-05.htm.

CHAPTER 6 (Half) Making the Case

1. Blair, T. *Making the Case for Britain in Europe*, Speech at London Business School, 27 July 1999, available at http://www.guardian.co.uk/business/1999/jul/27/emu.theeuro2, consulted 22.07.13.
2. Daddow, O. *New Labour and the European Union: Blair and Brown's Logic of History*, Manchester University Press, 2011.

3. Smith, J. *The New Bilateralism: The UK's Relations within the EU*, Chatham House, 2002.
4. Riddell, P. *The Unfulfilled Prime Minister: Tony Blair's Quest for a Legacy*, Politico's, 2005, p. 151.

CHAPTER 7 Reforming the Club Rules

1. Blair, T. *Speech on Britain and Europe*, Speech at the Old Library Cardiff, 28 November 2002.
2. Blair, *Speech on Britain and Europe*.
3. Fischer, J. *From Confederacy to Federation – Thoughts on the Finality of European Integration*, Speech at Humboldt University, 12 May 2000, available at http://germanhistorydocs.ghi-dc.org/sub_document.cfm?document_id= 3745, consulted 22.07.13.
4. Chirac, J. *Our Europe*, Speech to the Bundestag, 27 June 2000, available at http://mayapur.securesites.net/fedtrust/filepool/Essay_9.pdf, consulted 22.07.13.
5. Teasdale, A. and Bainbridge, T. *The Penguin Companion to European Union*, Penguin, 2012, pp. 462–469.
6. The European Commission first had nine members – one each for the Benelux countries and two for France, Germany and Italy. On the UK's accession in 1973, nine grew to 13. Denmark and Ireland had one commissioner, but the UK had two. With succeeding accessions, by 1999 the Commission had grown to 20, with Spain also having two commissioners. In 2000, with the EU12 accession likely within a decade, on unchanged rules, the Commission would have grown in size to 33 on the assumption that Poland would also be entitled to two commissioners. Most experts agreed that the workload of the Commission could be efficiently divided into 8–12 portfolios (though in some of these portfolios, such as trade, 'junior' commissioners could have usefully served as junior ministers). A smaller Commission would also better retain the concept of a 'college' where decisions were taken collectively. The larger the size of the Commission, the more decision-making depends on the lead given by the president.

CHAPTER 8 Reforming Member State Economies

1. Leonard, M. *Network Europe: The New Case for Europe*, The Foreign Policy Centre, 1999.
2. OECD. *The OECD Jobs Study: Facts, Analysis, Strategies*, Organisation for Economic Co-operation and Development, 1994, available at http://www.oecd.org/els/emp/1941679.pdf, consulted 15.10.13.
3. Sapir, A. *Globalisation and the Reform of European Social Models*, Bruegel, 8 September 2005, available at http://www.bruegel.org/publications/publica

tion%20detail/publication/31-globalisation-and-the-reform-of-european-social-models, consulted 15.10.13.

4. Sachs, J. '*Suffer the children, suffer the country*', *Project Syndicate*, 22 April 2013, available at http://www.project-syndicate.org/commentary/new-unicef-study-of-poor-children-in-rich-countries-by-jeffrey-d- -sachs, consulted 15.10.13.
5. Vandenbroucke, F. 'Europe: The social challenge. Defining the Union's social objective is a necessity rather than a luxury', *Observatoire Social Européen (OSE) Paper Series*, Opinion Paper No. 11, July 2012, p. 39.

CHAPTER 10 Blocked on the Euro

1. In the 1951 election Labour won its highest ever share of the vote, winning more votes than Winston Churchill's Conservatives, despite ending up with 17 fewer seats.
2. Straw, J. *Last Man Standing*, Macmillan, 2012, pp. 326–327.
3. Hain, P. *Outside In*, Biteback, 2012, p. 250.
4. The wrong time was 1989, not 1985 before the Lawson boom had begun to wreak havoc. The wrong rate was because sterling should have joined when sterling was more competitively valued on the foreign exchanges, not when it had soared as a result of the high interest rates necessary to choke off inflation. And the wrong reason was to enable Margaret Thatcher to announce an interest rate cut at the Conservative Party Conference in 1989.
5. HM Treasury. *UK Membership of the Single Currency: An Assessment of the Five Economic Tests*, House of Commons, June 2003, p. 6, available at http://news.bbc.co.uk/1/shared/spl/hi/europe/03/euro/pdf/final_assessment/03_1100.pdf, consulted 15.10.13.
6. The fall would be less than the differential with the ECB because once Britain was a member of the euro the ECB rate would be likely to rise somewhat in order to reflect monetary conditions across the enlarged euro area, now including the UK.

CHAPTER 11 A Glass Half Empty

1. Bulmer, S. 'New Labour, new European policy? Blair, Brown and utilitarian supranationalism', *Parliamentary Affairs*, 61(4), 2008, pp. 597–620.
2. James, S. and Oppermann, K. 'Blair and the European Union in the Blair legacy', in Terence Casey (ed.), *The Blair Legacy: Politics, Policy, Governance and Foreign Affairs*, Palgrave Macmillan, 2009, pp. 285–298.
3. Smith, *The New Bilateralism: The UK's Relations within the EU.*
4. Blair, T. *A Journey*, Arrow, 2011, pp. 531–543.
5. Powell, J. *The New Machiavelli: How to Wield Power in the Modern World*, Bodley Head, 2010, pp. 248, 251; Rawnsley, A. *The End of the Party: The Rise*

and Fall of New Labour, Penguin Viking, 2010, pp. 189, 361; Blair, *A Journey*, p. 535.

6. Blair, *A Journey*, p. 537.
7. Peston, R. *Brown's Britain*, Short Books, 2006, pp. 217, 237–238; Rawnsley, *The End of the Party: The Rise and Fall of New Labour*, p. 194.
8. Powell, *The New Machiavelli: How to Wield Power in the Modern World*, p. 255; Radice, G. *Trio: Inside the Blair, Brown, Mandelson Project*, I.B.Tauris, 2010, p. 176; Rawnsley, *The End of the Party: The Rise and Fall of New Labour*, p. 195.
9. Seldon, A. *Blair Unbound*, Pocket, 2008, p. 214.
10. Blair, T. Speech at the Polish Stock Exchange, Warsaw, 6 October 2000, available at http://tna.europarchive.org/20050302152644/http://www.strategy-unit.gov.uk/output/Page3384.asp, consulted 27.07.12.
11. Blair, T. *A Clear Course for Europe*, Speech in Cardiff, 28 November 2002, available at http://www.astrid-online.it/Riforma-de/Studi-e-ri/Archivio-2/A.TONY-BLAIR-Speech-on-Europe–Cardiff-28.11.2002.pdf, consulted 31.07.12.
12. Vargas-Silva, C. *Migration Flows of A8 and other EU Migrants to and from the UK*, Migration Observatory Briefing, 2012, available at http://www.migrationobservatory.ox.ac.uk/sites/files/migobs/Migration%20Flows%20of%20A8%20and%20other%20EU%20Migrants%20to%20and%20from%20the%20UK.pdf, consulted 20.09.12, p. 2.
13. OECD Economic Outlook, *Economic Outlook No. 73 – June 2003 – Annual Projections for OECD Countries*, Annex Table 1, available at http://stats.oecd.org/Index.aspx?DataSetCode=EO73_MAIN, consulted 30.07.13.
14. Brown, G. 'Old Europe's choice', *Wall Street Journal*, 16 October 2003.
15. Brown, G. *Daily Telegraph*, 5 November 2003.
16. Thompson, H. *No Way Back: The Legacy of a Financial Sector Debt Crisis*, Policy Network, 2012.
17. Gamble, A., Bush, J. and Elliott, L. *In or Out? Labour and the Euro*, Fabian Society, 2002.

Act Three: Cameron's Gamble

1. Ganesh, J. 'Tory conflagration has been postponed', *Financial Times*, 25 January 2013.

CHAPTER 12 The Unexpected Return of Europe to British Politics

1. Forsyth, J. 'Gove: I'd vote to leave the EU if referendum held today', *Spectator*, 12 May 2012.
2. HL Paper 124-II, p. 60.

3. Giles, C. and Parker, G. 'Osborne urges eurozone to "get a grip"', *Financial Times*, 20 July 2011.
4. YouGov. 'The Sun Survey results', 14–15 January 2013, available at http://cdn.yougov.com/cumulus_uploads/document/cfpryrmbka/YG-Archive-Pol-Sun-results-150113.pdf, consulted 06.08.13.
5. Stephens, P. 'The new prisoners of ideology', *Financial Times*, 3 January 2013.
6. Sky News. 'Cameron: No UK guarantee for foreign banks', *Sky News*, 29 June 2012, available at http://news.sky.com/story/953966/cameron-no-uk-guarantee-for-foreign-banks, consulted 30.07.13.

CHAPTER 13 Renegotiation and Referendum

1. Ganesh, J. 'Tory conflagration has been postponed', *Financial Times*, 25 January 2013.
2. The key to Wilson's successful 'renegotiation' was that, right at the start of the process, he persuaded the cabinet to rule out the possibility of treaty change. He had a much subtler sense of the politics of Europe than the vocal anti-marketeers of the time such as Tony Benn, Barbara Castle and Michael Foot. Cameron's cabinet may be full of wiser Euroscpetic vigilantes. Also at that time British entry was recent and the renegotiation was acceptable to our partners as 'unfinished business'; a renegotiation after 40 years of membership is an altogether different proposition.
3. CBI, *Our Global Future: The Business Vision for a Reformed EU*, 4 November 2013, available at http://www.cbi.org.uk/media/2451423/our_global_future.pdf, consulted 04.11.13.
4. Kirkegard, J. F. 'Cameron plays a weak hand, but don't bet on a Brexit', *Pederson Institute*, 24 January 2012.

CHAPTER 14 A Progressive Alternative

1. Marquand, D. *The End of the West: The Once and Future Europe*, Princeton, 2011.

Conclusion: Britain's Unresolved Choice

1. Milward, A. *The European Rescue of the Nation State*, Routledge, 1999.
2. Wall, *The Official History of Britain and the European Community, Vol. II: From Rejection to Referendum, 1963–1975*, p. 218.

Bibliography

Attlee, C., *Labour's Peace Aims*, London, 1939.

Baker, D. and Seawright, D. (eds), *Britain For and Against Europe: British Politics and the Question of European Integration*, Clarendon Press, 1998.

Bale, T., *The Conservative Party from Thatcher to Cameron*, Polity, 2010.

Bell, P., *The Labour Party in Opposition: 1970–1974*, Routledge, 2004.

Blair, T., Leader's Speech to Labour Party Conference, Blackpool, 1994, available at http://www.britishpolitical speech.org/speech-archive.htm?speech=200, consulted 20.09.12.

Blair, T., Leader's Speech to Labour Party Conference, Brighton, 1995, available at http://www.britishpoliticalspeech.org/speech-archive.htm?speech=201, consulted 20.09.12.

Blair, T., Leader's Speech to Labour Party Conference, Blackpool, 1996, available at http://www.britishpolitical speech.org/speech-archive.htm?speech=202, consulted 20.09.12.

Blair, T., Speech at Lord Mayor's Banquet, London, 10 November 1997.

Blair, T., *Making the Case for Britain in Europe*, Speech at London Business School, 27 July 1999, available at http://www.guardian.co.uk/business/1999/jul/27/emu.theeuro2, consulted 22.07.13.

Blair, T., Speech at the Polish Stock Exchange, Warsaw, 6 October 2000, available at http://tna.europarchive.org/20050302152644/http://www.strategy-unit.gov.uk/output/Page3384.asp, consulted 27.07.12.

Blair, T., Speech to the Royal Institution of International Affairs, 5 April 1995.

Blair, T., *Britain's Role in Europe*, Speech at European Research Institute, University of Birmingham, 23 November 2001, available at http://tna.europarchive.org/20050302152644/http://www.strategy-unit.gov.uk/output/Page1673.asp, consulted 31.07.12.

Blair, T., *A Clear Course for Europe*, Speech in Cardiff, 28 November 2002, available at http://www.astrid-online.it/Riforma-de/Studi-e-ri/Archivio-2/A.TONY-BLAIR-Speech-on-Europe–Cardiff-28.11.2002.pdf, consulted 31.07.12.

Blair, T., Speech on Britain and Europe at the Old Library, Cardiff, 28 November 2002.

Blair, T., *A Journey*, Arrow, 2011.

Blair, T. and Chirac, J., *Joint Declaration on European Defence*, British–French Summit, St Malo, 3–4 December 1998, available at http://www.iss.europa.eu/uploads/media/cp047e.pdf, consulted 22.07.13.

Brivati, B., *Hugh Gaitskell*, Richard Cohen, 1996.

Broad, R., *Labour's European Dilemmas*, Palgrave, 2001.

Brown, G., 'Old Europe's choice', *Wall Street Journal*, 16 October 2003.

Brown, G., *Daily Telegraph*, 5 November 2003.

Bullock, A., *Ernest Bevin: Foreign Secretary, 1945–1951*, Heinemann, 1983.

Bulmer, S., 'New Labour, New European policy? Blair, Brown and utilitarian supranationalism', *Parliamentary Affairs*, 61(4), pp. 597–620.

Cameron, D., *We Stand for Social Responsibility*, Speech to Conservative Party Conference, Bournemouth, 1 October 2006, available at http://www.conservatives.com/News/Speeches/2006/10/Cameron_We_stand_for_social_responsibility.aspx, consulted 19.07.13.

Cameron, D., *Foreign Policy in the National Interest*, Speech at Lord Mayor's Banquet, London, 14 November 2011, available at http://www.number10.gov.uk/news/lord-mayors-banquet, consulted 26.07.13.

Cameron, D. *EU Speech at Bloomberg*, Speech at Bloomberg's London Office, City Gate House, 23 January 2013, available at https://www.gov.uk/government/speeches/eu-speech-at-bloomberg, consulted 06.08.13.

Campbell, A. *The Blair Years: Extracts from the Alastair Campbell Diaries*, Knopf Publishing Group, 2007.

Campbell, J., *Roy Jenkins: A Biography*, International Affairs, 1983.

Camps, M., *Britain and the European Community 1955–63*, Princeton, 1964.

Castle, B., *The Castle Diaries 1964–1976*, Macmillan, 1990.

Chace, J., *Acheson*, New York, 1998.

Charlton, M., *The Price of Victory*, BBC Books, 1983.

Chirac, J., *Our Europe*, Speech to the Bundestag, 27 June 2000, available at http://mayapur.securesites.net/fedtrust/filepool/Essay_9.pdf, consulted 22.07.13.

Churchill, R. (ed.), *Europe Unite – Speeches: 1947 and 1948 by Winston Churchill*, Cassell, 1950.

Clarke, P., *The Last Thousand Days of the British Empire: Churchill, Roosevelt, and the Birth of the Pax Americana*, Bloomsbury, 2009.

Cole, G. D. H., *A History of the Labour Party from 1914*, Routledge, 1948.

Colley, L., *Britons: Forging the Nation*, Vintage, 1996.

Crosland, C. A. R., *The Future of Socialism*, Camelot, 1956.

Daddow, O., *New Labour and the European Union: Blair and Brown's Logic of History*, Manchester, 2011.

Dale, I. (ed.), *Conservative Party General Election Manifestos 1900–1997*, Routledge, 1999.

Dale, I. (ed.), *Labour Party General Election Manifestos 1900–1997*, Routledge, 2000.

Donoghue, B. and Jones, G., *Herbet Morrison: Portrait of a Politician*, Phoenix, 1973.

Dumbrell, J. and Schaefer, A., *America's Special Relationships*, Routledge, 2009.

Dyson, K. and Featherstone, K., *The Road to Maastricht*, Oxford, 2003.

Ellison, J., *Threatening Europe: Britain and the Creation of the European Community*, Macmillan, 2000.

Estorick, E., *Stafford Cripps: A Biography*, London, 1994.

EU, *Eurobarometer*, Spring 1997, Section 4.2, available at http://ec.europa.eu/public_opinion/archives/eb/eb47/eb47_en.pdf, consulted 22.07.13.

EU, *Eurobarometer*, Spring 2010, Section 2.1, available at http://ec.europa.eu/public_opinion/archives/eb/eb73/eb73_first_en.pdf, consulted 22.07.13.

Fischer, J., *From Confederacy to Federation – Thoughts on the Finality of European Integration*, Speech at Humboldt University, 12 May 2000, available at http://germanhistorydocs.ghi-dc.org/sub_document.cfm?document_id=3745, consulted 22.07.13.

Fowler, N., *A Political Suicide: The Conservatives' Voyage into the Wilderness*, Politico's, 2008.

Gaitskell, H., Speech to Labour Party Conference, Brighton, 1962, available at http://www.cvce.eu/obj/speech_by_hugh_gaitskell_3_october_1962-en-05f2996b-000b-4576-8b42-8069033a16f9.html, consulted 03.09.12.

Gaitskell, H., Memorandum to President Kennedy, 11 December 1962.

Gamble, A., *Between Europe and America*, Palgrave Macmillan, 2003.

Gamble, A., Bush, J. and Elliott, L., *In or Out? Labour and the Euro*, Fabian Society, 2002.

Ganesh, J., 'Tory conflagration has been postponed', *Financial Times*, 25 January 2013.

George, S., *An Awkward Partner: Britain in the European Community*, Oxford, 1998.

Giddens, A., *Turbulent and Mighty Continent: What Future for Europe?*, Polity Press, 2013.

Giles, C. and Parker, G., 'Osborne urges eurozone to "get a grip"', *Financial Times*, 20 July 2011.

Grant, C., *Delors: Inside the House that Jacques Built*, Nicholas Brealey, 1994.

Hain, P., *Outside In*, Biteback, 2012.

Hansard, HL Deb Series 5, Vol. 515, 11 May 1953, available at http://hansard.millbanksystems.com/sittings/1953/may/11, consulted 15.10.13.

Hansard, HoC, Columns 179–196, 23 February 1999, available at http://www.publications.parliament.uk/pa/cm199899/cmhansrd/vo990223/debtext/90223-05.htm, consulted 15.10.13.

Healey, D., *European Unity. A Statement by the National Executive Committee of the British Labour Party*, London, 1950.

HM Treasury, *UK Membership of the Single Currency: An Assessment of the Five Economic Tests*, House of Commons, June 2003, available at http://news.bbc.co.uk/1/shared/spl/hi/europe/03/euro/pdf/final_assessment/03_1100.pdf, 2003.

Hutton, W., *The State We're In*, Jonathan Cape, 1995.

James, S. and Oppermann, K., 'Blair and the European Union in the Blair legacy', in Casey, T. (ed.) *The Blair Legacy: Politics, Policy, Governance and Foreign Affairs*, Palgrave Macmillan, 2009.

Kaiser, W., *Using Europe, Abusing the Europeans*, Macmillan, 1996.

Leonard, M., *Network Europe: The New Case for Europe*, The Foreign Policy Centre, 1999.

Lodge, J. (ed.), *The 1989 Election of the European Parliament*, Macmillan, 1990.

MacArthur, B. (ed.), *The Penguin Book of Twentieth Century Speeches*, Penguin, 1999.

Macmillan, H., *Riding the Storm 1956–59*, Macmillan, 1971.

Major, J., *The Autobiography*, HarperCollins, 1999.

Milward, A. S., *The European Rescue of the Nation-State*, Routledge, 2000.

Milward, S., *The Rise and Fall of a National Strategy: The UK and The European Community Volume 1*, Routledge, 2002.

Morgan, K. O., *Keir Hardie*, Littlehampton, 1984.

Nairn, T., *The Left Against Europe*, Penguin, 1973.

OECD, *The OECD Jobs Study: Facts, Analysis, Strategies*, OECD (Organisation for Economic Co-operation and Development), 1994, available at http://www.oecd.org/els/emp/1941679.pdf, consulted 22.07.13.

OECD, 'Economic outlook (June 2003)', *Economic Outlook No. 73*, June 2003, *Annual Projections for OECD Countries*, Annex Table 1, available at http://stats.oecd.org/Index.aspx?DataSetCode=EO73_MAIN consulted 30.07.13.

Owen, G., *From Empire to Europe*, HarperCollins, 1999.

Peston, R., *Brown's Britain*, Short Books, 2006.

Pimlott, B., *Harold Wilson*, HarperCollins, 1992.

Pimlott, B. (ed.), *The Political Diary of Hugh Dalton*, Jonathan Cape, 1986.

Potthoff, H. and Miller, S., *The Social Democratic Party of Germany 1848–2005*, Dietz-Verlag, 2006.

Powell, J., *The New Machiavelli: How to Wield Power in the Modern World*, Bodley Head, 2010.

Radice, G., *The New Germans*, Michael Joseph, 1995.

Radice, G., *Friends & Rivals*, Little Brown, 2002.

Radice, G., *Trio: Inside the Blair, Brown, Mandelson Project*, I.B.Tauris, 2010.

Rawnsley, A., *The End of the Party: The Rise and Fall of New Labour*, Penguin Viking, 2010.

Richards, S., *Whatever it Takes*, HarperCollins, 2010.

Riddell, P., *The Thatcher Government*, Blackwell, 1985.

Riddell, P., *The Unfulfilled Prime Minister: Tony Blair's Quest for a Legacy*, Politico's, 2005.

Robinson, R. (ed.) *The Neo-Liberal Revolution*, Palgrave Macmillan, 2006.

Sachs, J., *Suffer the Children, Suffer the Country*, Project Syndicate, 2013.

Sapir, A. et al., *An Agenda for a Growing Europe*, Oxford University Press, 2003.

Sassoon, D., *One Hundred Years of Socialism: The West European Left in the Twentieth Century*, The New Press, 1996.

Seldon, A., *Blair Unbound*, Pocket, 2008.

Seldon, A. (ed.), *Blair's Britain 1997–2007*, Cambridge, 2007.

Smith, J., *The New Bilateralism: The UK's Relations within the EU*, Chatham House, 2002.

Stephens, P., 'Britain would have fared better in the euro', *Financial Times*, 14 February 2011.

Straw, J., *Last Man Standing*, Macmillan, 2012.

Stuart, M., *John Smith: A Life*, Politico's, 2005.

Sun, 'Why I love the pound', *Sun*, 17 April 1997.

Sun, 'The Sun backs Blair: Give change a chance', *the Sun*, 18 March 1997.

Sun, 'It's the Sun wot won it', *Sun*, 11 April 1992.

Teasdale, A. and Bainbridge, T., *The Penguin Companion to European Union*, Penguin, 2012.

Thatcher, M., Speech at the College of Europe, Bruges, 20 September 1988, available at http://www.margaretthatcher.org/document/107332, consulted 10.08.12, 1988.

Thompson, H., *No Way Back: the Legacy of a Financial Sector Debt Crisis*, Policy Network, 2012.

Thorpe, D. R., *Supermac: The Life of Harold Macmillan*, Chatto & Windus, 2010.

Turner, M. J., *Britain and the World in the Twentieth Century: Ever Decreasing Circles*, Continuum, 2010.

Vandenbroucke, F., 'Europe: The social challenge. Defining the Union's social objective is a necessity rather than a luxury', *Observatoire Social Européen (OSE) Paper Series*, Opinion Paper No. 11, July 2012.

Vargas-Silva, C., 'Migration flows of A8 and other EU migrants to and from the UK', in *Migration Observatory Briefing*, January 2012, available at http://www.migrationobservatory.ox.ac.uk/sites/files/migobs/Migration%20Flows%20of%20A8%20and%20other%20EU%20Migrants%20to%20and%20from%20the%20UK.pdf, consulted 20.09.12.

Wall, S., *A Stranger in Europe*, Oxford, 2008.

Wall, S., *The Official History of Britain and the European Community, Vol. II: From Rejection to Referendum*, 1963–1975, Routledge, 2012.

Weiler, P., *Ernest Bevin*, Manchester, 1993.

Williams, P. (ed.), *The Diary of Hugh Gaitskell*, Jonathan Cape, 1983.

Wood, A. (ed.), *The Times Guide to the European Parliament 1984*, Times Books, 1984.

YouGov, *If There Was a Referendum on Britain's Membership of the European Union, How Would You Vote?*, September 2010–January 2013, available at http://d25d2506sfb94s.cloudfront.net/cumulus_uploads/document/brs76vk9v0/YG-Archives-Pol-Trackers-Europe-210113.pdf, consulted 22.07.13.

Young, H., *This Blessed Plot: Britain and Europe from Churchill to Blair*, Methuen, 1998.

Index